THE MAKING OF THE MOVIE

THE MAKING OF THE MOVIE

By Jonathan Smith

Volume Two

RAISE THE TITANIC THE MAKING OF THE MOVIE

© 2022 By Jonathan Smith

All Rights Reserved.

No portion of this publication may be reproduced, stored, and/or copied electronically (except for academic use as a source), nor transmitted in any form or by any means without the prior written permission of the publisher and/or author.

Published in the United States of America by:

BearManor Media
1317 Edgewater Dr #110
Orlando FL 32804
bearmanormedia.com

Printed in the United States.

All photos used with permission.

Typesetting and layout by DataSmith Solutions

Cover by DataSmith Solutions and Jonathan Smith

ISBN — 978-1-62933-978-8

Acknowledgements

In the preparation of this book I have had the extreme pleasure of assistance from many sources from *Titanic* enthusiasts to those in the film industry. Without their help and support this book would not have come to its full fruition. For that I am eternally indebted to them.

Special gratitude goes to: actor David Selby who was always there to answer my questions and for taking the time to write the foreword for this book; FX legend John Richardson who was an email or phone call away to share his production adventures, tricks of the trade, support for my little book project and for the writing of the shared foreword; to Jeff Herne for his time in assisting with the editing; Jean Pierre Borg for his continued support and who is always there to help; Narcy Calamatta for his many tales from the production time in Malta; Ken Marschall for sharing his fascinating insights of working on the movie mod- el in California and for allowing many of his photographs to be reproduced here for the first time; artists Cyril Codus and Lionel Codus for their exceptional work and who are always there to assist come rain or shine. Geoffrey Mackrill for sharing his collection and stories of working on the production. And to my loving wife Toni Ann for putting up with my *Titanic* obsession and supporting me every step of the way.

I would also like to thank those who came forward to share their own collections, their own stories and their own memories. I apologise in advance if I have left anyone out. In no particular order: Jerry Jameson (director); John DeCuir. Jr (art director); David Harris (special effects); ITV Studios; Walter Winterburn; Simon Mills; Drew Struzan; Rob Burman (Burmans Studio); Doug Llewelyn (Doug Llewelyn Productions); Eugene Nesmeyanov; Stuart Williamson; Nick Stathopoulos; Geoff Leonard; Jon Burlingham; the late Robert Gibbons (*Titanic* historian); Sue Connelly; Gabriel Christopher- Cawood Waters; John Fry; Colin Cook; Steve Hall; Joe Sciberras; Mike Jones; Alan Quale; William Barney; Garth Thomas; Jim Olson; Dan Cherry; Jonathan Scott; the gravediggers of Southby graveyard; Peter Lewis; Elang Erlangga; Andy Tree; Angela Catherine; Tom Haight; Bill Thomas; Capt. Lawrence Dali; Ged Jones; Commodore Ronald Warwick; Mario Hristovski; Teresa Trower; Faye Taylor; Henry Brayshaw; Alan J. Adler; Kellen Butler (President and Director of *Friends of the Hunley, Inc.*); Mike Seares; Patrick Walsh; Selim San; Philip Kiel (President of *Photo-Sonics, Inc.*); Shane Strat- on; Leo Walker; Tom Wedge; Peter Lewis: William Van Dorp; *Marine Photos & Publishing Co*; the late Lawrence Suid; Tony Holt; Tommy Bernard; Kento Gebo (special FX artist); David Harris (special FX artist); the team at Network on Air; James Perkin; the late Steve Rigby (*Titanic* historian); Les Walker; William Brower; David Ashely Bubb; Adam Lively; Terry Moore; Charles Pellegrino; Walter Nones; Mike Branigan; Colten Vanosdale; Sandy Saling; Greg Nicholls; Delinda Peterson; David B. Reeves Cicero; Glen Barker; Alex McDonald; IMDb; Jim Scoular; Senthil Kumar and Ben and the team at BearManor Media for their hard work in bringing to life my dream.

I wish to dedicate this book to my mother and to my late father who was taken from me at such an early period of my life and age. As a child he pushed me to pursue my fascination with *Titanic* that soon became an obsession. Thank you for the childhood memories; the love and the reassurance that life, no matter the challenges, can be rewarding.

And lastly, the late Wayne Velero; fellow *Raise the Titanic* enthusiast, author and founder of the *Clive Cussler Collector's* Society. Wayne's energetic enthusiasm for collecting was second to none and I am proud to personally own some of his collection. I will always be grateful for his support for my book project from the offset. Thank you, Wayne, for everything you did and the memories you have left behind.

Go on an adventure behind the scenes on how the cult movie was made with this lavishly illustrated two-volume book set.

AVAILABLE FROM

WWW.BEARMANORMEDIA.COM

Contents

Acknowledgements V
Preface IX

Volume 2

Chapter 15 On Location 1
Chapter 16 The Curse of Cornwall 45
Chapter 17 Raising the Question on Reality 75
Chapter 18 Wreckcognising *Titanic* 107
Chapter 19 In Search of the *Titanic* 131
Chapter 20 *Raise the Titanic!* 175
Chapter 21 The Sounds of *Raise the Titanic* 263
Chapter 22 *Raise the Titanic* Uncovered 285
Chapter 23 Production Details 297
Chapter 24 Premiere, Charity Events and those
               Damned Critics 309
Chapter 25 The Art of *Raise the Titanic* 335
Chapter 26 It *would* have been easier if they had
               lowered the Atlantic 367
Chapter 27 Lost and Found 387
Chapter 28 The Last Voyage of the "unsinkable" *Titanic* 433
Chapter 29 Brewster's Vault: Collecting *Raise the Titanic* 465
Chapter 30 The Last Great Human Adventure 495

Afterword 507
Bibliography 509

Preface

Welcome back to *Raise the Titanic: The Making of the Movie*. In Volume One we delved into the legacy of the doomed liner; Lord Lew Grade who financed the motion picture; the best-selling author Clive Cussler who envisioned the raising of the wreck in the pages of his 1976 novel; the troubled production as directors came and went; the fascinating look into the building of the films iconic 55ft *Titanic* recreation and the many other vessels and models; the search and hiring of the stand-in *Titanic*; the construction and teething problems of the world's largest water tank in Malta; a look into the fictional salvage fleet who will help raise the *Titanic*; the intense problems that arose between the film studio and the United States military over the films cold-war setting portrayal on-screen; looking into the actors and characters of the movie including those approached and rejected, and an amazing behind the scenes look into the films infamous deleted 1912 prologue.

For Volume Two we dive into the depths of the black abyss as the impossible is made possible. Discover how they filmed the haunting underwater scenes; take a trip to the many filming locations around the world; be there in Cornwall as a fictional *Titanic* survivor reflects on the night the *Titanic* sank and how a vast storm nearly brought an end to filming. Take a journey to the *Titanic* and discover how experts had envisioned the wreck in the days before the ship's actual discovery in 1985 which lead to how movie makers presumed the boat would look after decades on the ocean floor; see how movie magic was created as the pristine *Titanic* is turned into the long lost liner; go into the recording studio for the recording of John Barry's hauntingly beautiful score; join the team as the secrets behind how they successfully raised the *Titanic* on the big screen is revealed for the first time. And if that isn't enough to whet the appetite, join the stars at the advanced screenings of the movie including the World Premiere; learn about the artists behind the amazing posters and artworks for the movie; take the uncharted voyage into the deleted scenes of *Raise the Titanic* that reveals a much different motion picture; read about the unfortunate implosion upon Lord Lew Grade, his company and the hostile takeover from the fallout from *Raise the Titanic*. And for the curious, we look into the four decades that have passed since the film's release, what became of the models and the first look into the future preservation of the mighty *Titanic* film model.

To find it in five-million-miles of the Atlantic.

To reach it thousands-of-feet below the surface.

And to finally bring it up.

It may be the last great human adventure of all time.

And you will be there to…

CHAPTER 15

On Location

"Are you telling me the army sent a guy up there seventy years ago to get a half-a-ton of Byzanium?"

Admiral James Sandecker

The first scenes put to film under director Jerry Jameson began at the soundstages of the CBS Studio Center facilities in Los Angeles using some of the interior submersible sets created by Mickey Michaels. Located at 4024 Radford Avenue, Studio City, California, the facilities offered not only the grounds for filming many popular television shows such as 3rd *Rock from the Sun, Brooklyn Nine-Nine, Falcons Crest, Hill Street Blues,* and *Will & Grace,* major feature films were also filmed there including *The Adams Family, Dr. Doolittle, Father of the Bride, Scream 3* and *The Muppet Movie.* An added bonus for the film was that Martin Starger's office for Marble Arch Productions was based at Studio Center. The film's opening segment consisting of interweaving period black and white photographs were created by titles designer Gene Kraft utilizing 16 photographs; 14 showing the construction and voyages of *Titanic* and her sister *Olympic,* and 2 generic photographs of musicians and ballroom dancers that bared no connection to the liners and which were supplied by *Titanic* historians Charles Ira Sachs and Robert Gibbons. Two soundstages were hired for filming the integral interior sets of the submersibles based on the production artwork from John DeCuir who had replaced Bill Creber following Stanley Kramer's departure from the production. Assisting DeCuir was Academy Award-nominated set decorator Mickey S. Michaels who had experience of working on *Airport* (1970) and *Airport '77* with Jerry Jameson.

For the realistic appearance of the sub interiors and the banks of computers and screens, Hewlett Packard, Sony and General Electric loaned to the production nearly $3m in equipment. Hewlett Packard, based then at Palo Alto, California, supplied $500,000 of computer systems while four of the company divisions from San Diego, Colorado, Oregon, and San Francisco assisted in the connecting up and programming of the systems including computer controllers, chart recorders, data plotters, loggers and screen displays. On loan from General Electric was their Diver Equivalent Manipulator System, DEMS for short, a highly expensive and sophisticated robotic arm and claw, which could pick up a teacup with such preciseness. The production team had great fun in using DEMS for the film's publicity by demonstrating at the CBS Studio Center with the device how it could, with great dexterity, pour tea from a teapot into a cup and saucer, sweep the studio floor with a brush, even opening zips on clothing, all under the watchful eye of the film's producer William Frye and special guest Lady Sarah Churchill, the grandniece of Winston Churchill. With publicity out of the way, the team could return to filming the device in the soundstage interior water tank which had been dressed to represent the bottom of the ocean floor as DEMS went to work to pluck free an encrusted musical cornet wedged between rocks signifying the first tangible trace to the wreck of the *Titanic*. The next stage for the DEMS were varying insert shots showing the device in action as it works on sealing up the gash on *Titanic*'s hull, filmed like that of the cornet, in the soundstage water tank with a section of the hull. With the sub interior sets completed and operational, the filming of scenes as subs crews glide over the ocean floor looking for the long-lost wreck and the latter scenes of the crew with Seagram trapped within the skylight on *Titanic* could now begin.

The last of the interior submersible scenes filmed were those of the demise of the D.S.V. *Starfish* after the crew comes into difficulty when they exceed the diving depth capabilities of the craft. The interior was lifted into place into the drained tank for the flooding of the set with a clear tank built around the open end of the set piece where camera crews would work. With Michael Ensign (Northhacker), Paul Tuerpe (Klink), and Trent Dolan (Isbell) within the interior set filming could begin as the *Starfish* descends to the bottom taking on water as both Beck and Isbell panic to release the subs inner sphere via the lever. To complete the scene a number of exterior shots showing the submersible miniature as it sank deeper, trailing a stream of bubbles behind it, to then finally implode, were filmed within the soundstage tank at the CBS Studio Center with the soundstage filming coming to an end in the first week of November 1979.

Autonetics Marine Systems Division, California

"Four hundred times we repeated this process and every time it landed within inches of the same spot," says Dr. Gene Seagram as the white model of the *Titanic* glides through the water to land on its marker on the bottom of the tank. During scouting for film locations for *Raise the Titanic,* members from Marble Arch Productions visited the annual Offshore Technology Conference in Houston where they were intrigued by the display of the Ocean Systems Engineering Compatibilities from AMSD and their large sonar pool at the Rockwell International Corporation. With their main head office in Anaheim, California, it was chosen for the location to film one of the film's integral scenes; the testing of a scale *Titanic* model to establish where the vessel had landed on the ocean floor. The sonar pool was rectangular in design with a length of 120ft, a width of 90ft, a depth of 30ft, and a holding capacity of 1.4 million gallons of water. It was spanned with a large walkway with an additional control room that measured 15ft in diameter. On October 25, 1979, the film crew arrived on-site at 1:30 pm with electrical equipment, camera vehicles, catering truck, wardrobe, make-up vehicles, and a dressing room trailer. By evening the usually tranquil surroundings of the sonar pool was buzzing with film crews as they floodlighted the location.

Three AMSD employees were chosen to appear in the scenes giving them their first taste of working for Hollywood. Selected were Al Stimpert, Bob Jones, and Jim Hull, who, having worked with the company for some considerable time, had a better understanding of the company's environment adding realism to the production. Between 7 pm and midnight, the actors rehearsed their scenes with filming starting at the pool at 12:30 am, continuing until 4:30 am. On hand was Ray Quiroz, who typed up last-minute revisions to the script and keeping a tab of the scenes, and providing descriptions of the scenes for the film's editor. Within the pool there sat a floating pontoon in which the scaled and perfectly weighted *Titanic* model sat to then be released by crew for its descent to the bottom. The sequences were filmed with underwater cameras set up by assistant cameramen Pat McGinnis and Dennis Matsudo. Upon completion of filming, and asked what he thought about his first time appearing in front of the camera, Al Stimpert said, "My back is sure sore – and my feet are killing me!"

Bronson Canyon, Griffith Park, Los Angeles

"HERE LIES SGT. JAKE HOBART UNITED STATES ARMY FROZE IN A STORM FEBRUARY 10, 1912". The inscription is burned into a section of a wooden crate and left with the body in the long-abandoned mine shaft on the island of Svlardov. Fans of the film may have been fooled into thinking that the deserted mine was created within a sound stage. Nothing could be further from the truth. While the location was outdoors, *Raise the Titanic* was never its first screen outing. Its nickname of the Batcave gives a hint to what it was famous for. Located at Hollywood hills Bronson Canyon in Griffith Park, Los Angeles, the cave was used for the entrance for Bruce Wayne's Batcave in the much-loved television series *Batman* (1966-1968). Given its unique appearance and location, it gave filmmakers the ideal opportunity to use the cave's natural features. The location would be transformed into the ice-laden surroundings of the long-abandoned mine shaft on the Russian island of Svlardov where the Byzanium was robbed from the earth. Before the actor Stewart Moss, the American agent named Koplin, could be filmed, the cave had to be miraculously turned into the dark cold setting of a mine located within the Arctic Circle.

The film's art director John DeCuir, Jr, and his team of set decorators set to work in achieving the illusion. To create the look a half-mile of the tunnel was coated with white plastic and clear plastic inserted to represent clear ice. On the floor of the cave was laid a series of narrow-gauge tracks with a gravel bed and a series of vertical wooden columns mimicking shoring timbers. To add realism 23 tons of real shaved ice was added within the confines of the cave giving more realism to the set. With the entrances of the cave sealed off, the production crew could film the scenes with Stewart Moss in character as he stumbled around the cave looking for traces of the Byzanium with his torch and Geiger counter. One last added feature was that of the frozen-in-time remains of Sgt. Jake Hobart, which had been painstakingly sculptured by the father and son duo of Tom and Rob Burman of The Burmans Studio, Inc of Van Nuys, California. The Burmans Studio are a well-established practical FX company that has worked on many blockbuster movies and hit television shows including *Planet of the Apes*, *Close Encounters of the Third Kind*, *Invasion of the Body Snatchers*, *The Goonies*, *The X-Files* series, *Grey's Anatomy*, and *Nip/Tuck*. Two figures were crafted for *Raise the Titanic* that also included that of the gaunt remains of Arthur Brewster that Gene Seagram nearly steps upon when entering the vault in the cargo hold of *Titanic*. The Burmans Studio was asked to create the film's characters in various stages of decomposition with their progress photographed for the film's producer and director to choose from.

The early look for Hobart was that of a largely decomposed body that was far removed from what was finally created and used on screen. The version that was selected was tremendously detailed and lifelike. Unfortunately, the figure was required to be set in a clear resin that would represent ice. But with the low lighting conditions combined with the camera angle shots and the heavy resin ice bath surrounding the body, the details were all but lost. Thankfully, the series of Polaroids taken of the progress of the figure have survived where they reveal the remarkable detail incorporated into Hobart. The Burmans version of Arthur Brewster would see the character undergo several variations from that of a nearly skeletal figure draped in clothing to that of a more sunken and mummified body before the progress of reshaping the face concluded with that of the look of a more slightly older gentleman. Both Hobart and Brewster were finished as full figures, articulated and dressed in period clothing that, like the wretched victim wearing them, had been aged accordingly. While Hobart was confined to the dressed cave at Bronson Canyon, Brewster was flown out to join the FX crews onboard the *Athinai* at Piraeus harbour in Greece and placed inside the John DeCuir's designed cargo hold vault with the apparently full wooden crates containing the gravel and Byzanium. Speaking of his time shooting the $80,000 scene at the Bronson Canyon caves, DeCuir later commented, "After shooting, we had to go in with scalding steam hoses, melt down the remains, and clean up the area. It took days."

Heather Island, Valdez-Cordova, Alaska

It was termed the "Assault on Heather Island" when 26 members of the film's production crew arrived for *Raise the Titanic* at Heather Island, Valdez-Cordova, Alaska, overlooking the Columbia Glacier in the waters of Heather Bay. Because this filming period was during winter, the exterior crew had been purposely narrowed down. The barren, snow-covered landscape had to look as authentic as possible. The island was to stand in for Svlardov in the opening scenes of the film as Koplin digs into the snow to reveal the entrance to the long abandoned mine shaft. The production team flew into Anchorage, Alaska, then onto Prince William Sound in Valdez, the southerly terminus for the Trans-Alaska Pipeline. Their arrival in January 1980 was hampered by bad weather as snow prevented them from flying onto Heather Island by a normal chartered plane. They succeeded in securing transportation to the location with helicopters, then pitched up at the Sheffield House in Valdez, which would become the crew and actor's headquarters during the filming process. Among the crew were four actors, three humans; Richard Jordan as Pitt, Stewart Moss as Koplin, and Michael Kalcsar as the Russian soldier. So, who was the fourth? It was Teddy, a breed of Anatolian Shepherd dog. The first of the scenes to be filmed was Moss, as he digs into the snow in search of the opening to the mineshaft. As the sequence plays out the view sweeps across from the mainland, following over Heather Bay to Heather Island with the mass of ice towards Columbia Glacier in the distance. The scene was to close as the helicopter comes down to the tree line of the island with Moss digging in the snow. That first day of filming went smoothly.

Then the weather hit again with heavy winds, rain, fog, and then snow, snow, and more snow. What they thought was going to be a simple shooting schedule turned into a major headache as the weather set and the production crew became snowed in and stranded due to helicopter flights being pulled. For five days the crew was stuck out in their makeshift mobile unit. The winter wear that was supplied to them by the wardrobe department was insufficient for the climate and thankfully, upon their arrival in Anchorage, the local Army-Navy Surplus Store in town opened early and supplied the crew with the appropriate winter clothing. A break in the weather had the crew and actors move on to the next leg of the movie for the filming of the chase sequence and the first appearance of Dirk Pitt out on the ice plain. With a window of clear weather, aerial shots were filmed from those of Pitt hauling Koplin across the ice and a sequence filmed out to sea of icebergs which were to be inserted into one of the films Atlantic Ocean scenes with Dirk Pitt and Gene Seagram. On the ice plains, Teddy the dog with actor Michael Kalcsar and Stuart Moss had done their sequence with stuntman Loren Janes on hand to assist as Koplin is shot and attacked. But as the scenes moved on to Jordan an unexpected turn of events occurred that nearly turned the filming into a disaster movie in its own right. As Jordan got into character and the cameras rolled, all were unaware of what was happening right behind them. A sudden loud crack followed by a rumbling growl marked the moment as a huge mass of ice sheared off from the glacier and collapsed down into the sea with a roar. Set decorator Mickey S. Michaels recalled the frightening New Year experience,

> "One gigantic piece of ice broke off the glacier, about 100 yards from where we were working on the island. When it hit the water and didn't come up right away, I shouted to the rest of the crew to take cover, figuring that when it did pop up, it would generate one hell of a wave. It sure did – two or three feet high, rolling over the point where eight guys and the dog were working. The cameraman dove for the lens. All of us got wet. Soaking. Then the weather socked in, and we were stranded there for four-half hours."

At first glance it appeared that the camera had taken the full brunt of both the wave and impact with the ice. Concerned for the film inside, the camera was placed within a bag full of saltwater. Michaels continued,

> "Once it's wet, you keep it that way until you can get to it. It took three men all night, once we got back to Valdez, to dismantle the camera and clean it up. The film, as it turned out, wasn't even wet."

With a lull in the weather, the crew took the opportunity to make a run for it as helicopters arrived to pick them up. The weather was still relatively bad and the journey back to Valdez had the tower guiding the pilot back into town by using the street layout, "Turn right at the water tank" joked Michaels. But they were not in the clear just yet as 18 of the 26-member skeleton crew, including actor Richard Jordan, were taken ill, being submitted to the infirmary as a severe case of flu brought on from filming in the warmer climate of Greece to suddenly being exposed to sub-zero temperatures of Alaska ravaged the team one after the other. Richard O'Connor later recalled the effects of the flu upon the team. "The cameraman got sick, I got sick – even the damned dog got sick." Before they left Valdez the bill for the aviation services had to be tallied and settled. For filming in Alaska, the team had been given a budget of $10,000 to cover *all* costs of the helicopters. But the hiring of the helicopters, the usage of extras that were brought in due to the storm, the fees they amassed over the five days being snowed in, and the hiring and then non-use of a fixed-wing plane came to $75,000. The whole opening segment that lasted three minutes went on to cost the production company a total of $300,000, over $120,000 more than originally budgeted.

Washington D.C.

Washington D.C. offered plenty to the production team during the filming of *Raise the Titanic* which not only benefitted the filming schedule, but also to cut back on expenditures for the production, from filming in the Chesapeake Bay area for the movies cringe-worthy "wormy on the hooky", to the typewriter soundtrack of the Washington Star headquarters. This part of the production would prove to be the lengthiest of the filming schedule for *Raise the Titanic*. The Meridian International Center located at 1630 North West of Crescent Place, Washington, doubled as the U.S.S.R. Embassy and which was used for the interior and exterior scenes including that of the party attended by Capt. Andre Prevlov when he is interrupted by Marganin reporting in that *Titanic* had been discovered, which leads to Prevlov delivering the ultimatum to leak the discovery to the press. Also filmed within the building was the double sweeping staircase where Prevlov asks Marganin about the Sicilian Defence chess player move. One last scene was filmed inside the library as Prevlov is questioned about the Byzanium hidden inside the cargo hold of the *Titanic*.

The National Trust for Historic Preservation, located at 1785, North West of Massachusetts Avenue, Washington, was scouted for use in the movie as the headquarters for NUMA and the offices of Admiral James Sandecker. Fans of the film will recognize the building in the scene where Dirk Pitt pulls up in his Porche 911 as Dana Archibold is seen leaving the offices to where they both engage in conversation. Constructed between 1917-1922, the building is also known as the McCormick Apartments and is the headquarters of the National Trust for Historic Preservation, which was founded in 1949 to preserve and protect irreplaceable buildings and landscapes.

The Mayflower Hotel, located at 1127 Connecticut Avenue, North West, Washington was the setting for the film's recognizable press conference conducted by Admiral Sandecker. The interior sequences were filmed inside the hotel's beautiful Presidential Dining Room, recently renamed as the Chinese Room, where Sandecker holds the question and answer session with the press before exiting the hotel, only to be hounded over the rumours of the Byzanium, which was filmed outside the hotel's main entrance. This historic hotel, built in 1925 by property developer Allen E. Walker, is the largest luxury hotel in the District of Columbia hosting such notable guests as Charles DeGaulle, John Wayne, James "Jimmy" Stewart, President Harry Truman, and even Winston Churchill. *Raise the Titanic* author Clive Cussler, who makes a brief cameo appearance in the role as one of the press reporters, commented at the time, "I felt on the outside, looking into myself,"

At the time of production on *Raise the Titanic* the problems overseas as the Soviet-Afgan war raged prevented scenes from being filmed at the White House as President Jimmy Carter acted upon such a crucial time in the nation's history. The decision was taken to film at two locations to complete the inserts that were to depict the White House connection to the story. Exteriors scenes were shot outside the grounds of the White House on Pennsylvania Avenue, including a gated entrance, but for what was to be the interior, the crew traveled to Morven Park in Leesburg, Virginia, and the former home of Thomas Swann, governor of Maryland from 1866 to 1869. This was largely due to the similarities of the building's design to that of the White House. With the exception of the actual location filmed in Washington, the interior scenes were removed during the editing of the movie.

Prospect House on 3508 Prospect Street, NW, in the Georgetown neighbourhood of Washington, designed by William Thornton in 1788, the architect behind the Capitol Building, acted as the home of Admiral Sandecker with its gardens being used for Dirk Pitt to deliver the news of the whereabouts of the last known trace of Byzanium.

"He put the ore in a vault and saw it lowered into the hold of a ship. And on April 10, 1912, the ship sailed…"

The sixteen-room 2-million-dollar property served as the home of Washington attorney David Shapiro and once was used as the presidential guesthouse when President Harry Truman lived at Blair House. The film crew arrived at an inconvenient occasion when a fund-raising event was taking place to raise proceeds for the Vietnamese boat people who fled Vietnam after the war. The event was attended by 150 of Washington's leading citizens including folk singer Joan Baez and Senator Edward Moore "Teddy" Kennedy.

Business magnet Joe Wheeler loaned his 89-foot luxury yacht *The Potomac* to Marble Arch Productions during the filming of *Raise the Titanic* with a price tag of $6,000 for one-day of filming, starting from the Capital Yacht Club and down the Potomac River. Wheeler asked that William Frye should make the cheque payable to the Special Olympics. The vessel acted as the Presidential yacht for the meeting with Pitt, Seagram, Sandecker, CIA Director Nicholson, General Busby, and Admiral Kemper and Pitt explains, "We don't go to the mountain. The mountain comes to us."

Washington's Dulles International Airport supplied Apron W at the south end of the airfield for the arrival of Dirk Pitt with the wounded Koplin who are greeted by Seagram and Sandecker. During a break between scenes, Robards was asked what it was about the role of Sandecker that intrigued him.

"Money! The actors in this film don't have much to do. They (motioning towards Selby and Jordan) have more to do. They have some character development. Sandecker is just the guy in charge of the project. He doesn't go from this to that or to learn anything. These guys are different. They have a little more growth. But Sandecker has none. He is an old establishment man who was a liaison, a liaison with the government and the Navy, and the president. He's an authority figure. Act the clout of authority, and that's it. It's hard to do."

From there the crew moved to the United States Naval Research Laboratory located on the South West of Overlook Avenue, Washington for the interior scenes to be filmed of Seagram demonstrating the potential of the laser defense system to Sandecker, Busby, Nicholson, and Kemper. The Cyclotron Research Facility department of the base housed complex laser system equipment under testing for medical surgery and all tested behind walls and doors eight feet in thickness to safeguard employees against radiation leakage. *Raise the Titanic* was the first movie to allow its production crew to film within the laboratory giving a unique insight for the audience to glimpse the future of this vital field in science. One segment that did not make it into the final cut of the movie was filmed at Andrews Air Force Base where Seagram and Sandecker are trying to explain to Pitt what C.I.A. Nicholson has done, trying to flush out a Soviet spy, and releasing the news to Russia of the project. "You mean they're willing to jeopardize this whole project just so they can play their damn games?", says Seagram in response to the CIA getting involved with the Sicilian Project.

The final shooting location took place at the cities Washington Star newsrooms. Located at the northwest end of Pennsylvania Avenue, the newspaper ran from 1852 to 1981 when the company went bankrupt. Originally, it was intended to be filmed using a cast of extras but the decision was taken to use 31 of the company's staff playing themselves with Marble Arch Productions paying them one and a half times their normal salary for the Sunday, November 18 filming. As the newsrooms did not open until 5 pm on Sunday, the shooting schedule had to take place before that time so as not to disrupt the running of the newsroom. It was a long day for the new extras as they paced around the offices in noise-cancelling clothing, but that's the sacrifice you have to make for fame and fortune.

Chapter 15: On Location • 7

All quiet please. Filming in progress on the CBS Studio Centre soundstage. *(ITC – Author's collection)*

The film's set decorator Mickey S. Michaels fools around with the DEMS robotic arm during preparations at the CBS Studio soundstage where some insert scenes were being filmed including the interior areas of the submersibles. *(Author's collection)*

The movies memorable opening montage was a selection of images edited into a sequence by Gene Kraft. But not all were of the *Titanic*. Going from left to right, top to bottom; The double bottom of *Olympic* takes shape; *Titanic* is ready for launch; The fourth funnel of *Olympic* arrives at the ship to be fitted; 1919 image of *Olympic* as she undergoes a post war refit; The propellers of *Olympic* in 1924; *Titanic* in the Belfast Graving Dock in March 1912;

Chapter 15: On Location

Olympic's starboard B-Deck promenade; The First Class Lounge of Olympic; Titanic steams out of Southampton; Four of the main decks of Olympic in 1911; Titanic begins her maiden voyage; Titanic in Belfast Lough during sea trials; Olympic 2nd class publicity brochure; 2nd class area of Titanic's boat deck; Dixieland Jazz Band in 1917; Passengers take to the dance floor of the Cunard liner Mauretania. (Images: Harland & Wolff/Museums of Northern Ireland/Author's collection)

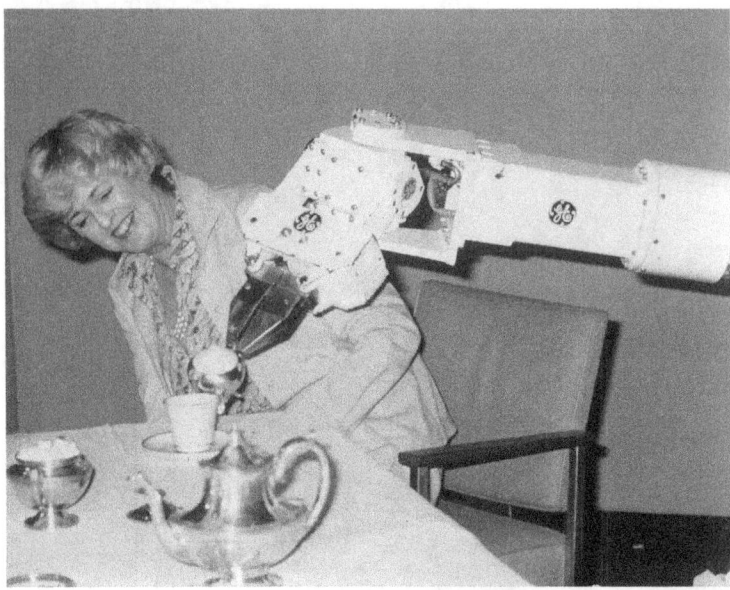

Tea for two? During a break in filming, the DEMS takes part in a spot of publicity for *Raise the Titanic*, Executive Producer William Frye and guest, Lady Sarah Churchill, grandniece of the late Winston Churchill, are served refreshments as part of a demonstration to how precise the robotic arm can be. *(Author's collection)*

Chapter 15: On Location • 11

The *Starfish* interior set was built inside one of the indoor filming tanks at the CBS Studio soundstage. When the time came to lens the flooding of the submersible, the actors played their parts and read their lines as the tank and set was flooded. *(ITC – Author's collection)*

This behind the scenes photograph shows how they filmed the scene through the safety glass of the soundstage tank as the actors play out the sequence as they struggle to pull the lever to release the cockpit sphere of the *Starfish*. (*Author's collection*)

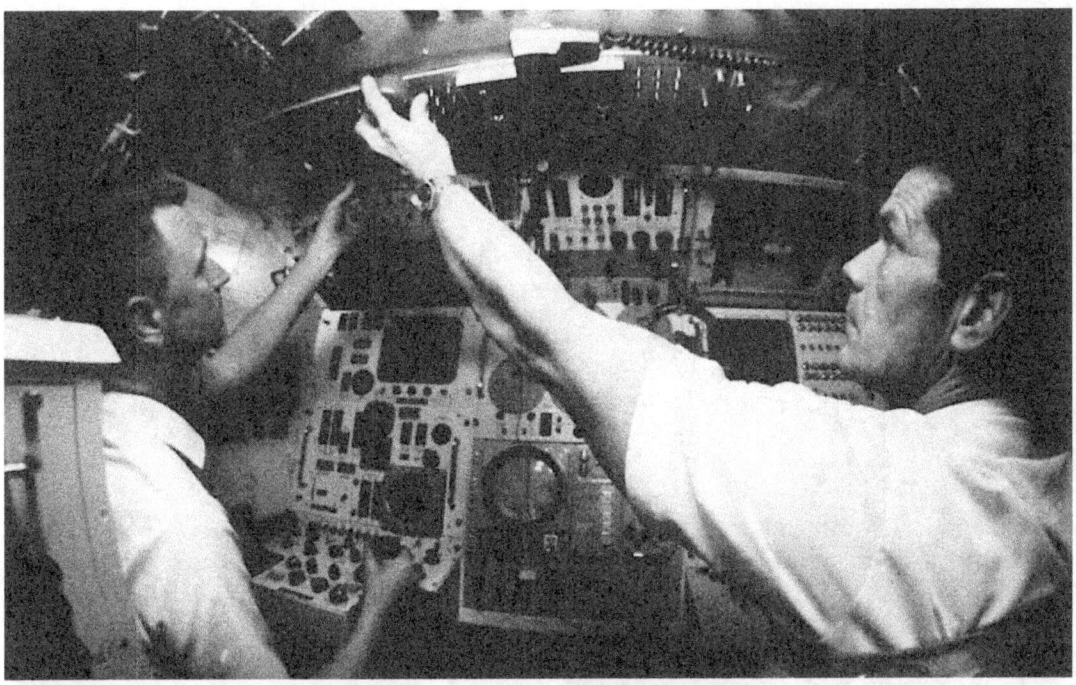
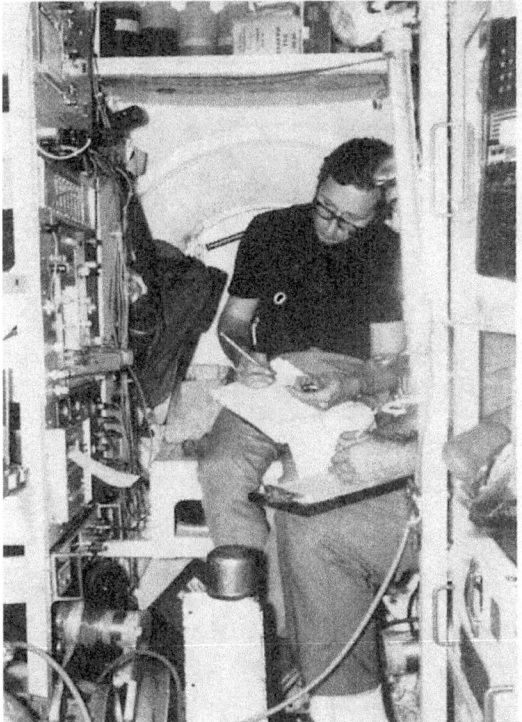

LEFT AND TOP: Lockheed publicity photographs from the late 1960s that show the interior of the real D.S.V. *Deep Quest* which would have been used as reference points for the recreations of the submersible interiors created by Mickey Michaels over at the CBS Studio Center. *(Lockheed – Author's collection)*

14 • *Raise The Titanic*

David Selby, Michael Pataki, Robert Broyles and Brendan Burns are thrown into danger when the *Deep Quest* gets stuck on the *Titanic*. *(ITC – Author's collection)*

"Two more weeks underwater and the submersibles crews will come after you with a harpoon." Series of candid photographs taken on-set of the submersible interiors at the CBS Studio Center soundstage. *Top left:* Mark L. Taylor and M. Emmet Walsh. *Top right*: Trent Dolan and Michael C. Gwynne. *Bottom left:* Dirk Blocker. *Bottom right:* Michael Pataki and Hilly Hicks. *(Author's collection)*

Chapter 15: On Location • 15

Director Jerry Jameson guides Richard Jordan through a scene in the interior set of the *Sea Cliff*. *(Author's collection)*

From left to right; Ken Place, Trent Dolan and Richard Jordan in the *Sea Cliff* interior set. *(ITC - Author's collection)*

The sonar pool at Rockwell International where the drop test *Titanic* model would be filmed. *(Author's collection)*

Bill Blackburn, set wardrobe man, affixes a company logo to the smock of Al Stimpert, one of the AMSD employees. *(Author's collection)*

Assistant Director Scott Easton (left) discusses a scene with three AMSD employees. *(Author's collection)*

The sonar pool all lit up during filming on *Raise the Titanic*. *(Author's collection)*

Jason Robards and David Selby with AMSD employees Al Stimpert (left), Bob Jones (centre) and Jim Hull. *(Author's collection)*

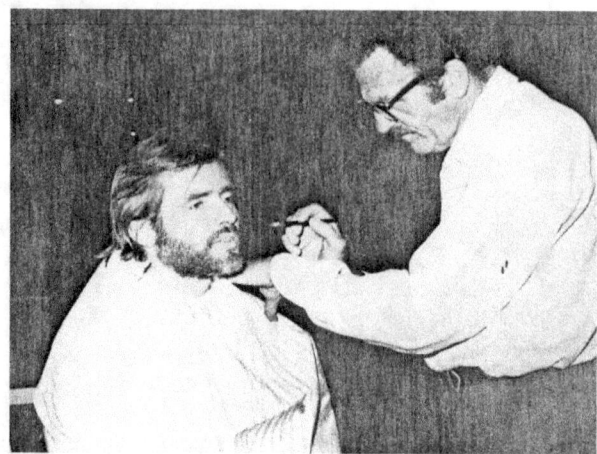
Makeup artist Bob Dawn transforms Richard Jordan into the character of Dirk Pitt. *(Author's collection)*

Chapter 15: On Location • 17

Jason Robards and William Frye discuss filming. *(Author's collection)*

Assistant cameraman Dennis Matsudo (left) and Pat McGinnis prepare an underwater camera for shooting. *(Author's collection)*

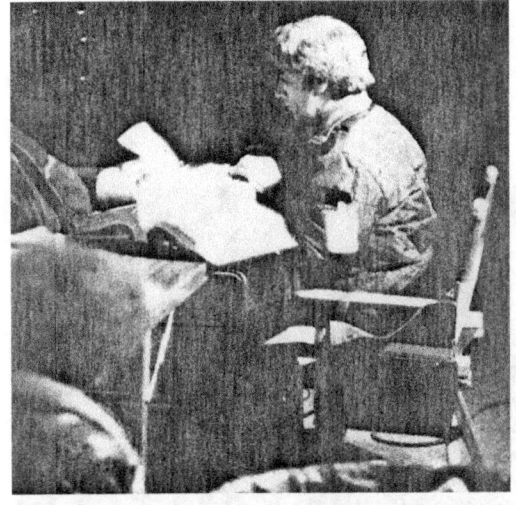

Script supervisor Ray Quiroz types up last-minute script revisions. He was also responsible for keeping track of the number of takes for each scene and provides brief descriptions of the scenes in their final form for the film editor. *(Author's collection)*

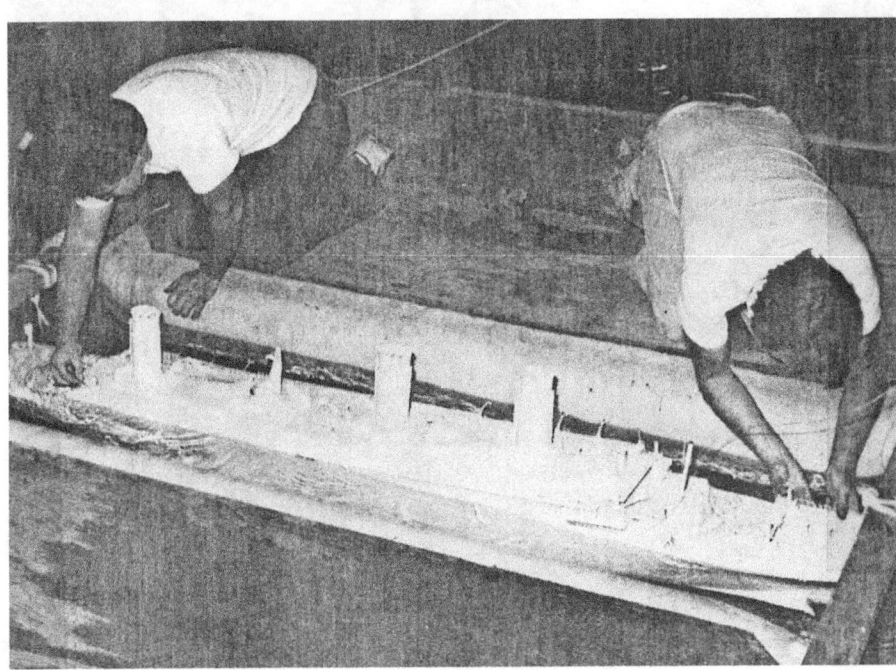

Crew prepare to launch the 9ft white drop-test model of the *Titanic* from the platform on the surface of the sonar pool. *(Author's collection)*

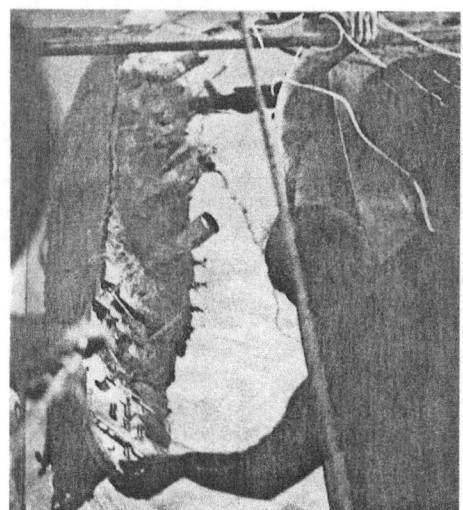

With the model's stern pitched up to simulate the sinking, the crew release the *Titanic* for its journey to the bottom of the tank. *(Author's collection)*

The scenes of Pitt, Seagram, Sandecker and Dr. Silverstein watching the drop-test unfolding on the monitors were shot in the main laboratory of Rockwell International. *(ITC – Author's collection)*

Holy Svlardov, Batman! The interior of the Bronson Canyon cave in Griffith Park, Los Angeles, that would become the cold entombed mine shaft of the Russian island that once was robbed of Byzanium. *(Photograph © Steven Miller)*

Chapter 15: On Location • 19

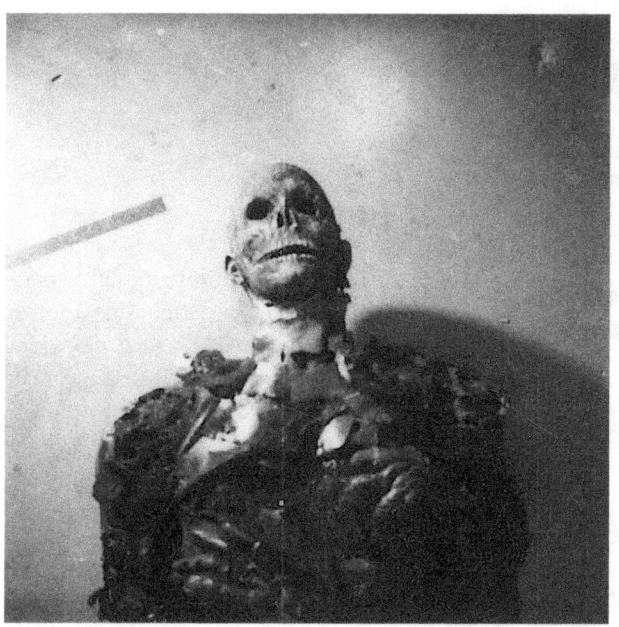

A very early rendering of the remains of Sgt. Jake Hobart that was created by Hollywood FX legends The Burman's Studio. *(Original Polaroid – Author's collection)*

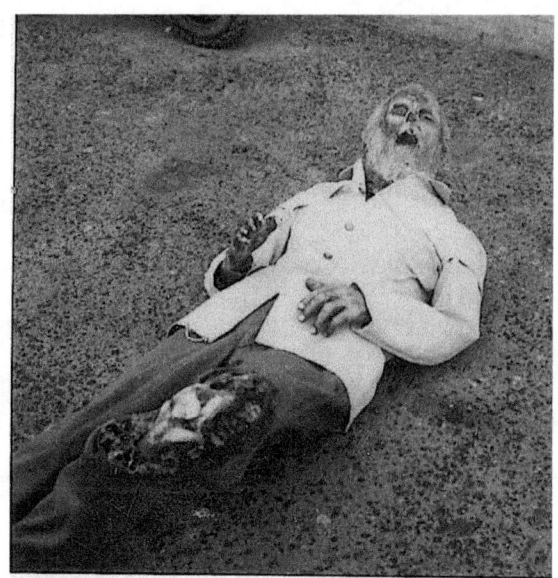

This Polaroid shows a second attempt by The Burman's Studio at creating Jake Hobart. What is of particular interest is the hand written details which indicate that *Raise the Titanic* originally was given a 15A certification. *(Original Polaroid – Author's collection)*

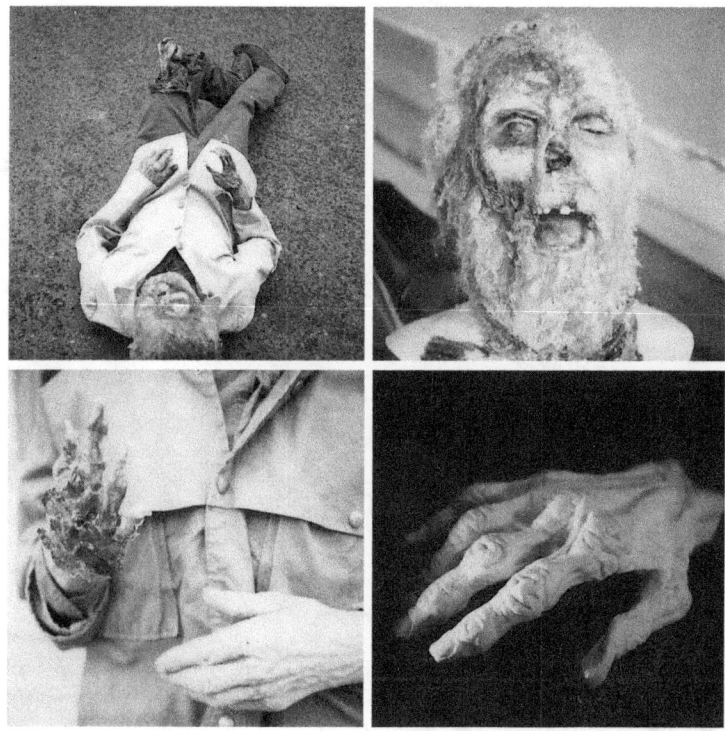

More views of The Burman's Studio second rendering of Jake Hobart. His change of appearance was largely down to the film studio who would check on the progress of the FX work, requesting tweaks here and there which they feel would better suit the film. *(Original Polaroid – Author's collection)*

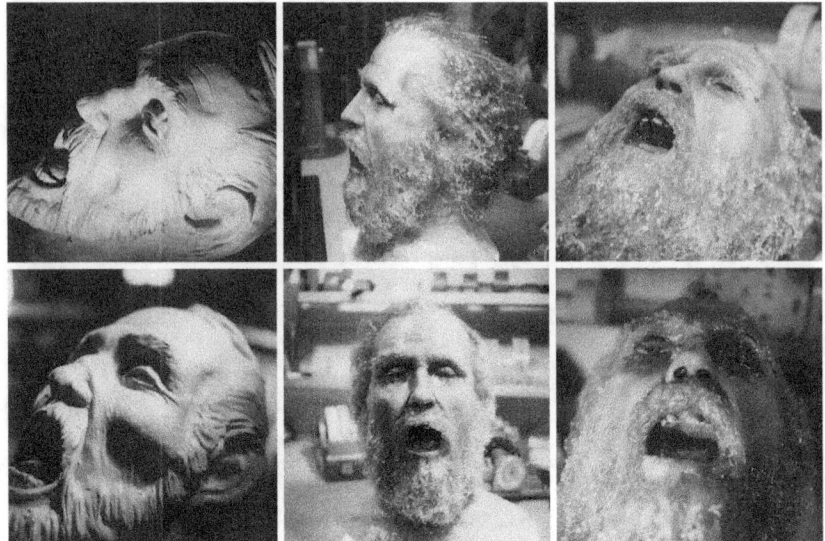

The studio approved final version of Jake Hobart including the ice chippings in his beard. Speaking on his work, Rob Burman of The Burman's Studio said "all those details would be lost when the body was finally entombed in the clear resin." *(Original Polaroid - Author's collection)*

Koplin (Stewart Moss) examines the remains of Hobart who has been frozen in time in a large block of ice within the mine shaft. *(ITC – Author's collection)*

The sun sets over the glaciers of Heather Island, January 1980. *(Author's collection)*

Chapter 15: On Location • 21

On the approach to Prince William Sound, Mickey Michaels snaps this view of the snow- and ice-covered landscape. *(Author's collection)*

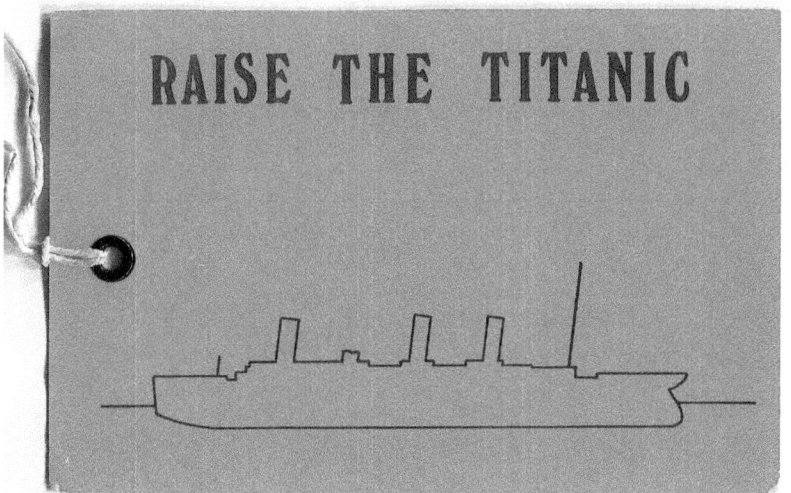
Original film crew equipment transportation label. *(Author's collection)*

Executive in Charge of Production Dick O'Connor wraps up warm for a day's filming on Heather Island for *Raise the Titanic*. *(Author's collection)*

Fuelling up the helicopter at Sheffield House. The craft was used to not only ferry crew and supplies out, but also to capture the aerial footage of the sweeping vista of the frozen island during the film's opening credits and the view of Pitt as he carries the wounded Koplin across the ice. *(Author's collection)*

Actor Michael Kalcsar and Teddy before they head out onto the glacier. *(Author's collection)*

Jerry Jameson (left) talks with Stewart Moss (centre) and Richard Jordan (right) over the sequence to be filmed for when Koplin is shot by the Russian sentry. *(Author's collection)*

The crew setting up to shoot the scenes with Michael Kalcsar, Teddy, Stewart Moss and Richard Jordan. *(Author's collection)*

Chapter 15: On Location • 23

Richard Jordan takes a cigarette break before the cameras start to roll. *(Author's collection)*

As the call of "Action!" rolls across the ice fields of the Columbia Glacier, Jordan gets into character and Pitt emerges from behind the ice, takes aim at the Russian sentry and his attack dog, and pulls the trigger. *(Author's collection)*

24 • *Raise The Titanic*

Jerry Jameson and Stewart Moss. *(Author's collection)*

Mickey Michaels captures the moment when mother nature turns on the film crew as sections of the glacier give way, crashing down into the ice strewn sea and sending a tidal surge of water racing towards the film crew to swamp the location. *(Author's collection)*

When the production gets snowed in at Sheffield House, those stranded they try to pass the time away. Jerry Jameson and Dick O'Connor resort to a game of pool in the camps recreational room. *(Author's collection)*

Meridian House, known in 1980 as the Meridian International Center, was the setting of the Washington U.S.S.R. Embassy. *(Photograph © Stephen Bobb Photography)*

The interior of the Meridian International Center dressed with film props to represent the U.S.S.R. Embassy. *(ITC – Author's collection)*

Actor Marvin Silbersher as Soviet Ambassador Antonov. *(ITC – Author's collection)*

The offices of the National Trust in Washington that doubled as the headquarters of NUMA. *(ITC/ITV Studios)*

The scene of Pitt (Richard Jordan) and Dana (Anne Archer) was filmed outside the offices of the National Trust at the junction of 18th Street & Massachusetts Avenue, North West. *(ITC – Author's collection)*

Chapter 15: On Location • 27

Dirk Pitt's Porche was a 1977 Turbo 930 Carrera. Hired from the owner through the Porche Club, the car was originally to be on set for an intended 21 days. Filming with the vehicle was completed in 6 days at a rate of $100 per day to the owner who was paid for a total of 11 days. Richard Jordan had a love-hate relationship with the sports car, finding the cramped driver's cockpit an issue for his 6ft frame. *(Porche advertisement – Author's collection)*

Publicity photograph of Richard Jordan that was taken inside one of the offices to the National Trust which doubled as Admiral Sandecker's NUMA office. *(ITC – Author's collection)*

The grand Mayflower Hotel in Washington. *(Period postcard – Author's collection)*

The Chinese Room at the Mayflower Hotel that was the setting for the press conference. *(Author's collection)*

Rare behind the scenes photograph taken during the filming of the press conference as Jason Robards delivers his lines from the podium. *(Author's collection)*

Author of *Raise the Titanic!* Clive Cussler who had an all too brief cameo role as a reporter at the press conference. *(Author's collection)*

Admiral Sandecker addresses the press on how NUMA plan to raise the *Titanic*. *(ITC – Author's collection)*

Chapter 15: On Location • 29

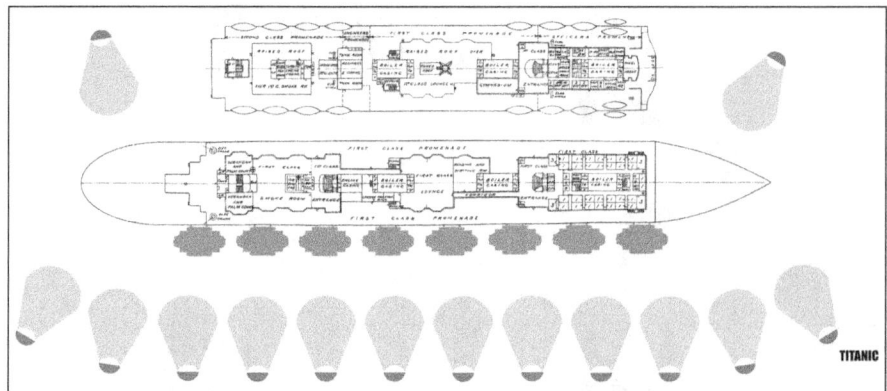

Press Conference Diagram #1 showing the location of the salvage tanks and lighting rig locations around the hull. *(Illustration © Jonathan Smith)*

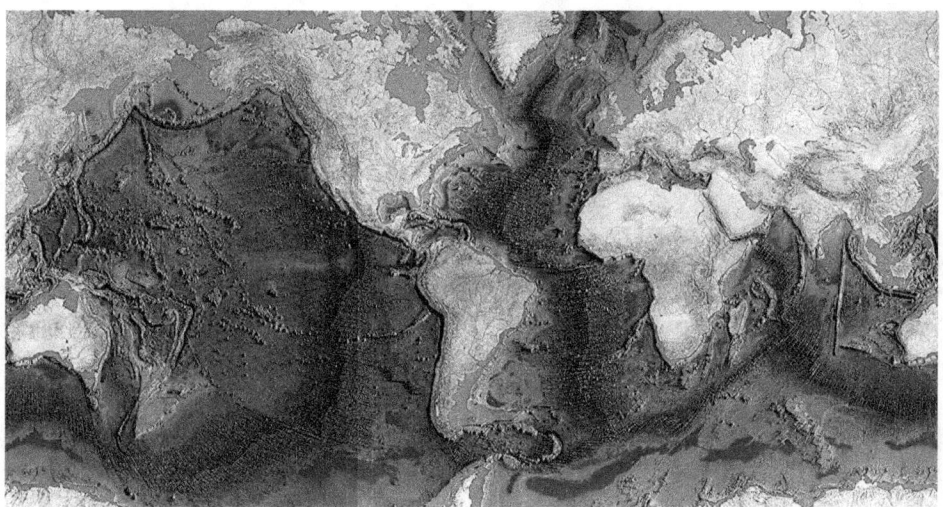

Press Conference Diagram #2 depicts the World Ocean Floor with the unique topographic research from Bruce C. Heezen and Marie Tharp. The data was then transformed into this amazing artwork by Heinrich Berann and Heinz Vielkind in 1970 and subsequently released in prints and postcards. *(Artwork © Heinrich Berann & Heinz Vielkind)*

Behind the scenes image of Robards with the miniature salvage tank. *(Author's collection)*

"The hull will be jarred loose from the bottom suction. And the *Titanic* will come to the surface." *(ITC – Author's collection)*

ABOVE: Sandecker (Robards) demonstrates to the press reporters how and where the salvage tanks will be attached to the wreck. TOP RIGHT: Sandecker then turns to lift the scale model of the *Titanic* from its stand to demonstrate how the ship will come to the surface. MIDDLE & BOTTOM RIGHT: Director Jerry Jameson watches on as Director of Photography Matthew F. Leonetti with the use of his 35mm Ultracam films the scene as Sandecker is mobbed by the press outside the Mayflower Hotel. *Raise the Titanic* was the first major film production where the newly developed Ultracam was used. *(Author's collection)*

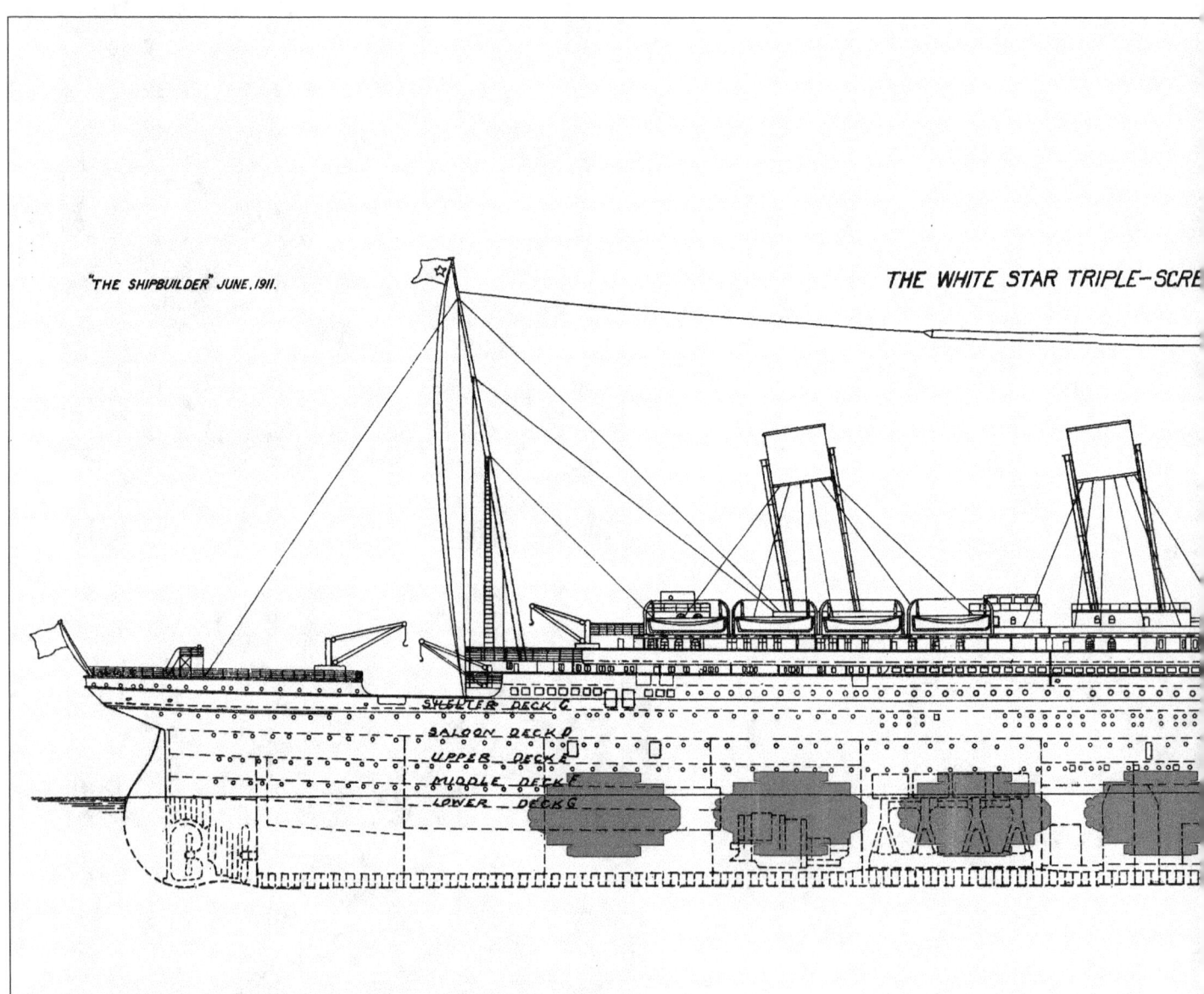

Press Conference Diagram #3 showing the starboard profile of the *Titanic* with the iceberg gash, missing funnel and the locations of the salvage tanks. *(Illustration © Jonathan Smith)*

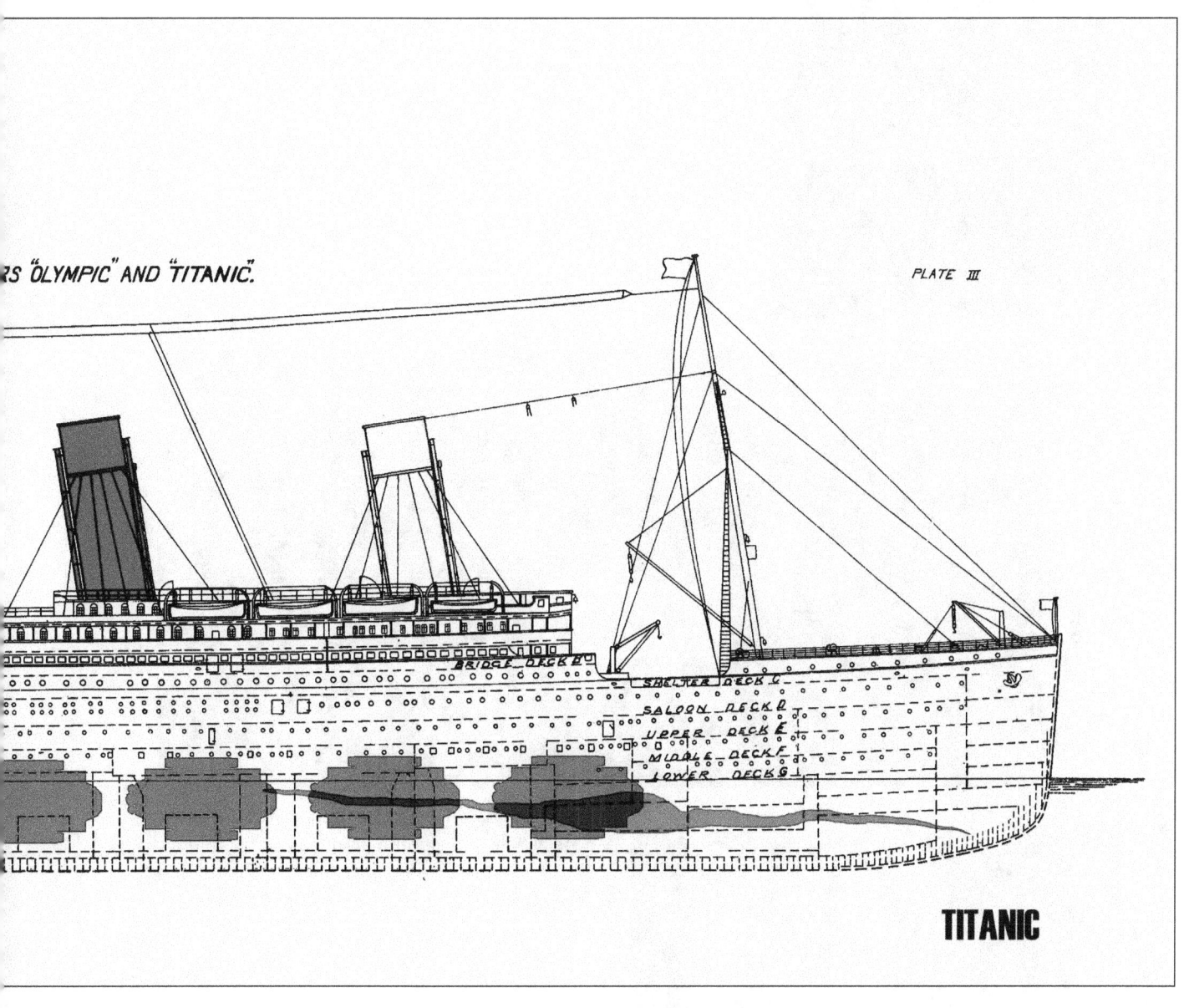

Rare candid photograph of Jason Robards with the 1:350th scale Entex *Titanic* model kit. Note the miniature salvage tank sitting on the table. *(Author's collection)*

BELOW: Morven Park mansion that doubled as the White House and used for some interior and exterior scenes with Jason Robards and David Selby. *(Postcard – Author's collection)*

Sandecker and Seagram leave the White House after trying to convince the president to go ahead with the Sicilian Project. *(ITC – Author collection)*

Chapter 15: On Location • 35

Prospect House that became the home of Admiral Sandecker. The property was used for both interior and exterior scenes; the latter being the sequence when Pitt drops the bombshell that the Byzanium was loaded aboard the *Titanic*. *(Library of Congress)*

ITC publicity photographs of David Selby taken in the gardens of Prospect House. *(ITC – Author's collection)*

The 89ft luxury yacht *The Potomac*. *(ITC/ITV Studios)*

Richard Jordan and Jason Robards take a lunch break between rehearsing lines for that evening's night shoot on board *The Potomac*. *(Author's collection)*

Robards looking serious in his role as Sandecker during filming on board *The Potomac*. *(ITC – Author's collection)*

Chapter 15: On Location • 37

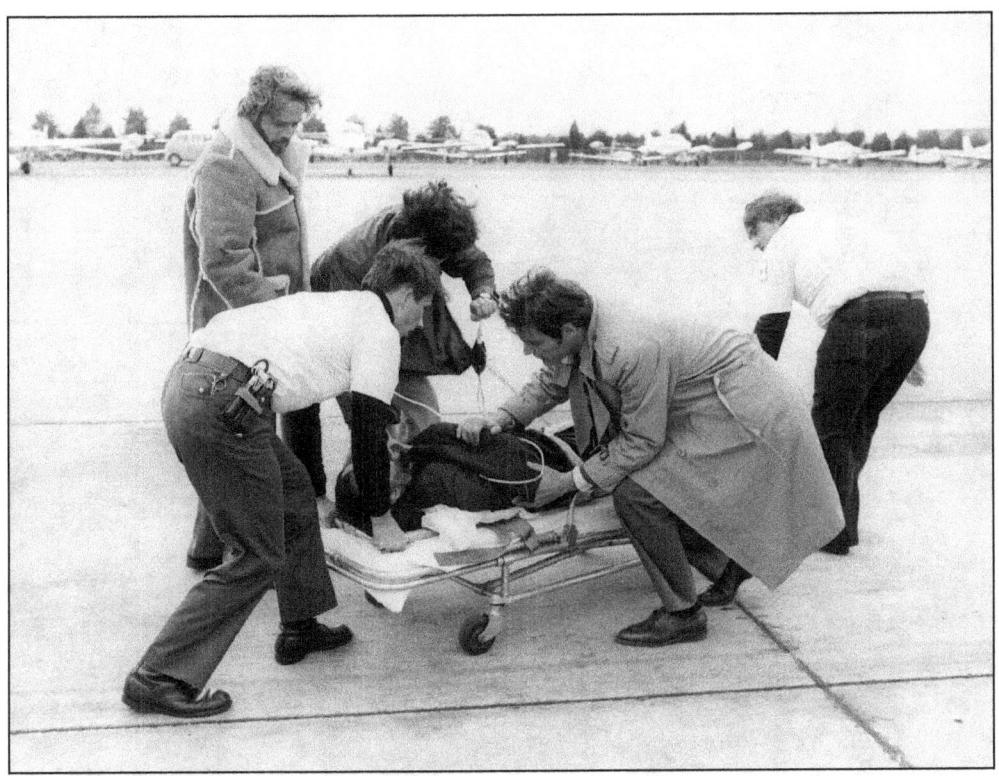
Seagram desperately tries to get answers from a semi-conscious Koplin, much to the annoyance of Dirk Pitt. *(ITC – Author's collection)*

Dr. Gene Seagram demonstrates the workings of his laser defence system. *(ITC – Author's collection)*

Rare behind the scenes on the filming of the laser system mock-up at The Cyclotron Research Facility. The scenes would eventually end up on the cutting room floor. Note the optic pattern that is being transmitted to the screen that shows the laser system rays spreading out to form the wall. *(Author's collection)*

Charles Macaulay as General Dale Busby and photographed within the grounds of the United States Naval Research Laboratory. *(ITC – Author's collection)*

Chapter 15: On Location • 39

Seagram demonstrating the potential of the laser defence system to Sandecker, Busby, Nicholson and Kemper. *(ITC – Author's collection)*

40 • *Raise The Titanic*

One of the conference rooms of the United States Naval Research Laboratory doubles as the main conference room at the NUMA headquarters. *(Patrick Walsh collection / Author's collection)*

Chapter 15: On Location • 41

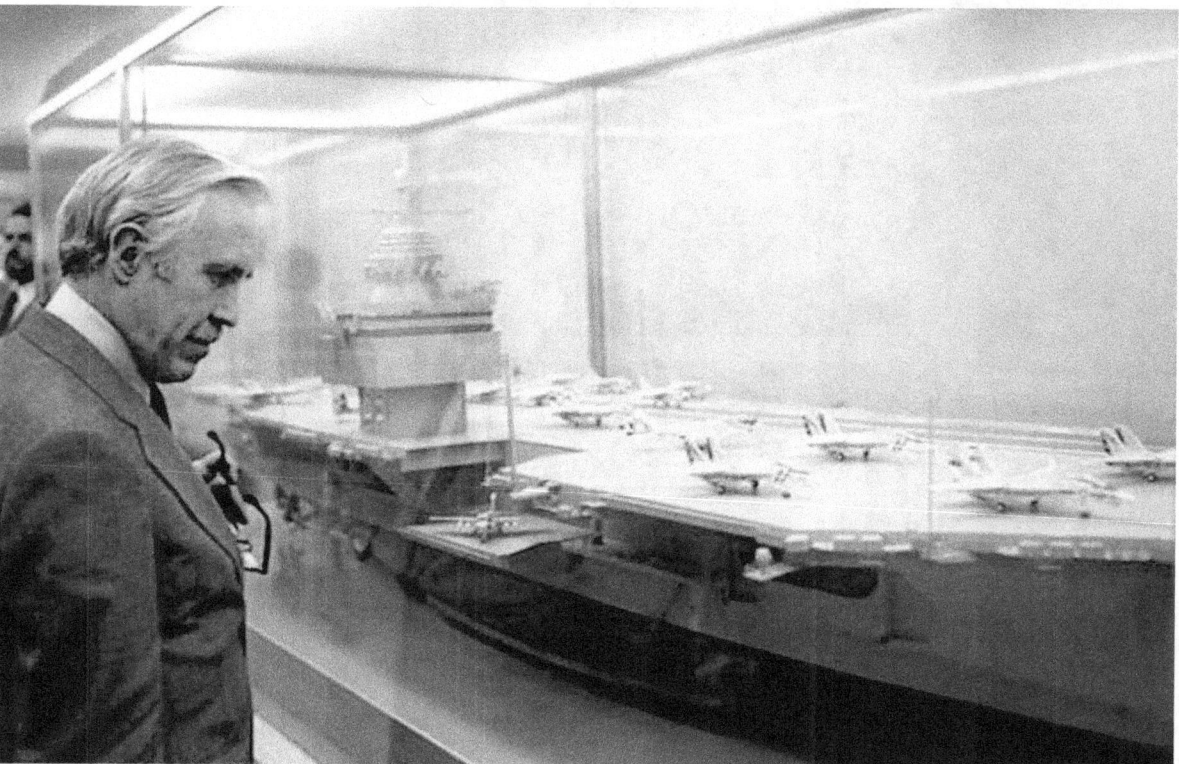

TOP and ABOVE: Pitt explains to the U.S. Navy and C.I.A. officials the importance of the project and the need to find and recover the *Titanic*. Jason Robards inspects a scale model of the *U.S.S. Enterprise* on display in the halls of the United States Naval Research buildings. *(Author's collection)*

42 • *Raise The Titanic*

One of the workshops of the United States Naval Research Laboratory being used as the restoration labs behind the preservation of the salvaged cornet. *(ITC – Author's collection)*

Chapter 15: On Location • 43

Gene arrives at the newspaper's office of *The Washington Star* to meet Dana. And the building as it appeared in 1921. *(ITC/ITV Studios/Library of Congress)*

Dana and Gene look skywards as a helicopter delivering a copy of *10 Easy Steps to Putting A Worm on A Hook* appears over the waters of the bay. *(Author's collection)*

Anne Archer as Dana Archibald photographed on the jetty at Calvert Bay. *(ITC – Author's collection)*

Chapter 16

The Curse of Cornwall

"One of the survivors is a man named Bigalow. He was a Junior Third Officer in charge of cargo and he's living in England someplace in Cornwall."

Admiral James Sandecker

"It's an odd thing you know. I've had a few ships shot out from under me. More than my share. Three in the 1914/18 fracas and two in 39/45. But all anybody ever asks me about is the *Titanic*." For the fictional location of Southby, the production team flew out to England and the south-westerly coast of St Ives in Cornwall, a small and picturesque seaside fishing town that lies on the coast of the Celtic Sea. This quaint little town, a firm favourite for many for their holiday destination due to the beautiful clarity of the waters, golden sand beaches, and stunning coastal views that are lined with whitewashed cottages and Victorian villas, has been awarded the honor of best UK seaside town three times during 2007, 2010 and 2011. And well deserved too. The origins of St Ives are attributed to the legend of the Irish Saint Ia of Cornwall, evangelist, and martyr in the 5th century. One of the most popular attractions along with the oldest building in the town, and in the whole of Cornwall, is the fisherman's pub The Sloop Inn which dates back to the year 1312. The pub with its adjacent restaurant is a blend of old and new with such character and charm that most visitors not accustomed to the sea would soon be converted. For the many, the pub, with its old-world style, could be just another seaside establishment catering for both residents and visitors to the town and harbour. But to the fans of *Raise the Titanic*, the pub is the retirement home of surviving crew member John Bigalow, wonderfully played by screen legend Alec Guinness.

The production crew's journey from London was during the early weeks of winter in December 1979. Their arrival between the dates of 10 – 14 December was poorly timed as the west coast of Great Britain bore the brunt of heavy gales with St Ives being battered with 85mph winds during one of the worst storms to hit the town in 135 years. But as the rains and heavy winds blew across the harbour and town the crew were safe and warm in the surroundings of the lavish Tregenna Castle hotel that sat high above the town. On Wednesday 12 December Jerry Jameson, accompanied by David Selby and Richard Jordan, made the 266-mile journey by train from London's Paddington Station to St Erth railway station located 4-miles from St Ives. Three primary locations, picked out by the scouting unit back in July, had been secured that included the town's harbour pier, The Sloop Inn, and the nearby Barnoon Cemetery with its cliff sides leading down to the peaceful sands of Porthmeor beach below.

A Single Bed that Beckons

Friday 14 December was a day of preparation for the crew before the first scenes were to be filmed that weekend. The following day Alec Guinness made the train journey from his London Westminster apartment to Cornwall; "I'm a senior citizen now – so I can travel half fare" he joked to Jerry Jameson on arrival to the picturesque coastal town. That same day the first of the sequences put to celluloid was filmed from the chartered helicopter that took off from Penzance heliport to capture the sweeping vista across the harbour and over to Smeaton's Pier. Sunday granted a day of rehearsals for Jordan, Guinness, and Selby allowing for The Sloop Inn to be finalized for filming. One embarrassing setback came when the ancient timbers of the snug were painted by the production crew. The result of decades of built-up of nicotine that had become etched into the timbers prevented the paint from drying. For the weeks to follow after filming the paint had to be washed off and the pubs seating covered in plastic until it was all rectified. Nothing was more glamorous than filming in winter, in England, during gales as winds whipped up icy cold spray from the choppy seas. But this was Hollywood. Cameras began to roll in the Sloop on Monday 17 December as Guinness and Jordan carried out their first scenes together, firstly at the bar with actress Nancy Nevinson and locals brought in as extras including The Sloop Inn regulars Bengy Penberthy and his wife Cissy, before moving into the seating area for Alec Guinness' fine delivery of Bigalow's heartwarming memory of his first love; *Titanic*. Nancy was no stranger to the story of *Titanic* having appeared that same year in the EMI production of *S.O.S. Titanic* playing the part of 1st class passenger Ida Straus. As Guinness approached the bar, he removed his cap and tossed it towards the coat hooks in a series of unsuccessful attempts to get it to land on one. After several takes, Guinness accepted defeat, although the extras seated around the bar area were delighted in having their drink glasses topped up for each take. Guinness and Jordan then move to the other side of the pub into the quaint disserted area named by Bigalow as his quarter-deck, which reveals his little museum of keepsakes of *Titanic* ephemera that adorn the walls and display case. While the Sloop maintained its original cottage style decor with handcut and carved timbered beamed walls and ceilings it still required something extra for the viewer to tie it together in being a retired sailor's home.

The props department from Pinewood Studios had made a large display board fabricated and finished with several cuttings from various issues of *The Titanic Commutator*, a magazine sold to members of the American-based *Titanic Historical Society*. In the center of the board was a color print depicting *Titanic*'s sister *Olympic* at sea in a beautiful sun setting that was copied from an original painting by *Titanic* artist Ken Marschall and presented to the late Ed Kamuda of the *Titanic Historical Society*. Later, during a screening of the movie in America, Ken was delighted to see his painting making a cameo appearance on the big screen. On the wall hung the prop department's glass-fronted display case housing a partially faded and moth-eaten White Star Line flag, folded up and mounted inside to emphasize the flag's large white star on the red background. The flag, often questioned on its authenticity, was a replica that was purposely made for the film production for both the sequences in Cornwall and when Pitt hangs the pennant from the stern of the raised liner. The final visual piece was a 30-inch model of the ill-fated *Titanic* in all her 1912 beauty. The model was a store-bought injection-moulded plastic model kit that was commercially on sale and produced by the American model kit manufacture Entex. The model was built as a visual aid by the prop department and was originally not intended for use in front of the camera. But that changed when Guinness requested its use when he recommended changing the scene from the character reminiscing the vessel's elegance by staring at the series of images on the wall to that of picking up the model. That change, although insignificant, worked better as it led to Guinness reaching out to open the display case and remove the pennant within to hand it to Jordan while delivering Bigalow's closing dialogue; "If you manage to bring her up again, maybe you'd put it back where it belongs."

The morning of Tuesday 18 December was cold, extremely overcast with winds lashing across the harbour from the approaching storm. But that day offered a break in the weather as director

Jerry Jameson, who had been counting down the hours, had his team set up the equipment to shoot the exterior sequences for the film starting with the open and exposed Smeaton's Pier. The pier was named after its builder John Smeaton who engineered its construction between 1767 and 1770. The pier unusually features two lighthouses with the first indicating the piers original constructed length of 120ft and the second, located at the very end of the pier, installed when it was extended by another 300ft during the 1890s. As Jordan and Guinness carried out their roles some of St Ives' residents were given the opportunity to be extras out on the pier as fishermen returning home with their catch of the day. From the pier, the camera crews moved back to The Sloop Inn to film a brief exterior shot of Guinness and Jordan as they walk towards the main door into the public house. Again, the local residents of St Ives were called upon to serve as extras while one of the film crew's own vehicles, a light green metallic Rover SD-1 V8, made its on-screen debut. The car was registered to ITC and used to speedily send completed film reels (rushes) to the Rank Studios for inspection. The unit then moved to Island Road and to the public carpark that was located at the foot of The Island hill for the final scenes to be filmed between Guinness, Jordan and briefly David Selby. The scene was to be the formal goodbye as Bigalow escorts Pitt to a waiting car that will whisk Pitt away to the airport for the flight back to the United States. Waiting at the car is Gene Seagram. As the two men walk towards the waiting vehicle, Jordan delivers his line, "This must be a pretty quiet life for a man like you?", Guinness replies, "God help a man who can't live by himself", "We all end up in a single bed sooner or later." Although the footage was cut, the audio did make it into the Cornwall segment of Pitt and Bigalow as they walk towards The Sloop Inn.

A Survivors Tale

With Guinness' performance on film, it must have come as a relief for the actors and crews to leave the cold openness of the pier and head indoors to the warmth of a well-deserved evening hot meal and drinks. One employee of the Bar Capri recalled the time when the actors and film unit came to dine in the restaurant. As the servers' shift had now come to an end for the day, the eagerly watching Sir Alec requested the employee to accompany him at his table. Guinness was not seated with the other actors or crew and was seemingly enjoying his own company up until that point. Asked as to why he was eating alone, Guinness remarked "I cannot abide watching Americans eat. They cut their food, change hands, and shovel it into their mouths." For his role as the fictional *Titanic* crewmember John Bigalow, Alec Guinness was paid £45,000 for the three days on location for *Raise the Titanic*. At the age of 65, Guinness had accumulated a lucrative filming career and yet despite his financial security brought about by the success of the *Star Wars* film trilogy and his performance in *Tinker Tailor Soldier Spy*, Guinness still found it hard to turn down any offers that came his way. As the camera rolled and Guinness delivered his lines, someone special was watching from the side lines who had lived through that tragic night of April 15, 1912. After learning of the filming going on in St Ives for a *Titanic* movie, local Cornish resident and *Titanic* survivor, William Rowe Richards, had travelled to the location to watch the events unfold. Richards was born on 1 April 1909 in Penzance and was the eldest son of James Sibley Richards and Emily Hocking-Richards. On 10 April 1912 William, his younger brother Sibley, and their mother boarded the *Titanic* at Southampton docks for the journey to New York to meet their father who had emigrated sometime before to set up their new home in Ohio. The voyage was originally to take place on board the White Star liner R.M.S. *Oceanic* until the cancelation brought about by the ending coal strikes of that year, which resulted in many vessels being laid-up in ports. With coal accumulated for *Titanic*'s maiden voyage now on board, passengers from other vessels were transferred to the new liner, including the Richards who received an upgrade to *Titanic*'s more spacious 2nd class accommodations.

Emily and her two sons were being accompanied on the voyage by their grandmother, Eliza, their uncle Richard and aunty Ellen. On the night of the disaster, Ellen rushed into the cabin to wake the family up with the news that the ship was sinking and that passengers and crew were being evacuated. Master William, his brother Sibley, mother, grandmother, and aunt were led to safety by being allowed to board lifeboat 4. Uncle Richard who was not permitted to enter would later perish in the sinking. The surviving family made it to New York on board the rescue ship *Carpathia* where they would remain in

Ohio until the end of 1914 where they returned home to Cornwall. The years that were to follow would see the brothers drift apart with William, in adulthood, marrying in May 1929. William served in the Royal Navy during World War II and assisted with the heroic evacuations at Dunkirk between May and June 1941. His latter years before retirement was that as a manager for a smoked salmon company during his time living in Carbis Bay in St Ives. During the filming of *Raise the Titanic,* he was approached to comment about the production and his connection to the disaster; "They'll have to build a bridge before I try and cross the Atlantic again", he said. The last few years of his life, William would frequently be asked to interviews as local media outlets covered the subject of *Titanic*, more so after her discovery in September 1985. Following a heart attack on 9 January 1988, William passed away at the age of 79. He is interred at Longstone Cemetery, Carbis Bay, Cornwall. When the movie had its UK premiere in London, William turned down the invitation to attend the gala event. It was then passed to younger brother Sibley, who accepted and attended the screening as a special guest of Lord Lew Grade. Sibley George Richards passed away aged 76 at his Penzance home on the 4 December 1987 and is interred at St Paul Cemetery in Cornwall.

"Thank God for Southby!"

Presented with the postcard, Seagram puzzles at the writing on the reverse. "Typical country church and graveyard in the county of Hampshire near the village of Southby." Pitt turns the card back around again to show the photographic image of an old English cemetery and chapel overlooking a rocky coastline. "Twenty miles from Southampton" replies Pitt. "We were wrong. We thought it was a man, but it's a place. Thank God for Southby." Before anyone reading this opens up a map of towns and villages in the United Kingdom in search of Southby your search will be in vain. During the scouting of locations for the film during the summer of 1979, the town of St Ives offered multiple spots for filming scenes which would cut back on transportation times and costs. Although the movie's closing sequences were filmed at Barnoon Cemetery close to the heart of the town, Barnoon was not the original location for Hobart's coffin and its deadly contents. Overlooking the beach to the east lies the aptly named The Island with its 15th century St. Nicholas stone-built chapel. The chapel sat alone on an elevated part of the island with a spectacular vista of the town and harbour to the south-west and the open waters of the Celtic Sea to the north. After lengthy discussions between the film studio and Penwith District Council, the grounds of the chapel were secured for filming. Due to the nature of the chapel and the adjacent sacred grounds permission was denied for any major construction work to be undertaken which included opening up the ground to simulate an open grave. Any close-up view needed of the grave and coffin would be completed within a sound stage.

From the props department at Pinewood studios came the series of fiberglass gravestones from previous productions, a long section of artificial stone wall with an arch, a coffin, and a production-created headstone bearing the name of Jake Hobart. As the film studio descended on the town on 10 December the carpenters set to work building their artificial graveyard to the side of St. Nicholas' chapel. With the wall, arch, and headstones secured in place all was left was for the actors and cameras to attend. The filming schedule for the graveyard scenes was set for Wednesday, 19 December. But the great British weather had other ideas. As heavy seas slammed the coastline and severe gales ripped across the town, the film crew could do nothing but watch the unfolding turmoil from the comforts of their lodgings. Then as the storms eased and the crews ventured back outdoors, they soon realized the destructive power of mother nature. The exposed crest of The Island had taken the full brunt of the winds with the roof of St. Nicholas chapel ripped away to expose the interior roof joists and scattering slate tiles and debris all around the grounds. To the side of the chapel, the film set had been unseated and lay across the grass while the numerous artificial gravestones lay either toppled or at grotesque angles. The untimely damage was a setback for the production as the entire scene of the discovery of the Byzanium in Hobart's grave was to be filmed at that one spot. Thankfully St Ives offered a secondary location with Barnoon Cemetery to the southwest. As emergency negotiations opened up with Penwith District Council the slight delay in filming did give the productions carpenters the chance to offer assistance in repairing the roof to the chapel while ITC offered to pay for the costs of the repairs.

Barnoon Cemetery
Take One

As cameras lensed Richard Jordan and Alec Guinness in town, an agreement had been settled to use Barnoon Cemetery. And by a quirk of fate, the use of a grave which had been opened up to allow for a burial that would take place on Thursday, 20 December. As a goodwill gesture, the film studios offered to pay for the burial costs, and with the agreeance with the family of the burial plot, time was of the essence. On the day of filming, executive of production Richard O'Connor gave the ultimatum to the crew that they had less than a day to get the scene to celluloid before the grave becomes occupied the following day. Not much was to be done with the grave other than to lay the Hobart headstone on the heap of earth and to the place Hobart's coffin inside the open grave. Wednesday morning, the crew were on location, and with the actors prepped the scenes could be filmed. Joining the plethora of crew was Richard Jordan, David Selby, British television actor John Barrett playing the part of the leading grave digger Nestor, and St Ives local, Tom Curnow as his work colleague. The sequence was to start with Hobart's coffin deep down in the opened grave as actor Barrett delivers the line "Just a moment sir. We'll carry over the lifting rig." As the two gravediggers exit the shot, Seagram steps forward with a metal detector, passes it over the coffin, and as it triggers the device he mutters "Jackpot!" From the direction of the chapel, the two gravediggers appear carrying some lifting apparatus. "Shall we lift it out then, sir?" asks Nestor. "I can't answer that" replies Pitt, "you'll have to ask Mr. Seagram." Getting no response Nestor asks one more time. "Do you want us to bring it on up?" After a long pause, Seagram replies with an abrupt "No". As the gravediggers stand immobile, Pitt and Seagram gather their belongings to then walk away from the grave and off towards a parked car.

"That's a wrap" shouts Jerry Jameson as the footage is quickly dispatched to the Rank Film Laboratories in Middlesex, then rushed out to London before being returned to Jerry Jameson during his stay at Tregenna Castle hotel. As filming came to a close in Cornwall, Barnoon was to reveal a real-life connection to *Titanic* as it is the final resting place of 2nd class passenger Mr. William Carbines who perished in the disaster. The crew of the cable-laying vessel C.S *Mackay-Bennett* was chartered by the White Star Line and sent out from Halifax harbour in Nova Scotia to recover *Titanic*'s victims which had drifted into shipping lanes. William's body was recovered and returned to his hometown of St Ives, where he was finally laid to rest on 30 May 1912. As the leading actors began their journey back to the United States to be with family and friends over Christmas, some of the film crew were treated to a special meal at Pinewood studios restaurant during the companies last day before closure over the festive period. All that was left to do now was to watch back the St Ives footage, rest up over the holidays and then get back to work with the important raising sequences with the miniatures over in Malta.

Barnoon Cemetery
Take Two

For the preview of previously filmed footage, Theatre 2 at Pinewood Studios had been booked for a two-hour period starting at 10.30 am on 20 December as crew and executives from ITC came to view the rushed-over St Ives footage before the facilities closed for Christmas. Among those present at the screening was Jerry Jameson, producer William Frye and the Deputy Managing Director of ITC, Bernard Kingham. As the screening began to roll and the sequences of St Ives flashed on the screen, they soon became to realize something was not right, as lines and a constant flickering appeared on the footage filmed at Barnoon Cemetery. The fault could have been overlooked if it had been confined to a few frames here and there, which could have been edited out. But the fault ran through the cemetery scenes to such an extent that the only way around it was to return to St Ives and re-shoot the entire cemetery sequence again. The decision was made to get Christmas out of the way, focus on the Malta tank filming, and get to the bottom of why the Cornwall footage became unusable. In the meantime, they could claim through the company's insurance the loss which in turn may ease the embarrassment of the additional expenditures that would undoubtedly follow.

On 23 January 1980, plans were put in motion for the return back to England for the crew and actors to reshoot the cemetery sequences. It all seemed to be going well with a new plot secured for filming the grave scene at Barnoon, the hire of equipment, fresh actors to play the gravediggers, and hopefully, a little better weather. Unfortunately, while Richard Jordan was available for the return, David Selby was committed to other film projects in New York and could not leave them until that contract was fulfilled. The only alternative now was to reschedule the Cornwall trip to the earliest convenience with all units and agents for the actors agreeing on the week commencing the 3rd March. In February the production unit had returned the faulty camera equipment to Technovision Cameras Ltd for tests to source the issue as to why the Barnoon Cemetery footage had become compromised. The reply back to ITC was one they would rather forget. The camera units being used were fitted with a feature that when operating in cold conditions, would allow for a built-in heater to switch on, warming the interior side of the camera body. This inbuilt device was operated by a battery pack that was removable and replaceable. The operator's guide that came with the equipment contained a step-by-step process on what to check before filming. Whether it was down to the mad rush in switching from St. Nicholas chapel to the new location at Barnoon, the battery supplied with the kit had not been installed and tested and so the unit ran cold. As the weather conditions at the time began to affect the unit the filming speed became compromised and unaware to the operator recorded at a slightly slower rate. The result would be a noticeable flicker effect on the celluloid. Then on 26 February came another disappointing outcome when the second camera unit returned to Technovision was found to be damaged. The 100mm lens was covered with a fine pitting on the outer glass which required replacing before it could be used again. The lens with a Tiffen 85 glass filter had to be shipped out from Japan to be replaced and repaired at a cost of £1,550 billed to ITC.

On Saturday 1 March, Jerry Jameson and Richard O'Connor arrived back in England for the reshoot at St Ives, followed thereafter with the director of photography Matthew Leonetti and actors David Selby and Richard Jordan touching down at Heathrow airport on Monday. The reshoot was to take place over two days with the first day of filming on Wednesday 5th starting just after 7.30 am. It seemed at first that the curse of Cornwall was to strike again as during the retake heavy rains and strong winds rolled in to batter the coastal town. Just after nine o'clock, Jameson gave word to close the set down, sending actors and crews back to the Tregenna Castle hotel to await a change in the weather. At 1.30 pm they all returned and the cameras began to roll again, albeit short-lived as the storms swept in again forcing them to abandon that day's filming. Yet again the foul elements of British weather put a stop to any usable footage that day. All they could do was hope that the following day, that last day, would result in something workable for the studio.

As daylight broke that morning of 6 March, so did the expectations of the crew as winds and rain continued to batter St Ives. The 8.30am call to the cemetery was cancelled as the film unit was forced to sit out the storm. Finally, a break in the weather allowed the unit to return to Barnoon and get that day's first take to film. The character of Nestor, the gravedigger with speaking lines, was changed from the original actor John Bennett, who could not attend the reshoot, to be replaced with another veteran British television screen actor, Roy Evans. St Ives resident, Tom Curnow, returned once again to reprise his role as the second gravedigger. This time around there was no open grave for the production to use and so the props department used the grass-covered paths that formed boundary lines between the burial plots. With the camera unit placed at a specific point, the pathways would be lost amongst the rows of headstones and with a spot chosen for the fake grave, the prop department laid down the raised bed of the grave and seated the fiberglass headstone. Along with a close-up of the grave, the whole prop blended in seamlessly with the rest of the hundreds of other burials. "This is the one, Jake Hobart. I'll go and get the shovels" says Nestor looking up from pages of the cemeteries plot lists. Seagram moves forwards and removing a Geiger counter from his bag proceeds to pass it over the grave as the unit's static voice confirms that 6-feet beneath his feet there lies the precious ore.

A few stops and starts did plague that afternoon as blustery winds drove across the exposed cemetery kicking up sea spray and rainwater which also brought a pause for a change to Richard Jordan's coat which had become wet from the nearby headstones. The final series of shots were to be of the departing Jordan and Selby as their characters walk the dirt path leading to the carpark and the awaiting car. The hired Titan crane was positioned on the open area of land known to the locals as The Green and which runs parallel with the residential road, Clodgy View, supported a high elevation overlooking part of Barnoon Cemetery capturing the storm whipped coast of the fictional Southby. As Seagram drops the Geiger counter back into his bag, Pitt begins to reminisce of the girl he recently bumped into who inquired if he had changed the world. "What did you say?" inquires Seagram as the two men walk the otherwise deserted path. Pitt's reply of being outnumbered was in keeping with his personality. But the winter of 79/80 became more challenging than anyone could have imagined. As the actors and crew made their way out of St Ives and towards the next chapter of the production, it was the weather that would be remembered for outnumbering those who were trying to raise the *Titanic*.

The Hobart Headstone Mystery

An odd enigma can be found on Hobart's headstone if you know where to look and quick enough to catch it. The inscription cut into the stone oddly reads;

JAKE HOBART

~

REST IN PEACE

~

AND CURSED BE HE WHO MOVES THESE BONES

~

DIED APRIL 3, 1913

But what is the significance of 1913? After all, *Titanic* sank on 15 April 1912. The viewer is lead to believe that Brewster buried the Byzanium in Southby before heading to Southampton to board *Titanic* with seven gravel filled boxes, because he was being followed. From Koplin's discovery, we know that Jake Hobart's actual body was discovered frozen in the mine on the Russian island and had been there since February 1912.

It does beg the question as to why the year 1913 was inscribed on the headstone to a grave that was occupied pre-April 10, 1912. Could it be that Brewster never put the Byzanium in the Southby grave in April 1912, leaving it in the hands of another American agent that is omitted from the story? Could it be that Brewster did indeed bury the Byzanium in the Southby grave in the days before heading to Southampton docks to board the *Titanic*, using the remoteness of the graveyard and purposely having 1913 put upon the headstone to throw anyone else off the scent should they come looking? Or could it be that someone at the film's prop department had messed up or picked up a pre-existing headstone that included the month, year and inscription and a blank space where a name should be and thought, "ah, to hell with it! This will do." Whatever the reason is behind the year 1913, one thing is certain, it makes no sense to the story and looks to be another film enigma that has no proper meaning. But given the amount of mishaps the production encountered; the 1913 inscription is most likely another victim to the curse of Cornwall.

1925 postcard looking out over the harbour and towards the pier. *(Author's collection)*

c1908 postcard of the historic The Sloop Inn. *(Author's collection)*

```
                    PIMLICO FILMS LIMITED

                     "RAISE THE TITANIC"

MOVEMENT ORDER NO. 2 - ST. IVES, CORNWALL, LOCATION    Issued: 10th Dec. 1979

MAIN UNIT DEPARTURE - THURSDAY THE 13TH DECEMBER 1979

APPROXIMATE DATE OF RETURN TO LONDON - THURSDAY THE 20TH DECEMBER 1979
_____

    HOTELS         TREGENNA CASTLE               MASTER ROBERTS
                   ST. IVES                      ST. IVES
                   CORNWALL                      CORNWALL
                   Tel.No: ST.IVES 5254 (073670) Tel.No: ST.IVES 6042
                   Telex: 45128

    ALLOCATION:    See Unit List Attached

    The Company is responsible only for room and breakfast. All other
    expenses incurred are the direct responsibility of unit members, and
    accounts should be settled before returning to London.

    Any telephone calls incurred on behalf of the Company should be
    submitted on petty cash vouchers for payment.

    FACILITIES AT TREGENNA:

        Production Office/Accounts - Small Dining Room on right of
                                     Main Entrance (Ernie Morris -
                                     Location Manager) in residence
                                     from Monday 10th December 1979
```

Section of the production movement order that listed film unit crews, actors and equipment destined for St Ives and the stunning grounds and buildings of the Tregenna Castle Hotel. *(Author's collection)*

Candid photograph of Richard Jordan during his stay at Tregenna Castle for the production of *Raise the Titanic*. *(Author's collection)*

Director Jerry Jameson during filming at St Ives in December 1979. *(ITC – Author's collection)*

British screen legend Alec Guinness as the fictional *Titanic* survivor John Bigalow. *(ITC – Author's collection)*

The calm before the storm. Alec Guinness braves the cold December weather for a series of publicity photographs for ITC the day before filming was to commence. That very evening the weather dramatically changed and St Ives was battered by the worst storms to hit the coastal town in decades. *(ITC – Author's collection)*

Veteran British television actress Nancy Nevinson as The Sloop Inn's barmaid Sarah Martindale. Nevinson was no stranger to the *Titanic* story having appeared in the 1979 EMI film *S.O.S. Titanic* as 1st class passenger Ida Straus. *(ITC & EMI)*

The bar area of the Sloop Inn has changed very little since 1980 with the exception of Perspex screens that were put in place during the summer 2020 Covid-19 pandemic. The narrow partition wall on the left separates the bar to the snug area of the establishment which now contains a number of tables for dining guests. It is in this area of the Sloop Inn where Alec Guinness would deliver his most memorable scene in the film. Note the *Raise the Titanic* replica model sitting on the bar table. *(Photograph © Andy Tree)*

Behind the scenes with Guinness and Jordan. *(Author's collection)*

Bigalow and Pitt wait for their pink gins. For those curious to know what the picture is that can be seen inside the miniature life ring hanging on the wall of the bar; it is a 1960s picture postcard of the Sloop Inn. *(Author's collection)*

56 • Raise The Titanic

Bigalow's memories of the tragic night of April 15 1912. All the items seen in the film were completely created for the scenes filmed in The Sloop Inn, including the image montage on the wall, the cased White Star Line flag and the model. *(ITC – Author's collection)*

Wonderful candid photograph of Alec Guinness resting between takes. All the images behind him were cut from various issues of *The Titanic Commutator*, the official magazine from the *Titanic Historical Society*. During the screening of *Raise the Titanic*, artist Ken Marschall said he was delighted to see a print of his *Olympic* painting being used in the scene. *(Author's collection)*

This series of behind the scenes publicity shots show Alec Guinness with the 30-inch scale Entex model kit of the *Titanic* built for the production and which would be used again in Washington during the press conference with Admiral Sandecker. *(Author's collection)*

Titanic's flag was a prop that was purposely made for the production. The prop was full size, machined sowed and artificially aged. It is not known what became of the prop once filming had come to an end on *Raise the Titanic*. *(ITC – Author's collection)*

The Sloop Inn as it is today. *(Photograph © Leo Walker)*

Smeaton Pier photographed during location scouting for the production around St Ives in the summer of 1979. *(ITC - Author's collection)*

December 1979 and Jerry Jameson lenses Richard Jordan and Alec Guinness on the exposed Smeaton Pier. *(On Location Magazine, August 1980 - Author's collection)*

58 • *Raise The Titanic*

Bigalow may be living the retired life on the coast. But even then, he cannot escape his past as he describes to Pitt the night the *Titanic* went down. The unusual item on the pier is a hand operated capstan that would have been used with a derrick to lift heavy cargo from boats alongside the pier. *(ITC/ITV Studios - Author's collection)*

Pitt and Bigalow walk towards The Sloop Inn. Although dialogue is heard during this scene, the dialogue was lifted from an unused scene with the audio carried over to the approach to the public house. *(ITC/ITV Studios)*

Emily Richards with her two sons, William (left) and his younger brother Sibley. From Penzance, Cornwall, the Richards were travelling 2nd class on board the *Titanic* with their destination being Akron in Ohio. *(Encyclopedia Titanica)*

William Rowe Richards at his Carbis Bay (St Ives) home in the mid 1980s. *(Author's collection)*

Sibley George Richards sometime in the 1960s. *(Encyclopedia Titanica)*

Sibley George Richards speaks with Lord Lew Grade at the UK premiere of *Raise the Titanic*. *(Jeanette Francis/Tony Richards collection)*

Seagram reads the fine print on the rear of the postcard found on the mummified remains of Arthur Brewster in *Titanic*'s vault. *(ITC – Author's collection)*

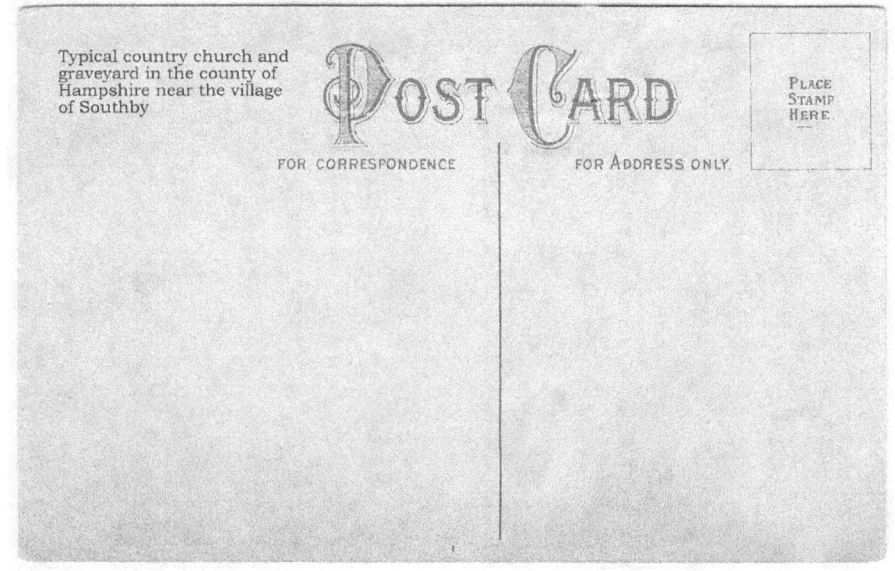

"Typical country church and graveyard in the county of Hampshire near the village of Southby". Faithful reproduction of Brewster's 1912. In reality the postcard in the film was completely mocked up for the production by the art department and shows a view of Barnoon Cemetery that sits overlooking the sea in the very heart of St Ives. *(Reproduction photograph © Tom Wedge 2020 – Postcard editing & reproduction created by Jonathan Smith and with kind permission from Tom Wedge)*

```
SCHEDULE
Friday, 14th Dec:      Preparations in Cornwall
Sat:    15th Dec:      HELICOPTER SHOT - Doubles on Quayside
Sunday, 16th Dec:      REST DAY    (Rehearsals with artistes)

Monday; 17th Dec:      INT. PUB              Loc:  Sloop Inn, The Quay
Tuesday,18th Dec:        "  /EXT. QUAY

Wed:    19th Dec:      EXT. CHURCHYARD       Loc:  St. Nicholas Chapel
                                                    The Island

Thurs:  20th Dec:      Return to London

Friday, 21st Dec:      American Unit to Greece

   NOTE:    Last two days subject to alteration of shooting
            not complete
```

Section from the movement order for St Ives, December 1979. Note the entry for the chapel. *(Author's collection)*

Two period postcards from 1911 of St. Nicholas chapel on The Island, St Ives. *(Author's collection)*

The Island with St. Nicholas chapel as photographed by the ITC production team from the chapel of Barnoon Cemetery. To the right of the chapel is Lamp Rock lookout station. Today the building is now the home of the National Coastwatch Institution. *(Author's collection)*

The graveyard set brought over from Pinewood Studios was erected on the sacred grounds to St. Nicholas with the fibreglass stone wall, arch, gravestones and grave markers giving an eerie look to a site that has no burials. *(Photograph © Bill Thomas)*

The weather battered St. Nicholas chapel with its roof ripped away by the storm. *(Photograph © Bill Thomas)*

```
c.c. Mr. Christopher, Mr. Cook,
     Mr. Kingham, Mr. Fitzsimon, Mr. Bloy, File.
```

PENWITH
PENWITH DISTRICT COUNCIL
St Clare PENZANCE Cornwall TR18 3DX
Tel Penzance 2341 STD 0736

D H Hosken D M A F Inst L Ex
District Secretary

Your ref
My ref   DHH/EBJ
Ask for
Ext
Date   16th January, 1980

Dear M/s Hall,

"Raise the Titanic"

Thank you for your letter of 11th January enclosing your cheque for £250 to cover the reinstatement of the car park and grassed area.

I confirm that this is in full and final settlement for the Island site being put back in good order.

Yours sincerely,

D.H.Hosken

District Secretary

With the St. Nicholas chapel site no longer viable for the production crew, the area was reinstated back to its original state and the bill settled with Penwith District Council. *(Author's collection)*

Barnoon Cemetery photographed in the summer of 1979 when ITC were looking for locations to film in St Ives. *(Author's collection)*

Film production crew survey the damage to the St. Nicholas *Raise the Titanic* set the morning after the storm. The ground is littered with broken roof slate tiles from the chapel, while a member of the crew can be seen propping up fallen fibreglass headstones with pieces of timber. *(Photograph © Bill Thomas)*

66 • *Raise The Titanic*

```
RAISE THE TITANIC - REV. 12/10/79                    140.  *
399   INSERT                                          399
          We SEE the card as he turns it over  A country church
          and graveyard  Sepia print.
                    SEAGRAM (O.S.)
                Southby...
                    PITT (O.S.)
                That's right.  Southby  He
                guessed wrong  It's not a man
                It's a place.  Twenty kilometers
                from Southhampton...
                                        DISSOLVE TO:

400   EXT. CHURCHYARD, ENGLAND - DAY                  400
          Exact duplicate of postcard.  We ZOOM TO A CLOSER SHOT.
          Seagram and Pitt by an open grave.  Two gravediggers
          there, NESTOR and QUINT   In b.g. a herd of sheep
          grazes

401   EXT CEMETERY - HIGH ANGLE                       401
          SHOOTING INTO grave, we SEE a long coffin-shaped box.
          Gravediggers shovel the last of the dirt off the top
          of it and crawl out of grave.

401A  TWO SHOT - THE GRAVEDIGGERS                     401A
                    NESTOR
                Just a moment, sir.  We'll carry
                over the lifting rig
          They move off.

402   ANGLE ON SEAGRAM                                402
          In b.g. we SEE gravediggers moving to lifting rig
          Seagram steps to edge of grave, metal detector in his
          hand  Pitt steps up, too, stands at his shoulder.
          They look at metal detector.

403   INSERT - METAL DETECTOR                         403
          The needle dances crazily.
```

```
RAISE THE TITANIC - REV. 12/10/79                    141.  *
404   TWO SHOT - SEAGRAM AND PITT                     404
                    PITT
                    (barely audible)
                Jackpot!
          The two men look at each other.  They've finally found
          what they're after.

404A  FULL SHOT                                       404A
          Gravediggers bring coffin-lifting apparatus to grave-
          side.

405   ANGLE ON GRAVEDIGGERS                           405
          as they arrive at graveside..  Nestor, the boss, looks
          at Pitt.
                    NESTOR
                Shall we lift it out then, sir?
                    PITT (O.S.)
                I can't answer that.

406   SINGLE ON PITT                                  406
                    PITT
                    (after a beat)
                ... you'll have to ask Mr Seagram.

407   TWO SHOT - PITT AND SEAGRAM                     407
                    PITT
                It's your baby, Gene.  Whether you
                like it or not.

408   EXTREME CLOSEUP - SEAGRAM                       408
          A long moment.  We HEAR the SHEEP in the background.
          Then...
                    NESTOR (O.S.)
                Do you want us to bring it on up?
                    SEAGRAM
                    (after another
                     long beat)
                No...
                    (shakes his head)
                No, I don't.
```

```
RAISE THE TITANIC - REV. 12/10/79                    141A. *
408A  CLOSEUP - PITT                                  408A
          No expression.  But nothing is lost on him.

409   FULL SHOT                                       409
          As diggers stand immobile beside grave, CAMERA MOVES
          BACK AND UP.  Seagram and Pitt turn from grave, walk
          back toward car.  We HEAR PITT CHUCKLE.
                    SEAGRAM (V.O.)
                What's so funny?

410   TRAVELLING TWO SHOT                             410
                    PITT
                I knew a girl once
                                        (CONTINUED)
```

```
RAISE THE TITANIC -  REV. 2/29/80                    142.
410   CONTINUED:                                      410
                    SEAGRAM
                I'll bet you did.
                    PITT
                One day she said to me, 'What
                happened to you?  I thought you
                were going to change the world.'
                    SEAGRAM
                What did you say?
                    PITT
                I said they had me out-numbered.
                    (BEAT)
                But I was wrong.
                    SEAGRAM
                    (AFTER A BEAT)
                Is that my lesson for the day.
                    PITT
                    (shakes his head)
                No more lessons...no more lectures.

411   FULL SHOT                                       411
                    SEAGRAM
                You mean school's out?
                    PITT
                You just graduated, professor.
          We PULL  UP AND BACK AS HIGH AS WE CAN GO as Pitt and
          Seagram get into car and start off down country road.
          MUSIC STARTS and we DISSOLVE THOROUGH TO WIDE SHOT of
          ocean.  In SLOW MOTION Titanic breaks through the
          water again.  As MUSIC SWELLS AND PEAKS we FREEZE
          FRAME, HOLDING Titanic at its highest point out of
          the water.  CLOSING CREDITS ROLL ACROSS THIS SHOT.
          As they END MUSIC FADES SLOWLY.  Final STILL SHOT of
          Titanic thrusting up out of water.  The last SOUND
          we HEAR is the soft thunder of KETTLE DRUMS as we:
                                        FADE TO BLACK.


                          THE END
```

The revised script for Southby graveyard, 12 October 1979. (Author's collection)

Chapter 16: The Curse of Cornwall • 67

New location but still in St Ives. The crew have moved over to Barnoon Cemetery to film with an opened grave. The window was narrow to film the desired sequence as the grave was required for a new burial. Despite the winds and rains that still battered the coastal town, the crew carried on regardless. At the grave stands David Selby and Richard Jordan as they look on as St Ives resident Tom Curnow removes the soil from within the grave as British screen actor John Barrett looks on. *(Patrick Walsh collection)*

At Southby graveyard, Pitt and Seagram watch as the gravedigger opens up the grave of Jake Hobart. As the shovel hits something solid, the outline of a coffin emerges. As the gravedigger exits, he is replaced by Seagram who clambers down and passes the Geiger counter over the stained wooden coffin. The device lights up as a static rhythm fills the air. "Jackpot!" exhales Seagram. *(ITC – Author's collection)*

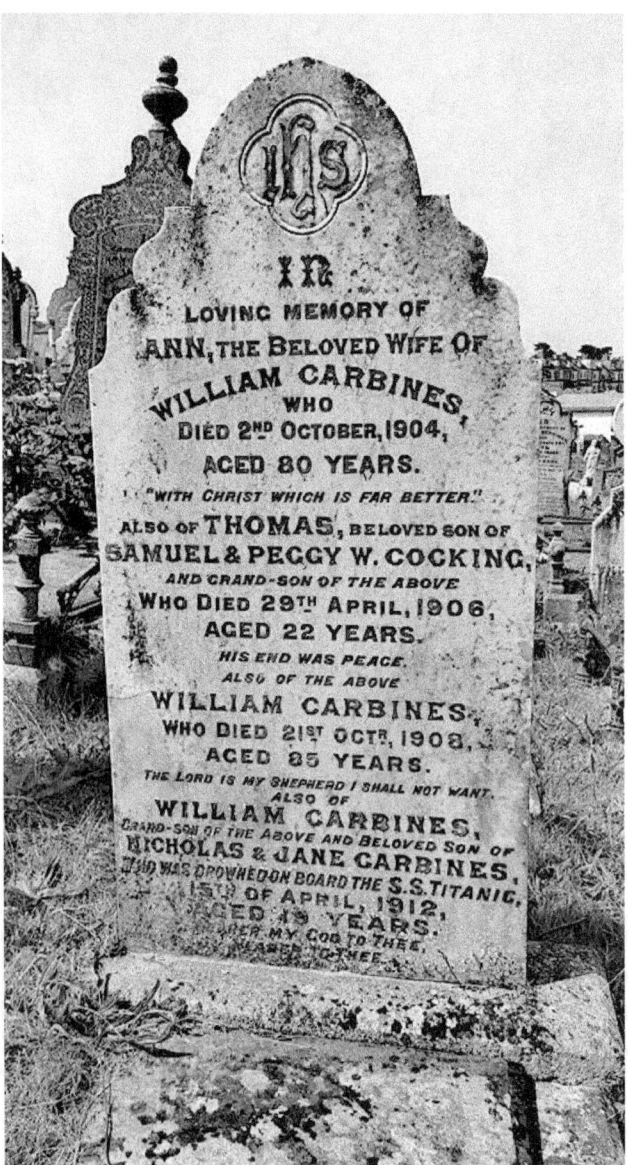

The grave of *Titanic* victim William Carbines who is interred at Barnoon Cemetery. *(Photograph © Angela Catherine)*

Over 500 mourners gather at Barnoon Cemetery during the funeral of William Carbines, 30 May 1912. *(Encyclopedia Titanica)*

```
Agents for:
MARBLE ARCH PRODUCTIONS INC.              11th February, 1980

J. Davies Esq.,
Department of Employment,
Overseas Labour Section,
Ebury Bridge House,
Ebury Bridge Road,
London, S.W.1.

Dear Mr. Davies,
                    "RAISE THE TITANIC"

Further to your letter dated 30th November, 1979, I must again
turn to you for help.

Our unit, suitably augmented with British Technicians, shot for four
days in Cornwall, and having wrapped and taken the crew and filmed
material to Athens, the Production Company finds that a considerable
part of the footage is unusable, due to a faulty camera. This will
necessitate re-shooting that sequence.

You will note that on this occasion, we have somewhat pared down the
the USA crew to key members only, per the attached list.

An added complication is that by the time we need him, Mr. David
Selby, one of the leading actors has different commitments, and will
be coming from New York. Incidentally, because of the high cost of
leading artists, you will readily understand that they are scheduled
such as to ensure that they are under contract when being filmed on,
and whenever possible not on the pay roll when scenes are being shot
in which they are not involved.

We are scheduling this reshoot for the week commencing 3rd March, 1980
so I think we need to plan engaging the British crew and equipment
before 1st March.

I have informed the Unions and the B.F.P.A. of our intentions, but
should you require any further information, please donnot hesitate to
contact me.

Yours sincerely,



Malcolm Christopher
Production Supervisor
```

```
Twickenham Film Studios
St. Margarets, Twickenham
Middlesex TW1 2AW, England
Tel: 01-892 4477
Telex: 8814497 TWIKST G
    Attn Technovision


Mr. Ron Cooke,
Pimlico Films,
c/o Pinewood Studios,
Pinewood Road, Iver Heath,
Iver, Bucks.                          16th April 1980


Dear Mr. Cooke,

          Following your recent telephone conversation I have
made enquiries and it would appear that the camera flicker
problems encountered during the Cornwall location of "Raise
the Titanic" during December 1979 were caused through the
camera not running to speed because of the cold conditions.
There were in fact heaters specially installed in the camera
and new heater batteries provided but, apparently, this facility
was not utilised.

          The camera was tested on its return and no faults
were found.

                              Yours faithfully,



                              Graeme D. Stubbings,
                              U.K. Manager.
```

On the 11 February 1980, following on from the discovery of unusable footage, ITC contacted the Department of Employment to secure the return of Richard Jordan and David Selby back to St Ives to reshoot sequences at the cemetery. It would not be until April when *Technovision* confirmed to what the problem was; a basic error contributed by the carelessness of the film unit. *(Author's collection)*

```
                        "RAISE THE TITANIC"

Further to our telephone conversation this morning, I now write to confirm
the details of arrivals of our American personnel:-

SATURDAY, 1st March

Mr. Richard O'Connor  )Arrive from Los Angeles on flight PANAM 120
(Producer)            )which is due in at 12.35 (midday).  We will
Mr. Jerry Jameson     )send car from International Car Hire to meet.
(Director             )

SUNDAY, 2nd March

Mr.&Mrs. Leonetti     )Arrive from Los Angeles on flight PANAM 120
Mr. Matsuda           )which is due in at 12.35 (midday).  We will
                       send car from International Car Hire to meet.

MONDAY, 3rd MARCH

Mr. Richard Jordan    )Arrive from New York on flight BA 178 which
Mr. David Selby       )is due at 21.50.
```

Movement order for the return back to St Ives, dated 27 February 1980. *(Author's collection)*

Daily Production Progress Report dated 6 March 1980. *(Author's collection)*

Richard Jordan and Roy Evans. *(ITC/ITV Studios)*

Chapter 16: The Curse of Cornwall • 71

	B & W PICTURE — NEGATIVE FILM FOOTAGE — SOUND							
WASTE	RESERVE & N/G	PRINT	TOTAL		TOTAL	PRINT	RESERVE & N/G	WASTE
	SEE FOOTAGES - DAY 2			PREVIOUSLY USED		1 roll		
				USED TO-DAY				
				TOTALS TO DATE				

STILLS	PREVIOUSLY TAKEN	TAKEN TO-DAY	TAKEN TO DATE

REMARKS

7.30/9.10a.m. waiting for rain to stop. Heavy, horizontal rain and force 7 wind caused abandonment of shooting at 9.10am. Unit returned to hotel. 1.30p.m. Unit left hotel to resume shooting. 4.50p.m. rainy and overcast. Unit wrapped.   NOTE: No PRINT on R/take 400B due to bad weather.

STILLS	PREVIOUSLY TAKEN	TAKEN TO-DAY	TAKEN TO DATE

REMARKS

7.30/9.10a.m. waiting for rain to stop. Heavy, horizontal rain and force 7 wind caused abandonment of shooting at 9.10am. Unit returned to hotel. 1.30p.m. Unit left hotel to resume shooting. 4.50p.m. rainy and overcast. Unit wrapped.   NOTE: No PRINT on R/take 400B due to bad weather.

	B & W PICTURE — NEGATIVE FILM FOOTAGE — SOUND							
WASTE	RESERVE & N/G	PRINT	TOTAL		TOTAL	PRINT	RESERVE & N/G	WASTE
440'	2810'	3890'	7140'	PREVIOUSLY USED**	1 roll			
				USED TO-DAY	6 rolls			
				TOTALS TO DATE	7 rolls			

STILLS	PREVIOUSLY TAKEN	TAKEN TO-DAY	TAKEN TO DATE

REMARKS

7.30-8.20am. Bad weather (rain and wind) resulted in unit standing by at hotel until signs of clearing. Left hotel at 8.20am (see above) Slated 400.400A & B (shot Wed. 5.3.80) n.g. as coat for Richard Jordan changed due to weather spots showing.
** Total footages for two days

Examples of the notes included on the production reports during filming at Barnoon Cemetery in March 1980. *(Author's collection)*

(Author's collection)

72 • *Raise The Titanic*

TOP: Pitt and Seagram make their way out of Southby graveyard. MIDDLE: The grass verge seen on screen opens out on to the private road leading down to the chapel and the adjacent carpark. LEFT: Hobart's headstone. *(ITC/ITV Studios – Photograph © Faye Taylor)*

Chapter 16: The Curse of Cornwall • 73

Some of the ITC production photographs taken in the summer of 1979 during the scouting of locations. *(Author's collection)*

CHAPTER 17

Raising the Question on Reality

"The Royal Mail Ship Titanic. Where is she now? And how do we get her up? That's our problem."

Dirk Pitt

The Atlantic Ocean is the second-largest ocean on the planet with an estimated 31,800,000 sq miles of surface. Its appearance is that of an S-shape stretching from the Arctic to Antarctic regions with North and South America to the west and Europe and Africa to the east. On average the floor of the Atlantic sits at 12,000ft with a crushing depth of 6,500 lbs. per sq. inch (3.5 tons). Ever since that bitterly cold night of April 15, 1912, *Titanic* has remained at 12,460ft down with the crushing amount of pressure upon her already twisted and broken hull. The first items ever recovered began with a series of dives in 1987. This prompted the conception of RMS *Titanic*, Inc which would oversee the controlled salvage rights of the wreck site. The company carried out several expeditions to *Titanic* during the years 1987, 1993, 1994, 1996, 1998, 2000, 2004, and their last exploration of the wreck in 2010 which resulted in the most advanced study to date with sophisticated high definition equipment. From 1987 to 2004 the company salvaged almost 5,000 artefacts. This large amount includes the items that were recovered in bulk such as passenger suitcases and travel trunks with all their contents or, as one recovery operation revealed, one of the kitchen sinks that was full of cutlery and pots. The recovery operations also included those of much more substantial artefacts; cast steel Welin lifeboat davit, one of her D-Deck shell doors, a 3-ton deck mounted mooring bollard and the largest item salvaged, the huge 17-ton starboard hull section that was given the nickname 'Big Piece', and which saw the light of day for the first time since 1912 when it was raised during the summer of 1998. The scene of the hull section as it broke the surface must have ignited memories of those who had previously watched *Raise the Titanic* as the rust-stained steel hull, brought up from the ocean floor with a series of diesel-filled lifting bags, was lifted from the Atlantic swells and lowered onto the deck of the recovery vessel. However, this was not the first attempt to salvage the 'Big Piece'.

In August 1996, a host of paying passengers on board the M.V. *Island Breeze* and the M.V. *Royal Majesty* watched the first attempt. Among them to pay respect during a memorial service were a host of well-known *Titanic* enthusiasts, historians, Walter MacQuitty the producer of the 1958 Rank movie *A Night to Remember*, and *Titanic* survivors Edith Brown Haisman, Michel Marcel Navratil, and Eleanor Johnson Shuman. The recovery process, watched by a large number of news outlets, turned to disaster when some of the lifting equipment attached to the 'Big Piece' gave way during the journey to the surface in the stormy seas, sending the hull section back down to the sea bed nearly 12,500ft down. While this was a costly and frustrating exercise for those involved in the recovery operations, thankfully the paying spectators on the other vessels had left the location when the storm descended. But as we entered a new decade the future of all these salvaged items comes into question after the salvor of possession went into administration leaving uncertainty for all the 5,000 items recovered. As more plans are made to dive the wreck of *Titanic*, to film and catalogue the condition of the wreck since the last expedition back in 2010, including a proposed plan to enter the bow section and remove crumbling remains of the Marconi radio equipment, *Titanic* herself is rapidly deteriorating as the marine microorganisms on the wreck are estimated to consume on average between 50 to 200 tons of iron from the metalwork per year dependent of oxygen content and organic materials filtering down from above. Given the rate of decay, it may be that by the year 2035, *Titanic* could entirely collapse in on herself. And judging by the small snippets of footage taken during the July 2021 dives to the wreck site, she is already entering that inevitable stage of decay.

It is hard to believe that from 1975 to 1985 the general census was still that of *Titanic* having survived intact, sitting upright on the ocean floor, just waiting for submersible crews to find her final resting place. Authors, marine experts, *Titanic* and ocean liner enthusiasts were confident that the liner was waiting to be found in a condition not changed from the night she slipped beneath the waves. Other notions were that the *Titanic* had landed on her side or that the sea bed was so soft she had all but vanished into the ooze. Regardless of survivor accounts, which lay claim that she broke apart during the final moments, were largely dismissed or regarded as sensationalism on the part of the survivors. How could such a mighty vessel, built from the finest materials, crafted by the hands of man, a ship regarded as being "unsinkable" have gone to the bottom of the North Atlantic in any other state than that of being in or near to intact? It was unthinkable. Incomprehensible, not to mention that the iceberg had to have ripped a huge gash in her starboard hull to have even sunk such a vessel as *Titanic*? The ship that "God himself could not sink." *Titanic* artist, Ken Marschall, had envisioned the liner intact based around the Clive Cussler novel; funnels ripped away, her masts reduced in size, lifeboat davits mangled, the bridge crushed. Her wooden decks rotting and covered with silt. And her hull blotched and streaked. If the stories of the liner breaking apart were ignored and those stories from other survivors that claim *Titanic* sank intact, this vision of *Titanic*'s wreck was more plausible than what would eventually appear on-screen. But this was Hollywood, and Hollywood often fails to follow its own script. Lew Grade's *Raise the Titanic* had to appear bold, fresh but oh-so-typically Hollywood. Science fiction rather than science fact. The time had now arrived to turn the beautiful *Titanic* model from her elegant 1912 livery to that of a shipwreck that has spent 68 years on the bottom of the North Atlantic Ocean.

In Search of Dreams

Going back to 1980, what was the general consensus of how the wreck of *Titanic* could have looked? Her real discovery was still five years away. The fictional aspect of *Raise the Titanic* is, after all, imagination going into overdrive for the sake of capturing the readers' attention. The many changes to the movie's screenplay were enough to suggest that not even *Titanic* herself would be put on screen in the way one would think. But for the art of movie-making, the imagination can run amok and create something amazing even if scientifically wrong. *Raise the Titanic* was no different. Before the *Titanic* model could be turned into the wreck it had to be established to what condition the wreck would be in terms of reality. Shallow water wrecks could give hints to some aspects of decay, the results of saltwater upon paintwork and steel, the types of marine life and growth. But *Titanic* was a wreck sitting 12,500ft down in the lifeless pitch-black abyss of a freezing cold ocean. It is no wonder why so many, even scholars, assumed that she would be intact and in remarkable condition. But for the camera, she *had* to appear as a wreck that was devoid of former glitz and glamour while maintaining those classic lines of an Edwardian steamship. To assist with this change, oceanographers and marine experts were called upon to advise with the film production.

Donald L. Keach was the former Lieutenant Commander of the U.S. Navy and who lead the dive operations with the *Trieste* during the summer of 1963 in search of the wrecked attack submarine U.S.S. *Thresher* at a depth of 8,400ft following its sinking that same year 190 miles off the coast of Cape Cod.

Lieutenant Commander Keach and his team were placed in harsh conditions within a vessel not built for such a research purpose. His commitment to the search was rewarded with the Navy Commendation Medal. Also joining Donald Keach as a technical advisor was another former *Trieste* member, Don Walsh. Lieutenant Walsh of the United States Navy was partnered with Jacques Piccard when they dived to a record-breaking depth of 35,813ft in the bathyscaphe *Trieste* at the Mariana Trench on January 23, 1960. His expertise in the field of oceanography and marine evolution secured a place within the films production department. His research was used as a basis towards aging the *Titanic* model to represent the wreck as close to studies of marine life and marine effect upon deep-water wrecks. In March 2012, Don Walsh became part of the team that oversaw the Mariana Trench Deep Sea Challenger mission that was performed by James Cameron, when the award-winning director carried out his solo dive to a spectacular record-breaking depth of 35,756ft.

Is it Feasible?

During the production shooting in San Diego between 27 November and 10 December 1979, both Don Walsh and Donald Keach were present on board the U.S navy vessels out in the bay as the film crews filmed exterior and interior shots for the movie. Both Walsh and Keach were approached to answer the questions on the reality of raising a wreck like the *Titanic*. While the movie was largely that of a work of fiction, the possibilities of a search and recovery mission to the wreck site of the *Titanic* was very much realistic as during the production of *Raise the Titanic*, Texan oil tycoon Jack Grimm, was already putting into place his expedition to go out during the summer of 1980 and find and photograph the remains of the *Titanic*. The prospects of such a wild and adventurous mission enticed many old and new schemes to the drawing board on how to raise the greatest of all lost ships. They still believed that the *Titanic* was sitting as near preserved as the night she sank just waiting for someone to find her and bring her up. And as the actors played out their roles in front of the camera for the sake of Hollywood, the experts were approached to give their verdicts on the reality of raising the *Titanic*. Donald Keach gave his account of the harsh environment of the underwater terrain where the *Titanic* now sits.

> "The deep ocean is not like anything that most of us have seen. The fact there is no sunlight penetration below about 1,800ft in the sea means there is no plant life. It is cold on the order of 30° Fahrenheit and there is very little oxygen at that depth. The animal life that's there, many of them have no eyes because they've become adjusted over generations of living in the dark. So, if I had to guess as to the shape of the *Titanic* might be in, I'd guess it's in very good shape."

Mike Harris, one of Jack Grimm's oceanographers and the expedition leader to the 1980 mission, went as far to say "I assume we will find a light layer of silt on the *Titanic* and the rest of it will be perfectly clean and almost as new as the day she sunk." Don Walsh was just as enthusiastic.

> "The evidence seems to indicate that she is probably is all in one piece, although she may have been holed. She pitched up vertically just as she went under. Some of the boilers may have come loose and gone through the front."

The logistics behind such an operation in salvaging a hulk like the *Titanic* were, to a degree, present during the film's production. But is it possible to raise the *Titanic*? Don Walsh believed so back in November 1979.

"It certainly is, if you don't ask the cost. All of the technologies that we tried to represent in this film, as technical advisors for the film, are here today or in the near future. If they're put together in the right way you could indeed raise the ship but it would be very costly. In fact, if the ship were rolled out of pure gold, if the hull were pure gold, you probably couldn't recover the cost of salvaging it. But it is feasible."

And how would they achieve such a monumental task? Based on the general census of the time that the *Titanic* was laying structurally sound on the sea bed in the same condition as the night she went down. And with a ton of money, experts to hand, and the most sophisticated technology, there may be a glimmer of hope that the unsinkable legend could be hauled up from the cold biting depths of the North Atlantic. The *Titanic*, they thought, sitting upright, would require the fabled 300ft iceberg gash cut in her side to be covered over. This would be done with a series of steel plates, dropped to the ocean floor, picked up by submersible crews, and welded in place over the gash. The experts envisioned pumping a liquefied material into the hull as one of the two main buoyancy aids. The liquid was a composite of synthesized materials that formed a durable foam based around Syntactic products of hollow spheres known as cenospheres or micro balloons, a product in use since 1955. Don Walsh describes the salvage procedure.

"This is a solid foam-like epoxy matrix which has small glass micro-spheres in it. These are embedded in this epoxy matrix and it makes large blocks of material. This would be pumped into the interior of the ship, all the voids, it will displace the water and this foam would then harden up in place and it would give buoyancy to the ship. In addition to the foam pumped inside the ship, you would also attach to the outside of the ship large gas generators; like balloons. Then at the proper time, these generators would be activated and they fill these balloons with gas and that will give the buoyancy to start to lift her off the bottom. And finally, to break her free of the bottom we'd use a series of explosive charges to break the suction from the bottom sediment to get her started, and then she'd hopefully come up."

For the time Don Walsh's concept was a very feasible idea considering what information they chose to go with, not just during the filming of *Raise the Titanic*, but the bona fide expedition being developed by Jack Grimm and Mike Harris. Unfortunately, the Jack Grimm expeditions of 1980, 1981, and 1983 failed to find the remains of the *Titanic*. But the public still showed much interest in her legacy and in turn, she still generated farcical stories from those wanting to find and raise her. And for many, it was still perceived that *Titanic* was intact and just waiting to be found. In May 1985 artist Ken Marschall went on to produce a painting that he could use to entice National Geographic into hiring him should any such expedition be mounted that coming summer. Ken depicted *Titanic* on the sea bed, listing slightly but still upright, masts intact and the third funnel still firmly seated on the deckhouse. It was hoped that if any expedition were mounted for that summer that he could illustrate the magazine. Little did Ken realize what the 1 September that year would bring to the masses of *Titanic* fanatics – all dreams of her being intact would soon become wishful thinking as her shattered remains were broadcast around the world. If only she looked like she did in *Raise the Titanic*!

Those ideas of filling the hull with ping pong balls, even pumping tons of Vaseline into the wreck and encasing the hull in a mesh and freezing the water to turn *Titanic* herself into ice, where she would pop to the surface, were to become a thing of the past. But even today there are those who firmly believe that *Titanic*'s hull can be salvaged, contrary to the mounting evidence accumulated since her discovery in 1985, that she is now far gone beyond any hope of salvage as the money, technology, and future preservations simply do not exist.

Titanic Found!

Fact v Fiction

The graveyard shift crew were spending yet another long night in the control cabin onboard the research vessel *Knorr*. Their eyes were transfixed on the monitors as a sled camera 12,460ft below them drifted lazily on its tether over the ocean floor relaying back to the ship an endless live feed of a baron muddy landscape. The crew was becoming accustomed to seeing mud, the scattering of glacial boulders, and the odd rat-tail fish that was oblivious to the intrusion from the *Argo* camera unit. Then the view changed. It was subtle at first, but enough for the weary crew to identify the items scattered about the sea bed as objects that should not be there; wine bottles, twisted fragments of steel beams, ceramic plates, the wire mesh remains of a bed mattress, and tons of coal. "Wreckage!", exclaimed crew member Bill Lange, followed by a crew member saying, "someone should go and get Bob." The curiosity of the ship's cook had gotten the better of him after hearing the shouts of excitement from the control cabin. After peering in, he was picked for his troubles and sent off to get Bob.

Dr. Robert "Bob" Ballard was still awake and reading in his quarters when the cook knocked on the door and delivered the message. As his reading material went flying in one direction, Bob went the other making the journey from his room to the control cabin in 30 seconds. Upon entering, the crew was replaying back a section of footage they had captured as the leader of the joint-French team, Jean-Louis Michel, stared at a page from a reprint of *The Shipbuilder* from 1911. "It's a boiler!" came the cry, "a boiler." And there on the monitor, through the haze of the ocean's depth, was the unmistakable shape of a ship's boiler sitting detached from the vessel it was once installed in. Looking from the book page to the screen Ballard couldn't believe his eyes as the two images matched perfectly. It was a boiler, a 50-ton single-ended Scotch marine boiler. But more importantly, *this* boiler belonged to the unsinkable legend, *Titanic*. Looking up at the clock on the control cabin wall the time read 1:04 a.m. on 1 September 1985. Ballard had *Argo* repositioned to nearly 100ft above the seafloor for the camera sled to continue its journey across the debris field as somewhere out there in that inky blackness lay the *Titanic*. The French-American team only had to wait for eight minutes to claim their prize as *Argo* passed within 12ft over the boat deck of the *Titanic*. The hours to follow had the team crisscrossing over the hull capturing as much video and photographic evidence that they could before the clock ticked down to them leaving the area and heading back to Woods Hole Oceanographic Institution. Even before September 1st had ended the news was leaked of the wreck's discovery with the headlines of TITANIC FOUND! making front-page news around the world.

Back at Woods Hole the images and video captured was scrutinized for gaining a better understanding of how the *Titanic* sank. It was clear that the journey from the surface to the seafloor was greatly destructive having ripped away her funnels, unseating many deck ventilators, and pulling apart the bridge area of the deckhouse. But it was the realization that *Titanic* had broken apart during her sinking that not only brought home the tremendous forces at play on the hull during the sinking, but it finally lay to rest once and for all that *Titanic* had indeed split apart like many survivors had claimed. What is remarkable about these claims is that before the wreck's discovery those passengers and crew who had survived *Titanic*'s sinking had been adamant about what they had witnessed. And yet they were ignored, despite the facts. As the decades passed the theory that the ship had sunk intact was supported by many authors and *Titanic* experts who continued to endorse the story that the mighty unsinkable *Titanic* pitched up on end and plunged beneath the surface intact. It was, if the horrors of the actual sinking are removed, a more elegant and fitting ending for such a grand ship.

And what about these facts? *Titanic*'s tell-tale sign of breaking up was documented on a more professional level the weeks after her sinking when the ship's owners, the White Star Line, charted vessels and crew to undertake the gruesome task of recovering the bodies of the dead that were being reported passing through shipping lanes. During their time at sea the vessels *Mackay-Bennett*, *Minia,* and *Montmagny* would pull from the freezing grasp of the North Atlantic the bodies of 328 men, women, and children. Initially, the recovery of the victims was primarily aimed towards the wealthy as the return home of loved ones was beneficial towards resolving disputes of estates. The bodies once recovered would be preserved in ice and brought to the port of Halifax in Nova Scotia where they would be passed onto relatives. The mortuaries and undertakers had grossly miscalculated the situation having supplied the vessels with embalming materials for the recovery of no more than 50 victims, the rest, they believed, would have been taken down with the *Titanic* or dispersed over hundreds of miles of ocean. The recovered victims were checked for identification and personal possessions of which all was to be documented. Those unidentified would be left nameless and assigned a number. In the case of bodies recovered that were badly decomposed or injured beyond recognition were given a ceremonial burial at sea. As crews faced the heart-rendering daily process of recovering the dead, they also seized upon the opportunity to break the grisly monotony of the task forced upon them by recovering any of the ship's debris that had drifted with the currents. Deck chairs, wall mounted oak cabinets, a huge section of panelling from the 1st class lounge, decorative oak inlay panels from the aft staircase, even heavy chairs from the D-Deck 1st class dining room, were all plucked from the waters with some of the wooden relics being fashioned into keepsakes of chessboards or cribbage boards. Before judging the crew too harshly for any attempts at profiteering from these recovered souvenirs, their actions can be excused. On the 17 April, they recovered the body of a two-year old. Later known as "The Unknown Child", the little boy was carefully brought to Halifax where the crew of the *Mackay-Bennett* paid for his headstone and burial at Fairview Cemetery. One last loving gesture from the crew was the placement upon his body of a copper pendant inscribed with the wording, "Our Babe".

As the items made their way off the ships in Halifax a number of them caught the attention of the press who added their recovery to the newspapers. It was no secret to where they came from and it was no secret that *Titanic* had broken apart during the sinking. *The Evening Bulletin* newspaper dated 19 April 1912 included an artist's rendering of the *Titanic* breaking in half between her second and third funnels to the bold headline of **TITANIC PLUNGES TO HER DOOM IN A SMOOTH STARLIT OCEAN**. As *Carpathia* carrying the 712 survivors made her way back to New York, one of the liner's 1st class passengers, Lewis Skidmore, put his artistic skills into action as survivor Jack Thayer described the events of the sinking. Skidmore's series of sketches were to include one of *Titanic* breaking in half based on Thayer's observation of seeing something large resurface where the bow should have been. It is questionable as to what exactly Thayer saw that night, maybe the collapsing forward two funnels or possibly the aft-end of the break-in *Titanic*'s bow which at the moment of separation was still visible on the ocean surface. We will never know. But what we are sure about is that Thayer was among many who that night was close enough to see the liner breaking her back before her stern disappeared.

Titanic's baker Charles Joughin stated in court that before he went out on the deck, he heard the tell-tale signs of interior spaces giving way while in the pantry on A-Deck. Major Arthur Peuchen described to the court that after the sinking, as he sat upon the upturned hull of the collapsible, he could see the striped pole of the C-Deck barbershop floating among the debris. Seaman Edward John Buley when questioned about the sinking told the court "Her rudder was clear of the water. You could hear the rush of machinery, and she parted in two, and the after part settled down again, and we thought the after part would float again." Quartermaster Arthur John Bright who was in lifeboat D witnessed *Titanic* from nearly 100 yards away telling the inquiry "she broke in two. All at once she seemed to go up on end, and come down about halfway", while Greaser Fredrick Scott spoke of seeing the ship break apart just behind the fourth funnel. Although Second Officer Charles Lightoller had already addressed the courts exclaiming that *Titanic* had sunk from beneath his feet "intact", further questioning about the sinking, he went on to explain that during the stages of loading and lowering the lifeboats, he witnessed the forward deck expansion joint flexing and opening up to the extent that the steel support wires to the number one funnel separated. As the funnels weight shifted it was sent toppling over to the port side of the bridge and down onto scores of people who seconds before had been washed off the boat deck into the sea as the *Titanic* took the sudden plunge forwards. While this somewhat minor detail of the sinking was to a degree irrelevant in the eyes of the courts in 1912, it was not until the discovery of the wreck in September 1985 when much of what was documented seventy-three years previously began to reveal that what these survivors had witnessed was largely ignored in favor of keeping the White Star Line in good light within the public's eye.

Over the next seven decades, the sinking became over-sensationalized on screen, within books, and in art, as her legacy began to take on a new characteristic. The horrors of that night were soon to be glamorized, romanticized, and even distorted to meet with the public's demand of something new or fresh on the subject. A lot of this blame stems from how the disaster was portrayed on the cinema screen with the releases of *Titanic* (1953), *A Night to Remember* (1958), and *S.O.S. Titanic* (1979) which took survivor and inquiry accounts and reshaped them for the screenplay and the production budget. What all these big studio productions shared was in having their *Titanic* sink intact. The fact they did it could be down to several reasons; budget, more workable model effects, or maybe just lazy research. *A Night to Remember* did give the audience something to think about with the collapse of the fourth funnel, the only time the story of *Titanic* was dramatized to be breaking apart during sinking at a time pre-wreck discovery. It was not until 1996 and the Konigsberg/Sanitsky Company mini-series *Titanic* for the Hallmark Entertainment network that became the first dramatization of the sinking to feature the ship actually breaking in half.

As part of the pre-production phase for *Raise the Titanic*, the studios turned to the British Inquiry reports as a source for information. It is clear that from the very start that *Titanic* had to be represented on screen as a complete fully hulled vessel. It was not only in keeping with how the wreck was portrayed within the pages of Clive Cussler's bestselling novel but how the liner was perceived by the experts of the day, based on first-hand accounts of survivors put to print in 1912. With such material to hand, how could anyone question to what state the real ship was in, when, after all, this was the mighty unsinkable *Titanic*, which according to the most reliable of sources, her surviving senior crew, she was still largely intact as she made that journey from the ocean surface to her final resting place 12,460ft down? The legend now outshined the realms of reality.

Raising Hopes

The idea of locating the *Titanic* was not the product of post-war technology. The first couple of days after the sinking, the family of John Jacob Astor, *Titanic*'s most illustrious passenger and who had been reported lost in the sinking, wanted his body retrieved from the wreck by any means necessary. Explosives would be dropped to the sunken *Titanic* and detonated blowing sections of the hull open. They thought that any bodies within the wreck would be freed to float to the surface where they would be retrieved and identified with hopes of laying claim to Astor's remains. Of course, it all depended on them knowing exactly where the wreck was. As if the idea wasn't foolhardy enough, it would have been short-lived when the news came of the successful recovery of his body by the crew of the *Mackay-Bennett* on 22 April.

It was in 1914 when the first idea was made public on the possibilities of locating and raising the hull of the *Titanic*. American architect, Charles A. Smith, devised a plan of building an unmanned submarine-type craft that would be fitted with electromagnetic devices and towed along the ocean floor where they believed the wreck was sitting. These powerful magnets when passed over the wreck would attach themselves to the hull, releasing a buoy to indicate at the surface where the wreck was situated. More of the magnets with fitted buoys and cables would be dropped to the wreck and then gathered together and connected to winches onboard a series of salvage vessels. Smith's idea was then to lift the hull from the sea bed and drag it to more shallow waters where the rest of the salvage attempt could be achieved with diving bells and their human operators. The aftermath of the great war, the deadly consequences of the 1918 Spanish flu pandemic, and the dawn of a new decade marked the end of Edwardian society and *Titanic* became just a distant memory.

It was around 1965 when the idea of finding and raising the *Titanic* began to circulate in the press when Douglass Woolley, founder of *The Titanic Salvage Company*, devised a scheme to secure the wreck, to find it and then subsequentially raise it with the objective to put the wreck on display in Liverpool as a floating museum. Woolley's proposal was to attach inflatable nylon balloons to the hull and fill them with gas to generate enough lift to bring her to the surface. It did seem plausible when tests carried out with small models in a water tank proved the idea worked. But despite Woolley laying claim to the wreck via a Jersey court ruling, several businessmen backing the project, the funds never materialized. And if that wasn't problematic enough the plan of inflating the balloons with gas fell flat when the process was calculated to take nearly ten years, not to mention they had not figured out how to get the gas into the balloons. Over a decade later Woolley was still pushing for financial support and backers as his operation *Titanic* was updated to a cost of £7m. In August 1977 it went to press that Woolley had a new partner at *The Titanic Salvage Company*, Arthur Hickie, a former Royal Navy diver who, at the time, was a truck driver for the Wolverhampton based BOC Gases, the United Kingdom's largest supplier of bottled industrial gas. Woolley predicted that *Titanic* was carrying gold and silver in her holds with an estimated value of £80m in 1977. Even if this had been true, which it wasn't, Woolley's £7m salvage costs were greatly under-priced as salvage experts had estimated such a scheme would cost in the region of $2 billion with that based on the technology existing at the time. Regardless, Woolley pursued his dream.

The new proposal was to assemble a wire mesh cage around the entire hull enclosing the *Titanic* within, to them pump liquid nitrogen into the hull and the exterior side within the mesh bubble, freezing the seawater and turning the *Titanic* into a 900ft iceberg that would become buoyant and float to the surface. How the wreck would be stabilized at the surface was never disclosed; if it was ever put to paper to begin with.

With the release of Clive Cussler's *Raise the Titanic* and preproduction beginning for the book's movie adaptation, the real-life scenarios of finding and raising the wreck seemed to never be out of print. While some wanted to bring the old girl up to sunlight again, others were more focused on finding the wreck and filming it. Again, a British company was reported to be putting together an expedition out into the Atlantic in search of the long-lost liner. *Seawise & Titanic Ltd* wanted to search the area during the summer of 1980 using technical data stemmed from a survey of the Atlantic by the Royal Navy in 1977. The SOLLIS PROJECT was a top-secret deep-sea sonar equipment test carried out by the Royal Navy in the search of a downed Russian nuclear submarine somewhere in the Atlantic off Greenland. What is interesting is that the tests led them close to the location where *Titanic* would be found eight years later by Ballard. But what is far more intriguing is that during those Royal Navy exercises, the equipment picked up two separate metal objects of considerable size on the ocean floor at the depth *Titanic* was thought to be resting. Of course, these locations were required to be documented due to their nature of being picked up by the sonar equipment, but whether or not the Royal Navy had put two and two together, these two sonar markers did not represent that of 883ft ocean liner. As to what they picked up? That remains classified until the year 2027. The information apparently shared with *Seawise & Titanic Ltd* formed the basis of their planned summer 1980 expedition. The story certainly caught the attention of the media when a lengthy article appeared in the October 1979 issue of the British culture magazine *Now!* The team would be led by ex-Royal Navy diving specialist John Grattan in which the team would locate the wreck at newly established coordinates and film her in her watery grave. Grattan would not disclose how he came in possession of the new material but his prominent background as a Commander in the Royal Navy may have led to disclosure from other sources. The summer of 1980 arrived on schedule, *Seawise & Titanic Ltd* did not as the expedition soon became scuppered due largely to the lack of financial support, or it may have been down to who the owner was of *Seawise & Titanic Ltd;* Mr. Woolley. Six decades have passed since Woolley came to light with his equally ill-fated schemes to find and raise the wreck and yet, despite his age, he still maintains those dreams. It doesn't matter how old you are or how preposterous your dream may be, we all have them and some do come true.

The Search Becomes a Reality

During those maddening times of the 1960s and 70s, one would think that the search for the *Titanic* was more for the benefits of being in the newspapers than any serious notion of searching for the legendary lost liner. While those who came forward had their personal agendas the almost weekly ritual of announcing them in the press began to weigh heavy on the public as the sinking of the *Titanic* was turning into a farcical race to find the ship. As the 1970s came to a close there were those who did have serious intentions. In 1978 Walt Disney Productions had intended to document the discovery and film the wreck after the company's senior executive Roy Disney was introduced to Robert Ballard during Ballard's time working at Woods Hole. Ballard's interest in looking for the ship began in 1973 on the back of working with the deep-sea submersible *Alvin*. The vessel's dive depth of 20,000ft was pivotal to any serious expeditions and if he could find the *Titanic,* the sub and its owners would make front-page news around the world. In 1977 Ballard became friends with long-time *Titanic* historian William Tantum, who, together, shared the desire in finding the wreck. The visit to Woods Hole by Roy Disney in May 1978 was positive, he favoured the idea of such an adventure and left to think it through. The following month he contacted Ballard with his decision. The upfront capital of $1.5 million was "not feasible for us to be involved". And so, Disney walked.

Watching from the side lines and waiting for his opportunity to step forth was Texas oil tycoon Jack Grimm. The flamboyant businessman had already made waves in the press with past expeditions to locate the fabled Noah's Ark in Turkey and deliver proof of the existence of Scotland's mystical Loch Ness monster and Nepal's Abominable Snowman. As he never delivered on the previous three it would be clear from the start that his summer 1980 expedition out to the last known position of the *Titanic* could end up the same way. As filmmakers were getting ready to screen the world premiere of *Raise the Titanic*, Grimm was preoccupied with dropping the sonar equipment into the Atlantic. Onboard the *H.J.W. Fay* the team of 23 scientists and 15 crew were struggling with the sled sonar as 50mph winds whipped up 12ft waves. Grimm had nearly $500,000 of invested contributions riding on the expedition and all the North Atlantic could do was refuse to give up its secrets by damaging the sonar. The *Fay* was originally due to dock in Boston during the first week of August until news came that Grimm had accepted defeat, and with just two days of fuel left and diminishing food supplies, they had no choice but to head back to port. There was however a glimmer of hope when during sonar scanning, they had a hit when an anomaly appeared. But they lost the target when the tail fin of the magnetometer got ripped away during a sharp turn brought about by the heavy seas on the towing cable. The worsening weather prevented any chance of obtaining photographic proof that it was *Titanic*. But that did not stop Grimm claiming in Texan ranch terms "the heifer is corralled in a canyon."

Grimm's premature announcement that he had found *Titanic* on 16 August 1980 was something that would eventually become costly over the course of the next three years. News agencies began to circulate the story that the expedition team had discovered the ship resting 12,000ft down at "latitude 41.46 North and longitude 50.14 West" but without any obtained imagery it could not be fully confirmed. One positive aspect of the expedition was that 500 square nautical miles had been mapped with 14 targets presenting possibilities of one of them being *Titanic*. The only way forward was to mount another trip to the area and resume the search. This time they hoped the weather would be more friendly. The June 1981 expedition onboard the research vessel *Gyre* had to hand a more robust sonar, the Scripps Deep Tow. Again, the weather turned but not before the previous year's 14 targets were found and identified as being natural features of the ocean floor. On the dockside in Boston Grimm addressed the press who had gathered there following on from his new claim that *Titanic* had finally been found. The apparent discovery was backed up with a photo-mosaic of an object which Grimm claimed was part of a propeller of *Titanic* still possibly attached to the main hull. Despite the crew of *Gyre* refusing to endorse Grimm's remarkable declaration, it was later perceived to be nothing more than an outcrop of the sea bed giving the illusion of a manmade structure. Grimm still refused to give up.

In July 1983 he tried one more time to prove that *Titanic* was somewhere out there in the area he had been surveying. What the expedition did prove was the bad luck that haunted Grimm and the crew as yet again the weather turned bad restricting the crew of the *Robert D. Conrad* and the deep tow system SeaMARC. As the storms pummelled the search area the decision was made to return to the safety of port adding Grimm's expedition to the list of his other failed endeavours. While Grimm had to come to terms with not being the discoverer of the Queen of the Ocean, he should be remembered for being the one who *nearly did,* as during the period following Ballard's successful expedition in 1985 it became apparent that the 1981 Grimm search had come within 1.5 miles of the wreck site. But more devastating for the Texan was that the SeaMARC had passed directly over the remains of the *Titanic*, and the onboard equipment failed to detect it.

It is without question that the joint French-American teams who found *Titanic* in September 1985 had on-hand the correspondence from naval resources documented during the 1970s and from the Jack Grimm expeditions of 1980, 81, and 83. Ballard was not the first on-site to begin the search for the wreck of *Titanic*. That honour went to the French team from IFREMER aboard their vessel *Le Suroit* in July 1985. The team was using a magnetometer that was trailed on a cable behind the vessel as it crossed selected areas of the ocean floor. Using such equipment had already proved unsuccessful during the Grimm expeditions, but yet they were confident that their updated equipment in use with current coordinates would produce something positive. Weather and time hampered the expedition as the SAR magnetometer was deployed time and time again in search of the wreck. The data sent back to the *Le Suroit* was fascinating but troubling as it revealed a picture of the ocean floor along *Titanic* Canyon had been destabilized from earthquakes that plagued the area. On 18 November 1929, a 7.2 magnitude quake was recorded in the Grand Banks lasting for almost a minute in duration. White Star Line's *Olympic*, the surviving older sister of *Titanic*, was on her westbound voyage from Southampton to New York at the time and was caught in the quake as the vessel vibrated from the shocks. The INFREMER crew were now concerned that the great quake of 1929 may have resulted in mudslides through the canyon burying anything in their wake, including the *Titanic*. By mid-August the crew of *Le Suroit* had found no traces of the wreck and with the window of opportunity diminishing quickly it was looking as if the *Titanic* would remain forever lost.

The arrival at the site of the American team on board the *Knorr* meant that both teams could now combine their data. It was evident that the use of the magnetometer was proving futile as Ballard opted in changing the search tactics from looking for one object, to that of searching for debris trails. It was perceived that *Titanic* being a single object of 883ft in length and 92ft in width, large as she was, was like searching for a needle in a haystack. Instead of looking for the hull of the *Titanic,* it was decided to look for the considerably larger debris trail that she left behind during her descent from the surface down to the ocean floor. *Titanic* was fitted with all types of deck fittings such as deck benches, ventilators, funnels. Her journey to the bottom surely resulted in much of this content being dispersed over a large area of the sea bed. The scatter pattern of debris would be far greater in size than that of the main hull. From the decks of the *Knorr* the camera sled *Argo* was dropped into the water and towed over the ocean floor as the crew gazed at the video monitors in the hunt for bread crumbs that would eventually lead them to the prize.

Shattered Dreams

That first week of September 1985 was a period that many long-time *Titanic* enthusiasts would never forget. The discovery of the wreck created mixed feelings from those of tremendous excitement to that of grave concerns as the position of the shattered remains now presented a time of exploitation. Images released from Woods Hole showed *Titanic* scattered over a huge area of the seafloor with thousands of artefacts that were once inside the luxury liner now spread over vast areas easily accessible for any expedition leaders to dive and retrieve. It also meant that the *Titanic* was no longer a single hull wreck and that either bow or stern could be salvaged more affordably and accordingly than previously thought. It didn't stop those coming forward with lavish schemes of salvage. Within days of her discovery being made public, British salvage expert John Pierce came forward with his plan of using a manned submersible to attach 90 inflatable bags to the bilge keel of the hull. His idea was upscaled from the salvage on the 21 August 1985 of the Greenpeace vessel *Rainbow Warrior* which had been attacked and sunk the month before by French saboteurs while she sat in Auckland Harbour. *Salvage Pacific Ltd* in Fiji supplied salvage airbags which had a lifting capacity of five tons each were attached to the starboard hull of the *Rainbow Warrior* and with her compartments pumped clear of water she was slowly brought to the surface. While they were successful in recovering the 418-ton vessel from shallow waters, *Warrior* was not in the same category as a deep-water wreck like the *Titanic*. Nonetheless, Pierce maintained it could be done.

Some schemes put forward on raising *Titanic* were audacious and borderline insane. One was to fill the hull with hundreds of thousands of ping pong balls to float the great liner to the surface while not taking into account that they would be crushed long before they even reached the wreck. A more practical idea came with filling the hull with Benthos glass spheres that would survive the pressures at 12,500ft. The estimated $238 million salvage bill was soon to scupper any such plan. The British eccentricity surfaced again in September 1985 when underwater engineer Tony Wakefield devised a plan of placing lifting bags under the hull and up the sides to create a cushioned cradle. He estimated that 180,000 tons of petroleum jelly, better known as Vaseline, would be pumped into the lifting bags creating a lift rate of 3ft per second. The ascent to the surface would be controlled by a series of additional trimming bags pumped with alcohol sent down through pipes from a platform vessel at the surface. This vessel would also double as a towing ship that would keep the wreck suspended at a depth of 200ft beneath the hull for the journey to Scotland, where they could lower the *Titanic* into a deep-water loch to begin preservation, turning the hull into a tourist attraction and clawing back the estimated £100m in salvage costs. The only advantage Wakefield had was that his company assisted with the raising in February 1985 of the Balao-class submarine *Santa Fe* which had been captured and scuttled while at the King Edward Point jetty of South Georgia docks by the British during the 1982 Falklands War conflict. The hull was partially raised, towed out to deeper waters and then scuttled. As the *Titanic* remains on the ocean floor, I guess all the ping pong balls, magnets and jars of Vaseline did more in raising eyebrows than raising the fabled shipwreck.

30 Years and Counting

If *Titanic*'s name alone was not enough to capture the imagination and take it into flights of fancy before her historic discovery, it is what the future holds since then which has secured her name in folklore for generations to come. The first grainy image of her twisted hull which circulated the world in September 1985 was just the beginning of an incredible journey on an unprecedented scale that allowed the wreck site to be catalogued in breath-taking detail. *Titanic* represented a cinematic elegance that studios liked. And in the wake of advancements in technology, the wreck quickly became the focal point in capturing the progressing state of decay inside and out. Robert Ballard's second outing to the wreck in June 1986 resulted in him and his crew becoming the first people to land down on the decks of the liner since her sinking. With the use of the submersible *Alvin* and the remote tethered camera unit named *Jason Junior,* they roamed the wreck photographing and filming her as she sat in the crushing pressures of the black abyss. The expeditions survey of the wreck hinted of the splendours that awaited future dives when Ballard descended the large opening of the grand staircase and caught on film the remains of the hand-carved oak deck supports and gilded and cut crystal light fittings that once adorned the ceiling of the staircase landings, now hanging suspended in time on their dislodged electrical wiring.

As Ballard said farewell to the wreck to begin the publication of his best-selling book *The Discovery of the Titanic*, the next chapter of *Titanic*'s discovery was now in progress, dividing opinions and kickstarting one of the most controversial periods in *Titanic*'s history. With financial backing, IFREMER began the recovery process of 1,800 items from the wreck and the surrounding debris fields, much to the horror of many survivors who openly objected to such deliberate acts of grave robbing. The start of a new decade had *Titanic* under the ownership of the newly formed RMS *Titanic*, Inc who was awarded the role of being the wreck Salvors of Possession, a title that meant that they and they alone were the only ones allowed to salvage anything from the wreck site. Their objectives were simple; to recover, to preserve, to protect, and to display the artefacts via exhibitions, or so they made the public believe. Over seventeen years the company would recover over 5,500 items from *Titanic* with only a small percentage of them ever going on public display. The costs alone of continuing recovery, preservation, and documentation began to weigh heavy on the company as directors came and went, eating into the profits with bankruptcy looming over them. These uncertainties not only had those questioning the future of the company but more importantly the concerns of the current list of recovered artefacts. Many supporters of these salvage operations still express to this day how much can be learned from the thousands of recovered items while not taking into account that *Titanic* was never the foremost symbol of Edwardian society, having played a very small part of it, not to mention that in learning from such artefacts they have to be accessible which for the past thirty years they have remained locked away from the public.

Of all the expeditions that have been carried out at the wreck since her discovery, two stand out as the most important of them all; the 2001 and 2005 dives by filmmaker James Cameron. He may be best remembered for giving movie fans such classics as *Terminator, Aliens, Avatar,* and his own take on the *Titanic* disaster, but to all the serious *Titanic* enthusiasts out there, it was his two ground breaking dives to the wreck that stand out. With the use of the Russian MIR submersibles, a huge lighting rig, and two microbot ROV cameras aptly named Jake and Elwood after the Blues Brothers, Cameron was able to penetrate interior spaces of *Titanic* revealing an enormous amount of well-preserved interior décor previously thought to have been consumed by marine organisms. The treasure trove of material caught on camera went on to form the basis of the book, DVD and Blu Ray releases entitled *Ghosts of the Abyss*. His return in 2005 was a continuation of the 2001 dives in establishing the capture of more interior footage in areas previously unexplored. There was a sad reflection in the dives as exterior imagery revealed how quickly *Titanic* was decaying and collapsing. But it was the tricky manoeuvre into the heart of the wreck to film the immaculate ceramic wall tiles of the cooling room of the 1st class Electric Baths. And yet, amongst all this decay, little pockets of the ship still retained the beauty and grandeur of a time long lost.

The reader may be interested to know that James Cameron was not the first Hollywood star with intentions to dive and film the wreck. A couple of weeks after Ballard had announced her discovery, screen legend Robert Wagner (*Titanic, The Towering Inferno, Hart to Hart*) went to press that he wanted to film and produce a documentary covering the filming and raising of the wreck that was in the planning stages by John Pierce. "I have been fascinated by the subject of the *Titanic* since my research for the movie," said Wagner. "It will be very exciting, win, lose or draw." It was neither as Wagner went on to can the project largely due to such lavish salvage operations not being practical or feasible.

RMS *Titanic*, Inc returned to the wreck site in the late summer of 2010 equipped with sophisticated mapping technology and, for the first time, full high definition cameras to capture the *Titanic* in stunning detail. The entire area, the ship, and the debris field were fully mapped creating unparalleled data that covered almost every single item from the ship sitting on the ocean floor. But with such extraordinary technology capturing the wreck in much minute detail came the realization that *Titanic* was a matter of years away from completely collapsing in on herself. The micro marine organism that thrives on the wreck in their billions continue to consume the metal composition reducing the stability of the steel to the point it is so thin and brittle in areas that the hull is expected to collapse within the next decade or two. The August 2019 exploration of the wreck marked the first manned dives to the *Titanic* in fourteen years. During the course of the five-day expedition, the wreck was filmed in 4K resolution with photoreal photogrammetry technology in preparation for creating highly detailed 3D models of the wreck for future studies. In 2020 controversy reared up again with the release in the press that a planned 2021 expedition by RMS *Titanic*, Inc were to dive the wreck and cut open areas to gain access to recover artefacts from within the ship. The Marconi Radio Room situated in the deckhouse of the Officers' Quarters on the crumbling boat deck is one designated spot for recovery as the rotten remains of the Marconi seem to be rich pickings for the company who want something new to display in their Las Vegas prime venue. As 2021 came to an end, so did the current need to retrieve the radio. The expedition was postponed indefinitely as objections were filed by the relatives of those who died in the disaster. Whether if you are for or against such operations it is becoming all too evident that as the years pass, as technology improves and as *Titanic* slowly peels apart, the idea of ever raising her is confined to the pages of books. What is alarming is the uncertainty of the future of the wreck. It is only a matter of time before those desensitized by progress will see *Titanic* as a continued source of income, dictating how she should be presented to the public and at what cost. It is fearful that as the years pass *Titanic* will go from being a wreck, the final resting place of hundreds, a grave marker to the 1,496 men, women, and children who perished on the Monday morning of 15 April 1912, to become the final symbol of greed and arrogance as the hull is torn apart in gaining access to any treasures hidden within the remains.

The idea of raising the *Titanic* will always be a work of fiction regardless of how many came forward over the years before her discovery with grandiose ideas of salvage. Reflecting on the "what-if" still produces a buzz of excitement; if only she had been found intact; if only the technology and money were there to raise her. It is that fantasy which continues to be thought-provoking, separating fact from fiction. *Raise the Titanic* is the ultimate escapism, a fantasy that defines "what-if". But in reality, the footage that we see is of a rusticle-encrusted collapsing wreck where the dignity of this once graceful ocean liner is now being broadcast around the world as a pile of collapsing junk, hauled up off the ocean floor in buckets and thrown on display like some money-orientated freak show. The beginning of a new decade has kicked off interest in the wreck as enthusiasts around the world mark the anniversary of her sinking in 2022. And with this new interest comes new technology and the opportunity for customers to travel down to the wreck site at a ticket price of $250,000 in a newly crafted submersible. If there is any hope that the *Titanic* will be left alone it is fading as quickly as the ship deteriorates. And the more she collapses, the more she exposes her riches, the more the salvors of possession will push to recover these artefacts to keep their company above water. Maybe one day the old girl will finally be left alone to the darkness and the inhabitants of the deep.

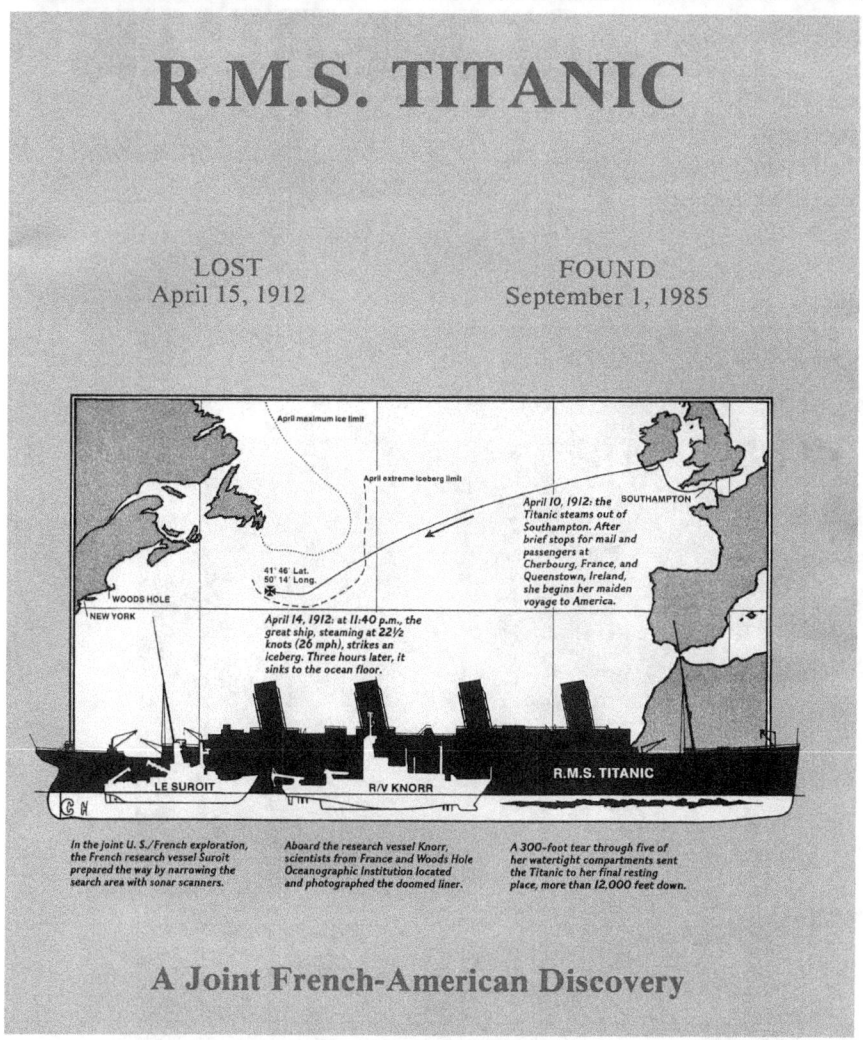

TOP: The remains of *Titanic's* bow section upon her discovery in September 1985. ABOVE: Press pack released by Woods Hole Oceanographic Institution in September 1985. *(Painting © Stuart Williamson / Author's collection)*

Original IFREMER crew jacket patch from the 1987 recovery expedition to the wreck site. *(Author's collection)*

Full colour supplement from October 1987 that was free with copies of the UK newspaper *Sunday Mirror*. The 15-page magazine is entirely devoted to artefacts brought up from the wreck during the 1987 recovery expedition by IFREMER. *(Author's collection)*

The intact *Titanic* pitches upright before sliding into the black freezing waters of the North Atlantic. This publicity still for the 1953 Fox production *TITANIC* did much to convince the general public into thinking that the liner had in fact sank in one piece. *(20th Century Fox - Author's collection)*

Chapter 17: Raising the Question on Reality • 89

A highly unusual and somewhat imaginative rendering of the wreck from the early 1980s depicting *Titanic* sitting actually upright. *(Charles Myer collection)*

Donald L. Keach who was one of two oceanographer advisors on the production. *(ITC / The Last Great Human Adventure promotional film – Author's collection)*

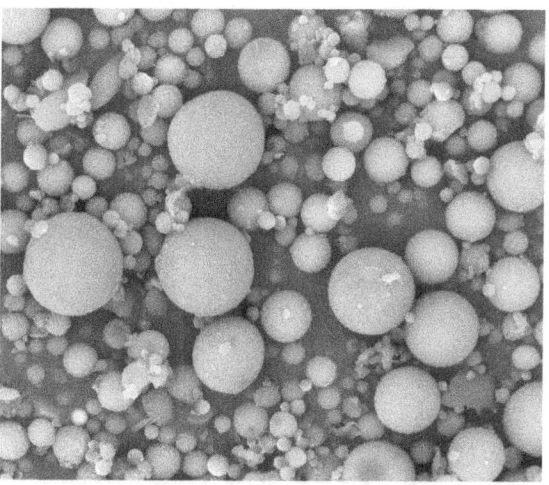

The mass-produced lightweight industrial composite of cenopsheres, otherwise known Syntactic foam. Each hollow sphere is less than 1mm in diameter and when combined with other liquids, such as epoxy compounds, it would congeal and harden. And being lighter than water and used in quantity, the composite could be pumped into a wreck, forcing out the water and adding buoyancy. *(Engineered Syntactic Systems)*

Publicity photograph of the deep-sea submersible *Trieste* in 1960. *(Author's collection)*

90 • Raise The Titanic

Don Walsh interviewed on board the *U.S.S. Denver* during filming off San Diego for *Raise the Titanic*. (ITC / The Last Great Human Adventure promotional film – Author's collection)

Millionaire businessman Jack Grimm in 1980 during his real-life quest to find the *Titanic*. (ITC / The Last Great Human Adventure promotional film – Author's collection)

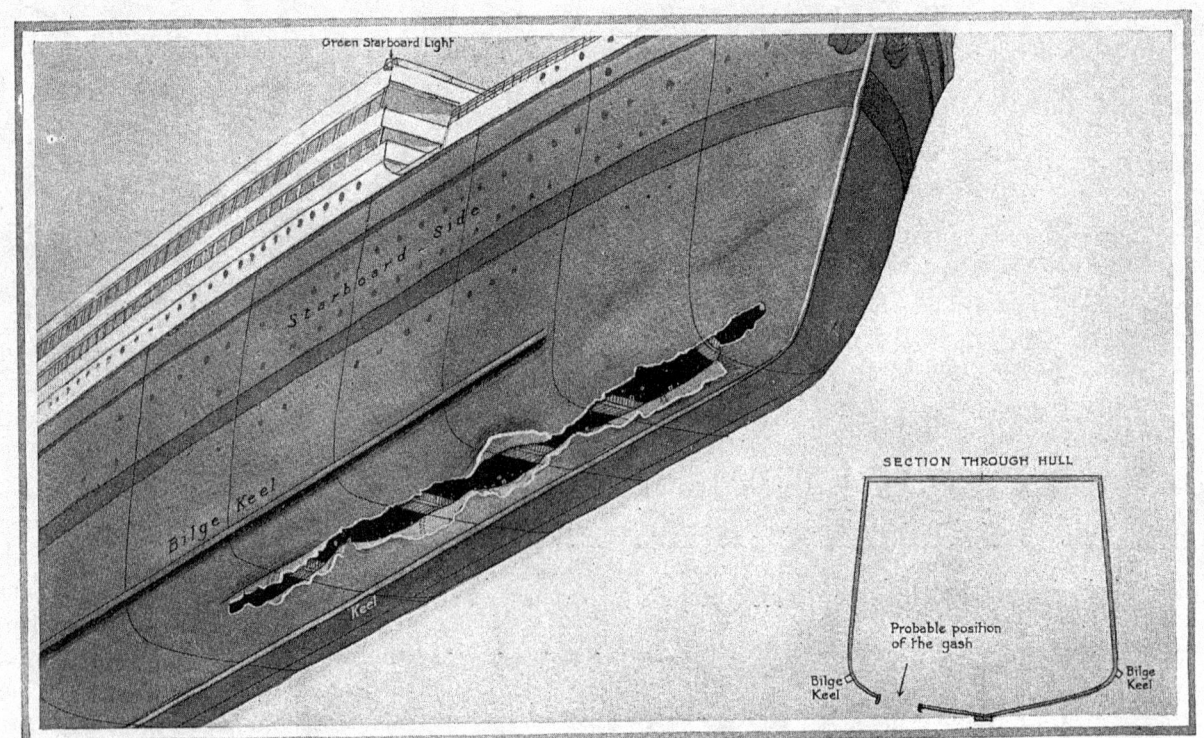

The beginning of a myth that would last decades. Within weeks following the disaster, a number of newspapers and magazines enthralled readers with lavish illustrations of what was perceived to have happened to the *Titanic*. During this time many myths were born including that of *Titanic* being ripped wide open by the iceberg resulting in a 300ft gash running down her lower starboard hull. What else could have sunk the unsinkable? This misconception remained as fact until the expeditions to the wreck site in the mid-1990s finally lay to rest that the *Titanic* suffered a number of puncture wounds and separation of plates. *(The Sphere, May 1912 – Author's collection)*

Chapter 17: Raising the Question on Reality • 91

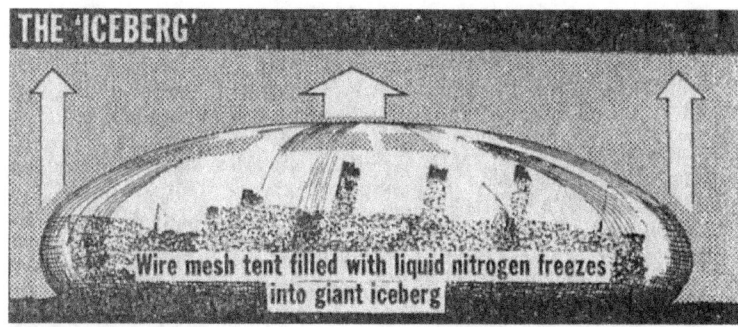

As the news spread on the 2 September 1985 that *Titanic* had been found, the fantasy of raising the wreck once again made headlines around the world with some that could have originated within the pages of a Jules Verne novel. *(The Sunday Times, 8 September 1985 – Author's collection)*

Salvage engineer Tony Wakefield's eye-opening plan to use 180,000 tons of a petroleum jelly-based product to raise the *Titanic*. *(Sunday Mirror, 8 September 1985 – Author's collection)*

John Pearce and Bernhardt Jones who envisioned salvaging *Titanic* by using a series of air bags attached to the hull. The bags would be designed to lift an estimated 500 tons per unit. *(Observer, 15 September 1985 – Author's collection)*

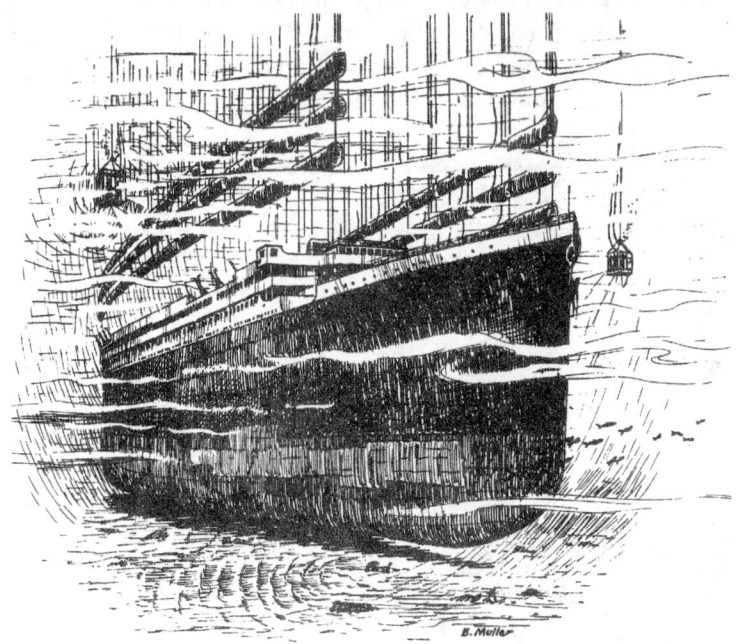

One of the many fanciful ideas from the 1970s to how *Titanic* would look and how she could be raised. *(Illustration © B. Muller – Bill Wormstedt collection)*

The discovery makes the news. This largely circulated image was mostly incorrectly identified by many newspapers and magazines as being a section of *Titanic*'s hull and railing. In fact, this image is taken directly over the starboard side of the boat deck where the bow and stern separated. The railing-like structure is the ripped out remains of the A-Deck promenade while the flat structure to the right is the raised roof over the 1st class lounge that sat between funnels two and three. *(Daily Mail, 6 September 1985 – Author's collection)*

Chapter 17: Raising the Question on Reality • 93

"SHE SLOWLY TILTED STRAIGHT ON END" DRAWN FOR "THE SPHERE" BY G. H. DAVIS

This G.A. Davies illustration created for *The Sphere* in May 1912 depicts *Titanic* pitched almost vertical during the ships final plunge. It was artworks such as this that fuelled the theories to come that *Titanic* had sank intact. *(Author's collection)*

Dramatic artist impression that was published in the 19 April, 1912 issue of the *Chicago Daily Tribune*. The fine print under the main header reads *"From a photograph of the Titanic and Description furnished by survivors who arrived last night on the* Carpathia.*" (Author's collection)*

This 1912 published postcard has an illustration by F.H. Chase and visibly shows *Titanic* breaking into two pieces. *(Author's collection)*

What is remarkable about this illustration from the 19 April 1912 is that not only does it show *Titanic* breaking in half, but recent studies of the wreck have revealed that *Titanic* did break her back forwards of the third funnel and not previously thought between funnels three and four as depicted in the 1997 James Cameron movie. *(Author's collection)*

One of the more popular 1912 illustrations is that of the Skidmore rendering. Lewis Skidmore was a passenger on board the *Carpathia* when the liner picked up the 712 survivors of the *Titanic*. Skidmore made these sketches based around the description of the sinking by survivor Jack Thayer. *(L'Illustration, 6 May, 1912 – Author's collection)*

A male *Titanic* victim is embalmed on the open deck of the cable ship C.S. *Mackay-Bennett*. After the body has been searched for identification and notes taken on possessions and condition, the bodies were placed into crude coffins and stored out on the vessels deck until the ship reached port. *(NSARM Photo Drawer - Transportation & Communication - Ships & Shipping - Titanic, no. 2 / neg. no.: N-0715)*

Horse drawn hearses line up on the quay at Halifax, Nova Scotia, as crews remove coffins containing victims of the *Titanic* disaster from the C.S. *Mackay-Bennett* as each victim is carried to the funeral parlour. *(NSARM Photo Drawer - Transportation & Communication - Ships & Shipping - Titanic, no. 3 / neg. no.: N-0332)*

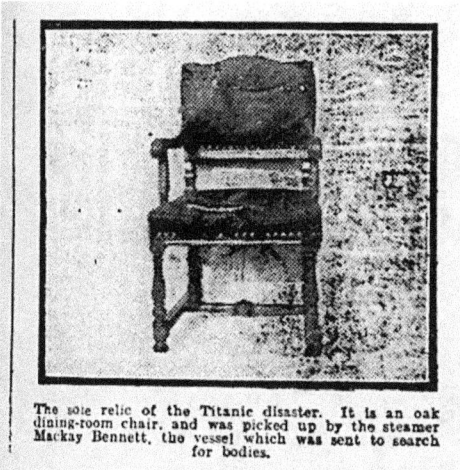

The sole relic of the Titanic disaster. It is an oak dining-room chair, and was picked up by the steamer Mackay Bennett, the vessel which was sent to search for bodies.

During the recovery process of bodies, the chartered vessels also recovered some of the artefacts found floating in the debris field that drifted. A large quantity of wooden items such as chairs, deck chairs and interior panelling was pulled from the water by crews of the *Mackay-Bennett* and the *Minia*. This extremely heavy solid oak dining room chair was spat out when the ship broke apart. The first-class dining room down on D-Deck was completely ripped apart when the ship broke her back. And for such a heavy item, and one that was anchored down to the floor of the room to prevent it moving in heavy seas, it could not have been carried out by any passenger or crewmember. *(Author's collection)*

Another relic from the *Titanic* that got spat out during the break-up. This large decorative panel once sat over the double door entrance into *Titanic*'s lavish 1st class lounge on A-Deck. As the ship ripped herself apart during the final plunge, the area of the break also went through the lounge detaching many items. Heavier items would sink to the sea floor, while others, such as those made of timber, were found to be floating, including this wall panel. *(Photograph © Lynda Hartigan)*

Titanic survivor Chief Baker Charles John Joughin. *(Encyclopedia Titanica)*

Titanic survivor Arthur Peuchen. *(Toronto Star)*

Titanic survivor Edward John Buley. *(Encyclopedia Titanica)*

Titanic survivor Arthur John Bright *(Author's collection)*

Titanic's Second Officer, Charles Herbert Lightoller (bowler and pipe) outside the courts of inquiry into the *Titanic* disaster. *(Author's collection)*

The first funnel collapses over to portside. *(Author's collection)*

Chapter 17: Raising the Question on Reality

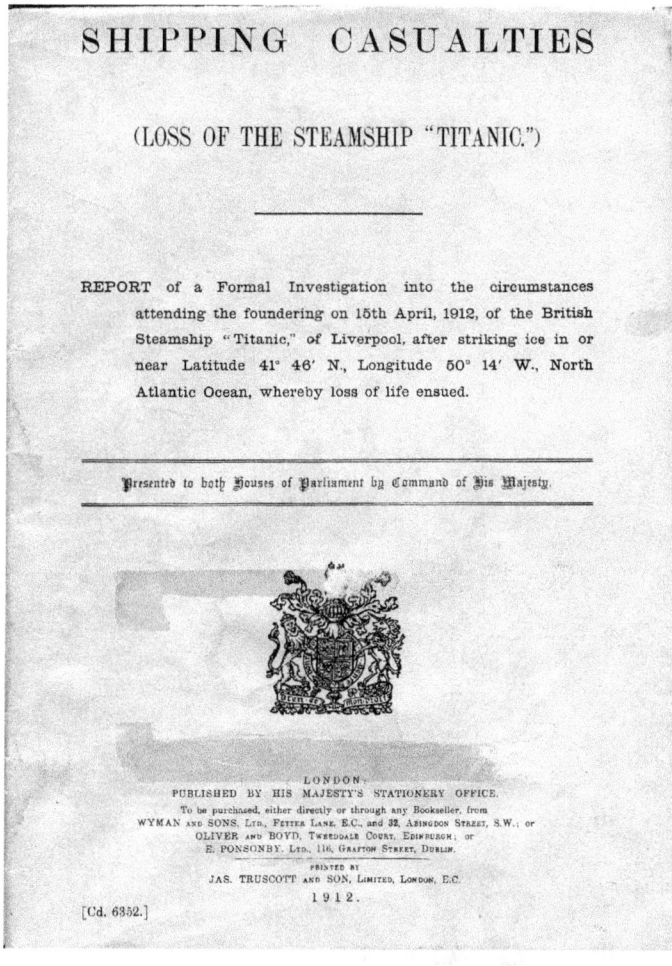

Documentation from the inquiry into the loss of the *Titanic*. Both the American and British inquiries were documented with witness statements put to record. Since the summer of 1912 these reports have been widely available to the public and can be an interesting look into the first and only voyage of the *Titanic*. However, over the decades, a lot of the reports have been misinterpreted by researchers and these have led to a number of errors that have appeared in books, documentaries and movies. *(Author's collection)*

Charles A. Smith's 1914 plan of locating and raising the wreck using a series of high-powered magnets that would be attached to the hull. At the surface a fleet of ships would lower cables down. Also attached with magnets, and when both meet, they would attach and the wreck could be winched upwards and carried to shallow waters and then onto New York. *(Author's collection)*

Douglas Woolley in 1970. *(Author's collection)*

Commander John Grattan of *Seawise & Titanic Ltd* in 1979. *(Now, 19-25 October, 1979 – Author's collection)*

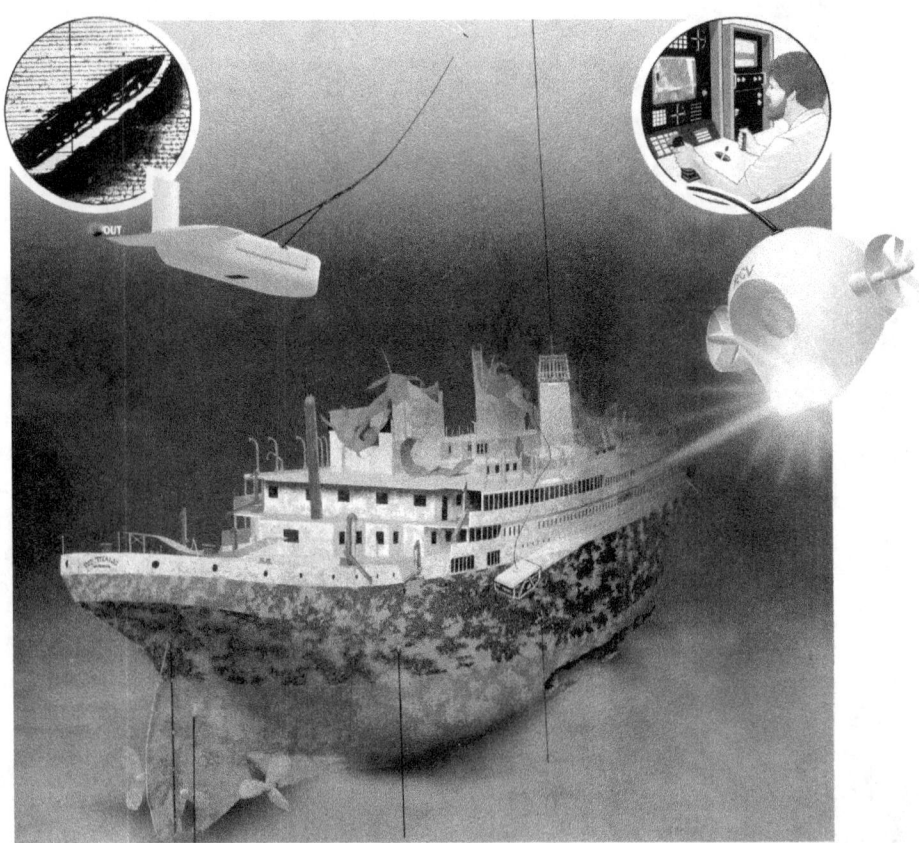

Artist impression to how *Seawise & Titanic Ltd* perceived the wreck to have looked in 1979. *(Artwork © David Case - Now, 19-25 -October, 1979 – Author's collection)*

Jack "Cadillac" Grimm; the business tycoon who failed to find the Loch Ness Monster, Noah's Ark and the Abominable Snowman. Now his sights were set on finding the legendary *Titanic*. *(Author's collection)*

The news on the possible discovery of the wreck makes headlines, 16 August 1980. Despite the best efforts of the crew of the *H.J.W. Fay*, whatever the anomaly was picked up on sonar, it was not the *Titanic*. *(Author's collection)*

We think we've got the Titanic!

Titanic... she hit an iceberg

By PHILIP FINN in New York

EXCITED members of an American search party reported last night that they believe they have found the wreck of the Titanic, which sank 68 years ago after hitting an iceberg on its maiden voyage to New York.

A sonar scanner located the evidently telltale outline 380 miles off the coast of Newfoundland.

"We think we've got the Titanic," said Mike Harris, one of the team aboard the research vessel HJW Fay, in a radio call to New York.

"We won't be sure until we send the television cameras down but the conar shows it's the righ length, right width and right height."

The cameras may be sent down today and, if the Titanic outline is confirmed, a submarine may follow next

Known

The scanner found the outline 12,000ft down at latitude 41.46 North and longitude 50.14 West—"not too far from the historic site where the ship went down," said Harris.

More than 1,500 people died when the "unsinkable" White Star liner sank on April 15, 1912. Although the location has been generally known, the vast depths in that part of the North Atlantic have previously prevented searchers from finding her.

The Fay expedition, financed by Texas oil millionaire Jack Grimm, has been closely monitored by a Soviet vessel.

Lost; then found; to be lost again. *(Daily Mail, 16 August, 1980 – Author's collection)*

Chapter 17: Raising the Question on Reality • 103

If only the Atlantic where *Titanic* sat was that shallow. This illustration from April 1980 does share some similarities to the real wreck in that the wreck is depicted broken in two main sections. *(Illustration © C.L. Lacroix – Science & Vie, April 1980 – Author's collection)*

Robert D. Ballard holds a press conference on the 11 September 1985 following the discovery of the *Titanic*. *(Original publicity photograph – Author's collection)*

R.V. *Atlantis II* and the D.S.V. *Alvin* in 1985. Both vessels would be used by Ballard during the first manned dives to the *Titanic* in July 1986. *(Postcard published by Plastichrome, Boston, MA – Author's collection)*

The wreck of the R.M.S. *Titanic*, September 1985. *(Painting © Stuart Williamson)*

Looking directly down on the forecastle of *Titanic* in September 1985 and the sediment covered anchors chains, windlasses and capstan. *(Woods Hole Oceanographic Institution Press Photograph – Author's collection)*

Chapter 17: Raising the Question on Reality • 105

Robert Wagner and Audrey Dalton on the set of the 1953 Fox production *TITANIC*. *(Author's collection)*

The prediction of exploitation of the wreck is clear in this cartoon from the 11 September 1985 issue of the *Miami Herald*. Two years later marked the first dives to the wreck site where nearly 700 items were pulled up from the debris field and, more to the dismay of many *Titanic* enthusiasts, items removed from the ship herself. *(Author's collection)*

Some 5,000 items have been removed from the wreck site since 1987 when the first dives began after Robert Ballard had completed his own survey of the wreck. The items recovered vary from those removed from the exposed debris field around the bow and stern of the *Titanic* to those found inside passenger luggage retrieved from the sediment including cut lead crystal tableware's, ladies hand mirror, playing cards, floor tiles, ceramic 3rd class soup bowls, decorative lead 1st class corridor vent grill, one of her sidelights (porthole) and even a well preserved hot water bottle. *(All photographs © Jonathan Smith)*

CHAPTER 18

Wreckcognising *Titanic*

"The model needed a lot of constant repair…"

FX Supervisor John Richardson

We now live in an age where special effects-laden feature films are so heavily crafted with computer technology that those types of films are taken for granted in delivering to the masses scenes that take the viewer beyond the realms of fantasy. The last *Titanic* movie to grace the big screen was James Cameron's blockbuster. The production was a glorious combination of physical special effects refined with the use of CGI. If that movie had been created today it is almost certain that the production would be largely computer generated. In 1979 the production crew on *Raise the Titanic* never had the luxury of such computer wizardry. What they did have was the best technology available to them; the best art direction; the best model FX unit, and pushing the film production into the category of the second most expensive feature film financed in the 70s after *Superman*.

Raise the Titanic was a monumental task from the offset. As 1980 dawned with a new year in a new decade, it was to deliver an intriguing year of motion pictures that would include *Airplane*, *The Shining*, *The Blues Brothers*, *The Elephant Man* and the second instalment of the *Star Wars* trilogy with *The Empire Strikes Back*. In a period long before the dawn of digital technology was to embrace Hollywood, films of varying calibre relied upon and utilized the astounding work of matte artists and scores of devoted personnel who painstakingly crafted amazing miniature work required to fool the audience. The disaster movie genre was the epitome of full-scale sets and practical miniature work with early movie productions such as *San Francisco* with Clark Gable as his character searches for the woman he loves as the city is destroyed by earthquake and fire. Or George C. Scott looking for a saboteur on board the soon to be doomed airship *Hindenburg*. There is no denying that the 1970s delivered some of the most dazzling disaster movies ever to grace the screen, from Irwin Allen capsizing the S.S. *Poseidon* or setting ablaze the world's tallest skyscraper in *The Towering Inferno*. And let's not forget Charlton Heston and George Kennedy helping the survivors after the "big one" levels Los Angeles in *Earthquake* or Sean Connery trying to make people realize that the earth is doomed in *Meteor*. While some disaster epics are best-remembered, others are more forgettable. *Beyond the Poseidon Adventure* with a rather shouty Michael Caine trying to locate precious bounty in the upturned hull of the liner as the supporting cast deliver a bland and tedious performance. At least it was not as bad as Caine's role as a scientist in *The Swarm* and his cringe-worthy delivery of, "We've been fighting a losing battle against the insects for fifteen years, but I never thought I'd see the final face-off in my lifetime. And I never dreamed, that it would turn out to be the bees. They've always been our friend."

One of the first films to incorporate CGI was Barry Levinson's 1985 action-adventure *Young Sherlock Holmes* in which Industrial Light and Magic spent four months creating the film's stain glass Knight window that comes to life to become the first-ever CGI character in motion picture history. Industrial Light and Magic was to deliver again in 1989 with the alien water tentacle for James Cameron's sci-fi masterpiece *The Abyss*. The film was Cameron's first outing with CGI before turning to his 1991 non-stop action blockbuster *Terminator 2*. But while CGI was still largely in its infancy those films still relied heavily on good old-fashioned practical work. The heavy usage of CGI can work wonders for broad sweeping aerial views of cityscapes or mythical worlds like those in Peter Jackson's *The Lord of the Rings* and *The Hobbit* trilogies. Catastrophe movies of today that include the 2009 Roland Emmerich disaster epic *2012* or Brad Peyton's 2015 earth-shattering *San Andreas* can reduce cities to rubble on-screen in seconds in terrifying detail, even if they appear somewhat overblown in destruction. But will these movies be as memorable and cherished for their special effects in 40-years' time? Sometimes the delivery from simplicity due to restrictions or restraints with miniature work can have a longer-lasting legacy on celluloid than that of a computer-animated scene purposely created to be photo-realistic that the mind knows it is faked when compared to the model work where the mind can differentiate that it is a miniature yet conclude it looks realistic as the model reacts to its surroundings.

The 1958 Rank Organisation adaptation of Walter Lord's *A Night to Remember* covering the *Titanic* disaster was achieved using a 40ft recreation of the liner built by Shawcraft Model Ltd in the United Kingdom that was based around the surviving 1910 shipbuilders display model of the *Olympic* and *Titanic*. The company name may be familiar to some as Shawcraft brought to life the Daleks for their on-screen presence in *Doctor Who*. Five years earlier Hollywood delivered the Twentieth Century Fox production of *Titanic* featuring Barbara Stanwyck and Clifton Webb alongside the workable 28ft replica of the liner. While the model work was of its time, based on the information available, these miniatures did share one thing in common in that these replicas were nowhere near a faithful recreation of the historical liner as they were littered with deck detailing errors or grossly scaled wrongly with funnels being too tall. Any studio post-1958 wanting to produce a new *Titanic* feature film needed to do the subject justice with a near-as faithful replica of the ship. Excluding the 1979 TV movie *S.O.S. Titanic* which utilized cutting room floor footage from *A Night to Remember* and the odd still photograph of a 20ft museum display model of the *Titanic*. It was not until 1977 during the production stages for *Raise the Titanic* that those involved brought the fabled liner to life in such minute detail that the ship, herself, would be represented on the screen correctly. Unfortunately for those wanting to see the disaster portrayed accurately on-screen the production was more about salvaging the liner than the sinking of it.

Titanic: 68 Years Later

As Grade deemed the prologue an unnecessary expenditure for ITC during the summer of 1979, Special & Mechanical Effects Supervisor John Richardson received the phone call asking for his assistance over in Malta to lead the film into its final stages of development. From there a new crew was assembled for the journey to Malta to carry out the extensive conversion of aging the *Titanic* model into that of a long-lost wreck that has spent nearly 70 years locked away in the depths of the North Atlantic. When the U.S team left in mid 1979, the model was to spend the next few months pushed to one side of the Marine studio of the Mediterranean Film Facility to await the arrival of Richardson and his team. As autumn broke the new crew had arrived at the studio to take up the next phase of the production. Uncovered now, the *Titanic* model was removed from the Marine studio and over to the surface tank for inspection and floatation testing. Things were not looking good. The interior installed tanks were struggling to keep the model stable to the point the model sank to rest on the floor of the surface tank. The existing tanks had to be replaced if the model unit wanted the *Titanic* model to float on the surface unaided for the sequences that involved the ship being caught up in the storm and the journey to New York with the tug boats.

Over the following days, the superstructure was removed along with the masts, forecastle, poop deck, both well decks, rudder, and propellers to leave the main hull in a minimal state of assembly for transportation. As some members of the model unit disassembled the *Titanic* replica, others carried out tests on the hull, experimenting with ways on how to age the model on a large scale when the hull had been fitted out. Stripped down to a minimum the hull was collected on a low-loader and road transported to Malta Docks where welders from the shipyard would install a new internal keel and fabricate new floatation tanks designed to be removed when they had served their purpose. A few weeks later the work had been completed and the hull was back on a low-loader for its return to the studio where, ceremoniously, the *Titanic* replica was craned from the trailer, sat down into its purpose-built transportation cradle, and towed into the interior of the Marine studio where it would undergo its extensive transformation to a wreck.

The overall look chosen for the model was a combination of research stemmed from marine experts Donald Keach and Don Walsh with subtle nods towards the Clive Cussler novel. The wreck had to retain almost all of the features that identified it as being *Titanic* but as a battered, rust-stained hulk cloaked in silt and marine growth after 68 years of deep-sea submersion. It was a time-consuming job but the crews must have felt some satisfaction as they set to work on breaking down the model with hammers and cutting tools. It was one sure-fire way of relieving stress. On the main hull, the lower starboard area was marked out for power tools to cut away the fiberglass hull where the iceberg damage would be modelled into the miniature. The iceberg gash was cut out from the hull starting from the location of the forepeak hold of the bow and stretching back to Boiler Room No. 5 just beneath the forward funnel. For now, the gash was nothing more than a gaping cavity that resembled nothing like the damage they thought the ship had sustained. And so, a series of internal vertical supports were created from timber to mimic the hull frames and edges of the bulkheads, secured down in place and where the hull plates would be affixed. Each plate was cut from an aluminium sheet and cut to scale to match those already modelled into the fiberglass hull. As each plate was offered up to the hull it was marked out where the damage would appear where the model FX unit could then shape the plate to appear as if something solid and heavy had been dragged down the side of the hull, pushing in the plates, opening up the joints and bending the steel-like plate inwards of the hull giving the impression the ship in that location had been ripped open with a can opener.

One necessary change was how the ship's name and port of registry were going to appear onscreen. On the model, the vessel's name and LIVERPOOL had already been cut into the fiberglass hull plate at the stern along with TITANIC on her bow, port, and starboard side, when the miniature was finished off in her 1912 appearance. With the lettering this way and the model now being aged, the FX materials being used would wash out the name, leaving it a struggle for the camera to pick up and removing the identity of the wreck in the scenes when she is discovered. Even though the lettering was nearly accurate to what they knew in 1979, from a movie-making standpoint it was not at all practical. It was decided to remodel the name and port of registry by creating a set of separate plates that could be attached to the hull and seated over the existing name. David Harris, one of the crew members of the model unit, created a master copy of the bow and stern plates and from the moulds produced several copies from a mixture of metal powder impregnated resin resulting in a plate with the letters raised and identifiable when the paint crews started on the aging process. As each plate was screwed onto the model it made things easier in case damage occurred during filming where the plate would be required to be swapped out with a new one.

Once the model unit had come to a decision on which angle to film the model in the tank, the aging process of the model saw a number of portholes down the starboard side of the hull blanked off from the inside, with the exception of D-Deck. As the model was to be filmed in slow-motion as it breached the surface of the tank, and with all camera units positioned to film only the port side of the model, the blanking off of portholes in the lower section of the hull on the starboard side meant that the water only had those purposely left open on the port side to exit the hull sustaining a higher and lengthier volume of water being filmed by the camera unit as it exits. It was the superstructure that underwent the most brutal of the transformations to the model. Railings on the deckhouses were crushed and buckled. The port side bulwark that sat between the forward and aft end lifeboat stations had been crushed down in the area where the number two funnel had made contact with it during its untimely collapse. The many sets of lifeboat davits had been set in varying poses, some still in their cranked-out positions, others cranked back up and twisted and many ripped away from their bases to be left strewn across areas of the Boat Deck. On the port side of the A-Deck promenade, one or two of the vertical supports had been cut and removed altogether while distressed pieces of material were tucked in beneath the upper Boat Deck supports and left to hang down. Hammers had been at work on the steel sides of the superstructure buckling and distorting the plates just beneath the promenade areas while many of the resin window frames that incorrectly outlined the windows of A and B- Deck had been ripped away giving an ununiformed appearance to what was once a sleek profile. The model's rear mast, more properly termed the mainmast, had been butchered with thirty inches of the top removed entirely.

The most dramatic change was with the number two funnel. The funnel had already been replicated with a spare shipped with the model from L.A to Malta that was used for the sinking prologue. The funnel, the unit built to follow suit with the other three funnels of the 1912 *Titanic*, had been bolted back down when the model went into dry storage following the return home of the U.S crews. The spare funnel that had been used for the sinking scene had been left to one side for the model unit to break down. With cutting tools to hand the model unit started to cut, chop and pull away sections of the funnel skin to resemble a tattered stump that still presented the *Titanic* as a four funnelled ocean liner. The FX unit had dressed the funnel with its broken inner skin, snapped off steam exhaust; a section of which can be seen laying across the Boat Deck during the fly-past, buckled remnants of internal crew ladders, supporting braces, and entangled rigging. The damage was simultaneously copied to the other funnel miniatures that had been built for when the submersible crews find the detached smokestack on the ocean floor in the scenes leading up to the discovery of the main hull. The three remaining funnels did not go unscathed either as the FX department warped a couple of the ladders that were fixed to the forward end of the funnels, tarnished the steam whistles, and unseated a number of the funnel cables to lay loosely hanging or be entwined around its nearby companion.

At the stern of the model, several passenger benches had been rearranged to appear pushed from their deck mountings while two of the benches had been completely unseated and wedged into the poop deck railing alongside a detached lifeboat davit. The railings around the deck and the docking bridge had been buckled along with a section of hull trim that had been detached and caught up in the railings. The Marconi aerial that stretched between the masts was detached with the forward part sitting on the port side Boat Deck outside the Officers' Quarters and the majority of the wires snaked along the length of the deck and down to the aft end of the superstructure with the aerial cable spreader resting across the pair of cargo cranes on the poop deck. One feature added to the stern was a water pump that sat out of sight beneath the steel of the poop deck with a small outlet to discharge a stream of water. In the aft well deck, the port side cargo crane had been completely removed including its mounting and leaving the starboard crane swung inboard with its cargo boom wedged against the superstructure. In the forward well deck sat a broken section of a cargo derrick from the forward mast and both the cargo cranes had been knocked backward with the boom of the portside crane buckled downwards towards the deck.

Venting Frustration

The forecastle deck at the bow was to undergo the most talked about changes that over 40 years later still has many fans of the film and *Titanic* subject debating furiously as to why these changes were ever carcarried out in the first place; the inclusion of mast vents. The real *Titanic* never had such ventilators on either side and forward on the centerline of the mast. Although many *Titanic* enthusiasts openly air their frustration to seeing them in place on the model, there is a simple explanation as to why the model unit had to include them on this replica – continuity. Once the *Athinai* had been secured over in Athens which came about *after* the sinking prologue with the miniatures had been completed, many of the storyboarded scenes to be filmed on the foredeck of the *Athinai* would reveal much of the former liners now static deck details, which had to match seamlessly with the miniatures over in Malta. While some ship fittings could be ignored, others, such as the combined cargo cranes with ventilators could not, as they served a role during the ongoing working conditions onboard the *Athinai*. Similar to *Titanic*, the *Athinai* had a cargo hold on the foredeck in which a pair of cargo derricks that sat either side of the forward mast would lift goods from the deck and down into the holds located decks below. Even though *Titanic* had one cargo hold on the forecastle and two others behind in the well deck, these holds could be worked with a large cargo derrick that sat at the rear of *Titanic*'s mast. A second derrick could be fitted to a bracket on the forward face of the mast for use in removing the No.1 cargo hold steel cover and load/unload goods from the holds below.

On *Athinai* the pair of ventilator derricks could not be removed as they were imperative in loading ship fittings removed from areas of the ship where scenes and *Titanic* sets would be filmed. If the production unit had gone ahead and removed them it would not only limit the safe storage of removed fittings in the holds, but it would result in a breach of contract between Marble Arch Productions and the brokers the courts selected to oversee the handling of the *Athinai*. The only option left to the model unit was to replicate them for the *Titanic* miniature. This also includes the single vent with the storage cradle for the cargo derricks to rest upon and the solid bulwark that sat at the tip of the bow. What comes more of a blow to *Titanic* enthusiasts is that after all the filming and editing had been completed the finished movie was to only show one scene where these ventilators are in plain sight for a mere 18 seconds. One other detail changed on the *Titanic* model was the elimination of the triangular-shaped anchor crane from the prow. In a reversal of historical accuracy, as *Athinai* had no such feature the crane was no longer needed on the *Titanic* miniature. One last addition to the forecastle on the model was a pair of water pipes, one per side, that ran from just behind the cut out for the center anchor and to finish just forward of the breakwaters to the No.1 cargo hold. These deck-mounted pipes, barely visible because of layers of sand spread out over the deck, were connected to a pumping system directly beneath the deck that forced water up into the pipes to spray seawater into the air when the tip of the prow emerges from the sea in a thunderous roar. The system was controlled by the model unit divers operating in the tank during the filming of the raising scenes. Once the bow shots were in the can the pump was removed for the continuation of filming the rest of the replica from the bridge area and back towards the stern.

Aged Beauty

The crucial part of the replicas aging process was getting the colours and textures right in representing a deep-water wreck after seven decades on the ocean floor. The texturing process from the keel upwards was a long and daunting task for all those involved. The paint FX to be applied had to remain on the model for the time frame the replica was being used. And whatever they were going to apply to the entire miniature, it had to be substantial enough that it remained intact on the prop at all time during submergence in the water and when the model was moved in and out of the tanks. The FX paint had to be robust, durable, easy to apply, and available in large quantities. Like mad scientists in their laboratory, the crew in the film studio paint shop began to mix up their special aging application using, well, anything they could lay their hands on. Liquid resin was the main bonding ingredient and once in a vat the other elements were thrown into the mix; sand, grit, sawdust, wood chippings. Once a curing agent was applied in the mix the lethal mixture was applied to the entire model with commercial hardware. Once the fx material had hardened the colour painting process could follow. The black livery of the hull was heavily washed out with browns acting as rust patches and staining, while sprayed layers of grey, blue tints that could be brushed to blend in with the textured hull giving an almost oily black look to the replica.

The superstructure and previously white sections were treated with light grey paint and textured again with varying browns brushed on giving the appearance of heavy surface rust and staining. The funnels were treated in the same manner as the hull and superstructure with a grey wash applied and varying browns acting as rust, discoloration, and staining. The attention to detail on the painting process was second to none with the incredible work by the paint crews being seen in all its glory during the fly-past scene in the finished movie. And it didn't stop there. Areas with deck fittings were picked out with little dabs here and there of green that looked like simulated marine algae; the propellers are one example of this aging process when the green coloration is highlighted by the artificial lights from the submersible models during the moment leading up to the big reveal of *Titanic*'s stern name plate. Unfortunately, the days the model was to sit submerged in the Mediterranean saltwater along with the rigors of being handled by the dive crews, small areas of the model's surface would soon begin to flake or peel and reveal the models original livery beneath. When the model sat on the ground around the tank it was easy for the FX artists to touch up the paint using a brush. But when the model had already been submerged and showed signs of paint fx deterioration that had to be addressed there and then, the production team could not afford to keep removing the model from the tank each time the camera unit picked up on an area of the model that had become affected by fx paint loss. John Richardson recalls one ingenious method of remedying the issues with the model while it was still on the bottom of the water-filled deep tank.

> "The model needed a lot of constant repairs. I devised a way to touch it up while it was on the bottom. I use to go down with a big jar of Vaseline and different coloured powders. By smearing the Vaseline onto the hull and then dabbing the powder into it you could actually paint over the defects and the bits that had come off and make it look reasonably good. That is what we had to do through the entire shoot."

Of course, the *Titanic* wreck would not be complete without her decks being thickly covered in layers of sediment. Sand brought into the studio grounds from the beach at Ramla l-Ħamra (Gozo) which was already in use in the deep tank to cover the artificial sea bed could be utilized for the decks of the *Titanic* model. Mixed in with Fuller's earth the sand and earth mixture once wet could be applied to the decks and compacted down in areas to form a build-up of sediment like snowdrifts. These built-up areas were also used to disguise small outlets that had been cut into the boat deck where pipework beneath the deck and out of camera sight would pump water up from the tank and out across the sediment-soaked decks.

Preparations for Salvage

With all the work completed with the model unit of the sequences leading up to the salvaging of the wreck, the next major change came about with the *Titanic* model and the deep tank facility. Back in the workshop, the huge *Titanic* model was again stripped back down. But not as severe as the first stages of the wreck transformation. With the superstructure, forecastle, poop deck, and well decks once again removed, the hull was open for work to start on removing the water tanks. The tanks installed had served their purpose in keeping the model weighted down at the bottom of the tank when the tank was filled. But the tanks were not substantial enough to be used for when the model was to be raised due to sudden pressure changes from sitting nearly 40ft down at the bottom of the tank and the sudden shift during the ascent to the surface. With the tanks removed additional support was added to the steel inner keel that would allow for the attachment point of the lifting rig and the addition of a buoyancy keel weight to prevent the *Titanic* model from shifting its weight once at the surface.

With the *Titanic* miniature undergoing its alterations, construction crews were busy at work at the bottom of the drained deep tank dismantling the cumbersome fiberglass sea bed, cutting it into moveable pieces where they would be dragged out of the tank and deposited off to the sides of the studio facility for recycling. The next step was to cut up the equally large steel-framed turntable and remove it completely from the floor of the tank so that the concrete base could be cleaned up for the installation of the lifting rig.

Raise the Titanic? It was beginning to look as if lowering the Atlantic would have been the cheaper option.

The 55ft *Titanic* in her 1912 livery sits in the surface tank at Malta during the June 1979 filming of the sinking sequence. Soon the model will be removed from the tank, put into studio and stripped down for its transformation into the movie wreck. *(Joe Sciberras collection)*

The death of airship passenger travel when the leviathan of the skies explodes in *The Hindenburg*. *(Author's collection)*

The cruise from hell as the liner *Poseidon* is capsized by a rogue wave on New Year's Eve. *(Author's collection)*

The earth trembles and skyscrapers topple in Universal Pictures epic disaster movie *Earthquake*. *(Author's collection)*

The beginning of an end? The birth of CGI in the movie industry started with the release of *Young Sherlock Holmes* in 1985. *(IMDb)*

Chapter 18: Wreckcognising *Titanic* • **115**

All aboard! Special & Mechanical Effects Supervisor John Richardson with one of the scale miniature three-panelled salvage lights. *(Author's collection)*

The *Titanic* replica inside the Marine studio at the Mediterranean Film Facility as it undergoes being broken down for the next stage of the production. *(Joe Sciberras collection)*

Special delivery. The hull of the *Titanic* is returned back to the studios after the new floatation tanks were fitted inside by steel fabricators over at Malta Docks. *(Author's collection)*

Outside of the Marine studio the hull sits on the low-loader awaiting personnel to move the monster model indoors for work to resume. Prior to being sent to the docks the model was completely stripped of all removable parts. This was done not only to give the fabricators room to work when installing the new tanks but also to prevent the model being picked of souvenirs that would be costly to replace. *(Author's collection)*

Chapter 18: Wreckcognising *Titanic* • 117

Not one to miss a photo opportunity, the model is photographed for the records with a signage board reading RAISE THE TITANIC VALETTA MALTA. Once the crane has lifted up the hull, the truck is removed and the whole model in its steel transportation cradle is lowered onto the ground. *(Author's collection)*

With the help of a small dumper truck, the model is pulled inside the Marine studio. Those curious to know as to what the painted backdrop is hanging on the wall; this was created for the science fiction series *The Martian Chronicles* which was filmed in Malta. *(Author's collection)*

Chapter 18: Wreckcognising *Titanic* • 119

With one last push the model is moved into position for the FX crew to begin the transformation. Before the hull was sent for the new tanks the FX department had already started testing in aging the model. The starboard side of the hull shows a mixture of paint applied that simulate rust and staining. However, the portside of the hull remained intact at this point. *(Author's collection)*

As no photographs are known to exist of the floatation tanks inside the hull of the model in 1980, this illustration gives a basic representation to where they were fitted and totalling of 8 tanks; 2 tanks sitting side by side. *(Illustration © Jonathan Smith)*

Two access panels were cut into the lower decks of the model that allowed a person to gain entry to the main pipework to the tanks inside the hull. The access points were located on the starboard side of the forward well deck (pictured) while the other was at the stern on the portside of the aft well deck. *(Joe Sciberras collection)*

One of the original unused stern name plates for the model that was made from resin. Several copies were made for the model and kept to one side in case one got damaged while filming. As each plate was held in place with screws, it was easier to switch a damaged one out for a new plate. These new plates for the stern and those on the bow also served another purpose in that the letters were purposely raised. When the FX paint was applied, the name and port of registry was still visible, something not possible with the original plates which would have been washed out when the FX paint was added. *(David Harris collection)*

Chapter 18: Wreckcognising *Titanic* • 121

The starboard bow name plate. *(Author's collection)*

Members of the FX crew apply touch-up coats of FX wreck paint to the hull. *(John Richardson collection)*

122 • Raise The Titanic

With the superstructure removed from the hull and sat upon the ground it made aging the model a lot easier for the crews. Not only could they apply the custom mixture of paints but also the build-up of sand on the decks and around the deckhouses. *(John Richardson collection)*

The twisted stump of *Titanic*'s second funnel. The out of place circular hole in the deckhouse directly beneath the funnel was access to a bolt that held the funnel in place. *(Author's collection)*

Chapter 18: Wreckcognising *Titanic* • **123**

Looking along the portside boat deck and deckhouse of the Officers' Quarters in its wrecked state. Note the lifting eye on the left. *(ITC – Author's collection)*

This behind the scenes photograph taken during lighting tests in the tank shows the detail of the eroded deck fitting on the wreck conversion. *(ITC – Author's collection)*

Area of the portside A-Deck promenade showing some of the vertical supports broken away and the sides of the superstructure buckled. *(Author's collection)*

The damaged bulwark on the portside of the boat deck and presumably done to tie-in from damage caused when the second funnel collapsed; although the sinking footage filmed in June 1979 had the funnel fall to starboard. *(Author's collection)*

Chapter 18: Wreckcognising *Titanic* • **125**

The stern with two dislodged deck benches and a lifeboat davit arm caught up in the railings. *(ITC – Author's collection)*

This view is looking from the starboard side of the model towards the remains of the second funnel. It also reveals the lengths the FX department went into breaking down the model and aging it. *(Author's collection)*

Love or loath them, they certainly make for a unique looking *Titanic*. Due to complications over in Piraeus with the former liner and the prevention of removing certain structures from the ship, continuity between the model and the *Athinai* meant that the FX department had to replica in miniature the solid bow bulkhead, single tall vent and the pair of cargo derricks with vent tops either side of the mast. *(ITC – Author's collection)*

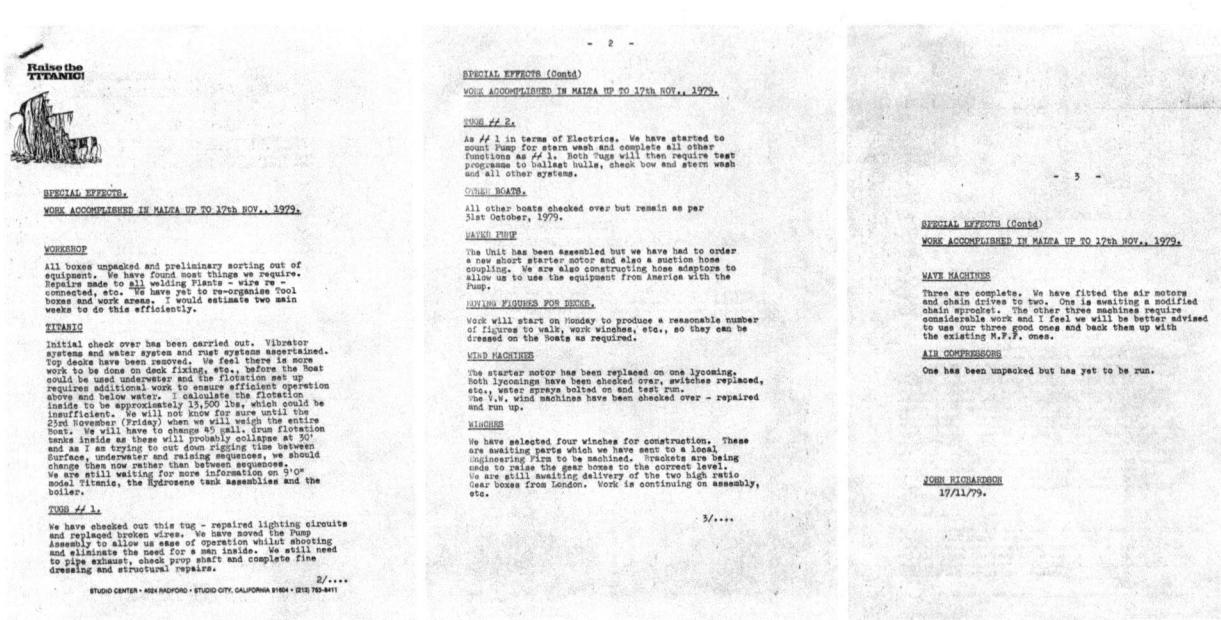

The model FX unit inspection sheets for works completed and awaiting. *(Author's collection)*

The *Titanic* model undergoes floatation tank tests in the surface tank. A number of the replica's details have been removed during the process; her masts, foredeck, poop deck. Even the forward skylight has been removed to expose the dome beneath. *(Mario Cassar collection)*

Unsinkable to the very end. The mighty *Titanic* model sits in the surface tank looking every part the movie star. *(John Richardson collection)*

CHAPTER 19

In Search of the *Titanic*

"We're talking about two miles underwater. Maybe more. Everything at that depth is a mystery. That hull could have wound up a couple of miles from where she disappeared."

Dirk Pitt

In 1998 James Cameron's *'Titanic'* dominated the box office boasting a monumental budget of $200m to bring the story of the most famous shipping disaster in maritime history to the big screen. The filming process documented the technological feats incorporated into such a movie with the visual effects and large-scale sets propelling the film production into one that would break new ground in special effects. Cameron's movie did include segments of the wreck using a mixture of actual footage he filmed in the summer of 1995 and sound stage work with a 1:20 scale wreck model of the bow that was suspended upside down in a rig in a smoke-filled room. The smoke environment mimicked water density while a model FX unit controlled the models of the submersibles via a special rig. And not once was that wreck model or the complete 45ft hero model of the liner ever placed in water. But eighteen years earlier the FX unit on Raise the Titanic had no such comforts and what the FX crews in Malta were to accomplish was something equally impressive as they began work on pulling off what was thought to be the impossible task of raising the *Titanic* – quite literally. Given the size of the model, its tremendous weight, and purposely submerged nearly 40ft down in water, this was no ordinary film shoot, and certainly one that had never been achieved before. This was breaking new ground in terms of special effects. But how were the filmmakers going to pull-off such a task?

North Atlantic Ocean, 12,480ft

Replicating the harsh environment of the North Atlantic Ocean at a depth of 12,500ft in a man-made tank that was only 36ft in depth was challenging enough for the production crew, let alone trying to get the right balance of the lighting in the tank to some degree workable that audiences would think that a great expanse of water had been used for the sequences. It was originally thought that filming at night would help with plunging the interior of the tank into darkness allowing for a more natural look to the underwaters shots. While a number of shots were filmed at night, the main bulk of what was captured on film was done during daylight hours. Night filming was not a welcoming decision as the idea of shooting for four months in Malta, at night, in a deep tank filled with cold water during the winter of late 1979 into 1980 was not a positive working environment for those who had to be submerged for long periods of time. With the production running over schedule and the principal actors now being lensed on location elsewhere, it was no longer an option to pack up for months of end and wait for the warm weather that summer would bring. The production issues were already at stake and the important scenes with the *Titanic* being discovered and raised had to be in the can by mid-spring if the studios wanted to complete on the advertised summer 1980 release for the movie. At the drawing board, the model FX unit was working on ideas on how to blackout the deep tank during daylight hours. One concept was for the use of expandable polystyrene balls that when poured onto the surface of the water they would broaden coverage and form a screen preventing light from entering the tank from the surface but at the same time allowing for crew and equipment to enter and exit the water. As the idea was passed about the FX unit it was decided the use of such material would not be a viable option as, despite the potential of success in shutting out the light, the quantity needed to cover the vast surface area of the tank when filled was too much of a burden for all working in and out of the tank. Coincidentally a similar method would be used during the filming of James Cameron's *The Abyss* when black Dylite was poured into the studio tank covering the surface of the water tank in round black spheres. Another idea from the FX unit was to cover the surface of the tank with canvas sheets attached to a series of floating pontoons. The idea, as practical as it was, did bring about some concerns that if for any emergency reasons the ascent from the floor of the tank to the surface could hamper or slow down recovery from the water should an accident or injury be sustained during filming. While incidents such as this were rare among the professionals in their field of work, they were still required to take into account potential freak incidents that could occur. It was essential to take into consideration a worst-case scenario if anything were to happen.

With the decision taken to use canvas screens to blackout the surface, the pontoons and the working arrangements of the screens were drafted up and fabrication work commenced. Each pontoon would be equipped with a walkway that allowed easy access for a crew member to walk along the upper exposed portion of the pontoon. The framework of the pontoon formed a portable bridge that was attached to a number of empty and sealed-up former oil drums that acted as floats. Each pontoon was an estimated 16ft in length and attached with ten floatation drums, five per side and attached to the underside of the walkway. Attached to the top edge of the walkway were pulleys that allowed for a cable to run out from that pontoon to the next set of pontoons meters away allowing for a rolled-up canvas sheet to be pulled along the cables like a roller blind and secured in place. Each 16ft pontoon could be locked into the next to form a bridge that spanned from the dry edge of the tank wall and out into the center of the tank where it would be secured in place to another larger island pontoon that was fitted with a shed-like structure that allowed for camera equipment and air tanks to be stored during the period of filming in the tank. The shed also contained a darkroom where used reels could be extracted from the camera, replaced with a new reel, and the used reel put into its canister before being sent off to the laboratory. With a line of these canvas covers stretched out across the surface of the tank and held in place with the floating pontoons, the end result was that of a tank with a covered surface area of about ninety percent. With the tank all but devoid of natural light the crews could get to work filming with the models.

The Submersibles

Deep Quest, *Sea Cliff*, *Turtle*, and *Starfish*

With the deep tank filled with an approximated 23 million litres of water, the model FX unit was expected to spend on average six to seven hours at a time submerged in water temperatures of fifty-five degrees. FX supervisor John Richardson alone logged over an incredible 450 hours in the water on the production of *Raise the Titanic*. Richardson still remembers the cold working conditions in the tank.

> "We use to wear woollen underwear beneath our dry suit. And yet we still lay there at the bottom of the tank and shiver. It was bloody cold!"

To cut back on time, divers would change their bottles while they were still at the bottom of the tank rather than the normal practice of coming to the surface, swapping them out, and heading back down. The working conditions in the deep tank did affect both divers and models. The combination of the tank's design, depth of the structure, and the difference in water pressure between the surface and that at the 36ft depth limit created a change in atmosphere that required alterations not just for the divers but also the *Titanic* and other models. Even the water itself proved to be a problem from the offset as the salt in the pumped-in Mediterranean waters created hurdles for the FX unit. The remote-controlled submersible miniatures, designed and built in California, had been fully tested in freshwater before being approved and crated up for the shipment to Malta. With initial dry tests carried out at the side of the tank to make sure that the motors, lights, and remotes worked without any issues, the model FX unit was soon to discover that the models had not been exposed to saltwater.

At first the submersible miniatures performed well. But soon they became sluggish, began to malfunction, then drop like some drunkard as the motors ground to a stop. Tests carried out in the workshops next to the tank facility revealed that the saltwater had corroded wiring and left an unwanted residue on the moving bushes and bearings of the motors and internal running gear, clogging and corroding the metalwork. Each time the models went into the water the units had to be cleaned and repaired afterward for the next day of filming. The mounting delays brought about by the models being serviced ended with the FX unit having built a small separate water tank measuring 30' x 30' at a depth of 9' that sat on the side of the deep tank where freshwater could be pumped in allowing for filming with the remote submersibles for certain shots where one or two of the subs were needed to be seen moving just a matter of feet above the ocean floor. These *Titanic*-less insert shots could be filmed at night with the subs being remotely operated, divers off to the side, and filmed in the freshwater tank that was partially dressed with a section of the artificial sea bed. With the saltwater damage still creating havoc with the sub miniatures, a late start filming in the new tank on the 5 April 1980 not only ended up with more delays as the subs broke down but things took a turn for the worse when one of the large lighting towers was accidentally knocked over, sending the lighting rig crashing down to strike the side of the freshwater tank, fracturing one of the glass panels that resulted in the crew abandoning and draining the tank.

While the production encountered its fair share of accidents with the models, there was an entirely intentional one; the filming of the demise of the D.S.V. *Starfish*. The scene was filmed in the freshwater tank with the fully remote-controlled submersible 1:16th scale miniature which had been altered to show the sub in distress as it takes on water and sinks before switching to another model for the subs catastrophic implosion. The full sub miniature had been rigged with a small hose that fed air into the model and with a small hole in the top of the subs sail hatch it allowed for the air to escape. With the divers in the water controlling the model's descent, the remote side to the model could have the internal lighting turned on and off to simulate the flickering of the electrics along with the ability of separate box structures replicating the subs main battery pods to be dropped to remove weight in conjunction with the screenplay. For the quick scene of the *Starfish* imploding another less detailed scale model was constructed and fitted to a stationary stabilizing rig that held the model in place. Where the model was to implode, it had been fitted with a charge and a series of break-away parts that were attached to a wire mechanism out of camera shot. As the sequence was filmed, the wires were pulled, the charge goes off, and the sub collapsed inwards of itself.

The clashes between the models and the FX unit saw a system put in place where the submersible models could be operated by a diver in the tank who would hand control the model while the camera unit filmed the miniature up close and, with caution, minimalizing capturing the diver in the shot. While it worked for some shots it did not always go according to plan. Any scenes that included a frame or two of one of the FX divers working the sub would be darkened in the editing stages of the sequences. The decision was an easy cop-out for the editing department as it made the job of removing anything that is not supposed to be there a simplified process by adjusting the lighting in post-production. Of course, carrying out such editing also meant that far too many underwater scenes in the movie were now so dark that detail was all but lost through the process. A number of sequences filmed in the deep tank with the submersibles and *Titanic* miniatures did not make the final cut of the film and ended up on the cutting room floor. Those familiar with the movie could reel off many if not all of the scenes that feature the miniatures; and there are plenty of them. But all those weeks filming in the tank did mean that many of the filmed and later deleted scenes resulted in a large number of sequences that were imperative to the story and now sadly lost. Using the finalized screenplay, the storyboards, model unit FX sheets, and some of the behind-the-scenes photographs give a clear indication of what was filmed with the submersibles that never made it to screen; for example, the subs finding one of the ships unseated boilers after the discovery of the smokestack; the subs picking up the steel plates dropped to the ocean floor, taking them over to the wreck and welding the plates over the iceberg damage; subs cutting small holes into *Titanic*'s hull and attaching the flexible pipes that will pump the buoyancy foam into the lower hull; welding the mounting frame to the ship's hull and picking up the Hydrozene tanks from around the wreck, taking them to the ship and attaching them to the mounting frames.

The entrapment of the *Deep Quest* was a part of the film that underwent several rewrites leading to locations on the *Titanic* being changed from that of the submersible becoming trapped under a pair of electric cargo crane jibs on the stern to that of getting wedged into the skylight over the grand staircase. It is unclear as to why they opted for moving the trapped *Deep Quest* from the stern of the *Titanic* to that of the skylight. The *Titanic* model, *Deep Quest* miniature, and the full-size *Deep Quest* replica were to hand during filming which makes one wonder why they went for the less dramatic skylight story. One theory is that the full-size sub-set used in the waters off San Diego with the U.S. Navy for a backdrop was already a done deal. Since there was no reason to send the sub-set over to Malta to film in the deep tank, and no actors were to travel to Malta for any scenes at the Mediterranean Film Facility, they were routed to Athens for the sequences filmed aboard the former cruise liner *Athinai*, while the practical effects with the miniatures were kept under wraps over in Malta. But the most likely explanation may be the work carried out in Athens with the *Athinai* when the stern deck originally budgeted was scrapped, eliminating the deck area, docking bridge and cargo cranes and reducing the set-piece down to a simple section of the liners 3rd class entrance. However, the *Deep Quest* sub-set could still have been transported to Athens and placed aboard the *Athinai* when the liner's stern decking was cleared to make way for filming with Richard Jordan as he ties the White Star Line pennant to the jack staff. Whatever the real reason is the move to the skylight went ahead and the decision was made to refit one of the *Deep Quest* models and build a new *Titanic* deckhouse and deck section in 1:16th scale for that sequence.

But why did the Deep Quest end up becoming wedged into a skylight on the *Titanic*? From the Navy ships on the surface, sixteen Hydrozene salvage tanks are dropped down to the ocean floor where they will be picked up by the sub crews and attached to the hull sides of the *Titanic*. But one of the tanks has drifted off course during its descent and lands on the deck of *Titanic*, seating itself into the buckled stump of the broken second funnel. *Deep Quest* and *Sea Cliff* come to inspect the downed salvage tank and, after hatching a plan, the crew decides to pull the lifting tank out and away from the funnel and carry it down to the sea bed. But the tank has become entangled in the funnel remains. With *Sea Cliff* pushing and *Deep Quest* pulling, both the subs go into full throttle to move the large tank. Suddenly, the tank breaks free and topples down onto the *Deep Quest*, pushing the submersible backward and into the steel weather covering of the dome over the grand staircase. Unable to free themselves the crew of the *Deep Quest* can only hope that Dirk Pitt comes up with a rapid solution to save them. Because of the nature of the scene with the model, it was easier for the FX department to build a section of the deckhouse with skylight and funnel remains instead of carrying out the filming with the large *Titanic* model. The model was to scale with that of the full 55ft replica and was perfectly copied in structure to represent the starboard side of the boat deck and deckhouse that contained the 1st class cabins, 1st class entrance, and the gymnasium. The deckhouse was detailed with matching ventilators with electric motors, stokehold vents, railings, skylight, and the twisted stump of the second funnel. The structure could be mounted upon a framework at the bottom of the tank with enough space below for a diver to work with the trapped *Deep Quest*. One major difference that was incorporated into the structure was the enlarging of the grand staircase skylight as the original did not give enough room to work with the trapped submersible. For continuity, the same skylight over on the 55ft *Titanic* replica was swapped out with a larger unit despite it being historically inaccurate.

One intriguing miniature built for the production was recently unearthed in Malta during the summer of 2020 after spending the past forty years locked away. A small-scale miniature of the hulls counter stern had been constructed from fiberglass and wood with resin mooring bitts detail and metal railings encircling the curvature of the poop deck. The miniature appears to have been originally constructed for use back in June 1979 for the all too brief shot of the stern of *Titanic* as it vanishes beneath the waves. During storage at the studio and with scenes being storyboarded showing the discovery of the wreck, the stern prop that was just sitting there doing nothing could be utilised for other scenes. Now aged with FX paint, it was to be used for the closing shot of the discovery of the wreck as the submersible lights pass over the nameplate revealing **TITANIC** and **LIVERPOOL** before abruptly cutting to the scene of the musical quartet playing at the Russian embassy party attended by Prevlov and Marganin. The miniature was of simple construction that was attached to an equally simple steel framework that allowed it to sit and be positioned accordingly on the bottom of the tank as a diver with a lighting rig swept the pair of sub lights across *Titanic*'s name. The effect itself was seamless and with the other scenes filmed with the complete 55ft *Titanic* replica and the *Deep Quest* and *Sea Cliff* models, it appeared as if that scene was filmed only using the large *Titanic* model.

"We got a floater!"

During the early stages of production as scenes were storyboarded, some sequences were to show the subs interacting with marine life in action scenes before *Titanic*'s discovery. To accomplish this, real fish were brought in for use in the 30' x 30' glass tank where the sub models, controlled by the crew, would work the miniatures in accordance to the storyboarded scene while the fish swam about. Freshwater young Leopard Sharks were brought over to Malta for use in the tank as this particular type of fish resembled a shark and when filmed with the submersible models their size could be passed off on film as a species of deep-water predator that was to scale with the submersibles. It was all going swimmingly until the fish were removed from their storage container and introduced into the tank. If the fish were happy to be out of their small crate to swim freely around in the large glass-sided tank, that happiness was short-lived. After being put in the tank and left to climatize to their new surroundings, the poor fish succumbed to the chlorinated water pumped into the tank, and eventually, the fish turned belly up and floated to the surface; probably the reason why "No animals, except fish, were harmed in the making of the motion picture" was not included in the end titles.

Dangerous Dives

The sea bed utilized in the film as the *Titanic* is prepared for salvage was a reworked set piece that was further adapted from the original intended design. Art director John DeCuir disliked the shape of the set-piece and worked with designing a new sea bed that would fit over the top of the existing build. The first sea bed bolted to the turntable contained miscalculations from the early days of production that did not take into account the change in weight with the model once sitting upon it. With additional welded extra supports, the turntable locked off, the first sea bed set adjusted to include access points, the newly constructed ocean floor could be assembled leaving a 3 feet aperture between the old and the new. Now strengthened the set could withstand the weight of the *Titanic* model and the change in pressure at the bottom once the tank had been filled with seawater. As the filming in the tank with the submersible miniatures had come to a close the next stage was to dress the *Titanic* with the salvage tanks for filming stage one of the salvage operation; triggering the explosives that will free her from the grip of the ocean bottom. Working with the model and artificial sea bed was challenging at the best of times while the set was dressed with rocks, tons of sand, and layers of Fuller's Earth. Each of the diving team working at the bottom of the tank would easily churn up the sand and earth as they moved about the submerged set which ended with a lapse of time if filming for a scene when kicked up sediment was required to settle back down before the cameras began to roll again. The diving team were now used to such working conditions and despite the hours logged for the team working in the tank and the years of experience between them, the environment was still unpredictable and anything untoward could easily happen, making for unpleasant circumstances, even those borderline dangerous. The filming of the segments as the explosives are placed around the hull to be blown and push *Titanic* up off the ocean floor was one case of how life-threatening the working conditions were in the tank.

To create the explosions the option to use actual explosive materials was completely out of the question being impractical and dangerous for the divers, camera crews, and equipment operating in that environment. John Richardson opted to use a combination of Aquaflex detonating fuse that produced a minimal explosive-type shock that created no damage to the set. In conjunction with the detonating fuse, compressed air was used to create the abrupt explosive burst, mixed in with photographic flash bulbs, giving the explosions their visual light. These elaborate pyro techniques represented the film's story as Pitt's salvage crew lay a total of eighty explosives in key locations around the lower hull of the *Titanic*. The explosives, placed on the ocean floor directly under *Titanic*'s keel and bilge keels would blow the sediment away and break the suction amassed over 68 years that had been holding *Titanic*'s huge tonnage to the sea bed, much in the same way that rocking a stranded car in mud would have. Once that suction had collapsed, the lifting equipment would take over and the *Titanic* would begin her ascent to the surface. But to achieve those scenes, access was required through the artificial sea bed and only possible through one access point in the underside of the stabilized turntable. Through the access point, the diver would be faced with a labyrinth of steel latticework that made up the turntable before coming to an open hatchway on the underside of the *first* fiberglass sea bed. From here the diver then had to pass through the two-feet-square hatch to gain access to the underside of the *second* fiberglass sea bed which, above it, sat the *Titanic*. The laying of the Aquaflex was a two-man job as one diver was needed to work in the claustrophobic space beneath the sea bed while another diver was positioned to work on the exposed surface around the rusting hulk of the *Titanic* model. With the use of just a torch, the diver beneath the sea bed worked in succession with the other diver who was passing a rod through a drilled hole where an air pipe would be passed through and also where a solenoid fitted to an air mortar would be seated. From there the air pipe, wires, and solenoids were buried beneath the Fuller's Earth followed by the divers moving onto the next location to repeat the process. Each time the sequence was recorded they had to do it all over again by heading back down to the sea bed set to rig up the next lot.

Model unit FX supervisor John Richardson was the one called upon to dive the tank and work on the tank floor installing the charges. The job was not for the faint hearted, as Richardson, working at a depth of 36ft and submerged in nine-million gallons of seawater, moved back and forth around the steel lattice frame of the turntable and in the confined space between the two sea floors while all the time kitted out in full diving gear including the air tank. Even with the best of intentions where sticking to Health & Safety was concerned it could never eliminate any potential accidents from ever occurring. Richardson recalls one of the terrifying incidents he encountered down at the bottom of the tank during the setting up of the charges.

> "I was the one who usually went down to do this because it's really difficult to get too. I got through the first sea bed and got up under the second sea bed when suddenly a whole lot of Fuller's Earth came down and completely clouded the water so I couldn't see anything. I tried to get back out and although there was a safety diver with me all he could see was the ends of my flippers. I got jammed because my air bottle caught up on the hatch of the first sea bed. I just couldn't move. Then my goggles got knocked from my face. I couldn't see anything because it was all cloudy. I was unable to signal to the safety diver that I needed help. In the end, I had to take my Aqua-lung off, pull it around in front of me, then take off my weight belt to help pull me back through the hatch. I got out and managed to get my mask back on along with my gear. I was so spooked about being trapped that I sat on the bottom for about ten minutes to get my cool back."

Following this scary experience, Richardson made his ascent to the surface of the tank as below his feet the displaced sand and Fuller's Earth settled back down again. Exiting the tank, he pondered over the events that just moments ago had him struggling for life.

> "I thought that if I don't get back down there right now, I'll never do it because I'll be too scared. And, so, I went back down and did it all over again. Things like this, they were happening all the time."

But not everything was so life-threatening, or serious, in the production of *Raise the Titanic*. Practical jokes lifted morale on set as a number of crew, including directors, became the subject of tomfoolery during filming. Director of the model unit in Malta, Ricou Browning, fell victim to a prank when one of the safety divers swam up behind him and cut through the hose connected to his headgear with a pair of bolt croppers while they were right in the middle of filming a scene. Browning, undeterred by the incident, did not stop and continued with the shoot by quickly removing his air cylinder and opening up the valve to breathe directly from the hose. The worst of the pranks played on the dive teams were the placement of coloured dyes in wet suits which resulted in tainting the colour of the diver's skin until it was washed off. It must have been a hysterical sight if a blue dye had been used turning the poor victim into someone resembling a Smurf.

At the end of filming in the tanks, the light heartedness continued over when a party organized at the Coxwain's Cabin located in Marsascala, Malta, which, ironically, was owned by Tony Whathem, who happened to be the dive master on *Raise the Titanic*. For the event, the film crew and guests went fancy dress, wearing period clothing similar to the attire of Edwardian life during the voyage of *Titanic* in 1912. And as food was scoffed and drinks were consumed on this particular last voyage, not once was an iceberg sighted that could sink these celebrations.

The first sea bed set, after completion, proved to be unreliable resulting in the set being ripped out and rebuilt to withstand the pressure in the tank and the weight of the *Titanic* model. *(Author's collection)*

Smoke for water special FX. Shot on a dry sound stage, model maker Mike Lynch makes final adjustments to the wreck of the *U.S.S Arizona* before filming what would become a modern-day scene for the 1999 Touchstone Pictures motion picture *Pearl Harbor*. The inclusion of smoke or haze, with coloured background lighting, would simulate a world beneath the surface of the ocean without the need of using any actual water. *(Image © Touchstone Pictures / Buena Vista Pictures / Jerry Bruckheimer Films)*

With the old sea bed removed, the floor of the tank was adapted to take a newly constructed frame with a series of fixed bolts added into the concrete base. From there the old turntable frame was reassembled and strengthened with additional supports and welded joints. On top of the turntable a new additional frame was constructed, raising the height of the sea bed from its original concept to a more substantial set piece. *(Author's collection)*

A section of newly constructed frame with a fibreglass sea bed piece attached to it is made ready to be craned down into the deep tank. *(Author's collection)*

 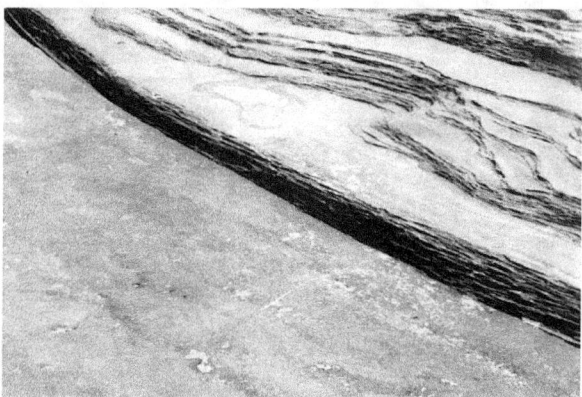

The fibreglass sea bed was designed to follow the inner contour of the deep tank's concrete floor. Once the sea bed was in place it was left to the FX crews to dress the set piece including covering the structure with tons of sand. While it looked authentic on screen, much of the set's details were lost beneath the layers of sand and minimal lighting conditions. *(Author's collection)*

The completed sea bed with the *Titanic* model resting upon it as the deep tank is filled. *(On Location, August 1980 – Author's collection)*

Assembled pontoons stored on the concourse around the tank await to be lifted into the tank once it is filled. The pontoons not only act as a floating bridge for crews to work from but they also double as securing points for the canvas covers that will be pulled out over the tank. *(Author's collection)*

Chapter 19: In Search of the *Titanic* • 143

The canvas blackout screens being pulled into place. *(Author's collection)*

The deep tank now covered with the canvas screens. The small hut in the middle was used by the camera unit as a floating darkroom where film reels could be changed out during the long hours filming in the tank. As the divers came up to the surface with the camera, the film would be removed, put into its storage can while a new film was loaded into the camera and passed back to the divers before they head back down to the bottom of the tank. *(John Richardson collection & Author's collection)*

This ITC company photograph of the models portside B-Deck with the #4 cargo hold demonstrates the effectiveness of filming in the tank at night while the blackout screens were in place. Despite a number of portable lights set up around the tank, the canvas screens are doing their job properly. *(ITC – Author's collection)*

Photo opportunity now over, the crew disperse to begin the impossible task of raising the *Titanic*. *(John Richardson collection)*

This artwork illustrates how the model sat on the bottom of the tank with its fibreglass sea bed. With a list to port, bow pushed down into the mud and the stern lifted up and resting on a rocky outcrop, the gap between the sea bed and the underneath of the hull around the stern allowed the camera crews to film around the ship's propellers and rudder. *(Illustration © Jonathan Smith)*

The *Titanic* model rests on the bottom of the deep tank during daylight hours. The outline of some of the pontoons can be seen while the bright light of the sun bursts down through an area of the tanks surface that has been opened up to allow the divers access in and out of the tank. *(Author's collection)*

Chapter 19: In Search of the *Titanic* • **147**

Draining the Atlantic. The impressive 55ft *Titanic* model sits with a heavy list to port on the sea bed set. The set was extremely well thought out with a section of a raised outcrop that allowed the stern of the model to be seated at an elevated position giving the camera unit an advantage of filming with the submersible models around the propellers of the wreck. To prevent the model from tipping over, two cables were fixed to anchors hidden down within the structure of the sea bed and locked in place with a hook passed through a porthole on C-Deck. Note the divers air tanks resting in the sand. *(John Richardson collection)*

148 • Raise The Titanic

Chapter 19: In Search of the Titanic • 149

During the building process of the new sea bed set, the model unit had to make sure the huge *Titanic* replica would sit correctly. To do this a wooden frame hull was made that was used in place of the heavy *Titanic* where the unit could work around the structure to get the set right. This photograph also reveals the set of 2x canyon walls that would be used as a backdrop for the sub miniatures as they drop down into the canyon that hides the wreck. And to right of the set piece is the remains of the broken second funnel laying on its side. At this stage the sand is yet to be added leaving the funnel sitting on top of the fibre glass sea bed. *(All photographs © Geoffrey Mackrill)*

After passing through the pump house and into the discharge pipes, the chlorinated filtered water is pumped into the tanks weir where it spills over the weir wall and down the interior side of the tank in a spectacular style. *(Photographs © Geoffrey Mackrill)*

Chapter 19: In Search of the *Titanic* • 151

With the stern of the model tilted upwards on the sea bed it gives the illusion the model is sinking in these behind the scenes shots of the tank being filled. *(Author's collection & Patrick Walsh collection)*

152 • *Raise The Titanic*

This is one of only a couple of known surviving original FX crew t-shirts that was created especially for them during the production of *Raise the Titanic* in Malta. Two types were made; blue for the dive team and yellow for the camera unit on the surface. (*Author's collection*)

From being the legendary movie monster in *The Creature from the Black Lagoon* to directing the underwater scenes for *Raise the Titanic*, Ricou Browning was the go-to expert for such challenging water filming sequences. (*Photograph © Collin Barnes*)

```
                                          INTER-OFFICE MEMO
Marble Arch    To:    ROBIN CLARK         Date:   November 30, 1979
Productions                               Copies: Ricou Browning
               From:  JOHN RICHARDSON              John De Cuir Jr.
                                                   Alex Weldon
                                                   Dick O'Connor
               Subject: SPECIAL EFFECTS REQUIREMENTS  Malcom Christopher
                        FOR MALTA

Priority            Diving Equipment & Sound Equipment
                    9' Model Titanic (painted)
                    Hyrozene tanks and operating equipment
                    Model Titanic boiler
                    Underwater drop lights
                    Miniature trumpets (with matching paint finish)
                    Foam pumping station (2 items) and hoses
                    Spare foam hose
                    Submersibles with 2 operators (to be in Malta by Jan. 1st)
                    Carbopol
                    Panel Adhesive  } as discussed with Alex Weldon
                    Capsules
                    Model Helicopters
                    Photographic cut out of Russian trawler 1/16" scale
Information on
Priority            Surface fleet markings
                    Photographic Coverage of L.P.D & Frigate
                    Explosive Probes
                    Foam type for Int Engine Room Seq. (model)
                    Clothing/Dressing of men on Titanic after surfacing
                    Funnel Capping
                    New York plate/matte requirements
                    Pennant that Pitt hangs on Titanic stern
                    Film clip of surface fleet at night
```

Correspondence from John Richardson to principle film personnel of the production in Malta dated 30 November 1979. The document lists some of the special effects required for filming at the deep and surface tanks at the Mediterranean Film Facility ahead of the all-important preparations in raising the ship. (*Author's collection*)

Original *Raise the Titanic* production used clapperboard. (*Liveauctioneers.com*)

Chapter 19: In Search of the *Titanic* • 153

John "Big John" McLoughlin (right) with one of the productions safety divers don their Poseidon diving suits for another day of filming in the deep tank. *(John Richardson collection)*

Titanic awaits the arrival of the dive teams. *(Author's collection)*

A member of the dive team appears more like someone from *Land of the Giants* as they pass over the sunken *Titanic*. *(ITC – Author's collection)*

TOP: Original John DeCuir production art of an early *Deep Quest* concept. What is interesting is that the craft was to have an attachment all-in-one workhorse with manipulators, video camera and welding torch. ABOVE: As the production changed so did the submersible as the existing submersible design for the Lockheed *Deep Quest* was chosen in favour and scaled down into 1/16 models. *(Author's collection – Photograph: Joe Sciberras collection)*

Chapter 19: In Search of the *Titanic* • 155

Courtney Brown holds one of the 1/16 scale *Sea Cliff* miniatures as model unit diver John McLoughlin looks on. *(On Location, August 1980 – Author's collection)*

Also on the bench in the workshop is one of the *Sea Cliff* miniatures. *(Joe Sciberras collection)*

The model unit put the submersibles *Sea Cliff* (D.S.V. 503) and *Turtle* through their paces in the deep tank during daylight hours. Built and tested in fresh water over in California, the submersible miniatures worked extremely well. But once in Malta and submerged in salt water, the salt began to clog up the workings of the models and erode the electronics to the point they went from being sluggish to requiring the helping hand of the divers; quite literally. *(John Richardson collection/Author's collection)*

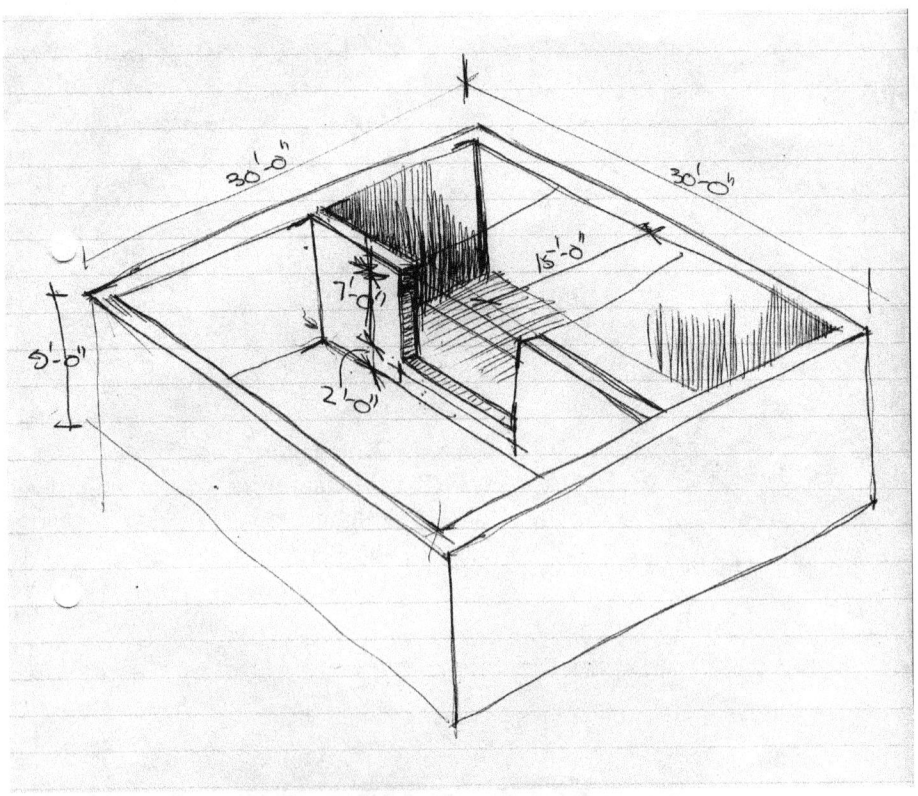

This production sketch is the only known documentation that shows the smaller third filming tank that was constructed and used on the asphalt outside the main office building to the deep tank facility. *(Author's collection)*

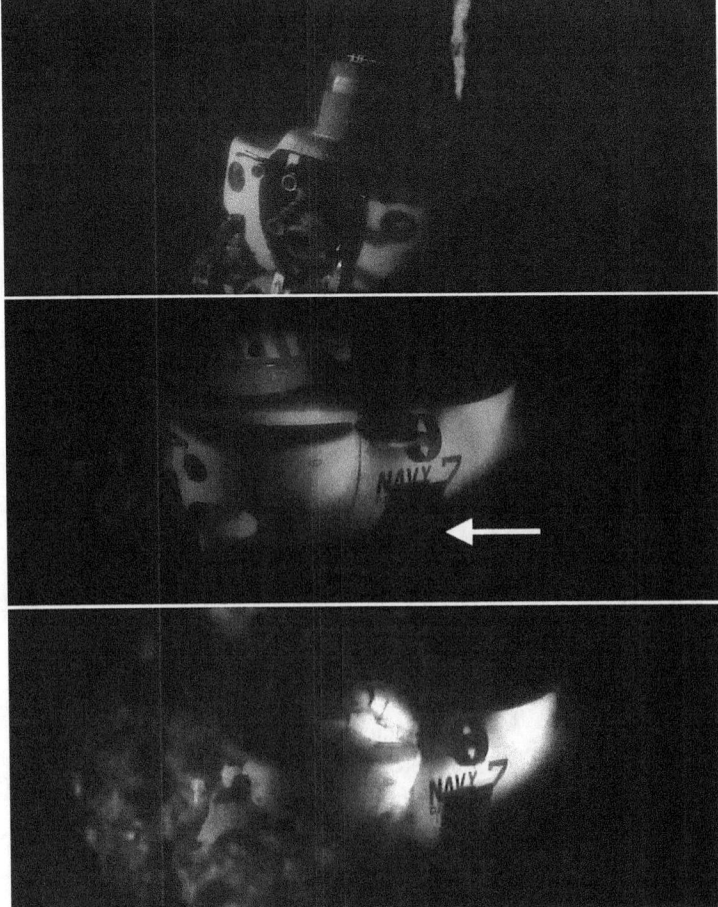

The demise of the *Starfish*. Two models were used for the sequence when *Starfish* floods and implodes. The first model was the hero miniature as it slowly drops to the ocean floor and rigged with an air hose to release the bubbles to simulate the hull leaking. The second model was the breakaway miniature that was secured in a clamp (indicated with the arrow) and rigged with a small charge that would emit small pieces of debris when the model is ripped apart. *(Author's collection)*

Chapter 19: In Search of the *Titanic*

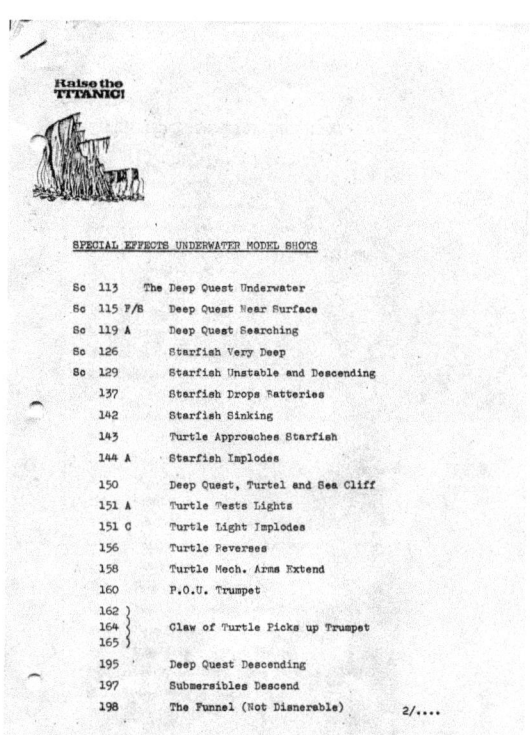
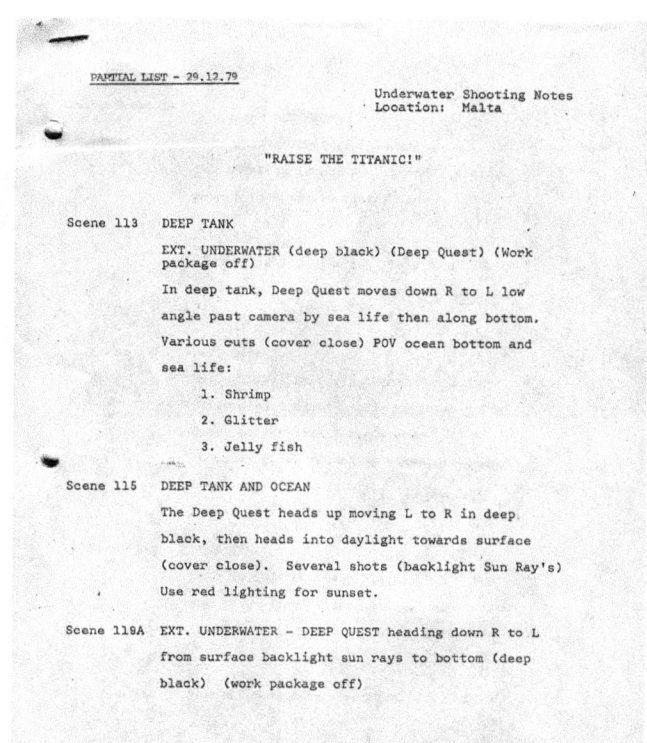

Part of the model FX filming list that includes the loss of the *Starfish* and her crew, the search for the *Titanic* and the discovery of her boiler. *(Author's collection)*

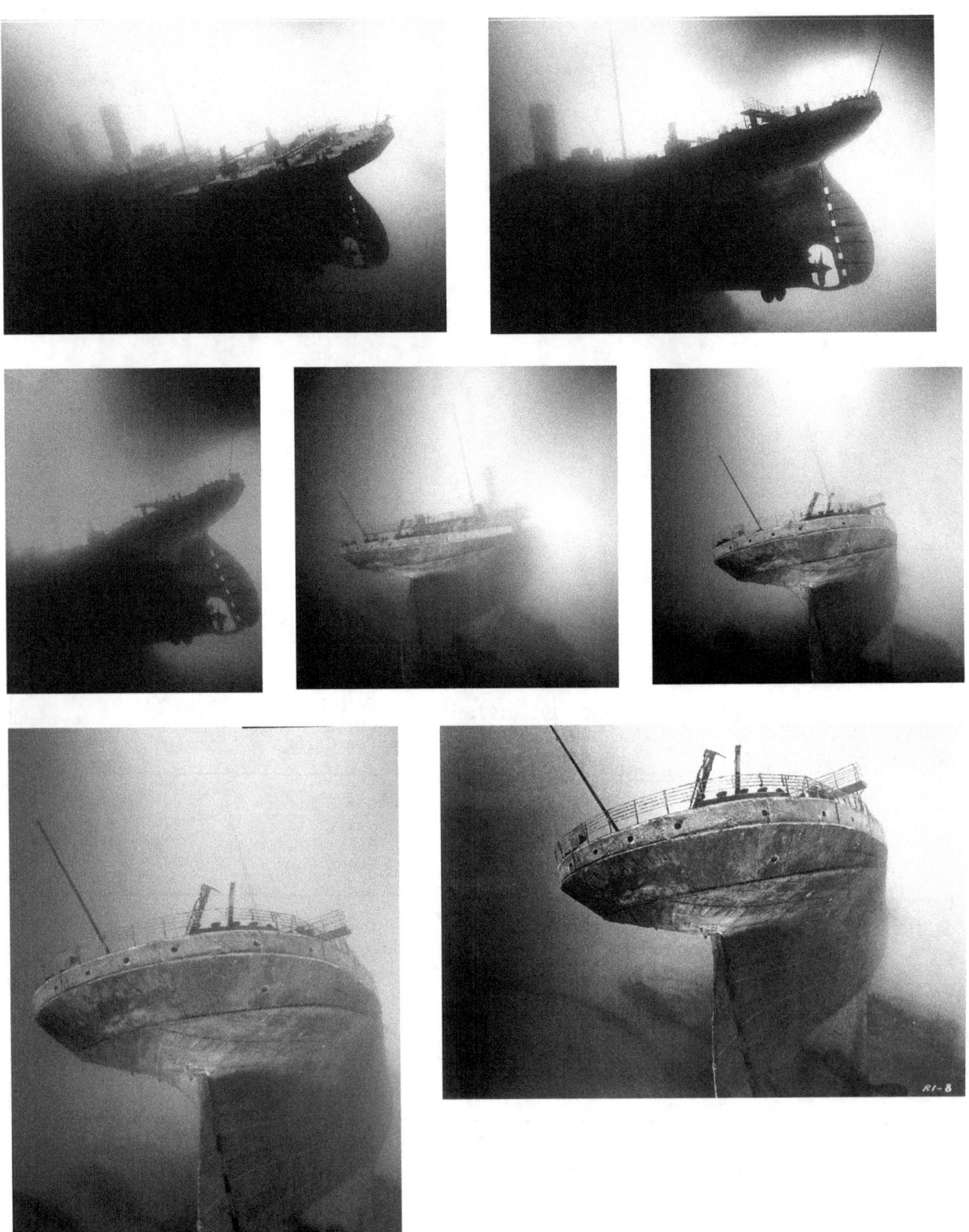

Sleeping beauty awaits to be awoken from the slumber of her cold and dark prison. *(ITC - Author's collection)*

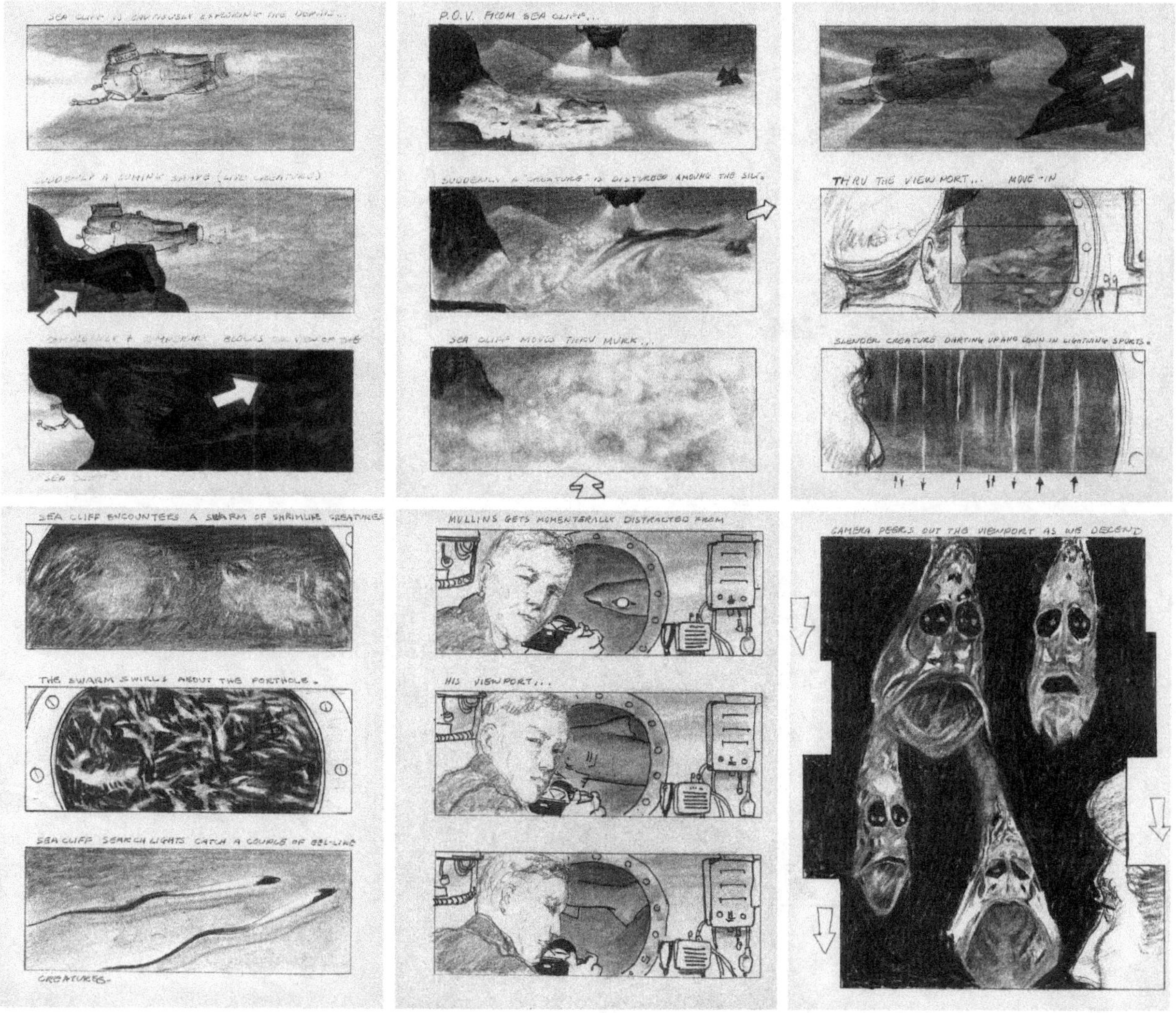

Chapter 19: In Search of the *Titanic* • 159

The search is on. This series of original storyboards were for a sequence as *Sea Cliff* scans the ocean floor in search of the wreck. From the viewport the crew witness the deep-sea marine life as creatures of all shapes and sizes are seen. From eel-like fish, deep water sharks and the nightmarish rattail fish. *(Author's collection)*

Production art of the *Sea Cliff/Turtle/Starfish* probing the depths. *(Author's collection)*

160 • *Raise The Titanic*

Deep Quest surfaces. *(Author's collection)*

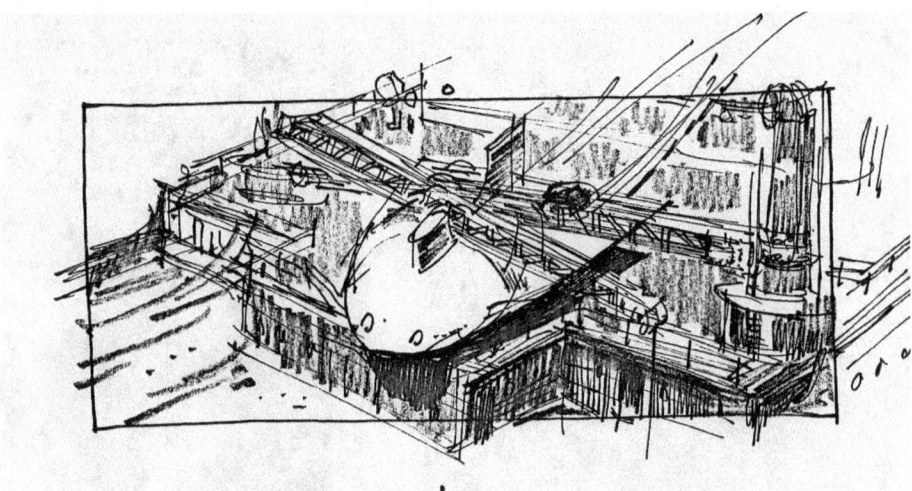

Early storyboards of the entrapment of the *Deep Quest* as the submersible gets jammed under a pair of electric cargo cranes on *Titanic*'s stern. *(Author's collection)*

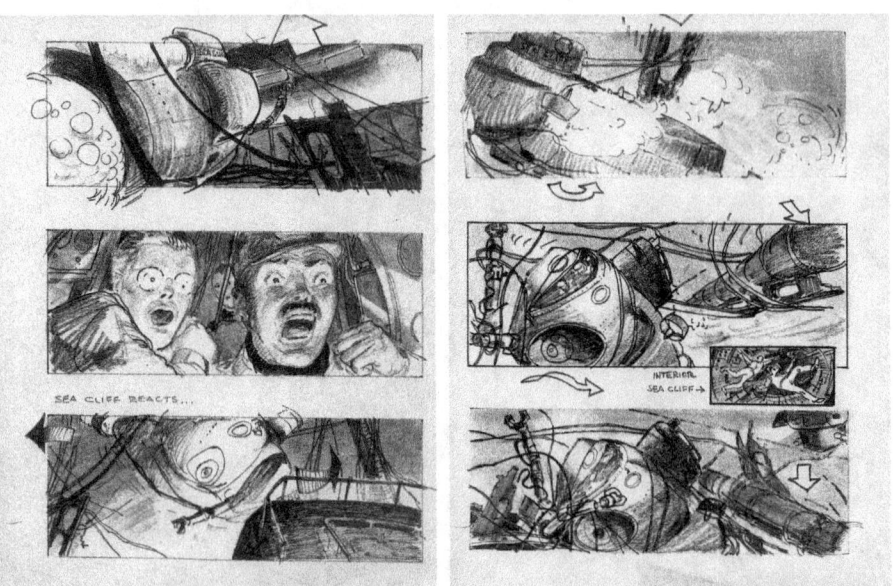

Another example of an early storyboarded sequence. This time it is the *Sea Cliff* that gets trapped. Working on the wreck, *Sea Cliff* manoeuvres around the towering funnels of the *Titanic*. As the sub passes by one stack it snags a piece of dislodged rigging that sends the *Sea Cliff* towards the remains of the broken funnel. As the crew watch on in horror, the *Sea Cliff* slams into a twisted funnel steam pipe to become entangled within the steelwork. *(Author's collection)*

The original skylight on the 55ft *Titanic* model during its construction in 1978. *(Photograph © Ken Marschall)*

The crushed original skylight on the *Titanic* model. *(Author's collection)*

162 • *Raise The Titanic*

Deep Quest lodged into the skylight over the Grand Staircase. *(ITC – Author's collection)*

Chapter 19: In Search of the *Titanic* • **163**

The model unit prepping and filming the *Deep Quest* model stuck in the skylight. It became clear that this approach did not work for Ricou Browning when the *Deep Quest* getting trapped shifted from the skylight of the 55ft *Titanic* model to a newly constructed set piece. *(ITC – Author's collection)*

A member of the model unit works on the deckhouse set built for filming the *Deep Quest* accident. *(ITC – Author's collection)*

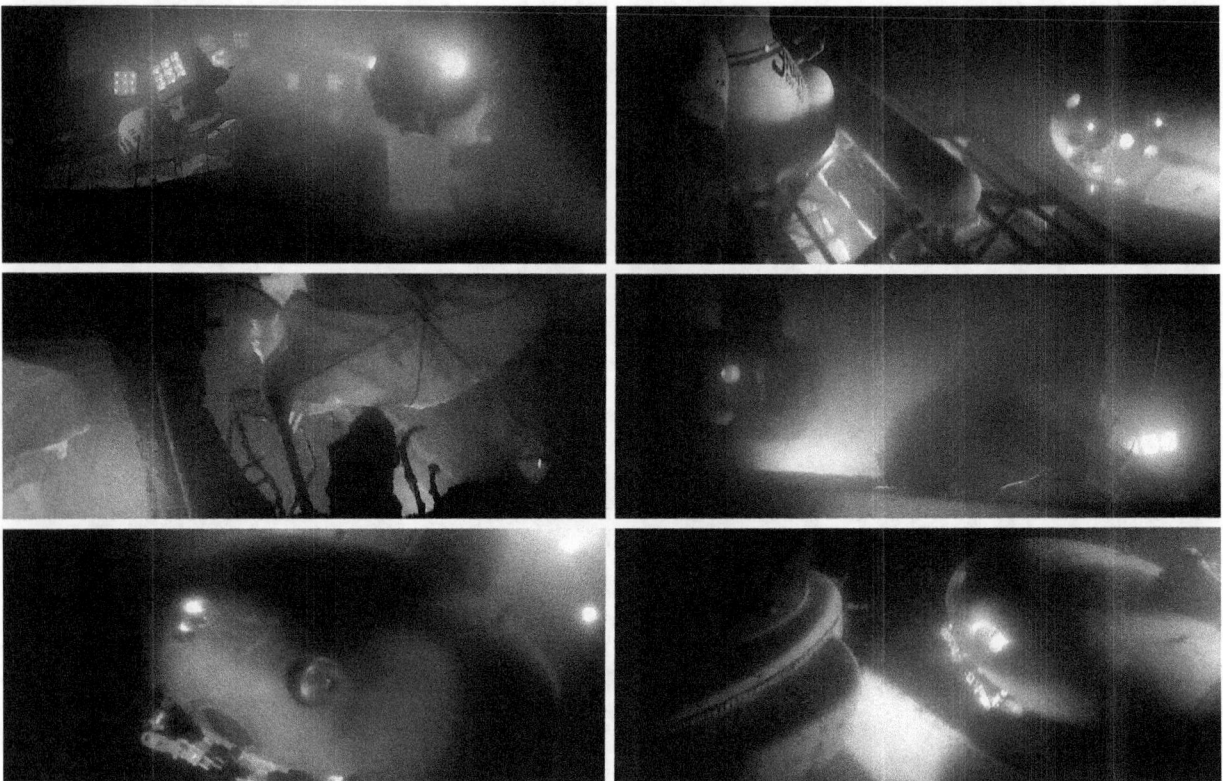

With the Hydrozene salvage tank wedged into the remains of the broken funnel, submersibles *Sea Cliff* and *Deep Quest* join forces to pull the tank free. But disaster unfolds as the tank tips forward to strike the *Deep Quest* and push the sub down into the skylight. These short scenes were all filmed using the deckhouse set featuring the larger skylight. *(ITC/ITV Studios)*

The remains of the boat deck and deckhouse that was constructed for use in filming close-up views of the trapped *Deep Quest*. When these photographs were taken in 1988 all of the smaller details such as vents, window frames, railings, skylight and funnels had long gone. The legs on the set piece allowed it to be raised up off the tank floor as a diver lay beneath operating the models. *(Photograph © Mike Seares)*

For continuity the original skylight on the *Titanic* model was switched out with a new larger unit in keeping with the deckhouse set piece. *(ITC – Author's collection)*

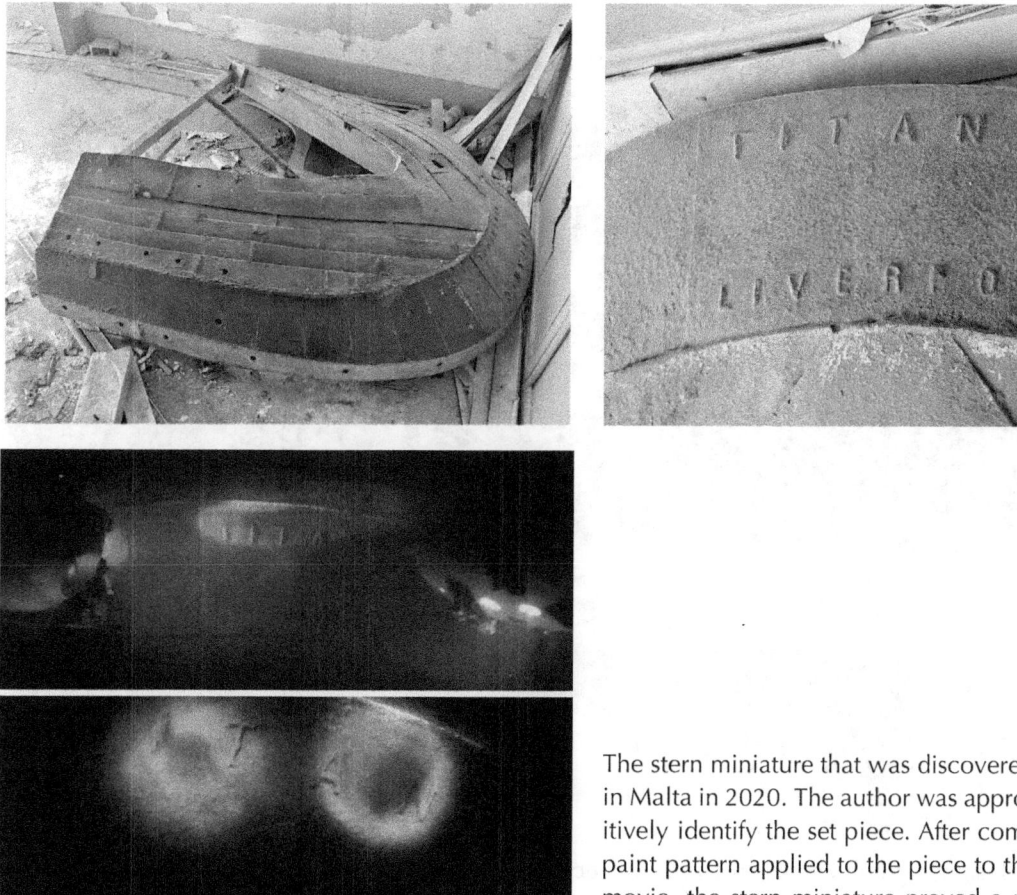

The stern miniature that was discovered in a lock-up in Malta in 2020. The author was approached to positively identify the set piece. After comparing the FX paint pattern applied to the piece to that seen in the movie, the stern miniature proved a perfect match. *(Photograph © Jean Pierre Borg & ITC/ITV Studio)*

One of the FX divers working with the *Turtle* in the 30' x 30' glass tank. *(John Richardson collection)*

Dangerous dives. This photograph was taken during the reconstruction of the sea bed set and shows the original ocean floor area and the newer set being built on top. Once the entire sea bed had been assembled, any work that involved divers having to venture beneath the set could become precarious. *(Author's collection)*

Two titans of the big screen. John Richardson with the unsinkable legend. *(ITC – Author's collection)*

This view of the drained deep tank shows some of the access points in the fibreglass sea bed. Once the tank was filled with 9 million gallons of water, the model sitting on the ocean floor and surrounded with tons of sand and Fuller's earth and the surface of the tank blacked out with the canvas covers, lighting conditions in the tank were reduced to a minimum with only the aid of a torch for Richardson to work his way around the mass of steel frames beneath the sea bed set. *(Author's collection)*

Beached Beauty

With a heavy list but still sitting up right, *Titanic* almost looks like some mystical mermaid left stranded upon the rocks of some distant shore. Once the model had been seated down on the sea bed set, her stern rested upon a rocky outcrop that left her rudder and propellers suspended high above the ocean floor, the heavy port list required a pair of securing cables on the starboard side of the model to prevent the 10-ton replica from keeling over. Once in place, FX crew could then dress the set with tons of sand before heading up to the concourse of the tank as the pump house opens up the valves to flood the tank for filming. This series of remarkable photographs hint towards the working conditions down in the tank and the many pieces of equipment needed for filming.

It was during these periods of when the model sat upon the set in an empty tank that the weight of the model was at it greatest. Lessons learned from the earlier ocean floor and turntable problems that resulted in the set being strengthened meant that the set could withstand the 10-ton model resting upon it when the tank was dry. Once the tank was filled, the model created a certain amount of buoyancy that helped reduce the risks of the set buckling. *(All photographs © Geoffrey Mackrill)*

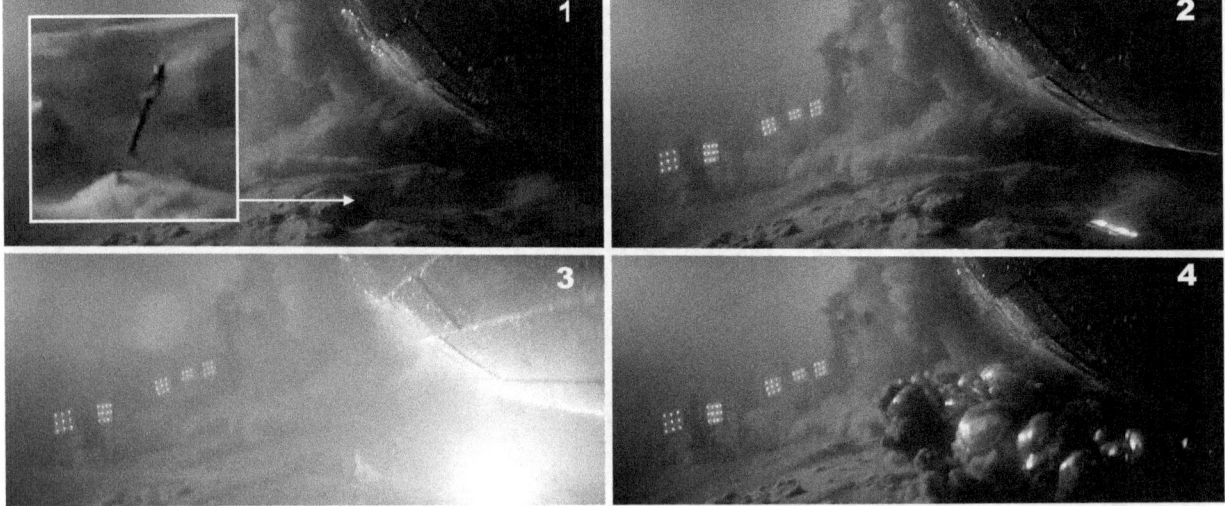

One of 100 to scale explosive pods sitting in the mixture of sand and Fullers earth around the hull of the *Titanic* model. (1) The prop explosive was not connected to any device other than wiring to work the flashing LED inside the top of the housing. (2) Positioned under the model and partially buried under the sand was a lighting rig made of camera flash bulbs in a housing that was connected to a controller operated by the FX diving team. The bulbs were to simulate the flash from the explosive going off. (3) As the explosive flash dies down, (4) the Aquaflex detonating fuse is triggered simultaneously setting off a release of compressed air to simulate the explosive force of the charge that will break the suction between the hull and the sea bed. *(Author's collection – ITC/ITV Studios)*

CHAPTER 20

Raise the Titanic!

"Ha! Are you talking about raising the Titanic? Can it be done?
A ship that big, down that deep?"

General Dale Busby

General Dale Busby's response to Pitt about raising *Titanic* is a memorable moment in the film. While Charles Macaulay's delivery is lifted from the pages of the script his line echoes a lot of truth. The raising of the *Titanic* is without question the most visually stunning part of the entire film; from the moment the mast exits the water to that last glimpse of the wreck fully afloat and surrounded by naval vessels. What was put to film in 1980 is far removed from Clive Cussler's all too brief passage in his 1976 novel. While descriptive enough for the reader, was it enough to visualize the scene with some sense of detail? The change from the wreck being raised stern first in the novel to bow-first was largely down to convenience, both for the handling of the large model and combined with the publicity required to advertise the film and its leading screen dominating star. The *Titanic* imagery had to be instantly recognised by the public as being the *Titanic*. Views of her, bursting up bow first with her name visible on her sides and her distinctive bridge and forward funnel, was more workable in selling the film than views of the ship being presented in a reversed sinking scenario.

Standing at the podium of the NUMA headquarters, Pitt addresses the senior officials from the Navy and CIA with his opening dialogue, "The Royal Mail Ship *Titanic*. Where is she now and how do we get her up?" That's a good question. The former has already been covered on how the *Titanic* was discovered and the preparations leading up to the salvage attempt. But how did they do it? Not the fictionalized characters in the film, but rather the FX unit.

Oddly, one of the most iconic moments of the film rarely gets asked on how the special effects were accomplished. Whether this is down to the viewer not wanting to know how the magician pulled off the magic trick, or because the process was never properly documented to begin with back in 1980 and publicly shared. The latter does warrant some truth as the film's production when made public during 1979 through to 1980 centered more towards the premise of the film's story, the actors, and the *Titanic* replica, without covering the techniques behind the special effects. In fact, almost all published material on the film between 1979 to 1981 never covered the films special effects other than a line or two. And then what was written was sparse. The information researched over the years that have gone into this book have come directly from those who worked on the film, who shared the same passion as me in finally documenting the remarkable practical effects of *Raise the Titanic*, and giving me access to the techniques used on the production from recently found production documents that reveal, for the first time, how they successfully raised the *Titanic*.

The Team Who Will *Raise the Titanic*

To raise this *Titanic*, it required a team of professionals in their designated expertise in the field of mechanical and visual effects. The production crew was expected to push the limits of filmmaking to bring to life the story from the combined pages of the screenplay, storyboards, and shooting notes for the movie's spectacular special effects. In 1997 during promoting his adaptation, James Cameron referred to the special effects in *Titanic* as "breaking new ground". But he had been pipped to the post when 17 years earlier, Alex Weldon, John Richardson, and their team, broke the mould in achieving an impossible feat by working with the world's largest *Titanic* miniature inside the world's largest water tank within the often harsh and unpredictable environment of actual water. What Weldon and his team were to accomplish had never been done before in movie-making history. It may sound cliché, but *Raise the Titanic* turned into a movie production where the special effects teams were faced with the task of actually raising the *Titanic* for real; day after day. A long-running joke began to circulate amongst the crew working at the Mediterranean Film Facility, that the job they faced in raising their movie *Titanic* was greater than raising the real thing. The film's Mechanical & Special Effects Supervisor John Richardson joked "It would be cheaper to lower the Atlantic than *Raise the Titanic*". In his 2019 book *Making Movie Magic*, Richardson continued to quip about Lew Grade stealing his line. It was, incorrectly, attributed to the television mogul. Lower the Atlantic? Richardson certainly had a valid point to make.

John Richardson is a BAFTA and Academy Award-winning British special effects designer to the film industry and has worked on some of the most recognizable and best-loved movies of our generation. His established career has seen him working on blockbusters from his first film *Casino Royale* (1967) working alongside his father, Cliff Richardson, who had worked on the effects for *The African Queen, Lawrence of Arabia, The Dirty Dozen,* and *Battle of Britain*. John would soon rise through the ranks of the film industry working on the family classic *The Railway Children* to the grittier *Rollerball* and horror classic *The Omen*. Action, adventure, and sci-fi include *A Bridge too Far, Warlords of Atlantis, Superman, Aliens, Willow, Cliffhanger, Starship Troopers, Deep Blue Sea,* and *Men in Black II*. John also had a successful career working on many of the James Bond series of films including *Moonraker, Octopussy, A View to a Kill,* and *Die Another Day*. And for today's families and younger audiences John brought his expertise to the much-loved Harry Potter film series starting with *Harry Potter and the Philosopher's Stone* right through to *The Deathly Hallows: Part 1* and *Part 2*.

In 1979 John was approached to head the team for the model FX unit for *Raise the Titanic* over in Malta, the filming duration in Greece and out in the Pacific Ocean with the U.S. Navy. His dedication to the film, to the industry, to his profession, was at a time when special effects miniatures ruled both the small and big screen, and *Raise the Titanic* was an extremely challenging project from start to finish. It was a gruelling four-month schedule for Richardson and his team as they pushed on to deliver the finished sequences with all the models in both the deep and surface tanks. As the U.S. crew left Malta in late summer 1979 after completing the 1912 prologue, Richardson teamed up with special effects legend Alex C. Weldon in bringing together their own team of experts for *Raise the Titanic*. Richardson and Weldon were to oversee the majority of the FX work for the production with Richardson concentrating on the more laborious mechanical and miniature work. Richardson and Weldon had to precisely calculate how they were going to pull off the movie's most costly and memorable sequence. To adapt the models, especially the large bulky *Titanic* replica, to film scenes with the model subs, model lights, model explosives, model salvage tanks and equipment, it would take a dozen or more personnel working together simultaneously in making sure everything comes together within budget and within the designated timescales. It was the gathering of the personnel who would achieve the goal of bringing *Titanic* to life, and to the surface, with the use of the technology available to them in 1980. Without the dedication of the movies FX crews, *Raise the Titanic*'s spectacular visionary could not have been achieved to the maximum effect that is so much loved to this day by fans and moviemakers.

The following is a list of known personnel who worked on the special effects in Malta during production on *Raise the Titanic*.

Leading Personnel

John Richardson *Special Effects/Mechanical Effects Supervisor* – Alex Weldon *Special Effects Supervisor* – Dick Frift *Construction Coordinator* – Ricou Browning *Malta Model Unit Director* – Bob Steadman *Director of Photography Malta Model Unit*

Special Effects Personnel

John Richardson – John Morris – Norman Baillie – Alan Barnard – Ron Cartwright – Gerry Ciantar – Tony Dunsterville – John Evans – David Harris – Tad Krzanowski – Ray Lovell – Ken Morris – Bob Simokovic – Ken Swenson – Bob Wilcox – Bob Worthington – Frank Foster – Lowell Draper (RC helicopter operator) – John Simone (RC helicopter operator) – John Stavros (RC helicopter operator)

Camera (model unit)

Bob Steadman – Mike Ferris – Paul Silberman – Montie Taylor – Steve Wolper

Divers (model unit)

Courtney Brown – Ricou Browning – John McLaughlin – Gavin McKinney – Tony Whathen

Construction

Dick Frift – Fred Morris – Harry Barnes – Harold Burst – Steve Court – Fred Crawford – George Dean – John Dearn – Fred Heyes – Tom Kavanagh – Ron Lenoir – Dick Morris – John Newell – Ron Newell – Ron O'Connor

***

More Lights, Camera and Action

The working conditions in the deep tank with the model were troublesome, as getting the atmospheric lighting right for the cameras was essential in capturing the look of the deep ocean while still giving the camera units enough light to capture the miniatures. The environment in the tank had to replicate the depth of the Atlantic at nearly 12,500ft while maintaining some form of visibility for the model unit and camera crews to work, but still cloaking the *Titanic* in darkness. For three weeks the crews worked tirelessly in the tank trying to get the lighting of the model to work in their favour. The issues they faced was in getting the separate lighting stands in a position that added some light to the model so cameras could pick up the haunting silhouette of the wreck on film while not being so glaringly obvious that a series of studio lighting rigs had been set up to illuminate the tank set and avoiding being picked up on camera. For three long weeks, the crews placed, relocated, and tested the tenacity of the lights in getting the balance right and eliminate all previous attempts of where the tank had been too dark to successfully capture the models on camera with some degree of detail.

It wasn't just working 36ft down that gave the crews a headache as working on the surface had its moments of frustration. The filming of the *Titanic* model during raising required dozens of angles and shots so that the editing department had additional material to fall back on should anything need removing because something unwanted or untoward appeared in-frame. Although tank personnel could control the working conditions in the tank, the Mediterranean backdrop afforded no such control when passing cruise liners, small craft and freight container ships sailed back and forth from the neighbouring Malta docks. It became a common occurrence in waiting for passing vessels to clear the shot before the camera started or resumed rolling. If one was to appear right at the moment the *Titanic* model is breaching the surface and the unmistakable silhouette of a ship not meant for the production was captured on camera in that shot, the action was stopped, the model paused, and if and when needed the model was either started back up from the point of being paused or it was sent back down to the bottom of the tank. And before the reader turns to the film with the hope of spotting a ship on the distant horizon, rest assured, none are seen. However, something unwelcomed does make an unscheduled cameo appearance during the raising of the *Titanic*. During the moment the bow claws skywards filling the right-hand side of the screen seconds before the John Barry score starts, a closer inspection of the tank's horizon point reveals the upper shoulders and head of two studio personnel who were standing in the spillway of the deep tank and watching the filming process of the model.

To capture the raising of the *Titanic* on film needed for the model unit and camera unit to work in harmony in achieving a realistic scenario of the story's most defining moment. At 1:16 scale, the *Titanic* model was large, but it also posed a problem in being built at the lower end of the spectrum scale for water droplets. Shots of the model filmed at a distance worked well as the eye had little to compare the scale between the model and the water. But as soon as the camera position shifted to a close-up view, a number of the shots soon emphasized the fact the viewer was watching a model and more so as the sequence was purposely slowed down so the water droplets remained in frame longer than normally expected. The earlier calculations on water scale were enough to satisfy many shots in the raising sequence even though one or two did validate the need for a larger *Titanic* model. The budget prevented that from ever happening. But it must be remembered that the 55ft model was never intended to be the raising model for the sequence. But given that what is seen on screen is the work of practical effects, those water droplets just feet away from the camera lens can be excused for being a little on the big side. The audience was expected to be too engrossed in that astonishing raising scene to even notice such minor errors. Oh, that magical scene. How can anyone not be stirred by that sequence?

The breath-taking shot of *Titanic* as she erupts from the ocean depths required a special camera which was designed to turn at a much higher rate of speed. Photo-Sonics, Inc of Chatsworth in California supplied one of their high-speed 35mm-4ER cameras which was one of only four in the world at the time of its production. The camera could achieve a working ratio of fifteen times the normal speed of a standard movie camera making it the perfect camera solution for effortless slow-motion filming. The 35mm-4ER used on *Raise the Titanic* captured the raising sequences at 360 frames per second (fps) which was an incredible 21,600rpm making it the fastest 35mm pin registered camera in existence. The design of the film transport containing 12 pull-down pins and 4 register pins meant that it could perform without fault at 360 fps. So versatile was the 35mm-4ER that it could run at 420fps and during its registered test speed it reached a maximum of 500fps. So acclaimed was the camera in the film industry that its design went on to win the Academy Award for Technical Achievement in 1988. Filming the sequence at such a high rate of speed meant that when played back at a normal pace, the footage was slowed down to run fluently without showing any signs of twitching or fluctuating. For low-level perspective in capturing the model bursting up from the water tank, the camera was mounted upon a floatable camera platform that was supported with floats, to allow the Photo-Sonics camera to float precisely at water level. In addition, the camera could be mounted to a platform that was hoisted by a crane and swung out over the tank at the distance required by the camera unit operating the equipment when capturing views of the model surfacing the tank meters beneath them.

The film's rolling end credits of the continuous birds-eye view of the rising *Titanic* from the water is a testament to the flawless workings of the Photo-Sonics 35mm-4ER camera. That single locked-off view was just one from a total of 55 times the model was raised to contribute to the film's three minutes, ten seconds of edge-of-the-seat escapism. And now the all-important question – what was the duration of the raising in real time? It may come as a shock but it was far quicker than expected. On average, the process, from the moment the top of the mast first appears, to when the model is fully exposed and sitting almost on a perfect keel, ranged between 12 to 15 seconds. It must be noted that the process of filming the underwater views of the model being raised to those of it seen at the surface was carried out on separate occasions and was never filmed as a single take.

During the 50+ times the *Titanic* model was raised, it was subjected to a punishing process of being catapulted from a depth of 11-meters and up through a vast volume of water and constantly changing pressure, and expected to work, without problem, time and time again. The FX team were not going to get a smooth voyage as the Mediterranean saltwater took its toll on the model. The length of time the *Titanic* replica was submerged in water combined with the pressure asserted upon the materials during the sudden blast from the bottom of the tank to the surface meant that some deck details would come loose and pop off during the rapid ascent as the glue that held them down reacted and softened in the saltwater. Another frequent issue they encountered was the model shedding its paint while in the tank. Richardson recalled the times the model was being touched up with paint both in and out of the water facility. With the model sitting on the side of the tank it could dry in the sunlight making the touch-up work easier. But there were times that some areas of the model required paint while it was still submerged under 9 million gallons of water. Richardson came to the rescue with his special paint mixture, diving down to the model, and with a tin and paintbrush in hand, he set about applying the paint mix to the model.

Designing the Unthinkable to Raise the Unsinkable

"Isn't that a beautiful son-of-a-bitch!", expresses Captain Joe Burke of the United States Navy, as *Titanic* rights herself moments after breaking the surface of the North Atlantic. Actor J.D. Cannon's line certainly sums up the view of such a majestic Edwardian ocean liner brought back from the dead. Although it was done through the process of movie magic, it was an incredible feat of engineering to begin with. Accomplishing such a grand practical effect in lifting what was essentially a 55ft boat was never going to be easy. In the case of this production, some elements of completing a special effect needed a more heavy handed approach that took them away from the normal standards of achieving an effect. What was not readily available to them in the FX stores resulted in going further afield to track down parts that can be adapted for use to finalise the sequence. The mechanics behind raising a huge 10-ton model boat was one such effect that needed a fresh approach. And given the size and weight of the model, the effect required a strong and highly stable mechanism that was expected to work time and time again with minimal problems. What was about to be achieved had never been done before… and has never been repeated since.

So, how do you get a huge 55ft, 10-ton model of the *Titanic* from the bottom of a very deep water tank and up through 9 million gallons of water through a depth of 36ft to the surface without mishap, and with the ability to do it time and time again on cue? Weldon and Richardson faced the challenge of devising a lifting mechanism that could move the model from one location point and up to a second location point while covering a distance of nearly fifty feet. One early idea pitched was for the floor of the tank to be dug out enough to allow for the construction of a ramp in which the FX department would sit the *Titanic* model upon the slope of the ramp and drag the model up and out of the tank to the surface. After much debate, it was concluded that this procedure would not only be too costly to achieve but also would be a ridiculous waste of resources in a sequence that could very well never be achieved properly.

With Weldon as the movie's principal model unit captain and Richardson as the leading practical mechanical FX unit supervisor, Richardson was handed the task of developing a fully workable system that could handle the weight of the large *Titanic* miniature, keep it stabilized and lift it clear to the surface of the tank and keep the miniature afloat once it was lifted. What they could not do was make it permanent as the lifting system needed to be removable as the *Titanic* miniature was required to be removed from the filming tank, worked on, and put into periods of storage. The final design that Richardson came up with was a lifting rig that would control the *Titanic* model from point 'A' of the tank floor to point 'B' at the surface directly 36ft straight up while all the time submerged in a colossal volume of water. The lifting rig design was more of a practical solution over that of attaching steel cables to the model and hauling it up via a heavy haulage crane swung out over the tank. Not only would the cables be exposed on film but the model could not be properly controlled, leading to problems for the crew working in the tank. The lifting rig was the most workable solution and the one that would be more beneficial to all the crews working on the production.

A pair of lifting keels fabricated from steel 'I' beams were cut to length and bolted to the underside of the *Titanic* hull and positioned on either side of the ship's keel with enough space between for the attachment of the main lifting rig. The pair of lifting keels, approximately 30ft in length, had securing bolts passed up through the fiberglass hull that would hold the keels to the inner steel framework that ran along the interior side of the hull just beneath the mounting points of the floatation tanks. Located forwards of the hull between the first and second funnel was the attachment point for the lifting arm. The arm was actually an extending heavy haulage hydraulic crane arm sourced from a local Maltese company and transported over to the studio. With a new attachment plate affixed to the one end of the crane arm and a substantial mounting point at the other, the crane arm could be secured to the lifting keels on the *Titanic* model with removable pins so the model could be removed from the tank while the crane arm remained attached to the mounting point at the bottom of the tank. At the tank floor, a steel frame and bed plate were constructed and locked down to the concrete floor of the tank. The frame included the crane arm mounting point with removable securing pins. With the one end of the crane arm attached to the tank floor and other end secured to the lifting keels on the *Titanic* model, the two main fixing points acted like a hinge that allowed for the model to start perfectly flat on the bottom of the tank, to then move forwards and up. All the time the crane arm would take the brunt of the models weight and pressure applied during the movement from the tank floor to the surface. Of course, this entire process could only be achieved with the full cooperation of the floatation tanks sitting inside the hull of the model and a series of cables attached to the lifting keels and passed through a pulley system along the bottom of the tank and up the tank sides to exit at ground level where the cables would be fed through a series of winches positioned around the edge of the tank.

With the mounting point of the crane arm located forwards of the hull, a section of the fiberglass hull bottom directly in line with the rear mast was removed giving access for counterbalance weight to be added and bolted to the steel frame inside the hull. This counterweight was important to the stability of the model once the entire hull had reached the surface of the tank during the ascent. To move such a large structure like that of the *Titanic* replica the mathematics had to be precise as the lifting gear had to withstand the weight and the overall control of the model making the equipment fully operational beyond its original capabilities in case anything unwarranted should ever occur. Richardson had to develop the lifting gear so it could be used as many times as needed while all the time being safe for the crews working with the model in and out of the tank. On paper, the design appears simple enough. But looks can be deceiving. Richardson devised a way that would bring the model up at an angle starting from its original seated position flat on the bottom of the tank. While the tank was big enough for surface shots its depth of 36ft was shallower than the overall length of the *Titanic* replica if it was stood up on end.

With the decision approved in having the model come up by the bow, the lifting rig had to move in a way that would allow the bow to move first, while the stern of the model was held down at the tank floor until the FX unit decided to release it. This manoeuvre would be controlled by the cables attached to the underside of the hull, and ran up and out of the tank to the winches. The cables worked in two sets with one attached to the bow-end of the lifting keel and the other, the stern cables, were attached to the aft end of the lifting keels. With each cable working independently from the safety of the concourse around the tank, it meant that the model unit had full control over the movement of the model from the moment it moved from the tank floor to its arrival at the surface. The final ingredient to the rig came from the eight lifting tanks seated four units per side within the hull of the *Titanic*. The tanks had to multitask when needed in keeping the model on the bottom of the tank, operated to lift the model and to then keep the model buoyant once at the surface. The FX department had designed the tanks so each unit could be fitted with air pipes where compressed air was fed down from the surface, into the tanks and through an air feed line operated from the side of the deep tank. As the air was pumped into each tank the water inside was forced out through an open vented system at the bottom of the tank, while excessive compressed air was released through a manifold at the top of each tank to stabilize the pressure within. With the water displaced and the tanks filled with the compressed air, the buoyancy aided in lifting the 10-ton hull to the surface. Once the hull had breached the surface then the valves would be closed sealing off the bottom of the tanks.

"We don't go to the mountain. The mountain comes to us."

Before the raising sequence could be filmed, the artificial sea bed had to be cut up and removed along with the steel framework that built up the turntable. With the work beginning in the last week of February, the clearing away of the set meant that the lifting rig could now be anchored securely to the concrete base of the tank floor without the FX model unit having concerns over movement. With the lifting rig assembled, the process of attaching the *Titanic* replica to it could begin. To explain the raising process of the model and the lifting rig it is presented here in a step-by-step format.

Step 1: With the deep tank completely drained of water, the *Titanic* model was brought to the tank side and lifted out of its transportable steel cradle with slings attached to a crane. The model was then swung out over the tank; lowered down over the lifting arm of the rig where the arm was bolted to the lifting keels on the underside of the hull.

Step 2: With the *Titanic* model attached to the lifting rig and seated horizontal to the tank floor, the bow-end and stern-end cables were attached to their mounting points on the lifting keel and ran up to the winch system on the concourse of the tank.

Step 3: From the concourse at the tank surface the air pipes were passed down and attached to the main inlet feed of the hull internal tanks.

Step 4: For the filming of the *Titanic* leaving the ocean floor, A simplified section of sea bed was pushed up to the hull bottom of *Titanic*'s bow and dressed with sand and the 1:16th scale lighting pods. (See *Step 6*)

Step 5: With the model seated to the lifting rig, anchorage cable fitted, air pipes, control cables and bow seafloor in place, the tank could now be filled with water.

Step 6: With the model unit and camera unit kitted up and in place at the bottom of the tank, the first sequence could be filmed. From the surface, the compressed air is piped down into the tanks to give buoyancy. At this stage, the tanks are only filled to give a partial lift for scenes of *Titanic*'s hull stirring from the sea bed. The anchor cables are removed and the control cables are played out from the surface allowing for the model to move a few feet before the air in the tanks is replaced with water for the hull to come back down again. With these scenes now filmed the model can be made ready for the complete lift from the tank floor to the tank surface.

The following process was to be carried out over several days resulting in multiple shots of the *Titanic* being filmed from within the tank, at the surface, and those aerial views that amounted to the model being raised an estimated 50+ times before all the desired camera angles had been accomplished.

Step 7: From the surface, the tanks are piped in with compressed air with a regular flow. With the water in the tanks pushed out and replaced with air, the *Titanic* is now ready to be lifted. With cameras rolling the anchor cables are first removed diverting the model's weight to the lifting arm and control cables. The first part of the model to be moved is the bow. With the cables holding down the stern, the bow cables are played out to allow for the bow to begin to rise. Once an angle of 20 degrees had been reached, the model, with its stern still secured down to the tank floor, had its forwards mast to breach the tank's surface at an increased 30-degree angle. With the mast now breached the cables at the stern can now be released sending the model, on its lifting arm, to follow the bow and exit the surface at an angle reduced back down to 15 degrees until the stern is completely exposed. The amount of time lapsed from the moment the bow is released to the stern being released and the model reaching and levelling off at the surface was dependent on the final release of those stern cables. A crucial procedure that had to be carried out every time the model was raised was the continuous venting of the air tanks during the ascent from the tank floor to the surface. Due to the sudden change of pressure at 36ft, the pressure upon the air tanks during the ascent to the surface would lead to the tanks imploding if not correctly regulated. Before the model was released for the journey to the surface the tanks filled with compressed air had the vents opened up resulting in a regulated flow of escaping air that prevented the tanks, manifolds, and pipes from giving way. Inadvertently, the escaping air as it flowed through the hull of the model and to pass through open portholes and windows added to the churning up of the water during the ascent and at the tank surface.

Step 8: Now at the surface the air tank valves are closed off sealing the air within the tanks allowing the model to float while still being attached to the lifting arm.

When filming with the model had come to a close whether it was for the day, a number of days or if repairs were needed to be carried out, the model was detached from the control cables, air pipes, and the lifting arm. With the slings placed around the hull, the *Titanic* was lifted out of the tank and seated down into its storage cradle until it was needed again.

Those Magnificent Men in their Flying Machines

The closure to the movie's raising sequence is the magnificent fly-past which treats the audience to a helicopter's perspective along the side of the salvaged *Titanic,* where her encrusted and rust-stained deckhouses, funnels, and mud strewn decks give tantalizing hints to the liner's former grandeur. The scene starts at the very tip of her stern, about 30ft above her deck, passing along her entire port side profile to gradually drop to deck level passing just meters away from the hull sides. To finally end with a view of the wreck surrounded by navy vessels as a pair of helicopters fly into view. One of them drops Pitt aboard the waterlogged derelict. Even in this state, something is mesmerizing about the ship's beauty that is hard to explain. There is something dreamlike about that scene; the water pouring out from windows and doorways, flowing like rivers to cascade down the side of the ship. The eye is magically drawn towards the details that were previously hidden in the darkness of the ocean's depths. The sequence is beautiful, romantic, artistic. To achieve this shot, the *Titanic* model had been moved over to the surface tank facility and connected up to water pumps and pipes that drew water up from the tank and out from the model. A boat with an outboard engine had been fitted with a film camera mounted to a small hand-operated camera crane. John Richardson took control of the boat's engine and the camera crane while colleague John Harris worked the camera. A couple of passes along the model's side was all it took to get the right angle and perspective for this unique glimpse of the model.

Prior to the *Titanic* model going into the surface tank for the filming of the sequence, the model underwent more alterations to the floatation system, as new sealed tanks replaced the previous units used for the raising of the model. During the changeover of the tanks, the hull and upper superstructure had been fitted with a new pumping system that drew water up from the surface tank, circulated it around pipes placed into the model, and exited through several points cut into the boat deck. With the pumps operating and the model's decks purposely wetted by FX crews working in the surface tank, the water drawn up was mixed with salt to add depth of scale and colour, then flushed out through the outlet ports discretely hidden under the wreck. The fly-past does reveal a little surprise - or two – when, as the camera nears the deckhouse of the third funnel, a little figurine can be seen moving on deck. The unnamed little workman is seen with his back to the camera busy operating a hand pump that is drawing water up out of *Titanic*'s hull to keep her afloat. Sometimes thought to be a joke, the little articulated figure was adapted from a garden windmill ornament. Known as a whirly-gig-wind-well, the decorative garden feature had been removed from its original crafted garden well and fixed down to a plate where it could be seated to the ships deck. A second workman is seen moments later on the aft end of the boat deck when the Sea King helicopter carrying crates hovers over *Titanic*'s stern. To make them move, the pumping station workman was water-powered by a simple paddle wheel that spun around when the prop was seated next to a water outlet built into the deck. As the water passed over the paddle wheel, the figure sprang into action.

The final shots filmed in the surface tank were those for the scenes proceeding the fly-past as *Titanic* is surrounded by the Sea King and Super Jolly Green Giant helicopters as the three United States Navy vessels, *Denver*, *Schenectady*, and the *Blakely/Carpenter* close in around the *Titanic*. As the Sea King hovers over the stern of the model, eagle-eyed viewers may have noticed a dark orange windsock fluttering on a piece of cable at the rear of the fourth funnel. The windsock helped professional remote-control operator John A. Simone, Jr in successfully working the miniature versions of both the S-61 Sea King and the Jolly Green Giant helicopters up and around the large *Titanic* miniature. Simone was already turning heads with his stunts becoming the National Helicopter Champion at the age of 20. In 1977 he founded the company R/C Helicopters, Inc in Hollywood as a remote-controlled stuntman for the film and television industry with the intense desire of becoming the leading pioneer of R/C helicopter units. Simone's on-screen debut began in 1974 when he provided his services operating the R/C helicopter in conjunction with the huge 90ft tall Glass Tower model skyscraper in the Irwin Allen production of *The Towering Inferno*. During filming on *Raise the Titanic*, Simone would spend two weeks in early 1980 working with the R/C models at the surface tank of Malta's Mediterranean Film Facility carrying out various stunts and manoeuvres with the helicopter miniatures; from loading boxes aboard the raised *Titanic* to crashing the helicopter into the sea bringing about the end of Captain Prevlov.

How Much?

On 13 July 1979, the hiring of the surface tank for the filming of the tugs with the *Titanic*, was scheduled for the period between 5 November to 16 December. That June the *Titanic* model had already been filmed for the movie's opening sequence in the surface tank for the brief prologue set in 1912. As work continued on the deep tank, the *Titanic* model had been put into storage in the film studio until the time was right for the conversion from the pristine ship into the wreck. In August, during preparations for the conversion, ITC signed the agreement in hiring the studio's Carpenter's Shop to double as the film productions Special Effects store facility at a weekly rate of £70. That September the hiring of the surface tank was pulled as delays completing the pump house to the deep tank added extra stress to the production on *Raise the Titanic*. The hire of the surface tank was essential for filming the *Titanic* miniatures with the pair of tug boats and the navy vessels. With the tank hire dates cancelled, there was no guarantee that another studio production could come in and snap up the tank facility. With pressure mounting to get the deep tank operational it was planned that a New Year's turnaround would see filming with the miniatures begin in the surface tank. In October 1979, ITC inquired about the use of the tank for a few months in early 1980, hoping to pencil in the hire of the facility as a priority. However, Lions Gate had already booked the tank for the period of 24 March to 17 May for the filming of their production, *Popeye*.

In desperation to get certain FX scenes filmed, ITC used the delays on the deep tank build as a bargaining chip in calling out the lack of interest in the production of *Raise the Titanic* from Malta's Department of Industry which the film company expressed should be doing more to support such a large film project. That November, ITC shifted their pitch on the hire of the surface tank suggesting that it should be loaned to them free of charge. The Board of Directors at the Mediterranean Film Facility were not impressed with the blatant attempt of piracy and rejected any such proposals of letting ITC have the tank for nothing. The first week of December, ITC received the verdict from the Board of Directors; the surface tank was booked in for use on the production of *Raise the Titanic* for 13 weeks between the dates of 2 December 1979 and finish on the 1 March 1980 at a reduced cost of £24k to ITC; that duration per the studios hire brochure would have come to £54k. The film company had no choice but to accept. The Mediterranean Film Facility also made it clear that any further delays on the film production that ran past the date of 2 March would result in the hire charges being processed at full rates. Finally, that December preparations began in getting the models, tank, and nearby buildings ready for filming in the surface tank.

Tugs to the Rescue

As the last of the Christmas turkey scraps made their way into trash cans, the filming of the wrecked *Titanic* with the tugs had now begun. The sequences needed to show the tugs taking control of the raised liner for the journey to New York, along with a number of scenes of the wreck battling the choppy waters as the hurricane descends upon the salvage fleet. As January opened a new decade, filming in the surface tank was going well as the model unit filmed the tug boats leading the storm-battered *Titanic* from her raising grounds. These initial first attempts of filming the departure for New York had the two tugs set up on either side of *Titanic*'s bow. The 1:16 scale tugs were still largely in their U.S-built state except for a few minimal changes with deck details and the addition of water pumps to add wash as the model moved through the water. With wind machines producing the stormy seas and with the scenes filmed as day-for-night; a technique of using a darkened filter, the model unit could film the required shots as the tugs, positioned either side of the *Titanic*, battle the storm and clash with the sides of the liner. Things took a turn for the worse when during filming on 31 January, the crane used in lifting the larger miniatures into their storage cradles after filming, somehow ended up in the tank and spilling oil into the water. Through the night the studio personnel worked hard in retrieving the crane, removing the oil, and reinstating the water for filming the following day.

As changes came about with the screenplay it reflected upon certain scenes previously filmed becoming redundant and newer scenes planned in replacing those discarded. Yet again, the *Titanic* and the two tugs were back in the surface tank for the reshoot of scenes that would make up views of *Titanic* being towed into New York. This time around the tug boats had been given a make-over with the two craft sporting a new colour scheme with the previously grey hull being replaced with a matt black finish. Out on the water the tugs had been placed in a new juxtaposition with one at the bow and the other placed at the stern. Whether this decision was more in keeping with reality as the *Titanic* would have had no working engines and rudder or whether it just looked better on screen, the decision was better and one that made more sense. With this set-up of the tugs and the *Titanic*, the sequences were filmed based on the storyboarded scenes from those of the salvage fleet seen from the water to those filmed from a camera crane swung out over the tank. With the shots in the can, it was left to the matte artists and their skills in taking New York matte works and bringing them together with the footage filmed in the Malta tanks and the earlier shots by Stanley Kramer and create a seamless transition between the miniatures, matte paintings, and live-action plates.

The Lost Fleet of *Raise the Titanic*

There were two model vessels that never made it to screen, even though they were both fully built, story boarded, and included in the story. Like the rest of the miniatures built to match the *Titanic* replica, ITC also had commissioned in 1:16 scale a New York Fireboat and a fourth navy ship; the U.S.S. *Pigeon*. Built with the rest of the ship models at the CBS Studio Center in Los Angeles, the models were fully operational and extremely well detailed. The Fireboat had been completed with a water pumping system that once the model had been placed in the water tank the pumping equipment fitted to the underside of the hull would draw water up and direct it through a series of firefighting hoses and nozzles located on the upper deck of the vessel. The model was to play a key role in the New York arrival sequence with the model being filmed shooting streams of water into the air in the surface tank in Malta as part of the *Titanic* and tugs ceremonial procession past the Statue of Liberty and the trip to Brooklyn. What is known of the model is that it arrived in Malta with the shipment of other miniatures, and there the story ends. It is unclear if they ever put the model in the tank and filmed it or whether it became another surplus to requirements prop that at the time of order was thought to be a worthwhile addition, only to lose out in the end as circumstances with the production changed. The model remained in storage at the Mediterranean Film Facility to become part of the inventory of items left at the studio when filming was completed on the production. The fate of the model is unknown.

Like the rest of the Navy ship models the U.S.S. *Pigeon* had been planned for use in scenes that required the miniatures to complement shots with the raised *Titanic*. The model, although well detailed, had not been fully completed when it left Los Angeles for the shipment over to Malta. The check reports on the 16ft model when it arrived at the film studio indicated that the model was without any operation internal electrics and had not been fitted with any water ballast system or engine mountings. As production costs increased it would seem that talks between the FX model unit and ITC stalled when it came down to throwing more money in getting the *Pigeon* fully working for screen time. Whatever the intended outcome was to be, the model was never used having been put into dry storage as production continued. The decision to not use it may have been swayed by the filming taking place in San Diego, as of the four Navy ships replicated for use in *Raise the Titanic*, the *Pigeon* was the only vessel not on the shooting schedule with the U.S. Navy. The combination of the film studio not being able to secure the hire of the real *Pigeon* during the November 27 to December 10 filming could have been what prompted the studio to leave the miniature on dry land. The fate of the *Pigeon* was the same as the rest of the ship models built for the production. The size of the miniature meant it could not be kept in dry storage and it too was moved outside and left to deteriorate in the studio backlot at the mercy of the Maltese weather, where it remained with the rest of the Navy model hulls throughout the 1990s until they were removed from the studio grounds and destroyed.

"A SIXTY-EIGHT YEAR OLD WRECK RISES TO STARDOM" But how did they do it? Let's find out. *(Daily Mirror, 28 May 1980 – Author's collection)*

Despite the level of special effects used in *Raise the Titanic*, not one single publication was ever released that covered how the miniature work was done. Film magazines only went to the extent of using a simple synopsis of the film story accompanied with a few publicity images. The only magazine to include some filming details, albeit kept to a minimum, was *On Location* from August 1980. But even then, the publication did not go into any detail on the film and repeating content which had already been put to print in small newspaper articles. *(On Location, August 1980 – Author's collection)*

The crew in the tank prepare for another day of filming. *(John Richardson collection)*

RAISE THE TITANIC   MALTA, 21st JANUARY, 1980

LIST OF LOCAL PERSONNEL AS AT W/E 20th JANUARY, 1980

Special Effects	12	
Carpenters	11	
S/by Labourers	8	Temporary
Special Effects - Cleaners	8	Temporary
Security	7	On Shifts
Deep Water Tank (Maintenance + Cleaners)	6	
Pump House (Operating)	5	
Plasterers	4	
Painters	3	
Catering	3	
Riggers	2	
Electricians	2	
First Aid	2	On Shifts
Accounts Secretary	1	
Buyer	1	
Cleaner	1	
Facilities Cleaner/Security	1	
Production Runner	1	
Time Keeper	1	Shared Basis
Water Chemical Treatment	1	Part-time
TOTAL	80	

Raise the Titanic document of personnel numbers working on the production in Malta during the 20 January 1980. *(Author's collection)*

188 • *Raise The Titanic*

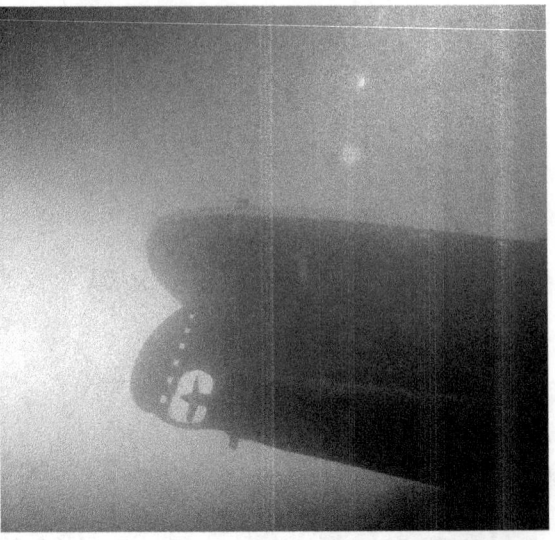

One of the major problems working in the tank with the huge *Titanic* model was getting the lighting right to the point that the ship lay cloaked in a controlled darkness that also had to work with the camera crews. *(ITC – Author's collection*

Chapter 20: Raise the Titanic! • 189

Working in the tank was particularly challenging for the film unit. It would take them nearly three weeks to get the light right down at the bottom before any cameras began to roll. *(ITC – Author's collection)*

Deep Quest takes a closer look at the dislodged funnel resting on the ocean floor. For the discovery of the funnel, two miniatures were built and filmed. The largest of the two was used for this scene as Pitt identifies the encrusted cyndrical object resting on the sea bed. Only half of the upper section of the funnel was built. *(ITC - Author's collection)*

190 • *Raise The Titanic*

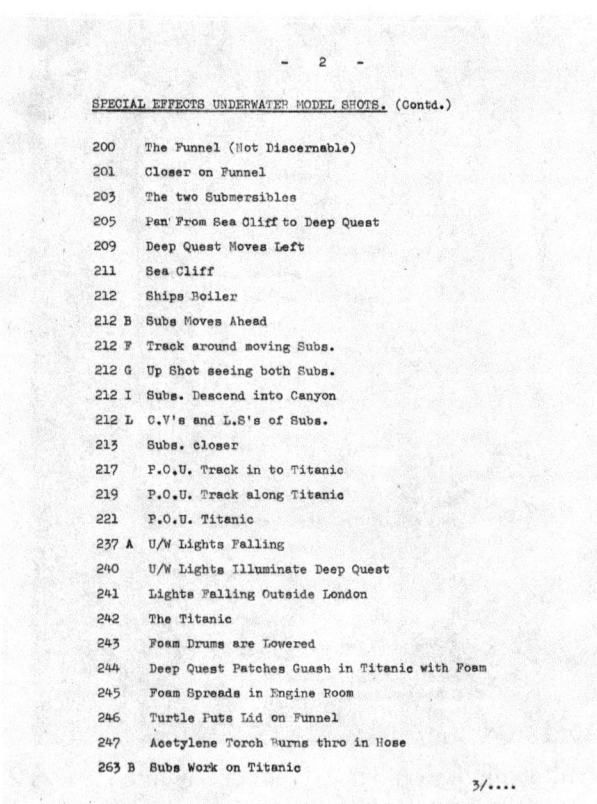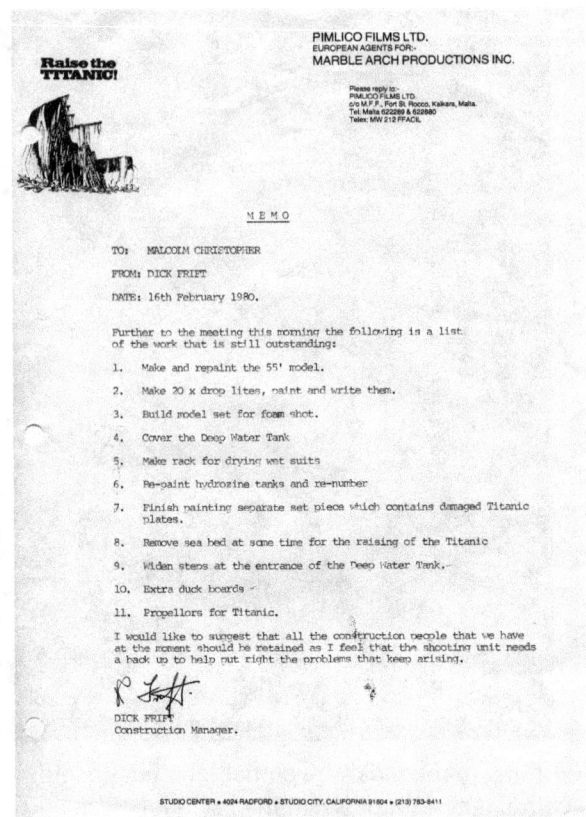

One of the pages from the model FX filming schedules for *Raise the Titanic* with all work being carried out in the deep tank, surface tank and additional inserts in the 30′ x 30′ mini tank. *(Author's collection)*

Victim to the heavy editing. At first glance it looks like something has been accidentally spilled over the ocean floor set. But what you see here has been purposely placed. This rare glimpse into the filming stages of the production shows an array of polished rocks arranged in an area of the sea bed that was used for a sequence when the submersible crews stumble upon a huge boulder field while searching the depths for the *Titanic*. The boulder field scene was to be accompanied by Dirk Pitt explaining that passing icebergs in the Labrador Current would drop their cargo of prehistoric rocks as the icy monsters melted. *(Photograph © Geoffrey Mackrill)*

STARTED	FINISHING DATE		SCENE NUMBERS	
ESTIMATED DAYS	LOCATION OF WORK/SET		COMPLETED	
DAYS TO DATE	SMALL SURFACE TANK NO. 1		Extra cover for 154-162 pages 37-39	
REMAINING DAYS	M.F.F.		PART 212pt.	
DAYS OVER / UNDER	KALKARA MALTA			

TIME		SCRIPT SCENES						
			SCRIPT		EXTRA		RETAKES	
CALL	08.00		NUMBER	MINUTES	NUMBER	MINUTES	NUMBER	MINUTES
1st SET UP COMPLETED	12.15		24				3	
LUNCH FROM	1.25	PREVIOUSLY TAKEN	-				-	
TO	2.15	TAKEN TO-DAY						
UNIT DISMISSED	2.45	TAKEN TO DATE	24				3	
TOTAL HOURS		TO BE TAKEN			DAILY AVERAGES, OVERALL:			
		TOTAL SCRIPT SCENES			STUDIO:		LOCATION:	

ACTION PROPS AND EFFECTS	SLATE NUMBERS		STILLS			
Deep Quest	UW181A/UW182A		B & W		COLOUR	
Sea Cliff		PREVIOUSLY TAKEN	2		2	
Turtle		TAKEN TO-DAY	-		-	
	SET UPS: 2	TAKEN TO DATE	2		2	

PICTURE				FILM FOOTAGES		SOUND		
WASTE	RES'VE & N.G.	PRINT	TOTAL		PRINT	MASTER ROLLS	¼" TAPE	
6886	74650	114744	196340	PREVIOUSLY USED				
40	320	290	650	USED TO-DAY				
6926	74970	115034	196990	TOTALS TO DATE				
SHORT ENDS:	22410 (Total S/E's)				WASTE:			

```
08.00 Unit Call                              REMARKS   ROLLS IN HAND
08.05 -
11.05 Setting up & lighting S1.UW181A                  96 x 1000'
11.15 Rehearsing S1. UW181A                           194 x  400'
11.30 Started shooting S1. UW181A
12.05 Trouble with model - removed from tank & mended  1.25 Lunch
12.15 Resumed shooting S1.UW 181A.                     2.15 Setting up & lighting UW182A in
12.20 Set up & lit UW 182A                                  mini tank
12.30 Glass on tank broke due to light being           2.45 shooting UW 182A
      knocked against glass.Diver Gavin McKinney       2.45 Wrap
      ordered out of tank and Unit abandoned
      Insert Tank. Tank then emptied                           PRODUCTION MANAGER
                                                               RAY FRIFT
```

Daily filming sheet for the film. At the bottom is listed the problems they had with the model submersibles and the damage sustained to the glass mini tank. *(Author's collection)*

A rare view taken of the *Titanic* model from the sea bed set inside the drained deep tank. At her bow and wearing the dark coat is John Richardson who is busy working the sand with a shovel as a member of the FX team brings bucket after bucket of the sediment to be dumped on the sea bed set. What is just about visible in this shot is the iceberg damage to the hull. Although the census at the time of filming was that the *Titanic* had sustained a 300-feet gash in her side, the damage incorporated into the hull was not to that extent coming short of its scaled down 300-feet representation. *(John Richardson collection)*

This rare photograph shows the extent of the damage to the hull of *Titanic* following the brief encounter with the iceberg some 68 years earlier. The damage was created by cutting out a section of the fibreglass hull, adding internal bracing and fixing in place aluminium plates which had been cut to size to match the existing plating and then buckled into shape. The end result was the wound that would eventually claim her unsinkability. *(Photograph © Geoffrey Mackrill)*

Filming is paused as outgoing traffic from Malta Docks pass by. *(ITC – Author's collection)*

It may have been the world's largest replica of the *Titanic*, but even at this scale, water droplets proved to be an issue with some close-up shots. Looking like snow, the droplets seen here were still airborne following the release of water through a set of pipes secured to the deck of the model that gave a good effect of a water eruption as the tip of the bow emerges from the sea. The pipes only vented water for a couple of seconds. But given how quickly the model exited the tank it was not long enough for the spray to settle down and clear the view of the camera lens. *(ITC/ITV Studios – Author's collection)*

The bows of the model showing the pair of spray pipes fixed flush with the deck. *(Author's collection / Mario Cassar collection)*

The bow of the model with the spray pump removed and sitting on the model's deck. *(Author's collection)*

Chapter 20: Raise the Titanic! • 197

The award-winning Photo-Sonics 35mm-4ER high speed camera that was used on *Raise the Titanic* to capture the movies iconic salvage scene. *(Photograph courtesy of Philip Kiel, Photo-Sonics, Ltd, California)*

The film transport of the Photo-Sonics 35mm-4ER. *(Photograph courtesy of Philip Kiel, Photo-Sonics, Ltd, California)*

The pair of Photo-Sonics 35mm-4ER's in full operational mode filming the crucial raising shots. *(Photograph © Jeff Paynter)*

Chapter 20: Raise the Titanic! • 201

The *Titanic* has been lifted clear of its transportation cradle and is in the process of being swung out over the deep tank. One interesting feature seen here on the model are the rows of salvage plates that are secured in place over the iceberg gash in the lower hull. In the foreground are a set of wooden makeshift racks for the divers Poseidon wetsuits to dry. *(Photograph © Geoffrey Mackrill)*

SC. 244 -

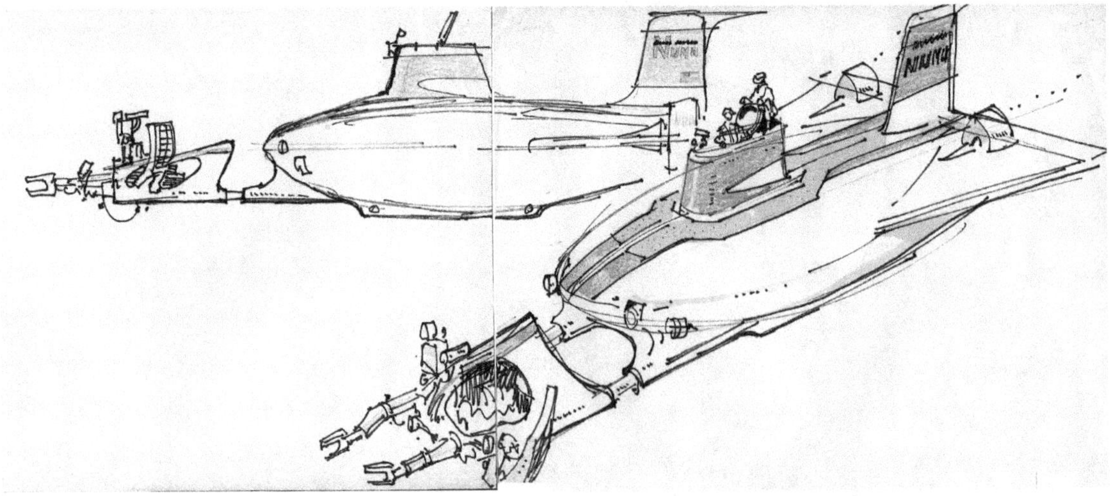

Applying a plaster to the wound. Before she can be raised, *Titanic* has to be patched up. This storyboard for the film shows the plating over of the iceberg damage to the hull. This was to be achieved by the *Deep Quest* where a welding device named *Rufus* would be connected to the front of the submersible. As both *Turtle* and *Sea Cliff* position each plate to the hull, *Deep Quest* with *Rufus* then start welding the plates in place. The scenes were filmed but eventually cut during the final stages of editing. *(Concept artwork © John DeCuir - Author's collection)*

Chapter 20: Raise the Titanic! • **203**

LEFT and ABOVE: The camera unit film the submersible *Sea Cliff* for the scene where the salvage crews carry out last minute checks on the plated over iceberg gash. *(ITC – Author's collection)*

204 • Raise The Titanic

ITC publicity photograph of the model that not only reveals the salvage tanks in place but also the salvage plates over the iceberg damage. *(ITC – Author's collection)*

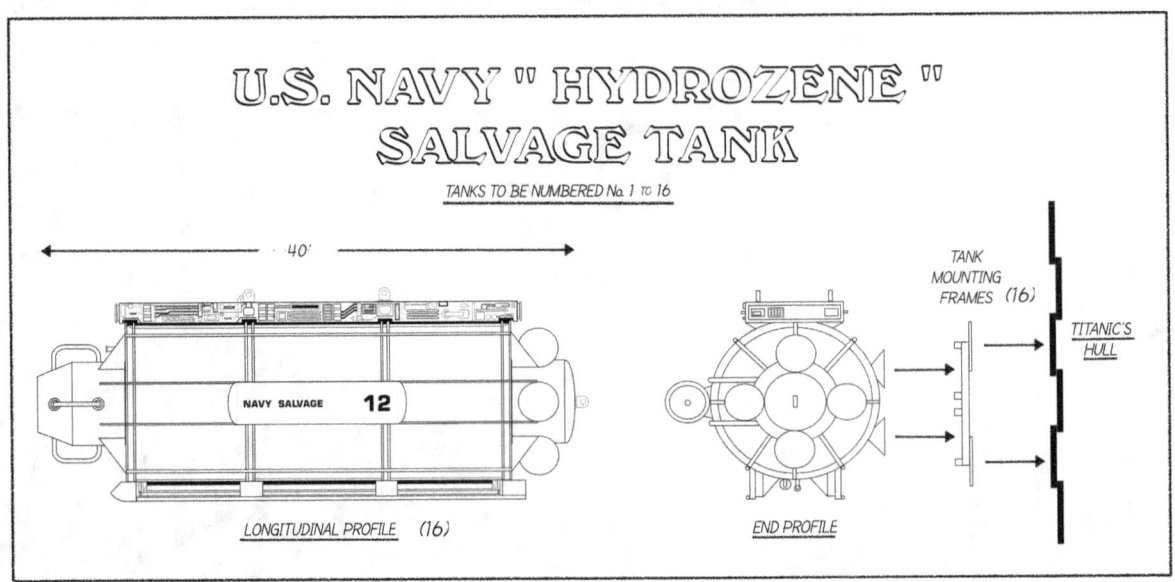

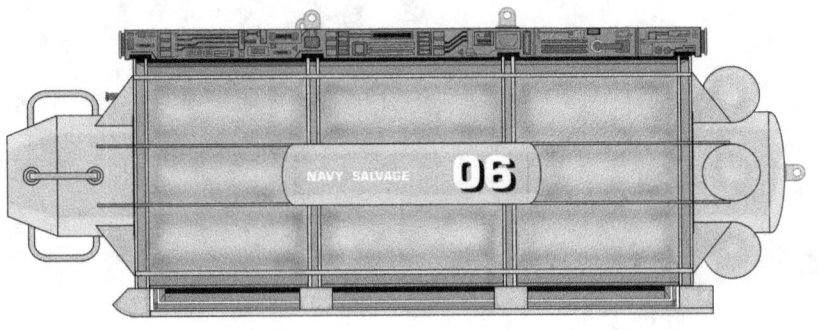

Plan and artwork of the fictional 40ft U.S. Navy "Hydrozene" salvage tank. *(Illustration © Jonathan Smith)*

Chapter 20: Raise the Titanic! • **205**

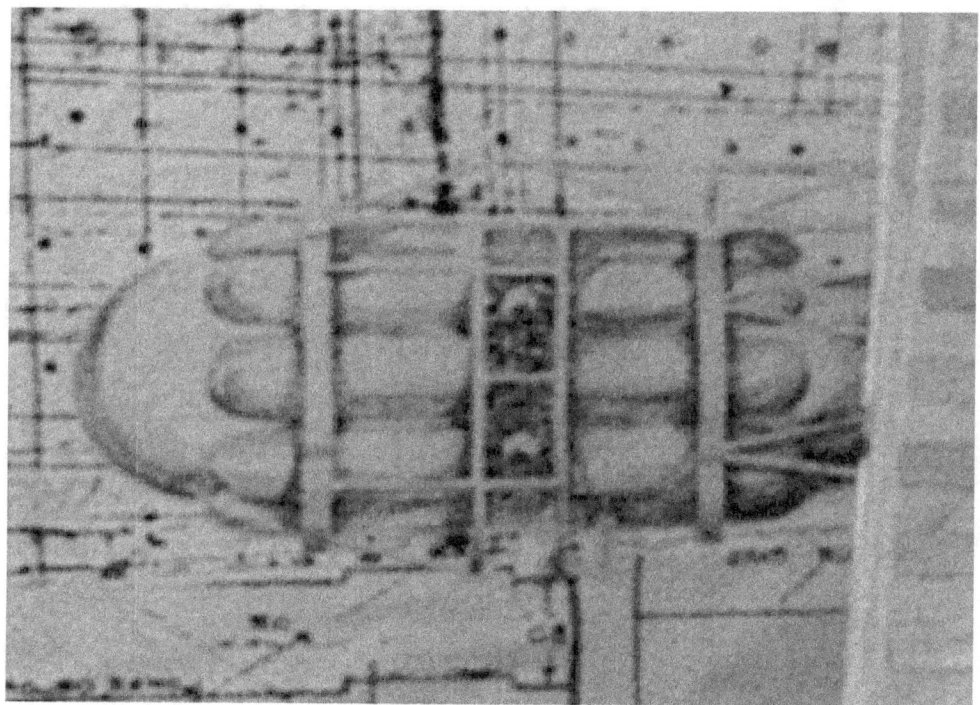

One of the early designs of the Hydrozene salvage tank as envisioned by the U.S model crews in 1977. *(Photograph © Ken Marschall)*

One of the 1:16th scale Hydrozene tanks sits on the side of the deep tank. At a scale of 1:16, matching the scale of the big *Titanic* replica, each one of these tanks measured 30 inches in length. *(John Richardson collection)*

"Start the countdown." The model unit film the scenes of the tanks being activated as the gas bags inside each tank is filled. In reality they used compressed air fed from a number of tanks operated by the divers who were resting above the model out of camera shot. *(ITC – Author's collection)*

Chapter 20: *Raise the Titanic!* • 207

Before the *Titanic* model could be raised, the huge artificial sea bed had to be completely removed. With cutting equipment, crews began the long job of cutting the structure into manageable pieces that would be lifted up out of the deep tank. (*Author's collection*)

Fiction vs. fiction. TOP: The *Titanic* of 1912 adapted to resemble the liner as she could have appeared in the movie for the sinking prologue. ABOVE: It is a stark contrast to how she did appear in the 1980 movie with this illustration depicting the liner as the wreck from *Raise the Titanic*. *(Artwork © Cyril Codus – Author's collection)*

Work continues to cut away the sea bed set. Once the tank floor had been cleared, the next major phase for the film was the installation of the lifting rig. *(Photograph © Jeff Paynter)*

"Control, this is *Deep Quest*. The ocean floor just disappeared. We're going down until we can find it again." One set piece of interest that was used in the deep tank alongside the sea bed set was this small rocky outcrop. Built and positioned to one side of the tank floor, the fibreglass set was used for the sequence leading up to the discovery of the *Titanic*. With the funnel found and logged, *Deep Quest* and *Sea Cliff* continue their search. But when the trail goes cold and the subs draw to a stop, the ocean floor suddenly collapses revealing a canyon. Pitt radios through what has just happened before taking the *Deep Quest* over the ridge and down into the unknown. For the shots of the ocean floor giving way in a cloud of sediment, a camera unit was positioned to the right of the set with the camera trained on the steps of the canyon wall. Out of camera shot a member of the unit then poured sand down the canyon wall. *(Author's collection)*

Chapter 20: *Raise the Titanic!* • 211

This photograph of the model reveals the exterior keel and its counter weight attached to an area of the hull bottom cut out at the stern. At the bow can be seen three air pipes to the tanks and the main fixing point to where the model would be attached to the lifting arm. As the model is being removed from the tank, the lifting arm has been detached when the model sat at the bottom of the tank. *(TOP: Author's collection / BOTTOM: Author's collection / Photograph © Jean Pierre Borg / Illustration © Jonathan Smith)*

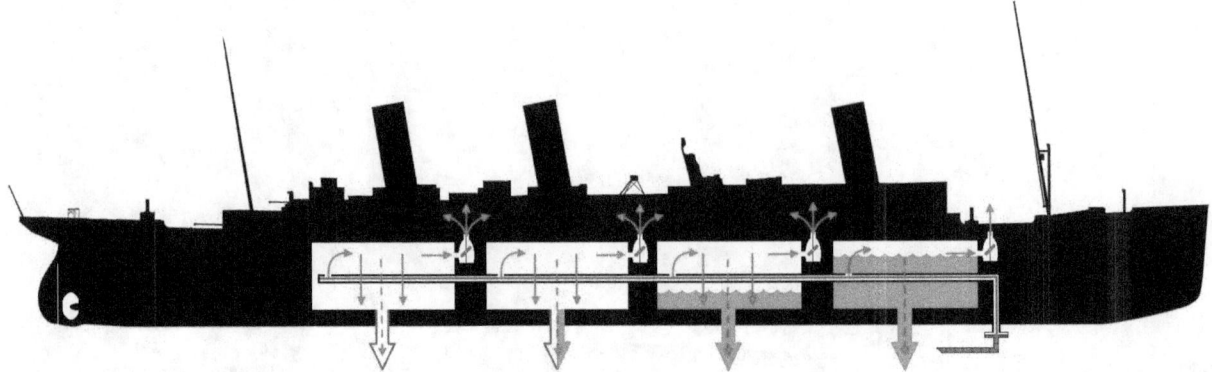

The model was fitted out with eight open vented floatation tanks; four units per side. The tanks played a double role in being filled with water to keep the model on the bottom of the tank to then be quickly drained of water that was replaced with compressed air to add instant buoyancy. One of the main issues addressed in working with the model for the film's famous raising sequences was the prevention of the tanks imploding. The sudden change in pressure from being submerged 36-feet down to then be catapulted to the surface in such a quick time meant that the floatation tanks had to be constantly venting from the bottom of the tank to when the model levelled off at the surface. *(Illustration © Jonathan Smith)*

Surviving pair of the raising floatation tanks inside the hull in 1993. *(Photograph © Simon Mills)*

Chapter 20: *Raise the Titanic!* • **213**

The scene of the churning up of the ocean surface as *Titanic* begins to appear from the depths was not part of the films FX shots. With Photo-Sonics cameras rolling and the water in the floatation tanks within the model being expelled and replaced with air, the venting air as it reached the surface of the tank created a tumult in the water. The churning and bubbling water created its very own effect that worked well on screen and added to the startling illusion of something monstrous about to appear from below. *(Frift Family Archive & ITC/ITV Studios)*

Bruce Hill, cinemaphotographer in charge of the Photo-Sonics camera systems, prepares one of the cameras that is housed in its waterproof container. As the crews are working on *Raise the Titanic*, a printed note that reads "The *Titanic* gets a new captain" has been stuck to the side of the camera housing. *(Photograph © Jeff Paynter)*

Your eyes are not deceiving you. The *Titanic* model really is sticking out of the tank with her stern in the air. This photo is a rare glimpse into the early stages of testing the lifting rig with the model. What makes this image interesting is that the model is rigged up with water pouring from the model's decks. While it is not erupting up from the tank, it is surfacing rather slowly while being test filmed with both Photo-Sonic cameras. The positioning of the model being filmed from the starboard side with the portside facing out over the sea convinces me that they did indeed take it seriously at first in having the wreck raised stern first like the Cussler novel before opting for the more photographic bow-up. *(Photograph © Jeff Paynter)*

Hey, ho! Up she rises. Testing the huge *Titanic* model in the deep tank. *(Photograph © Geoffrey Mackrill)*

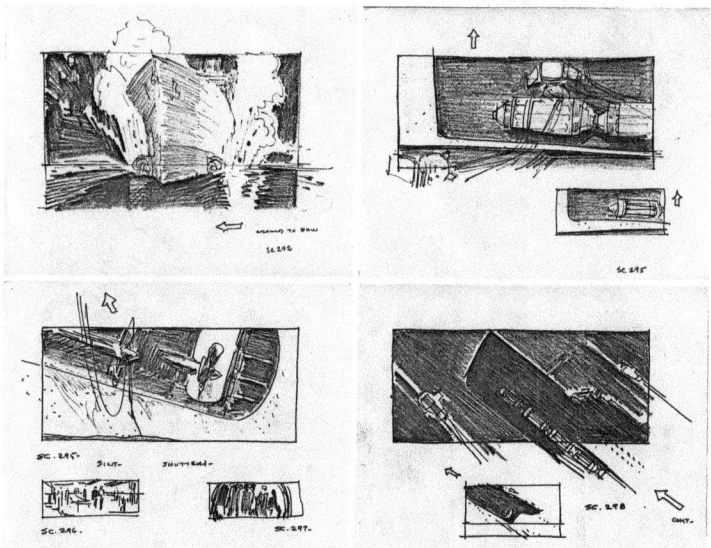

Storyboards for the sequence of *Titanic* pulling free from the ocean floor to begin the long journey to the surface. *(Author's collection)*

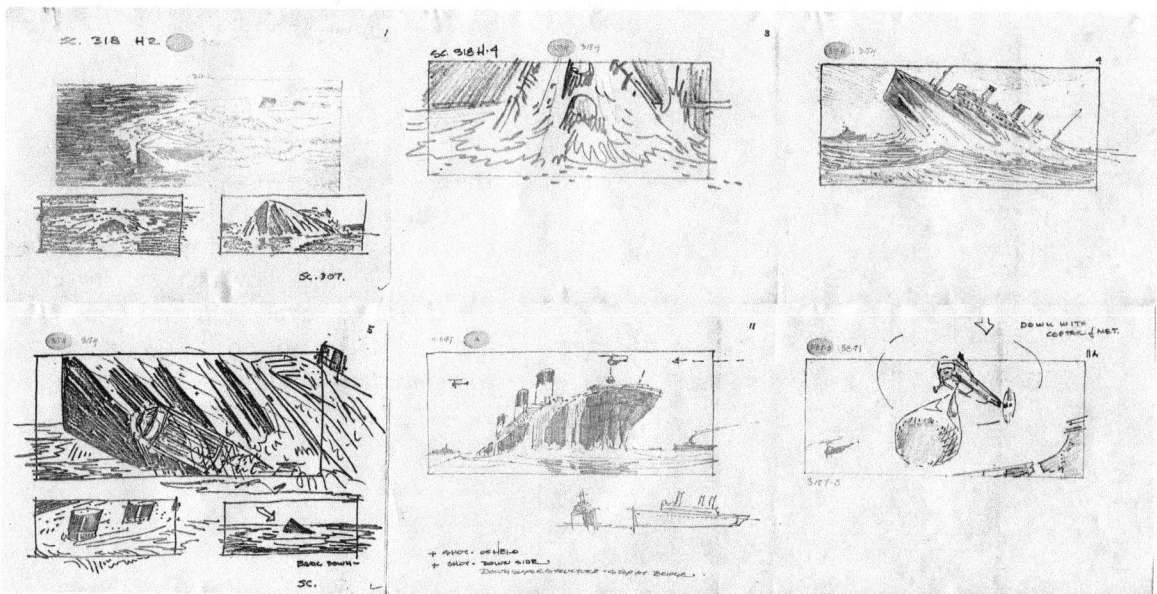

Storyboarding the raising of the *Titanic*. The scenes here are very similar to what is seen in the film with the exception of one. Scene 318H has *Titanic* vanishing beneath the waves after she levels off. Just the tops of her three remaining funnels can be seen. She then bobs back up to the surface as the salvage tanks take over. *(Author's collection)*

John Richardson (right, in glasses) and his team get ready to *Raise the Titanic!* *(John Richardson collection)*

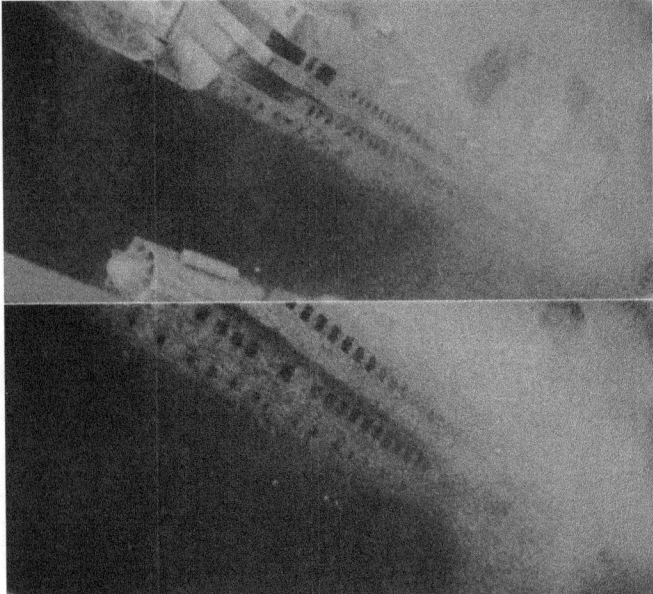

The repainted 9-feet "drop-test" *Titanic* model in its guise as the aged wreck complete with salvage tanks. The model was used for several close-up shots showing the entire ship as it hurtles to the surface. Only two shots made it into the final cut of the film. *(John Richardson collection & Author's collection)*

Chapter 20: Raise the Titanic! • 217

Getting ready to make movie magic. *(John Richardson collection)*

Capturing the overhead shots of the surfacing model. *(Photograph © Jeff Paynter)*

Up from the depths. Lost for 68 years, the legendary *Titanic* reaches sunlight once again. *(ITC – Author's collection)*

The model photographed from the floating pontoon. *(Mario Cassar collection)*

Stunning view of the surfacing *Titanic* replica. *(Mario Cassar collection)*

The model levels off just seconds after breaking the surface of the deep tank. *(Photograph © Jeff Paynter)*

Another break in filming to allow two cruise liners outbound from Malta Docks to pass by. Note the 30-inch salvage tank sitting on the wall of the steps into the tank. *(Photograph © Jeff Paynter)*

Using the crane platform to photograph the model. *(Photograph © Jeff Paynter)*

The *Titanic* rests on the surface of the deep tank. To the left can be seen the wave machine. Just behind it in the surface tank is one of the sets for the motion picture *Popeye*. *(Photograph © Jeff Paynter)*

Interesting aerial shot of the deep tank with the *Titanic* model. *(Author's collection)*

After being pushed to the side of the tank, lifting straps have been passed under the hull and connected to the crane for lifting the 10-ton *Titanic* out of the tank and seated down into its wheeled cradle. *(Photograph © Jeff Paynter & Author's collection)*

222 • *Raise The Titanic*

The *U.S.S. Denver* floats in the deep tank while crews reverse the *U.S.S. Schenectady* into the water. Note the huge wave-maker machine and the aircraft engine powered wind machines. *(Photograph © Geoffrey Mackrill)*

At first glance there may not be anything untoward with this shot of the model. But what makes this photograph unique is that the model is exiting the water at a much steeper angle compared to how she appears on screen. *(ITC – Author's collection)*

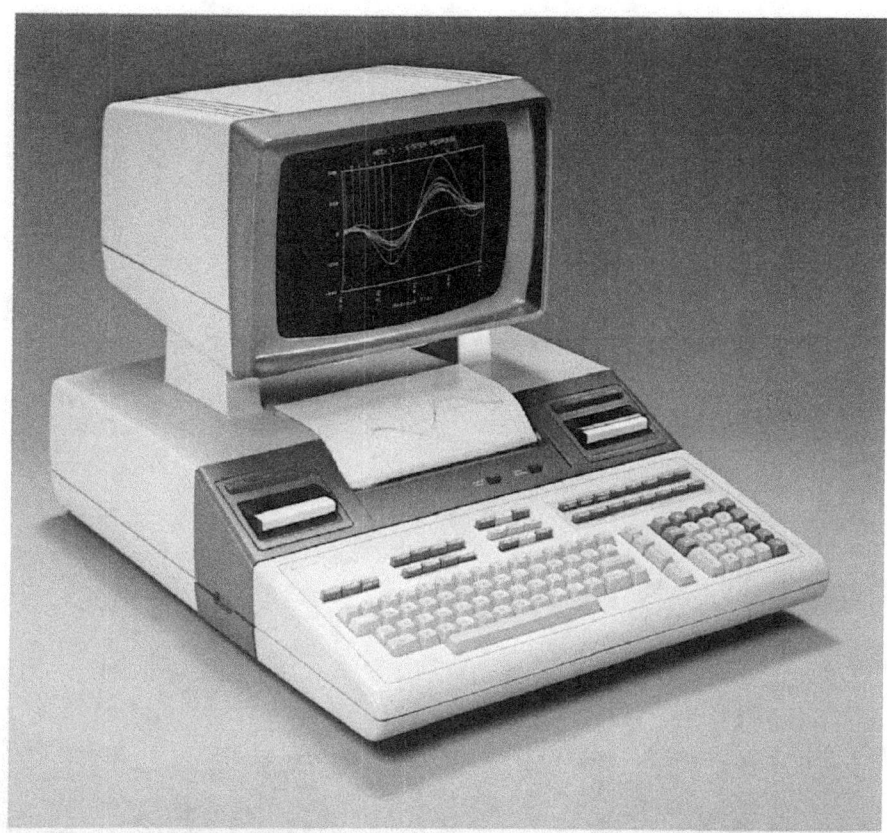
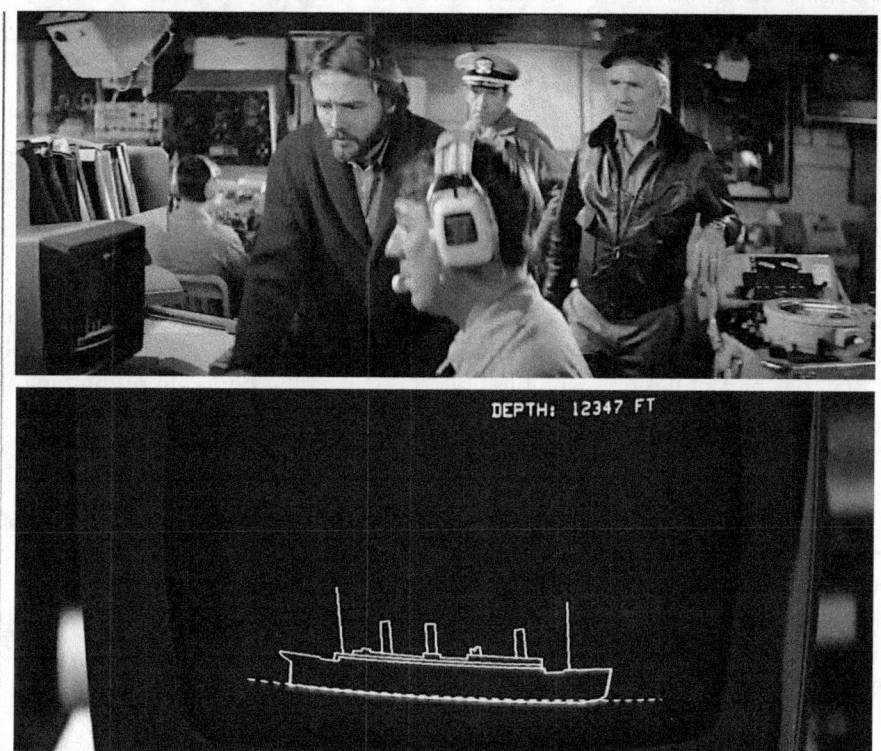

Dirk Pitt and his team monitor the movement of the *Titanic* as she begins to stir. Hewlett-Packard loaned ITC/Marble Arch Productions one of their HP 9845B models for use in the movie. *(ITC – Author's collection)*

224 • *Raise The Titanic*

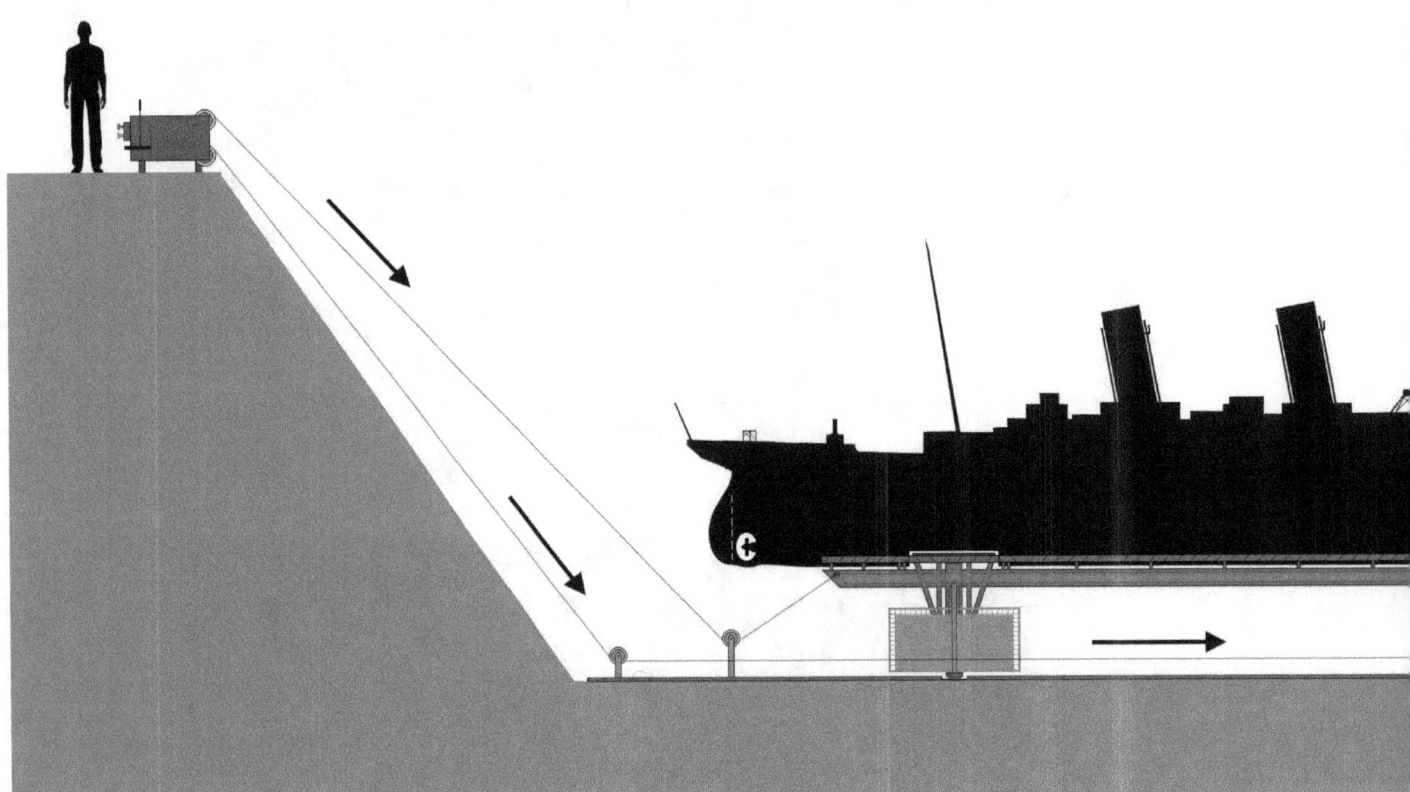

As no photographs are known to exist of the model attached to the lifting rig, this illustration demonstrates how the lifting rig would have looked. The main lifting arm, a former heavy-haulage crane jib, was attached to a pivot head that was part of the rig assembly bolted down to the concrete of the tank floor and put in place after the ocean floor set had been removed. The *Titanic* model would be lowered down into the tank and connected to the end of the altered crane jib head while the tank remained empty. Once the model was secured in place, the control cables were attached to the mounting points on the crane jib directly beneath the *Titanic's* hull and ran through a series of pulleys on the tank floor and up the sides of the tank to a hand-controlled winch. With removable cables in place to hold the model down to the tank floor, the model's internal floatation tanks were connected up to the flexible pipes going up to the surface of the tank and the steel tanks had their vents opened up to allow to flood when the deep tank was filled with water. As the deep tank filled, the model would remain in place upon the lifting rig on the tank floor. *(Illustration © Jonathan Smith)*

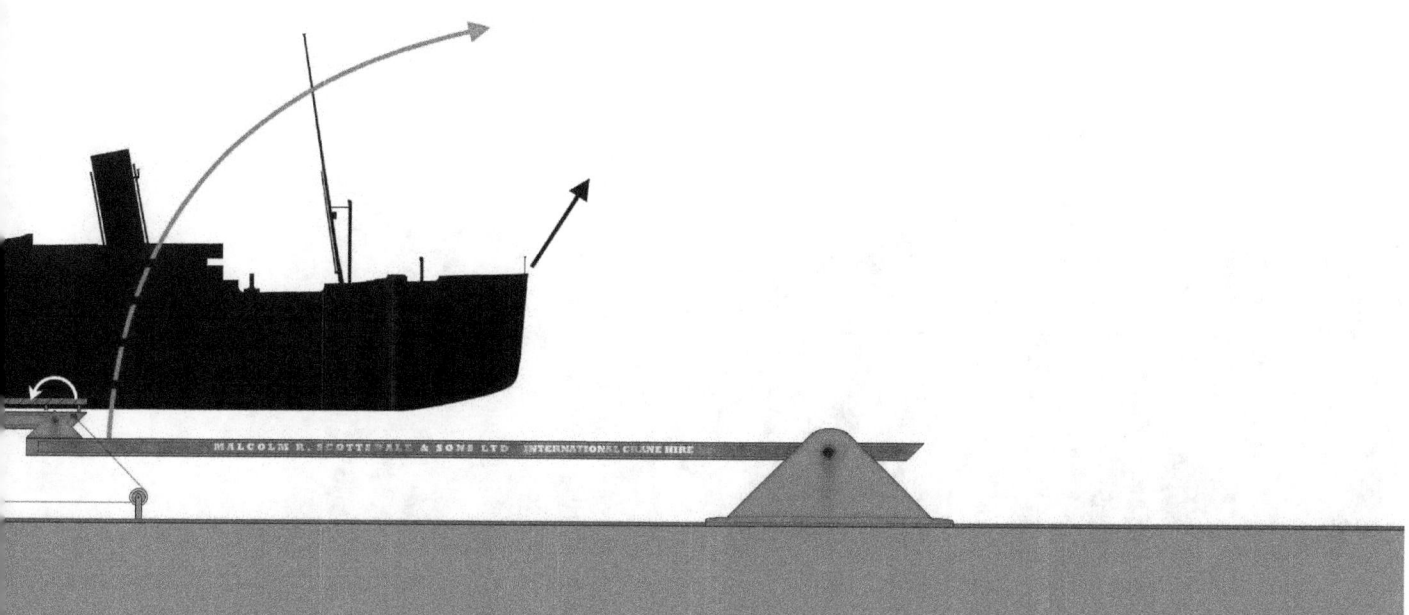

226 • *Raise The Titanic*

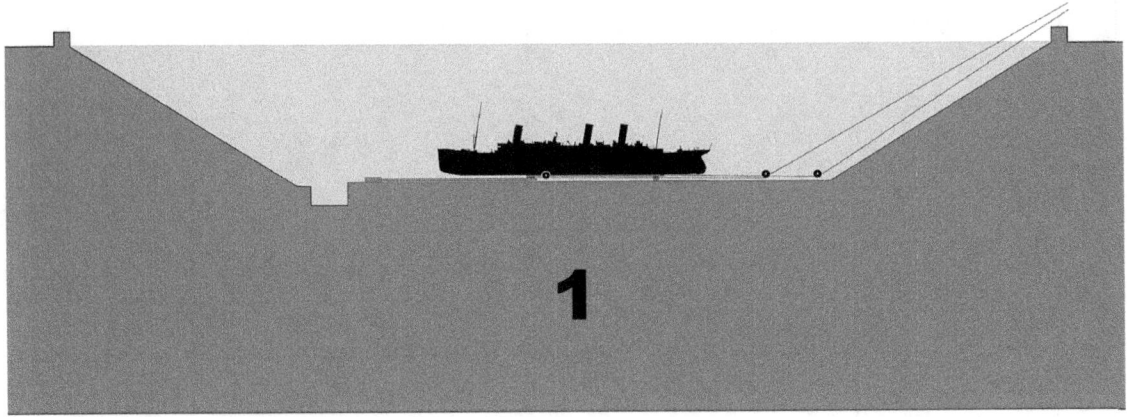

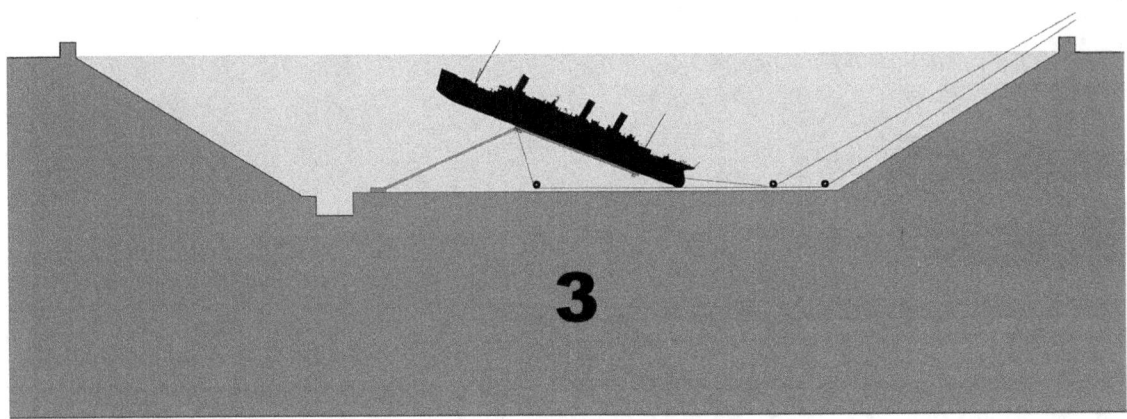

How they did the unthinkable and raised the unsinkable. (1) Starting flat on the bottom of the tank, the hull tanks are filled with compressed air adding buoyancy to the model. (2) The anchor lines holding the model to the bottom are removed and the control cables attached to the bow end of the lifting rig are played out allowing the bow to rise. (3) As the bow begins to emerge at the surface, the control cables at the stern of the model continue to hold the stern area down. (4) As the rest of the tanks are replaced with compressed air, continuously

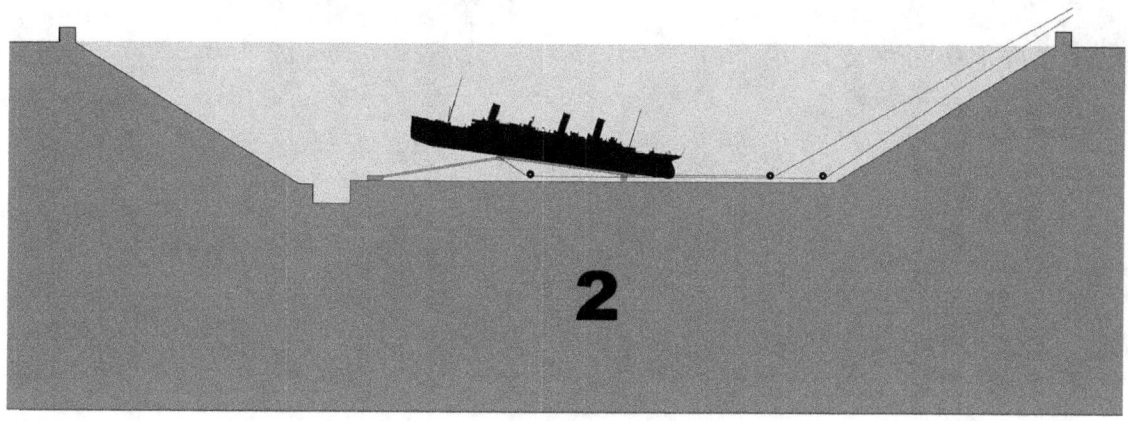

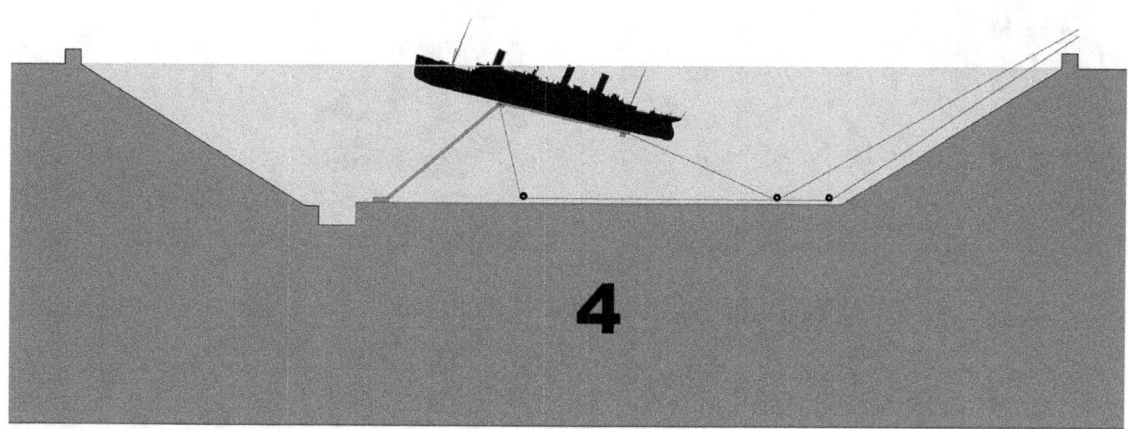

venting all the way to the surface to prevent imploding, the stern control cables are played out to allow the stern to rise. (5) Now fully buoyant because of the internal tanks filled with air, the model attached to the lifting rig and cables is allowed to level off and rise. (6) Each lifting process from the tank floor to the surface lasted 12 – 15 seconds. The model was then sent back down to the bottom of the tank again to repeat the process. *(Illustration © Jonathan Smith)*

Chapter 20: Raise the Titanic! • 229

Chapter 20: *Raise the Titanic!* • **231**

(ITC – Author's collection)

Chapter 20: *Raise the Titanic!* • **233**

Another blatant error in the film is that you never see the *Titanic* model afloat with any of the salvage tanks attached. This rendering shows how the *Titanic* in the film would have looked if the tanks had been present. *(Artwork © Cyril Codus - Edited by Jonathan Smith)*

Storyboard showing the original end titles for the film. Taken from the final draft of the screenplay, the ending was to stop when *Titanic* was at her highest point out of the sea, to freeze frame. The credits would continue to roll on the screen. *(Author's collection)*

(ITC / Author's collection)

Many die-hard *Titanic* enthusiasts were not keen on the additional vents and bow bulkhead that was incorporated into the model. With a little editing by the author, those *Athinai* continuity features have been digitally removed to make the model more historically accurate. *(Edited by Jonathan Smith)*

ABOVE: Mike Ferris and Bob Steadman in the surface tank prepping cameras to film the miniatures. LEFT: With the model now moved over to the surface tank, the crew prepare to film scenes with the navy ships and helicopters post salvaging of the *Titanic*. *(John Richardson collection)*

The *Carpenter* sits in its cradle awaiting to be lifted into the tank where she joined the *Schenectady* and some unwanted maritime guests. *(Joe Sciberras collection)*

One of the storyboards for the fly-past scene of the raised *Titanic*. *(Author's collection)*

In the surface tank as the model unit wet the model before the pumps are started in preparation to film the fly-past sequence. *(ITC – Author's collection)*

Chapter 20: *Raise the Titanic!* • 239

The water pumped up out of the surface tank and up through the model to be vented out on deck had salt added to the mix in a tank located just beneath the deck to give a better sense of scale with the *Titanic* miniature. As the water was piped through to the tank, the tank filled with table salt, would churn and mix with the salt and the water exiting out over the deck would flow with rivers of white frothing water. *(ITC/ITV Studios)*

Some readers may already be familiar with the little man that quickly appears in the fly-past scene. He is one of several figures that were used on the model representing salvage crew working the deck mounted pumps. The little man started life as a garden ornament, a mechanical wind spinner that operated a windmill. The figure was removed from its windmill, mounted to a new base and fixed to a box dressed as a pump that had a hidden paddle mechanism inside that spun as the water passed over it making it appear as if the crew member is busy working the pump. *(ITC/ITV Studios – Author's collection)*

The *Titanic* model is made ready for the filming with the RC helicopters. *(Author's collection)*

The RC Sea King and Jolly Super Green Giant helicopters spring into action. *(Frift Family Archive)*

John A. Simone, Jr operating the scale replica of the helicopter in the 1983 motion picture *Blue Thunder*. *(Columbia Inc publicity photograph – Author's collection)*

Operated by John A. Simone, Jr the Sea King helicopter approaches the *Titanic* model for a series of takes. *(Mario Cassar collection)*

The Sea King hovers just short of the starboard aft end of the boat deck. Note the wind sock that has been fixed to a line. The wind sock aided Simone during operating the RC helicopters in visualising wind direction blowing across the tank and reducing the risk of crashing the helicopters into the model. *(Author's collection)*

The Sea King, with Pitt on board, approaches *Titanic*. Around the wreck sits (left to right) the *Denver*, *Carpenter* and the photographic board (not a model) of the Russian ship *Mikhail Kurkov*. *(Joe Sciberras collection)*

242 • Raise The Titanic

Chapter 20: Raise the Titanic! • 243

The Sea King, piloted by John A. Simone, takes off and flies around the *Titanic* as the model unit and camera unit film the miniatures over in the nearby surface tank. *(All photographs © Geoffrey Mackrill)*

Model unit diver Courtney Brown pulls the *Titanic* model out into the middle of the surface tank for a day of filming. *(ITC – Author's collection)*

One of the most iconic and most published photographs. Courtney Brown, like the protagonist from Gulliver's Travels, tows the *Titanic* model out into the tank. *(ITC – Author's collection)*

The mighty *Titanic* afloat in the surface tank. The two items that look like rope hanging down the side of the hull directly beneath the broken funnel is actually rubber pipe that is part of the model FX dressing on the model. A number of these pipes can be seen laid out across the deck or stored on deckhouse roofs. These pipes formed part of the salvage pumps built to scale with the *Titanic* model and were used to dress the model to mimic the pumps and hoses pumping water from the waterlogged wreck. Note Courtney Brown clinging on to the stern of the model. *(ITC – Author's collection)*

FX supervisor John Richardson boards the *Titanic* and retrieves a stray model lighting salvage pod that had somehow got hooked up in the model. *(ITC – Author's collection)*

Chapter 20: *Raise the Titanic!* • **247**

What a lovely thing she was. The *Titanic* sits out in the surface tank to await the nest stage of filming. *(Author's collection & Patrick Walsh collection)*

The deep sea Navy tugs undergo a fresh coat of paint before heading out to the surface tank for the filming of the towing scenes. The tugs were the same models that were built in California. With Jerry Jameson on the film and the decision to use real tugs over in Greece, the models underwent some transformation to match the full-size vessels. The pipework seen exiting the bows of the models is part of the pumping system which drew water up out of the tank and sprayed it lightly to the surface around the bow and stern of the model to give the impression that the model is moving. *(ITC – Author's collection)*

The *Titanic* model awaits the tugs to be placed into the surface tank for the filming of the towing sequences. *(Author's collection)*

Chapter 20: *Raise the Titanic!* • **249**

John Richardson prepares one of the tugs for the coming scenes to be filmed. *(ITC – Author's collection)*

View from the surface of the tank from the location of the tug boat. *(Author's collection)*

Testing the positioning of the tugs with the first at the bow now connected up.
(Mario Cassar collection)

252 • *Raise The Titanic*

(Photographs © Geoffrey Mackrill)

Chapter 20: Raise the Titanic! • 253

Working on the mechanics of the tugs out in the surface tank. *(John Richardson collection)*

The tugs are repositioned once again. *(Author's collection)*

To move the *Titanic* and the tugs, the models were connected to cables that were fed through a towing machine that was operated by the side of the surface tank. *(ITC – Author's collection)*

Getting ready to film the tugs.
(John Richardson collection)

Guided by tugs, the *Titanic* starts her long journey to New York.
(ITC – Author's collection)

Better late than never. The scenes of *Titanic* entering New York for the journey up to the Brooklyn dockyards were created using photographs taken with the *Titanic* and tug models in the surface tank. Five views are seen that include the *Titanic,* four of which are the models with the exception of one aerial view which utilises a matte painting of the ship with tugs. One example of the model work is presented here. (1) Using footage taken in July 1977 at New York's Son of Op Sail, the live plate is captured first. (2) Nearly three years after being filmed, the footage is to have inserted the matte FX using a still image of the *Titanic* and tug models in the surface tank in Malta. (3) With the vessels isolated and the image transferred to glass, the live plate and matte image (4) are layered to form a single shot. Unfortunately, this shot resulted in *Titanic* appearing on screen far too small. *(Author's collection)*

Titanic under tow. *(ITC – Author's collection)*

The letter from ITC Entertainment Ltd company secretary L.E. Thompson to the Mediterranean Film Facility dated 19 May 1980 outlining that the filming of *Raise the Titanic* had now come to a close and that the deep tank was being handed over to the studio. *(Author's collection)*

Please reply to:-
PIMLICO FILMS LTD.
c/o M.F.F., Fort St. Rocco, Kalkara, Malta.
Tel: Malta 622289 & 622880
Telex: MW 212 FFACIL

20th May 1980

The Commissioner of Police,
Police G.H.Q.,
Floriana.

Dear Sir,

Now that the work on "Raise The Titanic" in Malta is coming to an end, I would like to take the opportunity on behalf of Pimlico Films Ltd and myself to thank you for all your help and co-operation during our stay here.

Please pass on our thanks and good wishes to the many officers who have been concerned with our company particularly the officers in the central immigration office and the Cospicua division.

I hope we have the opportunity to work in Malta again.

Yours sincerely
for and on behalf of
Pimlico Films Ltd

MIKE HIGGINS
Unit Location Manager.

STUDIO CENTER • 4024 RADFORD • STUDIO CITY, CALIFORNIA 91604 • (213) 763-8411

This letter dated 20 May 1980 was sent to the Maltese Commissioner of Police, thanking the police for their co-operation during the filming at the Mediterranean Film Facility. *(Author's collection)*

Even in her distressed state, the *Titanic* model still oozed charm and beauty. This rare photograph taken while filming was coming to a close reveal the majestic lines and minute detail that makes you look twice; reassuring yourself that what you are seeing is nothing more than a miniature. *(Author's collection)*

Assistant Editor for the Malta Editorial Department on *Raise the Titanic*, Geoffrey Mackrill, is pictured at work on a Hollywood 35mm Moviola inside the editing room, essentially a small single building that contained the editing and viewing room, which was erected just a matter of metres from the deep tank. The machine, with its distinctive green paint, featured a set of arms where 1000ft reels could be loaded and edited via a set of foot pedals located at floor level that allowed the reel to move backwards and forwards while the editor viewed the scenes via the viewfinder. With a sequence completed, the footage could be viewed by the director in the adjacent room where, once passed, it would be sent to the studios main editing department for consideration and use. Unfortunately for this production, much of what left Malta ended up on the cutting room floor over in Los Angeles. *(Photographs © Geoffrey Mackrill)*

It is 1988 and the stripped hulls of the navy fleet are pictured decaying on studio backlot adjacent to the Marine studio. *(Photograph © Mike Seares)*

The fibreglass hull remains of the three U.S Navy vessels from *Raise the Titanic* photographed in 1996 as they lay dumped in the studio backlot in Malta. *(Photograph © Simon Mills)*

(Painting © Codus Lionel 2022 – Courtesy of the authors collection – Prints available from www.raisethetitanic.co.uk)

CHAPTER 21

The Sounds of *Raise the Titanic*

"I never wanted to work for anybody else; I always wanted to be my own boss."

John Barry

Pitch the question to any fan of the film on what is their most memorable scene and almost every time it will be answered with the raising sequence accompanied by John Barry's score. There is no denying that the moment *Titanic* sores high into the sky and the brass instruments of the orchestra begin to play the opening bars of the main theme, the hairs on the back of your neck stand upon end. That score alone is as popular as the film is regarded as a flop among critics. And yet of the positive reviews the film receives, it is for John Barry's stunning soundtrack. At the time of production on *Raise the Titanic* there were a number of well-established composers that ITC could have turned to. During the 1970s John Williams was still a prominently fresh-faced composer known to movie audiences with his success of scoring *The Poseidon Adventure, Earthquake, Jaws, Star Wars, Close Encounters of the Third Kind* and *Superman*. Williams, like many other motion picture composers, had a certain signature to their scoring that correlated that music to that artist in much the same fashion as instantly recognising the trade mark sounds of Ennio Morricone and Jerry Goldsmith. One has to wonder to what those three icons of the industry could have created for *Raise the Titanic* if they had been signed up. Lew Grade kept it British with approaching one of England's best loved film composers who could deliver an adventurous score of outstanding quality. What John Barry was to produce became not only one of the most beautiful orchestral recordings ever crafted for a motion picture, but also one of the most sought-after soundtracks for collectors all around the world.

Mr Bond, I Presume?

Barry was born John Barry Prendergast in York, England on November 3, 1933 and was the youngest of three children. His father Jack Prendergast was a projectionist at the Rialto Cinema in York which would give the young John his early experiences of the big screen extravaganza, while his mother, Doris, was an accomplished concert pianist. His father went on to own a chain of cinemas across the north of England

and with his mother's musical flare it was easy to see that those musical tastes were to influence Barry as a youngster. At the age of nine Barry would undertake piano lessons where he recalled in later life that if he played the wrong chord his teacher, Miss Baird, would strike him across the knuckles with a stick. But that did not deter the young Barry from his dreams of being a professional musician. Barry had one drawback in his life in that he had a poor memory. With this he turned his attention away from the piano to concentrate more on the trumpet after discovering in his teens his passion for jazz music. During his teenage years he was still expected to work with his family at the cinemas which benefited him greatly, not only being able to watch the newest releases on celluloid, but it meant that by the age of fourteen he could operate a projection room on his own.

His schooling days were spent at the Bar Convent Catholic Junior School, later followed by St. Peters Public School. Upon leaving, he joined his father again in the family business. But his passion for music was always with him, and his father could see this. Barry reached out to Dr Francis Jackson, organist, composer and the director of music for the Cathedral and Metropolitan Church of Saint Peter in York, more commonly known as York Minister. Dr Jackson agreed to teach the young Barry the fundamentals of harmony, counterpoint and the appreciation of choral music. In this position Barry could achieve his goal of becoming the musician and composer he longed to be. In 1952 at the age of 19, Barry served in the British Army as part of the National Service during the peacetime conscription after World War II, leading him to join the Green Howard regiment for three years. After completing his initial training, he spent the early part of his army years in serving in Egypt where he had his own audience to hand along with fellow musicians who would participate in his musical arrangements even leading a full military band. Following his demobilisation and return to York in 1955, he would gather up some of his ex-army colleagues and with other local musicians to form his band John Barry and the Seven.

In 1957 his father Jack lent his son the sum of £5,000 to move Barry and his band down to London where he could cut a couple of demos to send onto Jack Good, the producer of the BBC programme *Six-Five Special*. Their popularity would soon see record labels such as Decca, Parlophone and EMI reaching out to sign up Barry. It was Parlophone who would sign him up with the first single released in 1957. By 1958 John Barry's music was making an impact in the British singles charts and even at the bands early stage, Barry was being looked at for a role as an arranger. Under the guise of the John Barry Seven by 1959, Barry was constrained to musical commitments working with Adam Faith while still being required to run his own band. In February 1960 Columbia Records had signed up Barry where, finally, the recognition he deserved would spark a period of record singles to reach the Top 10 singles chart in Great Britain following airing on the BBC flagship programme *Juke Box Jury*. With his undeniable flare for composing and arranging, Barry was in popular demand with many record companies. The year 1962 would become the career changing period in Barry's life when he answered the telephone to Noel Rogers, the head of publishing for the United Artists Music in London.

The United Artists Corporation was working on a brand-new film franchise based on the spy novels by Ian Fleming. For *Dr No*, the first in the series of James Bond movies, the film company wanted a signature tune that symbolises the movies main character. At this point of production, they were not happy with Monty Norman's original theme. With Barry's experience with arranging he was called upon to totally re-work the theme. Barry, without seeing a single frame of the film, worked the entire weekend on the track in which he opted for a Henry Mancini *Peter Gunn* style composition with Barry's orchestral flare added into the recording. The characteristic guitar riff performed by Vic Flick was likened by the film's producer Albert R. Broccoli, more specifically the opening few bars. The original Norman riff was scored an octave higher and Broccoli requested it dropped an octave, giving the tune a more ominous feel, which worked incredibly well. Recorded at Abby Road studios the finished John Barry track is as well known as James Bond himself. Impressed with Barry's working style and commitment, Broccoli had no hesitation to get Barry involved with the second Bond movie *From Russia with Love*.

During Barry's long career scoring Bond, it is *Goldfinger* that Barry considered his best in capturing the essence of 007. The soundtrack sales of the film even knocked The Beatles album *A Hard Day's Night* from the top spot in the LP charts. Even being the in-house composer for 007, there was no stopping Barry as he went onto scoring other films outside of the world of Bond; *Zulu, The Ipcress File, Born Free, Midnight Cowboy, King Kong, The Black Hole, Body Heat, Out of Africa, Dances with Wolves, Indecent Proposal,*

Mercury Rising and *Enigma* released in 2001. John Barry's music has always had a certain defining characteristic quality to the recordings that many composers back then, even today, cannot capture. His scores were soothing and poignant with deep basses and strings sections that climb and climb as harmonic tones from trumpets and trombones pierce through with rich tonal charm and grace. Barry was in a unique group of composers who with the aid of his compositions could move the viewer even if the films moving pictures struggled to do so. Barry could make the most mundane scene burst out from the screen with his scoring flare.

During his illustrious career, Barry would receive five Academy Awards, the first BAFTA award for film scoring, Grammy awards and ten Golden Globe nominations winning one for his *Out of Africa* (1986). In 1999 John Barry was made an Officer of the Order of the British Empire when he received an OBE at Buckingham Palace for his services to the music industry. In 2005 he then went on to receive the prestigious BAFTA Academy Fellowship Award. During his time composing for the film industry he did get the chance to appear on screen as himself when he appeared as the conductor of the orchestra for the 1987 James Bond movie *The Living Daylights* which starred Timothy Dalton. In 1975 Barry moved from Great Britain to live in the United States with his new residency in Oyster Bay, New York, alongside his fourth wife Laurie. John Barry died on the 30 January 2011 at the age of 77 from heart complications. Barry's enduring legacy is permanently engraved into the world of cinema and music defining him as one of the greatest modern-day composers of our time. He still remains to this day the composer's composer.

Scoring *Raise the Titanic*: Part One

John Barry's first outing with Lew Grade and ITC came in mid 1971 when he was approached by Grade's company to compose the opening score to the ITC action comedy series *The Persuaders!* that starred Roger Moore and Tony Curtis. With Grade's previous astounding track record of adventure series that include *The Prisoner* and *Danger Man*, *The Persuaders!* was hailed as "the most ambitious and most expensive of Sir Lew Grade's international action adventure series." It is not known exactly to why Grade picked Barry to score *Raise the Titanic*, but one thing is for sure, Grade clearly appreciated Barry and his symphonic repertoire as following the '*Titanic*' project he wanted Barry to work on the soundtrack for Grade's next movie, *The Legend of the Lone Ranger*. Barry came on board *Raise the Titanic* in late February 1980 with him drafting up the score at his New York home with the recording sessions to take place at The Burbank Studios in California. The two main sound stages of the studio sit uniformed within the film facilities that the complex was built for. Opened in 1938 the facility started out as the NBC Radio Networks to branch out into television in 1949 and progress through the decades to become the home of many best loved shows including *The Tonight Show* with the legendary Johnny Carson. With a name change to The Burbank Studio the sound stages were fitted out with the latest state-of-the-art recording equipment allowing for the use of not only catering for smaller musicians but the larger footprint allowed for recording orchestral arrangements for both television and motion pictures.

The *Raise the Titanic* recording sessions took place at the Burbank scoring stage during the period of June 2 to June 13 and again on 7 and 8 of July, 1980, with Barry conducting up to 90 members of the orchestra over the thirteen days of the sessions. The return to the studio at the end of the first week of July was cutting things incredibly fine as the world premiere was just twenty-one days away. At the mixing desk was veteran sound engineer Daniel Wallin who during his lengthy career worked on over 500 feature films. With each session recorded to master tapes, Wallin and music editor Kenneth Hall would layer the tracks together. One studio attendee in the scoring stage control room recalled the time when a particular section was troublesome for the solo trumpet player as take after take was required before the desired recording was approved. Once the entire score had been put to master tapes it was then sent over to Glen Glenn Sound studio in Hollywood for the final mixing and editing into the movie by Wallin and Hall.

The finished soundtrack for *Raise the Titanic* went on to become an entity in its own right that worked as both a score for the movie and also a musical suite that can be appreciated entirely separate from the motion picture. It was that latter appreciation to the score that fans of Barry's works preferred and praised the most, although there is no denying that while the wrecks raising is visually breath-taking, it is Barry's signature tune that ties the whole sequence together. With "Memories" Barry chose to give his *Titanic* the musical emotion signifying the liners once opulent past as Alec Guinness' character reminisces of the grandeur of *Titanic* which reappears later in the film as Dirk Pitt sloshes his way around the sodden interior. One thing is certain, Barry's trademark sounds and musical nuances are present from start to finish including recognisable plucked harp strings that reflect back to the Bond franchise. Barry found the concept inspiring enough to score without getting caught up in the sub-plots of the Clive Cussler novel or the films production from ITC. One aspect of the score which stands out is Barry's understanding of how the subject should sound. For the movie Barry gave *Titanic* two defining signature tunes that are so different in contrast but characterises the wreck between the two stages of the story. "The *Titanic* Uncovered" is a haunting piece that summarises the hellish depths of the ocean at 12,500 feet down as the subs with their crew skim over the sea bed in search for the wreck. The opening bars with the deep basses accompanied by the gentle weave back and forth of the horn section could easily fit within the confines of a horror movie. The string section affirms the excitement of the crews as the sub's equipment begins to pick something up looming within the blackness. Suddenly it changes to a beautiful euphony as the audience is treated to tantalising glimpses of the silt covered ship. Then as the momentum increases and the strings become richer and fuller, we are treated to the grand reveal of *Titanic*'s stern nameplate confirming what we already knew but still eagerly waiting for. This nearly four-minute track epitomizes everything that is *Titanic* as a long-lost wreck and the unforgiving environment that she is locked within. The key to that lock comes with the Barry's second signature track. Simply titled *"Raise the Titanic"* it symbolises everything about the ship as she was in 1912 to her magnificent resurrection and final journey to New York. If *Titanic* had a beating heart it would beat to the rhythm of this joyous and, dare I say, uplifting track.

Missed Opportunity?

Given Barry's impressive back catalogue of film soundtracks, it would appear that the release of *Raise the Titanic* was going to be an open and shut case. There were plans for a motion picture soundtrack to be released on vinyl and audio tapes for the latter part of 1980. It was in London during October 1980 when *Raise the Titanic* had its Dominion Theatre press screening that the score was being represented by the PR department of ITC. In their possession was a copy of the original audio on tape which they passed from executive to executive following the screening. The general census, it would seem, was that upon the success of the production the box office figures would warrant a fully supported release. As the weeks passed and winter began to fall it was becoming all too clear that the poor takings at theatres across America and eventually the United Kingdom had sealed the fate of any possible commercial sale. Even the release of the movie on VHS and laserdisc from 1982 onwards failed to deliver the original score that John Barry movie fans so longed for. But were other factors at play?

 U.S. entertainment magazine *Variety* published an article on the 2 July 1980 on the fluctuating business projects over at AFD. Lew Grade had already committed over $30m in *Raise the Titanic* and its success would pave the way for future releases through Grade's companies. Grade did not stop with television entertainment and motion pictures. He also invested in the music industry, mainly the distribution of recordings. By the mid 1960s, Grade's ATV company had purchased the main bulk of the shares to the British Pye Company; manufacturer of television sets and radios. Grade restructured the company to become Pye Records, a brand name it kept until the late 1970s. By the time that *Raise the Titanic* was in production, Pye Records had been restructured once again by Grade as he merged Pye Records in with his other notable entertainment company Marble Arch Productions to become Marble Arch Records. Through 1979 into 1980, Marble Arch Records and Grade's other entertainment company Precision Records & Tapes, had lost an estimated £1.3m in sales. With *Raise the Titanic* being an ITC/Grade adventure, Grade wanted to keep it typically British with releases of the film on varying medias of the time. As the film faltered on the big screen, Grade went ahead and created Precision Video Entertainment that would cover the UK distribution of the movie on home video sales during late 1981. It would appear that Grade had already thought ahead with putting the films score to records and tape before the film had made it to video.

The score would be covered by Grade and released on his own label of either Marble Arch Records or Precision Records & Tapes. The Dominion Theatre screening of the movie in October 1980 had already drawn up some interest in a potential release of the films score. But it never came into being. Something stopped Grade in his tracks prompting him to drop the release once and for all. While no explanation exists, certainly not directly from the man himself, some hints to his reasoning appear in that *Variety* article from July 1980. As the newly formed Marble Arch Records struggled, Grade turned to RCA Records for help. They obliged and both companies merged to become RCA Records-PRT (PRT being Precision Records & Tapes). With the already escalating costs in bringing *Raise the Titanic* to the big screen, Grade's companies were already facing over £12m in overhead debts. Company records of expenses must have weighed heavy on Grade as new faces came to the table to help. It was clear come mid-1980 that Grade's music industry was struggling. But with RCA now backing Grade, the funds were still not present as the heavy start-up of the newly formed partnership meant that some projects would have to be dropped due to lack of funding. John Barry's score to *Raise the Titanic* became a victim of this partnership decision.

You may be wondering as to why no other record labels picked up the recordings for release. Being bad for business springs to mind. If the company behind the movie is not willing to invest, then that alone rings alarm bells. Grade's track record with starting – then merging – then collapsing companies – did little to encourage others to invest in such business relations. And with *Raise the Titanic* being branded as an over-hyped and over-expensive movie, the jury was still out on if the film itself would claw back the £25m already invested. It was a gamble that many felt was unnecessary and one not to commit too if they saw very little in the way of return. And so, the tapes were put to one side and forgotten about, during which the film proved itself to be the financial disaster it had been envisioned to be. But for some, the production turned into a financial nightmare, while for others it was a lucky escape.

Scoring *Raise the Titanic*: Part Two

As 1980 came to an end an unexpected oddity emerged as the film began to get a positive reception over in Japan. The Japanese love for western produced movies resulted in *Raise the Titanic* breaking box office records for that year to quickly become one of the largest grossing films in Japan. To get around copyright infringements in place as the film was still showing on screens, the Seven Seas record label from King Record Co of Tokyo put to 45rpm vinyl single *Main Theme from "Raise the Titanic"*. Although the sleeve featured a publicity still for the movie, the music within was not John Barry. What was released was a copy of Barry's now much-loved theme orchestrated by Larry Nelson and performed by the Larry Nelson Orchestra. This somewhat obscure and now collectible release was the only release at the time of the films screening that featured music as heard in the movie. While it was not a carbon-copy of Barry's original it was a lovingly reproduced copy. Simultaneously, another 45rpm vinyl single was released on the Japanese record label Eastworld and titled *Titanic Forever*. This rather puzzling release was more of a lament to the disaster and shares no connection to the film production other than the sleeve featuring official artwork from the movie; essentially a blatant cash-in on the *Titanic* subject. The Larry Nelson Orchestra version of the main theme was rereleased again in Japan and this time appearing on Japanese movie score compilation albums between 1981 to 1983 on the Seven Seas label. The first LP to include the track was The Newest Themes '81 followed again the following year on The Newest Themes '82 edition. The track was released yet again in 1983 on yet another unofficial compilation titled *The Great Movie Themes, Volume 1*.

And now for the all-important question. What became of the original studio recording sessions of John Barry's *Raise the Titanic*? Since 1980 fans of both Barry and the movie have longed for the original score to be released. But while the film may not have been the success it was hoped for, the four decades that have passed have failed to unearth these precious recordings. In 1991 an unofficial bootleg release on audio tape of the original John Barry *Raise the Titanic* 'suite' was released by Video Vaudeville in the UK. The suite had a running time of a little over eight-minutes and comprised of the tracks 'The *Titanic*

Uncovered', 'Blowing the Tanks', 'Russian Threat' and 'End Titles'. While the tracks were the original Barry score, they had been re-orchestrated specifically for the suite to blend seamlessly with one another into a single track and done during the Burbank sessions as Barry not only worked on *Raise the Titanic* but also scoring for *Inside Movies* and *Somewhere in Time*. The bootleg release on audio tape was the only time that Barry's *Titanic* score, or part of it, was ever publicly released. The fact that since 1980 no copies have ever surfaced of Barry's original recordings, even during the hype of *Titanic*'s discovery in 1985, the subsequent recovery expeditions through the 1990s and the world-wide phenomena of the James Cameron movie, those studio master tapes never saw the light of day. Their absence over the past forty-years can only signify that they were either destroyed or, hopefully, remain hidden away waiting to be discovered just like the real namesake from the movie.

From my own personal correspondence between the studios that own the film rights and during the 2007 and 2015 periods where I assisted with special features for the British film and television distributor Network on Air for the release of *Raise the Titanic* on disc, the only known recordings that exist in the archives are those consisting of the Music & Effects tracks that form the movies audio tapes. These very recordings were made available to Network on Air where the music score was isolated with all actors' speech and sound effects, with exception of just one track, having been removed for better listening and added to the disc as part of the special features. The end result was that of the only known release of a near complete soundtrack, albeit in mono, of Barry's legendary score for *Raise the Titanic*. Of those tapes which are known to have survived; they are as follows.

3x Music & Effects dub reels: chapter's 1-15 on half-inch tape
UK full trailer m/e on quarter inch tape
3-track m/e 35mm tape
4-track Dolby Stereo 35mm tape

It comes to no surprise that during the films editing stages certain scenes which ended up on the cutting room floor also contained pieces of Barry's score that never became available to the public. These lost-tracks are as desirable as the original studio session recordings. While the released theatrical version of the movie on the 2015 Network on Air disc contains Barry's studio score, these forgotten tracks are still out there waiting to be publicly released. While no written material on Barry or the films score mentions these tracks, it is without doubt that many do not even realise that they once existed, taking what they hear in the movie as the full score. These incredibly elusive tracks did make an appearance in an early 1980 joint twenty-minute promotional film produced by ITC and *Titanic*1980,Inc outlining that coming July real life expedition to find the wreck of *Titanic* funded by Texan oil tycoon Jack Grimm. The mockumentary style feature titled *The Last Great Human Adventure* was used as part of selling the film production of *Raise the Titanic* to potential investors to the Grimm expedition during the release on the big screen of the movie. Four previously unused tracks appear in the production ranging from ten-seconds to over one-minute durations. It would appear that these tracks formed the basis of scenes cut from the final edits of the film. Other than their use in this mockumentary they have not appeared anywhere else since. With the whereabouts of the original studio session masters unknown and without them coming to light following John Barry's death in January 2011, fans can only speculate to where they could possibly be or if these recordings ever survived over the course of the forty-years now passed. Maybe one day the original masters will be discovered, including all the sessions, the deleted tracks and the suite, allowing fans the chance to finally have the definitive soundtrack recording in their music library.

Following the 1999 Nic Raine rerecording sessions of the score for the Silva Screen label, Barry went on to show his gratitude towards the score, the fans and for Nic Raine:

> "I did enjoy doing the score, although the movie didn't get the audience they thought they were going to get. But there was some interesting stuff in that movie. Take the idea of that story; forget about the movie – just the idea of going down there and bringing this historic thing back up to the world; that alone is fascinating! You could write a musical suite on the emotions of that, without

a movie. It's an interesting, haunting theme of a past generation, of something that happened in the world, in the history books. The mind jumps all over those very fertile thoughts of what that would be like, before you actually get into the movie. It's very consoling to think that you wrote something that stands up, whatever that means! It must be something that stands the test of time, as music, or otherwise I don't think that record companies would be expending this money on the actual recording, artwork and promotion."

Boom, Rattle and Crash

With the score complete the next stage was sound design and mixing. Daniel Wallin and Kenneth Hall who had worked together editing Barry's score were tasked with adding the sound effects, created by Ross Taylor, into the movie. The process was undertaken at Glen Glenn Studio in Los Angeles during July 1980 with a quick turnaround as the world premiere was merely days away. The sound effects for any movie is a crucial part of the production if the studios want the audience to believe in what they are seeing on screen. For *Raise the Titanic* a number of sound effects are easily distinguishable; the submersible sonar pings or the booming reports from the explosives used to dislodge the hull free of the sea bed. Those booming explosive sounds originally came from Irwin Allen's 1974 disaster blockbuster *The Towering Inferno* with the FX audio taken from the movies closing segment of when the water tanks above the grand Promenade Room are blown up to release a million gallons of water to drench the skyscrapers consuming fire. But some effects were sourced from other unlikely productions. To give *Titanic* a voice as she hurtles towards the surface to erupt from the depths, she lets out an almost vocal animal-like groan. The effect was not original to *Raise the Titanic* having originated several years before by sound effects artist Jerry Christian for the 1971 Steven Spielberg movie *Duel*.

The production was Spielberg's first main stream movie and was based on the short story written by Richard Matheson. The movie portrays a lone businessman, played by Dennis Weaver, who when driving to a business trip becomes stalked by a psychopathic driver of a 1955 Peterbilt tanker truck who, when overtaken by Weaver, begins a terrifying cat and mouse chase around the lonely remote Californian roads. The end of the film draws to a close as Weaver's character who is now physically and mentally drained confronts the demon truck close to a deserted ravine. Wedging his briefcase over the vehicle's accelerator pedal he dives from the car just in time as it ploughs headlong into the speeding truck. As the car bursts into flames, blocking the truck driver's view ahead of him, it is all too late as the truck careers off the dirt road to plunge over the cliff edge in a cloud of smoke and dust. The slow-motion sequence of the huge truck tumbling out of control down the walls of the ravine was accompanied with a sound effects of buckling and twisting metal mixed in with a long slow chorus of deep growls as if it were some wounded beast in its death throes. The sound was achieved by recording to tape the engine of a dirt track motorcycle being revved up. The recording was then slowed down and rerecorded with additional added reverb, sustain and delay effects. The end result was something grotesque in nature but also familiar to the ear. As the sound reels were archived for other uses, Ross Taylor picked them up and recorded them to tape at Glen Glenn Studios for use in *Raise the Titanic*. The sound effect was not to end with 'Titanic' as the following year it appeared once again in the two-part drama *Goliath Awaits*, a science fiction inspired film about people surviving within a bubble inside the sunken ocean liner S.S. *Goliath* which had been torpedoed during the Second World War.

One frequently used effect was that of a recording of a metal door with its latch being closed with a defining heavy *glunk*! Using the studios editing techniques the audio could be slowed and stretched out according to where it was to be placed within a scene. Another sound featured in *Raise the Titanic* and again later in *Goliath Awaits* was that of metal being dragged and mixed in with the sounds of railroad trucks being shunted. The sound of the trucks cumbersome metal trucks as they begin to move was ideal for the sound of *Titanic* as she begins to shift from her slumber. Recordings were made of metal doors being opened on squeaky hinges and a series of metal components being dropped onto sheet metal that would go on to represent *Titanic*'s hull plates and hull frames as they move and contort during her raising. The final sound ingredient inserted into the audio mix would continue through the raising sequence starting from the moment the hull begins to move from the sea bed to the moment she is fully up on the surface. The continuously flowing low bass rumble is that of a musical note created on a synthesizer with both modulation and white noise added to give that low bottom rumble and a high hissing pitch courtesy of the white noise. A similar technique was used for the earths rumbling sound for the 1974 Universal Pictures disaster movie *Earthquake* that starred Charlton Heston and George Kennedy. This time around it was a shipwreck that went bump in the night.

Raine in Prague

Conductor and composer Nic Raine concluded in 1999 while re-recording the soundtrack, that after all the considerable time that he alone has put into searching for the session tapes, including hours spent going through crate after crate of material stored at Heathrow airport in London, it is thought the original master tapes are somewhat "mislaid". London born Raine is a multi-talented musician, composer and arranger with a diverse background having worked with Howard Blake, Maurice Jarre, Michael Kamen, Elmer Bernstein, Hans Zimmer and John Barry; the latter working relationship resulted in two James Bond movie scores; *A View to a Kill* and *The Living Daylights*. Before turning his attention to recreating Barry's '*Titanic*', Raine had previously tested the waters with his remake of Barry's lessor known suite from *Raise the Titanic* which Raine recorded in 1993 during early collaborations with Silva Screen Records Ltd. The suite had a running time of 8m:27s and consisted of the tracks Barry re-orchestrated during the 1980 Burbank sessions and lovingly recreated by Raine. The track had a public release on the 1998 Silva Screen release *The Disasters! Movie Music Album* in which Raine with The City of Prague Philharmonic orchestra performed a series of classic disaster movie scores including those from *The Poseidon Adventure, A Night to Remember, Twister, Earthquake, The Hindenburg* and a number of other well-known disaster films.

The five-day recording sessions began on the 9 June 1999 at the Smecky Music Studios that is located in the heart of Prague. The scoring stage is highly prized by recording artists for its size in accommodating a full symphony orchestra with choir and the state-of-the-art equipment allowing for high definition recordings. Raine's work with The City of Prague Philharmonic produced an album consisting of the movies 15 tracks resulting in a respectable running time of 50m:21s in such definition and clarity that it can almost make up for the disappearance of the original Barry masters; almost. The recording is without doubt sublime and displays Raine's remarkable attention to detail in recreating one of Barry's most sought after soundtracks. It is possible that during the sessions Raine had to hand copies of Barry's original score sheets as the final product is crafted perfectly in a way that the sessions were not accomplished by watching the original movie and going by ear to score sheet. The score however is without fault as one of two tracks suffer from tempo issues and omit certain Barry'esque tones that are dominant in the films original score. Regardless of these minor faults, this is after all a rerecording carried out with such passion and professionalism, they can be excused and each track appreciated for what they are. Even if John Barry himself stood upon that podium during these sessions it would be highly unlikely that the re-recording's would have been carried out with such note for note perfection as to the original. In late 1999 the album was released on compact disc under the title of *John Barry Raise the Titanic: The Complete Film Score* on the Silva Screen label. It was now down to the fans of both film and artists if the twenty-year wait was indeed worth it. During 2001 Silva Screen released the four-disc boxset *John Barry: The Collection* comprising of 56 tracks rerecorded by The City of Prague Philharmonic and conducted by Nic Raine. Among the wealth of titles covering Barry's established career, *Raise the Titanic* made an appearance in a new suite by Raine. With a running time of 9m:27s the piece brought together the tracks To Cornwall, Dog Attack, The *Titanic* Uncovered, Russian Threat and the films End Titles. The last release containing tracks from Raine's *Raise the Titanic* recordings came with the 2014 deluxe boxset of *The Music of John Barry: The Definitive Collection* that included 7 tracks from the previously released 1999 complete film score.

In 2001 BBC Radio York went on to pay tribute to their famous son with a special live concert at the Grand Opera House of an evening devoted entirely to the music of John Barry. Of the music performed by the National Film Festival Orchestra which was conducted by John Morris, the American film, television and Broadway composer, *Raise the Titanic* got a well-deserved airing with other beloved tracks from Barry's Bond years and those from *The Lion in Winter* and *Indecent Proposal* productions. In 2013 *Raise the Titanic* was performed live during the 4 October Royal Albert Hall concert of *The Very Best of John Barry* where the first half of the performance was closed with the movies iconic main theme performed by the Royal Philharmonic Orchestra and conducted by Nic Raine. While this show was recorded by Raine, it is yet to be released publicly. With the increasing revival of classic albums on vinyl, Silva Screen transferred their original 1999 Prague recordings of the score pressed to LP for a 2016 release. Of their two releases of the score it is the vinyl and the alternative downloads which are more accessible to the public as the original compact disc version is now out of print.

John Barry with the Moviola machine in late 1967. The device allowed the film editor to view the footage during the editing process. *(Author's collection)*

Barry composing the soundtrack for the 1977 EMI motion picture *The Deep*. *(Casablanca Filmworks)*

Barry on the podium during the recording sessions of the James Bond movie *You Only Live Twice* at CTS Bayswater, England. *(www.filmscoremonthly.com)*

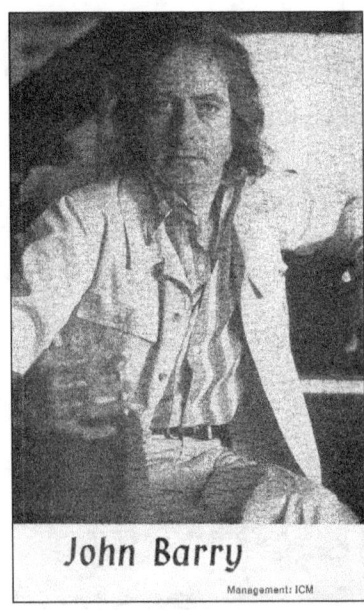

Publicity card of Barry around 1973. *(Author's collection)*

Raise the Titanic scoring mixer Dan Wallin at work on the Quad/Eight Electronics mixing desk at The Burbank Studios. *(Author's collection)*

The former Glen Glenn Sound headquarters in Hollywood where the Barry score and sound FX for *Raise the Titanic* was mixed and edited. *(Author's collection)*

The Burbank Studios in the San Fernanda Valley in the 1960s. The studio today is the home to Warner Bros. *(Author's collection)*

Steven Spielberg's first movie *Duel* would later lend some of its creepy sound FX to *Raise the Titanic* with the ominous animal-like growl. *(IMDb)*

The 1981 science fiction drama *Goliath Awaits* also went on to use some of the creaking railroad rolling stock that was used in *Raise the Titanic*. Co-incidentally, this poster for the TV-movie features an adapted model of the *Titanic*. *(Author's collection)*

274 • *Raise The Titanic*

LEFT: The audio recording of the low rumble of an earthquake from the 1974 motion picture *Earthquake* would be reused again six years later as the background noise of *Titanic* heading towards the surface. *(MCA Records)*

RIGHT: Publicity card of Nic Raine. *(Author's collection)*

Interior of Smecky Studios in Prague where the rerecording of *Raise the Titanic* conducted by Nic Raine was recorded in June 1999. *(www.smeckymusicstudio.com)*

Chapter 21: The Sounds of *Raise the Titanic* • 275

Silva America – SSD 1102

Silva Screen – SILLP319

Test Pressing – SILLP-319

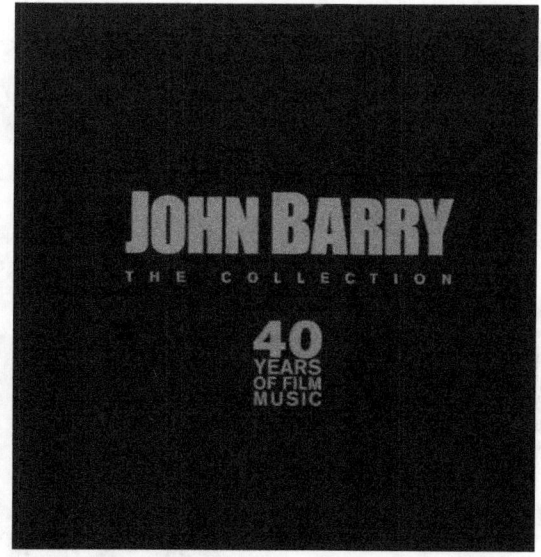
Silva Screen Records – FILMXCD 349

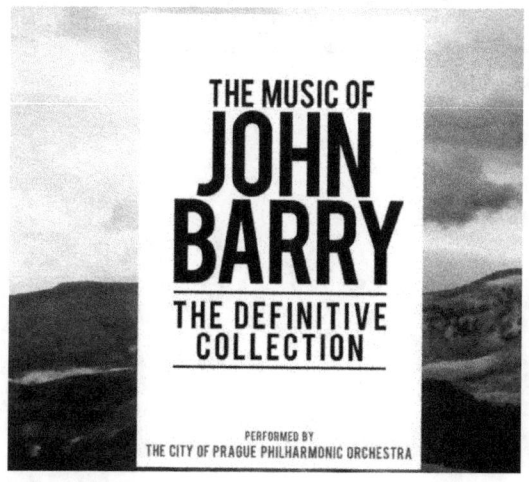
Silva Screen Records – SILCD 1445

Silva Screen Records – FILMCD 301

Raise The Titanic

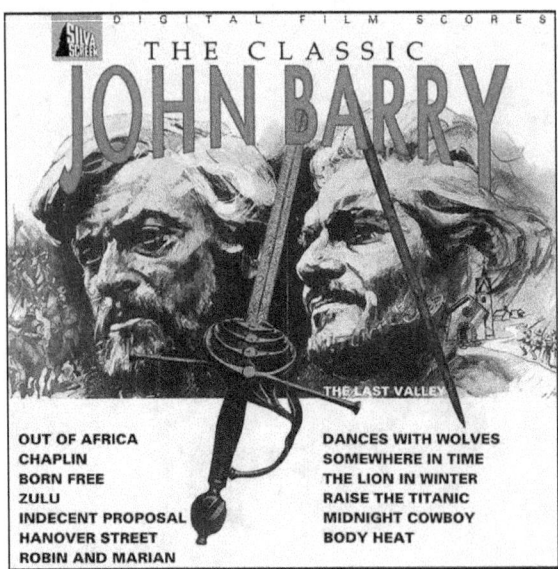
Silva Screen Records – FILMCS 141

Network on Air – Blu-ray 7957070 / DVD 7954201

Video Vaudeville bootleg cassette

Seven Seas – K07S-9003

Eastworld – EWS-17072

Chapter 21: The Sounds of *Raise the Titanic* • 277

Not on Label – DLP 105

BSX Records – BSXCD 8905

United Artists Records – K16P-4035

Seven Seas – K16P-4056-57

Seven Seas – K16P-4031

The Official Releases

John Barry Raise the Titanic: The Complete Film Score
The City of Prague Philharmonic.
Conducted by Nic Raine

Label: Silva America – SSD 1102
Format: Compact Disc, HDCD, Album, Multichannel
Country: United States
Released: 1999
Genre: Classical, Stage & Screen
Style: Modern, Neo-Classical, Score
www.silvascreen.com

Other Formats
Silva Screen – FILMCD 319
Country: United Kingdom
Released: 1999
Silva Screen – SILLP319 [vinyl]
Country: Europe
Released: 2016 [see 2016 entry below]

Track list
1: Prelude   1:58
2: Main Title / The Mine Shaft   3:16
3: The Sicilian Project / Dog Attack   2:33
4: The Sicilian Defence / Southby / "The Mountain Comes to Us"   3:06
5: "We're in Business"   1:45
6: To Cornwall / "All That's Left" [Memories of the *Titanic*]   2:27
7: Deep Quest / Flood!   5:26
8: Finding the Cornet / Spy on Board / The Smoke Stack   4:53
9: The *Titanic* Uncovered   3:58
10: Gene Explores the *Titanic* / Deep Quest Trapped   3:43
11: Rescue Attempt / Blowing the Tanks   3:50
12: Raise the *Titanic* / Deep Quest Saved   3:32
13: Memories of the *Titanic*   2:10
14: Russian Threat / The *Titanic* Enters New York Harbor   2:58
15: "Thank God for Southby" / In the graveyard / End Titles   4:46

Credits
Co-producer – Geoff Leonard, Paul Bateman
Conductor, Orchestrated By, Score Editor [Score Reconstruction] – Nic Raine
Contractor [Orchestra] – Rudolph Wiederman
Coordinator [Release Coordination] – David Stoner
Design – Colin Parker
Edited By, Mastered By – Gareth Williams (3), Ian Shepherd
Engineer [Assistant] – Jan "Honza" Hotzner
Engineer [Digital Recording] – John Luard Timperley
Executive-Producer – Reynold Da Silva
Leader [Orchestra] – Vladimir Pilar
Album Liner Notes – David Wishart

Orchestra – The City Of Prague Philharmonic
Producer – James Fitzpatrick
Soloist, Alto Saxophone – Jan Smolik

Notes
Dolby Surround Encoded
Score of the movie "*Raise the Titanic*" directed by Jerry Jameson (1980).
Recorded at Smecky Studios, Prague, June 1999.
Edited & Mastered at SRT / St.Ives / Cambridge.
Manuscript Coordination: Rutland Music / Tadlow Music.
Score published by ATV / Sony Music.

Authors note: It must be noted that the compact disc release contains a glaring typo on the rear inlay sleeve in that the full track listing consists of 15 tracks whereas what is printed states that 16 tracks are present. The missing printed track number 14 is completely missing.

2016 Vinyl
Label: Silva Screen SILLP319
Format: Vinyl (12-inch format)
Country: United States / Europe
Released: 2016
Genre: Classical, Stage & Screen
Style: Modern, Neo-Classical, Score
www.silvascreen.com

A Side
A1: Prelude
A2: Main Title / The Mine Shaft
A3: The Sicilian Project / Dog Attack
A4: The Sicilian Defence / Southby / "The Mountain Comes to Us"
A5: "We're in Business"
A6: To Cornwall / "All That's Left" [Memories of the *Titanic*]
A7: Deep Quest / Flood!
A8: Finding the Cornet / Spy on Board / The Smoke Stack

B Side
B1: The *Titanic* Uncovered
B2: Gene Explores the *Titanic* / Deep Quest Trapped
B3: Rescue Attempt / Blowing the Tanks
B4: Raise the *Titanic* / Deep Quest Saved
B5: Memories of the *Titanic*
B6: Russian Threat / The *Titanic* Enters New York Harbor
B7: "Thank God for Southby" / In the graveyard / End Titles

Credits
Conductor, Orchestrated By, Score Editor [Score Reconstruction] – Nic Raine
Orchestra – The City Of Prague Philharmonic
Leader [Orchestra] – Vladimir Pilar
Soloist, Alto Saxophone – Jan Smolik
Contractor [Orchestra] – Rudolph Wiederman
Producer – James Fitzpatrick

Raise The Titanic

Executive-Producer – Reynold Da Silva & David Stoner
Associate-Producers – Geoff Leonard & Paul Bateman
Release co-ordinator – Anna Harvey
Artwork – Stuart Ford

Notes
Recorded at Smecky Studios, Prague, June 1999.
Digital Recording Engineer – John Luard Timperley
Assistant Engineer – Jan "Honza" Holzmer
Editing, Dolby Surround Mastering – Gareth Williams & Ian Shepherd at SRT / St.Ives / Cambridge.
Manuscript Co-ordination: Rutland Music / Tadlow Music.
Score published by ATV / Sony Music.

2016 Vinyl "Test Pressing" SILLP 319
Test Pressing white label / Blank white card sleeve / Stickered
Format: Vinyl [12-inch format]
Country: Europe
Released: 2016
Genre: Classical, Stage & Screen
Style: Modern, Neo-Classical, Score

A Side
A1: Prelude
A2: Main Title / The Mine Shaft
A3: The Sicilian Project / Dog Attack
A4: The Sicilian Defence / Southby / "The Mountain Comes to Us"
A5: "We're in Business"
A6: To Cornwall / "All That's Left" [Memories of the *Titanic*]
A7: Deep Quest / Flood!
A8: Finding the Cornet / Spy on Board / The Smoke Stack

B Side
B1: The *Titanic* Uncovered
B2: Gene Explores the *Titanic* / Deep Quest Trapped
B3: Rescue Attempt / Blowing the Tanks
B4: Raise the *Titanic* / Deep Quest Saved
B5: Memories of the *Titanic*
B6: Russian Threat / The *Titanic* Enters New York Harbor
B7: "Thank God for Southby" / In the graveyard / End Titles

John Barry: The Collection - 40 Years of Film Music
Label: Silva Screen Records FILMXCD 349
Format: 4 x Compact Disc, HDCD, Compilation
Country: United Kingdom
Released: 2001
Genre: Stage & Screen
Style: Themes & Score
www.silvascreen.com

Disc 3
10: *Raise the Titanic* [suite] To Cornwall / Dog Attack / The *Titanic* Uncovered / Russian Threat / End Titles   9:27

Composer – John Barry
Conductor – Nic Raine
Orchestra – The City of Prague Philharmonic

The Music of John Barry: The Definitive Collection
Label: Silva Screen Records SILCD 1445
Format: 6 x Compact Disc, HDCD, Compilation
Country: United Kingdom
Released: 2014
Genre: Stage & Screen
www.silvascreen.com
Disc 5: 1978 - 1983

Track Numbers:
7:   Raise the *Titanic* Prelude
8:   Main Tile / The Mine Shaft
9:   To Cornwall / All That's Left [Memories of the *Titanic*]
10: The *Titanic* Uncovered
11: Raise the *Titanic* / Deep Quest Saved
12: Memories of the *Titanic*
Composer – John Barry
Conductor – Nic Raine
Orchestra – The City of Prague Philharmonic

The Disasters! Movie Music Album
Label: Silva Screen Records FILMCD 301
Format: Compact Disc, HDCD
Country: United Kingdom
Released: 1998
Genre: Stage & Screen
Style: Themes & Score
www.silvascreen.com

Track
7: Raise the *Titanic* [suite] The *Titanic* Uncovered / Rescue Attempt / Blowing the Tanks / Russian Threat / End Titles   8:27

Composer – John Barry
Conductor – Nic Raine
Orchestra – The City of Prague Philharmonic

The Classic John Barry
Label: Silva Screen Records FILMCD 141
Format: Compact Disc
Country: United Kingdom
Released: 1993
Genre: Stage & Screen
Style: Themes & Score

Track
10: Raise the *Titanic* [suite] The *Titanic* Uncovered / Rescue Attempt / Blowing the Tanks / Russian Threat / End Titles   8:29

Raise the Titanic *Network on Air* DVD / Blu-Ray Original John Barry Score
Distributor: Network on Air
Format: DVD / Blu-Ray 7957070 – DVD 7954201
Regional Format: PAL Region 2 [UK]
Country: United Kingdom
Released: 2015
Genre: Adventure
www.networkonair.com

Product Contents: Film / UK Theatrical Trailer / 15 Page Booklet / Inlay Notes / Press Material [PDF] / Time-Lapse *Titanic* Photo Album / Jonathan Smith *Raise the Titanic* Image Gallery / John Barry Music Score

Music Score Notes: Original isolated mono tracks of the John Barry *Raise the Titanic* original score.

Music Tracks & Cues
1: Opening Montage 1:55
2: Opening Title 1:35
3: Looking for Byzanium – Jake Hobart 1:30
4: The Sicilian Project – Svardlov 1:30
5: Rescue 0:57
6: The Sicilian Defence 0:20
7: Southby 0:48
8: "Are you talking about raising the *Titanic*?" 1:52
9: To Cornwall – Bigalow 0:25
10: Memories of the *Titanic* 1:37
11: In Search of the *Titanic* – Deep Quest, Turtle & Starfish 1:28
12: In Search of the *Titanic* 1:48
13: Starfish Implodes 1:58
14: In Search of the *Titanic* – Horn 1:24
15: Interference? 1:00
16: In Search of the *Titanic* – "I think we're smelling something" 0:43
17: In Search of the *Titanic* – "It's a Smoke Stack" 1:47
18: In Search of the *Titanic* – "The ocean floor just disappeared" 4:36
19: Examining *Titanic* 1:02
20: Code from Denver 0:34
21: Fixing the Ballast Tanks 3:04
22: Fixing Explosives & Inflating Ballast 4:12
23: *Titanic* on the Surface 0:47
24: Raising the Pennant 0:30
25: Distress Call 0:22
26: End Titles 3:12

Unofficial / Bootlegs

Raise the Titanic / John Barry
1991 audio cassette
Released by Video Vaudeville, Folkstone, Kent (privately produced bootleg)
Catalogue number – no number
One track – *Raise the Titanic Suite* (A - side)

Raise the Titanic (Main Theme)
7" vinyl
Larry Nelson Orchestra
Label: Seven Seas – K07S-9003
Release: 1980
Country: Japan
A – Side: *Raise the Titanic* (Main Theme)
B - Side: *Titanic* Forever

Titanic Forever
7" vinyl
Label: Eastworld – EWS-17072
Released: 1980
Country – Japan
A – Side: *Titanic* Forever
B – Side: *Titanic* Forever (instrumental)

Missing: The Great Movie Themes: Volume 1
Vinyl LP
Label: Not on Label – DLP 105
Country: U.S
B – Side – Track 1: *Raise the Titanic* (Larry Nelson Orchestra)

Titanic: An Epic Musical Voyage
Compact Disc
Label: BSX Records – BSXCD 8905
Released: 2012
Country: U.S.
Track 13: Suite from *Raise the Titanic* (performed by the White Star Chamber Orchestra)

Action Themes '81
Vinyl LP
Label: United Artists Records – K16P-4035
Country: 1981
Released: 1981
B – Side: Track 10: *Raise the Titanic* (Main Theme) (Larry Nelson Orchestra)

The Newest Themes '82
Vinyl LP
Label: Seven Seas – K16P-4056-57
Country: Japan
Released: 1981
A – Side: Track 3: *Raise the Titanic* (Main Theme) (Larry Nelson Orchestra)

The Newest Themes '81
Vinyl LP
Label: Seven Seas – K16P-4031
Country: Japan
Released: 1981
A – Side: Track 5: *Raise the Titanic* (Main Theme) (Larry Nelson Orchestra)

Chapter 22

Raise the Titanic Uncovered

"With the BAND still PLAYING, tiny lifeboats jammed with the people pulling away as quickly as possible, the Titanic slowly up-ends itself and with a ponderous, somehow sensual shudder, it gives up the struggle and slides slowly down into the black. As WE PULL UP AND BACK only the icebergs are left. And the scattered lifeboats and the faint SOUND of CHILDREN CRYING"

Scene 12, Revised Final Draft, August 27, 1979

The following are a mixture of newly descriptive scenes taken from the August 27, 1979 Revised Final Draft of the screenplay by Adam Kennedy and adapted here to give the reader a more contemporary story setting of each scene. While these do not represent the whole film production for *Raise the Titanic*, they do give a general idea of what was envisioned for the film adaptation of Clive Cussler's story.

The use of **EXT** and **INT** represent exterior and interior scenes.

Scene 1-13: EXT. NORTH ATLANTIC – NIGHT

The movies original prologue begins on the cold night of April 14, 1912, as the view opens to a sea dotted with icebergs. Then from the blackness of the night the sounds of a ships bell cuts open the silence, followed closely by the shouts of men, screams of women, grinding and crunching of metal. On the boat deck chaos and panic ensues as passengers are seen stumbling and falling to the sounds of the orchestra playing out on deck. Suddenly, an overcrowded lifeboat filled with women and children gives way as the ropes snap, sending the occupants of the boat tumbling into the sea. As *Titanic* tilts downward the scenes shift to a man pushing his way through the crowd. He is a bearded man, grey hair, in his fifties, short and weary looking. He pushes his way from the deck back into the interior of the ship where he bumps into a crewmember who is checking staterooms for slow moving passengers. The bearded man produces a short-barrelled gun from his jacket and forces the young crewmember to take him down to the cargo holds. When they arrive, the crewmember unlocks the door to the hold. On the boat deck the pandemonium continues as *Titanic* dips lower and distress rockets burst into the sky. In the cargo hold the bearded man releases the crewmember from his duty then pulls a set of keys from his pocket. Finding the right key, he stands at the large eight-foot square vault and unlocks the vault door muttering the words "Thank God for Southby." The final scenes show a reverse shot of the crew member paused in a passage doorway as the bearded man's whisper slowly emerges again, "Thank… God… for… Southby…" A wide-angle view reveals *Titanic* as she upends and slides beneath the waters. With the sound of kettledrums building the view cuts to a shot of *Titanic* as she settles down on the ocean floor. With her hull creaking as the liner rests in her watery grave, the titles **RAISE THE TITANIC** role up onto the screen as the view fades into darkness.

Scene 14: EXT. WASHINGTON D.C., WHITE HOUSE – DAY

In the final edit of the film the rolling title of **RAISE THE TITANIC** cuts to an aerial view of the snow-covered island of Svlardov as Koplin digs in the snow, trying to find the hidden entrance to the mine shaft. Scene 14 opens with Sandecker and Seagram as they leave the White House in Washington. They discuss the problem of the president going public with the Sicilian Project, as seen in the final edit of the film, but this time appearing before the view of Koplin on the Russian island. The scene then cuts to the laser laboratory as they discuss further with government officials using an electronic map and a working mock-up of the laser system. After admitting that they sent a man to Svlardov, the scene then cuts to Koplin digging in the snow while trying to find the mine and its contents. Upon the discovery of the frozen remain of Jake Hobart the scene shifts to Koplin being chased by the Russian soldier. As Koplin is brought down by a bullet the next gunshot takes down the soldier. From among the ice Pitt emerges with his gun. The scene fades to black.

Scene 36: INT. OFFICE

This scene was set at the interior office of the Russian Embassy in Washington as Prevlov and Marganin look through a number of aerial photographs and a map scattered on the office desk. Marganin explains that one of the photograph's has captured what appears to be an American ship with a helicopter flying out from Svlardov, under the radar, and that the passengers on board may have been responsible in killing the Russian soldier.

Scene 37: EXT. ANDREWS AIR FORCE BASE – NIGHT

It is evening and a limousine enters onto the grounds of the air base, passing Air Force One to then pull up to a small terminal area. As a guard salutes, Sandecker and Seagram exit the car and walk through the terminal onto the tarmac where a small jet that has landed. Sandecker explains to Seagram that Pitt had got the wounded Koplin off the island, killing a soldier in the process and getting the job done. As they approach the jet, Pitt appears in the doorway to explain the situation regarding Koplin.

Scene 56-56a: INT. SANDECKE'S HOME – NIGHT

At the private residence of Admiral Sandecker, Pitt is discussing the project in the kitchen following a meal. As Pitt jokes about wanting Sherlock Holmes on the job to help in finding the Byzanium, Sandecker reassures Pitt that he is the right man for the job. Pitt then requests that Sandecker keeps Seagram at distance. Pitt explains that the only lead they have is the dead Jake Hobart and being that he was an army man, any further information would be classified and held in the Army Archives.

Scene 67-68: INT. ARCHIVES READING ROOM

At the National Archives, Pitt goes through the contents of a strong box containing Code Six material. He is watched on by two official looking gentlemen who persist in giving Pitt orders to the length of time he has with the secret documents contained within the box. Pitt becomes agitated with the two men watching over him and so he asserts his own authority making it clear to them that he is there under the orders of General Wiggin and he will take whatever time there is in searching for the right information.

Scene 69: EXT. VIRGINIAN SHORELINE – DAY

Dana and Gene emerge from the house and proceed to walk towards a jetty. As they walk, Dana questions Gene that if she has three worms, she'll catch just three fish. Gene jokingly responds with maths. He tries to change the topic of conversation expressing that the morning doesn't feel like Christmas. As

Dana jokes about him going for a swim, he laughs. "There is life in the old man after all", says Dana as they near the end of the jetty before asking Gene if he would put the worm on the hook.

Scene 74-76: EXT. SANDECKER'S GEORGETOWN HOME

Pitt addresses Sandecker and Seagram on the material he found in the files, building a mental picture of Arthur Brewster and the way the gentleman operated. Brewster was a con-man with the expertise in mining and who travelled the world looking for rare minerals to profiteer from. Brewster was assigned by the army to look for the Byzanium. The army had deemed the ore to be more powerful than radium. He took the money from the army and proceeded to Svlardov. After making a deal with the Russian government, Brewster and his team mined out the ore and sent it on its journey. But Brewster was double-crossed by his Russian contact. In retaliation, Brewster and his team were pursued across Europe by armed Russian agents.

The rest of the sequence in the garden followed to what is used in the movie with the exception of one scene. The three men leave the garden and enter the home going to the library where Pitt continues the story of Brewster transporting the boxes of ore from Scotland down to Southampton. As Pitt explains of Brewster buying a walk-in vault Sandecker makes the connection. Pitt confirms that the vault was lowered on board the *Titanic*.

Scene 80: EXT. POTOMAC YACHT BASIN – NIGHT

This scene was a continuation to the yacht sequence when Pitt, Sandecker and Seagram try and convince CIA Nicholson and General Busby that the *Titanic* must be raised... "Ha! Are you talking about raising the *Titanic*?" With the yacht now moored, Busby and Nicholson walk back to their cars discussing the Byzanium. But Nicholson hints at the mineral's deadly potential.

Scene 86-87: EXT. SANDECKER'S OFFICE BUILDING - DAY

As Pitt and Dana talk on the sidewalk with Pitt joking about trying to fix the world five years ago, Dana questions Pitt about how he became to know about her and Gene. Pitt answers that he tried to keep track of her career with the news offices. Dana excuses herself saying she has to leave for a press conference. The two then say their goodbye's.

Scene 89: INT. COMMUNICATIONS ROOM – SOVIET EMBASSY

Prevlov and Marganin look through a set of photographs that confirm to the two men the story of an old abandoned mine having been discovered on the island of Svlardov. The report indicates that the tools and equipment found within the mine were American, proving that U.S personnel had been there looking for a mineral known as Byzanium.

Scene 92: INT. SANDECKER'S OFFICE – FULL SHOT

Out on the street as Sandecker exits his car, and as Seagram and Pitt clash in Sandecker's office over the president's time in answering "yes" or "no", Seagram continues to make it clear to Pitt just how important the Sicilian Project is to him. As the two men discuss the project, differing on opinions on whom is selling the project to whom, Pitt tries to warn Seagram that sometimes a job never goes according to plan. The conversation is cut short as Sandecker opens the door and steps into the office to deliver the good news.

Scene 97: INT. SUBMERSIBLE HANGER

The beginning to this scene originally had Pitt and Vinnie Walker talking deep sea exploration. Walker asks Pitt to what it is they were looking for this time. Pitt responds that the exercise was to search for a derelict and that is all he can disclose due to the sensitive nature of the project. Captain Burke appears and greets Pitt with, "They tell me you're the boss of this operation."

Scene 112d-112e: EXT. FIELDS – HIGH ANGLE – DAY

After survivor Bigalow has handed the White Star Line flag to Pitt, to then pause with his glass of brandy, the scene cuts to a high angle exterior shot of Bigalow escorting Pitt back to his hired car. As they walk, Pitt tells Bigalow how he likes Cornwall. Bigalow responds in saying that is the reason to why he picked it… to be by the sea. Pitt asks if Bigalow ever feels lonely. He responds with, "All of us end up in a single bed sooner or later". While that scene was cut, the audio was carried over and edited into the footage of Pitt and Bigalow approaching the Sloop Inn pub after their talk on the harbour pier.

Scene 113: EXT. UNDERWATER – DAY

Out of the blackness of the North Atlantic appears the deep-sea submersible *Deep Quest* as it explores the ocean floor at a depth of 12,420ft. Inside are four crewmembers, Munk, Merker, Willis and Woodson. As the sub glides over the sea bed, the men inside are seen at work on the controls and peering through the viewports.

Scene 114: INT. DEEP QUEST

Merker begins to ask to what it is they are looking for. As Woodson responds telling Merker they are looking for whatever is down there, Merker continues with his rant exclaiming that if he spends another week underwater, he would end up talking to the plants. Munk jokes that they don't have any to hand. The conversation is abruptly cut as Willis announces that Pitt has arrived.

Scene 119: INT. SOVIET EMBASSY – DAY

Inside the communications room of the Russian embassy, Prevlov and Marganin discuss Sandecker and his connection to the Sicilian Project, linking his agency to that of a fleet of U.S Navy vessels out in the North Atlantic. Prevlov poses the question as to why Seagram, a scientist, is also linked to the salvage fleet.

Scene 123-124b: INT. COMMUNICATION CENTER – PENTAGON & COMMUNICATIONS CENTER – MODOC

Inside the communication rooms of the Pentagon, Seagram is on the telephone to Pitt who is out in the Atlantic on board the *Modoc*. Seagram insists that the sub crews are looking in the right place based on the calculations from Dr. Silverstein. Pitt, looking towards a map of locations marked off, tells Seagram they have been at that location for six days and found nothing. Seagram hands the phone to Sandecker who proceeds to explain to Pitt they are doing their best. But Pitt is not satisfied and asks Sandecker to apply pressure on the guys and get the right data as, after three-weeks, the sub crews are asking questions as to what they are looking for.

Scene 125: EXT. WASHINGTON D.C – DAY

Sandecker and C.I.A. director Nicholson are in Lafayette Park. Nicholson informs Sandecker that the president has given approval to the Sicilian Project. But the C.I.A. want the Byzanium, regardless. Sandecker is angered by the forceful approach from Nicholson as the C.I.A. director informs Sandecker that they can no longer fool the KGB and that by securing the Sicilian Project, America will have additional powers over the Soviet Union.

Scene 126: EXT. UNDERWATER – DAY

The *Starfish* is approaching 12,200ft. Inside, her crew are throwing out all kinds of banter; from complaining about feeling like guinea pigs, to getting five meals a day for the troubles. Suddenly, they are interrupted by a high-pitched hiss, followed by water escaping with force from a pressure pipe on the submersible's bulkhead. The *Starfish* is leaking.

Scene 146: INT. PITT'S STATEROOM – DAY

Pitt is getting changed following showering. Walker steps into the cabin to see how Pitt is after the death of the *Starfish* crew. As Pitt starts throwing clothing into a bag for a trip to Washington, he turns to Walker. "The only thing I ever hated about sea duty. When the shit hits the fan and you need to get drunk, you can't do it."

Scene 147a: EXT. ROCKWELL SONAR POOL

Before Pitt, Seagram, Sandecker and Dr. Silverstein watch another test run of the *Titanic* model free-falling in the testing tank, Pitt confronts Seagram with a fuller conversation about being out in the North Atlantic and searching the ocean depths, expressing that Seagram and Silverstein are screwing around with computers while for five weeks the sub crews have been searching around the clock and that they are no better off than when they first started. Pitt is angered that his team are risking their lives under two-miles of water before reminding them that the project has already claimed three lives.

Scene 151-165: EXT. UNDERWATER – TURTLE

Deep Quest, Sea Cliff and *Turtle* are running tests as they search the ocean floor. On board the *Turtle* the crew talk amongst themselves, curious as to why they have been told to move to another location miles away. As they run an exterior search light test the lighting rigs suddenly shut down with a bang as the waters pressure eats up the lights. Disappointed to what just occurred, Walker requests permission to surface. As they prepare to ascend, a buzzer in the sub's cockpit sounds, signalling that the subs metal detector has passed over something metallic. Postponing the journey back to the surface they continue on in their search for the metal object. Then, below them, something appears, wedged into the rocks scattered on the sea bed. Walker thinks it is a bell. As Drummer moves the articulated arms over the object to pluck it free, Walker identifies it as being something like a horn.

Scene 168: INT. VOGEL'S OFFICE LAB

Dr. Vogel reaches down into a vat and pulls up a musical instrument. As he slowly turns to Pitt, Sandecker and Seagram, Vogel explains the special nature of this trumpet. In an almost eccentric manner, Vogel proceeds to glamorise the musical instrument, its craftsmanship, its purpose. He then reads out the presentation inscription cut into the instrument. Vogel explains that the name on the trumpet is that of Graham Farley, the trumpet player on the *Titanic*. As Pitt asks for confirmation, Vogel reassures him that the documentation is correct and that the trumpet was *the* trumpet that Farley played as the *Titanic* went down. Sandecker is finally happy that they are looking in the right area. But Pitt doesn't share the enthusiasm of Sandecker and Seagram butting in saying they are not looking for trumpets, but a ship nine-hundred feet long. "Let's locate the *Titanic* first. Then we can start patting ourselves on the back", says Pitt.

Scene 173-175: EXT. ANDREWS AIRFIELD – WASHINGTON – TERMINAL – NIGHT

On the tarmac of the airfield, Seagram is learning from Sandecker and Pitt what C.I.A. Nicholson has done on leaking the information on the Sicilian Project to Russia in the hopes of flushing out a Soviet spy. Seagram is angry. A member of the airfield personnel approaches Pitt to tell him that the helicopter is fuelled and ready for the nearly five-hour flight out to the salvage fleet in the Atlantic.

Scene 177-178: EXT. NORTH ATLANTIC – WIDE SHOT – DAY

It is just after dawn and the helicopter carrying Pitt and Seagram are closing in on the salvage fleet. Below them through the mist of the early day can be seen a flotilla of icebergs. Pitt explains to Seagram the terminology of the graveyard of the icebergs as the ice passes on down through the Labrador Current to meet their death in warmer waters. As the helicopter drops down, the salvage fleet appear on the horizon.

Scene 1982-183: INT – CABIN

Turning from his cabin window, Seagram suddenly drops the question to Pitt about Pitt not saying anything about knowing Dana. While Seagram finds it strange that Pitt never said anything previously, it is Pitt who finds it even stranger that he needed to say anything at all.

Scene 185: EXT. OCEAN SURFACE – DAY

Down in the depths of the North Atlantic the subs are still searching. On the surface, the salvage crews are busy on board the vessels. From an area onboard the ship, Seagram watches the daily routine of life on board the vessel.

Scene 189-190: EXT. DECK – COMMUNICATIONS ROOM

On the deck of one of the navy vessels is a mysterious man. He is hidden within the shadow of the night. In his hand is a small electronic device. A close-up of his hand shows it to be a device like a calculator as the man's fingers travel from button to button. As the view pans away from the man at the ships railing and out over the sea, another vessel can be seen in the darkness some several-hundred metres away. It is the Russian research vessel *Mikhail Kurcov*. As the camera zooms in towards a lighted porthole it reveals the interior of a communications room as an officer sits beside an array of electronic equipment listening to the message as the device next to him records it.

Scene 209-212a: EXT. INT. OCEAN FLOOR – HIGH ANGLE

Following the discovery of the broken off smokestack with control acknowledging Pitt's position of the debris, the scene cuts to the two subs as they continue on across the ocean floor. Bohannon calls out that the sonar has picked up another reading of a large object ahead. Pitt asks Walker over in *Sea Cliff* to what it is, Walker responds saying it looks like a "tank of some kind". Then from the darkness a ships boiler comes into view. Walker calls out "It's a boiler. It's a ships boiler!" The scene then shifts back to Pitt, "I think maybe we're gonna get lucky".

Scene 212b- 212g: EXT. INT. – OCEAN BOTTOM

After they pass by the boiler, the readings then come to a stop. The sub crews continue on with the search. Pitt asks his crew what they think of the following discoveries of the funnel and boiler. Bohannon responds that it's the same old story, "we're picking up apples but we can't find the tree." Pitt radios to control that they are continuing the search, "There's got to be a big hunk of iron down here someplace." Merker cuts in with that the metal detector is picking up nothing, "not even a fish." As the readings are dead the subs are brought to a stop. Moments later the ocean floor gives way in a cloud of sediment.

Scene 219-221: EXT. OCEAN FLOOR – THEIR POV

This was to be the original intended sequence of the unveiling of *Titanic*'s wreck that differs somewhat from was eventually used in the film. The subs come upon the wreck at her bows to slowly move along the hull giving fleeting glimpses of portholes, railings and masts. As Pitt looks out of the subs viewport the faint audible music of "Autumn" (Songe d'Automne), the last known piece of music played by *Titanic*'s orchestra as the ship went down, emanates from the wreck. The scene fades off with the audible electronic static sounds.

Scene 222-227: EXT. INT. NATIONAL GALLERY, WASHINGTON

This scene differs to that used in the film as Marganin exits from a cab, walks into the building and, after spotting Prevlov, takes him to one side to inform him of *Titanic*'s discovery. Prevlov tells Marganin to leak the story to the press.

Scene 233: INT. DANA'S OFFICE – NIGHT

The sequence of Gene confronting Dana about the leaked story differs to what is seen in the movie. Instead of Gene heading on down the building's stairs, he heads for the elevator. Dana tries to explain to Gene about her past relationship with Pitt and to why she did not stay with him. As Gene reacts, Dana angrily defends her position, "If it's not *your* way, it's no way. Is that it?" She continues to explain to the now silent Seagram telling him that he has to live with the fact that Dana and Pitt were once close. Remaining silent, Gene steps into the lift and the doors close.

Scene 234-235: INT. CORRIDOR, OCEANOGRAPHIC HEADQUARTERS

The press conference was originally to be held at the NUMA headquarters as Sandecker answers the press questions on the discovery and planned salvage of the *Titanic*. As he leaves the room, he is followed by the press who hound him for information about the top-secret project by the navy and the rumours of the mineral Byzanium. The scene abruptly ends when Sandecker fails to answer the question put to him about the mineral being more powerful than the Hiroshima bomb.

Scene 237a-247: OCEAN FLOOR

The following sequence was to be a major factor in the movie that was to show the early stages of the salvage operation in progress. It opens with little red lights appearing in the ocean's blackness as a series of portable lights are dropped to the sea bed emitting great waves of light. At the surface from the stern of the naval vessel *Modoc*, a pair of lighting rigs are seen being dropped into the water to start their journey to the bottom. As the lighting rigs open and release their lights, it picks up *Titanic* and the subs working around her hull. The scene shifts to Pitt at the controls of the *Deep Quest* as it moves along the jagged iceberg gash in the hull as Pitt inspects the damage. At the surface great lengths of piping for the syntactic foam are being dropped into the sea and brought down to the wreck site and manoeuvred into position by the submersibles. Pitt and Isbell in the *Deep Quest* are busy placing metal plates over the iceberg gash, welding them into place as the syntactic foam is pumped into the hull to harden. As more hoses are connected and more foam is pumped into the wreck the more water is displaced as it bubbles from within. Above the wreck the *Turtle* works on capping the tops of the three remaining funnels.

Scene 255: EXT. FLOTILLA – NIGHT

It is quiet on board the navy vessels as ship's crew are resting or asleep in their bunks. A static blip breaks the silence. Appearing from the night is the black silhouette of a man who is operating the handheld electronic device.

Scene 260: INT. CAPT. BURKE'S QUARTERS – DAY

In the private quarters of Captain Burke's cabin, Seagram is briefing Pitt and Burke that Nicholson swears the C.I.A. did not leak the Byzanium story, and that it wasn't the Pentagon or the White House, but thinks there is someone on the ship feeding information to the nearby Russian vessel.

Scene 261-262: EXT. MODOC – CAPRICORN - DAY

As more lighting rigs are dropped down to the wreck, crews continue to work on the hoses and tanks for the foam.

Scene 263-263a: INT. EXT. PENTAGON – MODOC

In the Pentagon conference room, Sandecker is in talks with C.I.A. Nicholson who informs him that the code signal picked up has variations of a code used by the North Vietnamese. Sandecker requests a call to be made to Pitt out in the North Atlantic. Onboard the *Modoc* Pitt is talking to Burke about Sandecker putting into place a triple security check procedure on every person working on the salvage project.

Scene 263b: EXT. UNDERWATER

Around the wreck of the *Titanic*, the subs *Turtle* and *Deep Quest* continue their work moving around a piece of complex welding equipment and welding the plates over the iceberg damage. The *Sea Cliff* is also busy handling lengths of hose for the salvage foam.

Scene 263c: MODOC – DAY

Pitt, Seagram and Burke are standing at the stern of the *Modoc* as they watch the incoming helicopter with Sandecker on board. Burke asks Pitt to what Sandecker has found out. Pitt's reply is that whatever it is, Sandecker has "got his teeth into something."

Scene 265-266: EXT. AFTER DECK – MODOC

Merker has been exposed as being the Russian spy. Handcuffed, he is walked to the helicopter. As the helicopter lifts off from the stern of the *Modoc*, Pitt, Sandecker and Seagram look on and begin questioning the extent of the damage caused by Merker. Meanwhile, the weather is changing as the sea become rougher and the wind speed increased, marking the approaching storm.

Scene 267-268: EXT. MODOC – DECK

Pitt and Sandecker exit out on deck as heavy winds batter down upon the salvage fleet. Pitt informs Sandecker that he does not like how the weather has turned, but Sandecker reassures him that Navy Weather reports the storm will pass to the north and miss them.

Scene 271-273: INT. DEEP QUEST

Seagram is on board the *Deep Quest* as it moves over the *Titanic*. Munk asks Seagram about his first dive; "There's no time like the first time. How'd it look to you?" "Nothing like I expected", replies Seagram. To his side is crewmember Willis who interrupts, "It gives me the willies, you know, that?" He continues. "Just thinking about all the people that went down in that thing. A floating palace they called it. Diamonds and gold and women in fur coats. Drinking champagne and laughing it up."

Scene 274-279: UNDERWATER – TURTLE – DEEP QUEST

Down at the wreck, one of the foam hoses has broken away from the hull and is snaking back and forth. *Turtle* informs *Deep Quest* that the pipe pumping the foam into the wreck has blown free during the storm. *Deep Quest* moves in to lasso the hose but the arm of the sub gets caught up in the dancing steel cables to the hose. As the crew put the sub into reverse it suddenly breaks free from the cable. However, the motors have been put to full and send the sub hurtling backwards into a skylight on the *Titanic*, wedging the sub into the steel structure trapping the sub and its crew. Munk radios through "Control… this is *Deep Quest*. We're in trouble down here. We're hung up and can't get lose." *Turtle* comes into view alongside the stricken sub as Pitt surveys the situation. But there is nothing he can do and so begins the journey back to the surface.

Scene 287-287a: EXT. INT. DEEP QUEST

Trapped in the *Deep Quest*, a panicked Kiel says "Jesus… we're up the creek." Seagram is calmer, "No, we're not. Pitt'll come up with something."

Scene 291: EXT. PITT

As explosives are put into containers to be dropped to the ocean floor, Pitt is seen at the stern railing of *Modoc* looking down into the water and muttering "Seagram, you chowderhead."

Scene 292-296: INT. DEEP QUEST

On board the *Deep Quest* the crew are trying to stay calm as the situation gets worse. "It's like we're squeezed in a goddamn vice or something" says Willis as Kiel continues in trying to make the radio work. Munk is repeatedly talking into the mic, "*Deep Quest* to Control… *Deep Quest* to Control." Suddenly lights flicker, a flash of red light and buzzing noises cut the atmosphere. On the heels of the electrical short the cockpit fills with smoke as the batteries leak pushing the crew to don masks.

Scene 297-305: UNDERWATER – SEA CLIFF – DEEP QUEST

Bohannon is at the controls of the *Sea Cliff* as the crew try in vain to free the trapped *Deep Quest*. Using the grappling arm of the sub, Bohannon repeatedly fails in trying to pull the sub free from the skylight. As time ticks away the crew of the *Deep Quest* begin to succumb to the cold as their air supply quickly fades.

Scene 306-310: INT. SEA CLIFF - MODOC

Bohannon is connecting up the explosive charge cables to the explosives that are being laid around the hull of the *Titanic*, linking them all together before he activates the charge. On the surface aboard the *Modoc*, Pitt radios through that they are setting up eighty charges. Pitt explains on the open channel to the subs how to set up the charges and how many to be placed at what locations while demanding they do it within an hour.

Scene 312a-314: INT. DEEP QUEST

Kiel has managed to get the radio working. Hearing Pitt's voice, Seagram takes to the radio to ask what is happening up there. Pitt responds that "Everything's on the rails" and that the odds are on Seagram's side, promising him he'll be home for supper. Pitt then hangs up the phone to give the order to activate the charges. Back on board the *Deep Quest,* Kiel is concerned that they are being left alone and that the others are giving up on them.

Scene 318c: CONTROL ROOM

As the last of the explosives sound off and Sandecker cheerfully responds "Something's happening… Something's moving down there", Walker also joins in, "Come on, you mother-grabber…" Chavaz who is sitting at the control panel shouts aloud "She's coming! She's coming! Sure, as hell!" Pitt responds "Goddamn it… we *did* it."

Scene 318p-318s: EXT. OCEAN – MODOC

As the crew are rescued from the *Deep Quest,* they are hoisted aboard the rescue helicopter and flown back to the *Modoc* where they are greeted by Pitt and Sandecker. Pitt greets Seagram "How'd you like your first submersible trip?" Seagram replies, quoting something that Sandecker had previously said to him, "Things don't always pan out the way you want them to." As *Titanic* floats nearby she is watched by the crew of the Russian research vessel *Mikhail Kurkov*.

Scene 318t: EXT. OCEAN – TITANIC – NIGHT

The weather is quickly changing as the navy vessels close in around the raised *Titanic*. Nearby sits the *Mikhail Kurkov*.

Scene 319-322: EXT. DECK – TITANIC – NIGHT

There is much activity on the decks of the *Titanic* as pumps are busy drawing water up from within the ship. As Pitt arrives onboard the wreck, the storm is now much stronger. He walks towards the stern and pulls from his jacket the White Star Line flag that Bigalow had given to him. Working with the rusty cable, Pitt ties it to the shattered stub of the stern mast.

Scene 323-324: EXT. DECK – TITANIC

Crews are unable to get the hatch cover to the cargo hold open. Pitt responds that they will have to wait until they get to New York where they have better equipment. Sandecker informs Pitt of the approaching storm which has changed course and is now heading straight for them.

Scene 325-326b: INT. SOVIET EMBASSY - ANTONOV'S OFFICE

Prevlov, Marganin and Antonov are watching a news report on the television as the commentator reports "It is certainly the most remarkable event in the history of marine salvage. The *Titanic* has been raised from the bottom of the ocean… and will soon be coming into New York harbour." As the news report continues, Antonov switches the TV off and turns to Prevlov asking as to when he plans on leaving for the trip to the Atlantic. Prevlov explains he will be aboard the *Mikhail Kurcov* and that the plan is perfect. "One way or the other we terminate the Sicilian Project."

Scene 327-328: EXT. TITANIC – OCEAN

The *Titanic* is being pitched about in the stormy sea as Sandecker approaches Pitt asking to where the tugs are. Pitt responds that they, like the other vessels, are fighting the bad weather. Sandecker asks Pitt how *Titanic* is holding up, "Walker say's we're losing a foot or more every twenty-four hours."

Scene 330: INT. SOVIET EMBASSY - ANTONOV'S OFFICE

Antonov is confronting Marganin over a document containing highly incriminating evidence against Prevlov that suggests Prevlov wants the Byzanium for *other* things. Feeling that he is being questioned also, Marganin assures Antonov that his source is completely reliable.

Scene 331-332: MIKHAIL KURKOV – DAY

The helicopter with Prevlov on board arrives at the *Mikhail Kurkov* as the weather intensifies. The vessel's master, Captain Parotkin, greets Prevlov saying that he picked a bad time to arrive. Prevlov replies "The *best* time. We're counting on this storm."

Scene 333-335: TITANIC - TUG BOATS

The two tugs arrive to draw alongside the derelict *Titanic*. One of the tug captains talks with Pitt and Sandecker. The tug captain waves off the storm as Pitt asks about the approaching hurricane, "Due to hit in twenty-four hours." "Maybe less" states Sandecker. Pitt asks the tug captain to connect up to the *Titanic,* but Sandecker suggests that the salvage vessels should leave the area. Pitt insists that the U.S. destroyer should remain behind to keep them company.

Scene 336: ON BOARD MIKHAIL KORKOV

As Parotkin and Prevlov watch the salvage vessels leave, Prevlov remarks "They're making it easier than I thought. They're leaving the *Titanic* all by herself." Parotkin points out that the U.S destroyer is staying. "Not for long. When they hear our distress signal, she will leave too" says Prevlov.

Scene 337-339: EXT. INT. TITANIC – McNAUGHTON

The tug crews are battling the storm as they try to get cables hooked up to the *Titanic*. Over on the navy ship *McNaughton* the radio operator picks up a distress call. On board the *Titanic*, Pitt spots the *McNaughton* moving away and comes out on deck to ask Sandecker as to why the ship is leaving.

Scene 344: PAROTKIN AND PREVLOV

Prevlov watches through binoculars as the U.S. destroyer steams out from the area. As the vessel disappears, Prevlov pans across the ocean to the *Titanic*. Turning to Parotkin he asks the captain to send out the message to Sandecker asking to board the derelict.

Scene 346: EXT. DECK – MIKHAIL KURKOV

On board the *Mikhail Kurkov,* Prevlov gives Parotkin instructions, "If anything goes wrong… if you haven't heard from me by 2100 hours…" Parotkin interrupts, "I know what to do." Prevlov heads out to board the helicopter.

Scene 347-366e: PITT AND PREVLOV

The helicopter lands down on *Titanic*'s deck as Prevlov is greeted by Pitt, Sandecker and Seagram. Battling the winds, the four men make their way to the ship's ballroom. Prevlov wastes no time in getting to the point, offering Pitt and his crew the safety of the Russian ship during the hurricane. Pitt responds with a blunt "no". Prevlov continues to offer assistance stating that once the storm has passed, Pitt and his team would be put into rafts, given food and water to await the arrival of American ships. Pitt tells Prevlov that *Titanic* will ride out the storm. Prevlov changes his tone. He tells them about Russia knowing about the Byzanium, that is was stolen from Russian territory and that Russia wants it back. Prevlov continues his threat with motioning to the *Mikhail Kurkov* delivering an ultimatum that if the *Titanic* isn't handed over then the vessel will be sunk. Seagram questions Prevlov over wanting the Byzanium, but Prevlov reassures him that Russia wants it for its potential to protect the country. "Sure, and the moon is made of green cheese" jokes Pitt. Prevlov cuts him short "You can make jokes if you like. But the clock keeps ticking."

One of Pitt's salvage crew runs into the room to deliver an urgent message. "The weather's coming in fast. All hells gonna break loose." Sandecker confronts Prevlov stating that he knew what Russia were up to and that he has evidence in Washington that Prevlov has been passing information to American intelligence since 1974. Sandecker then offers asylum to Prevlov saying he doesn't have much choice. Turning to his watch, Prevlov replies "But you don't have *any* choice." But Sandecker is the one with all the cards. He guides Prevlov to a porthole asking him to take a look. Between them and the Russian vessel is a U.S. submarine which has positioned itself parallel with the Russian ship. "Like I said, Captain… you don't have much choice." Prevlov knows he has lost. Defeated he exits the ballroom and runs to the helicopter boarding the craft for the journey back to the *Mikhail Kurkov*.

Scene 369: EXT. OCEAN

With Prevlov on board, the helicopter lifts off from the deck of the *Titanic*. But the pilot is struggling with the cross winds. As the helicopter battles with the storm, the pilot loses control of the craft. The engine suddenly cuts out and the helicopter slams down into the sea, sinking out of sight.

Scene 371-375: EXT. INT, THE STORM

Titanic is now in the heart of the storm. Chaos unfolds on board as the derelict is pitched about sending crew healing this way and that. As the sequence fades out, the next scene fades in to reveal a grey day. Slowly we pan across the sea to reveal a battered and listing *Titanic* with the two tugs slowly pulling the raised liner southward towards her New York destination.

Scene 382-383: EXT. DECK – NIGHT – DAY

It is late at night and Seagram and Pitt are walking towards the stern of the *Titanic*. Seagram is holding a paper cup and a bottle of champagne and is clearly drunk. Pitt is not drinking. Both men share a joke or two as Seagram admits that he wants to be like Pitt; confident, level headed. As the scene fades out from night turning to day, there is a sudden burst of a ships whistle to reveal *Titanic* as she is towed under the Verazzano Bridge and serenaded by smaller craft, fire boats and the screaming crowds on the Battery. The *Titanic* has finally made it to New York.

Scene 384-385: EXT. NEW YORK DOCKSIDE

With *Titanic* tied up to the dockside, Pitt and Seagram attempt to leave the ship only to be swamped by press reporters. As Pitt manages to squeeze through, he stumbles into Dana who asks him as to where Seagram is. "I'm not here on business" says Dana. As she walks away from Pitt, Seagram appears on the dockside where the couple then embrace.

Scene 389-394: INT. CARGO HOLD – BALLROOM

As crew members continue to carry out boxes of gravel from the vault, Seagram and Sandecker discuss as to what went wrong. Overhearing the conversation, Pitt steps forwards and picks up Brewster's bag.

He speaks confidently that the paperwork in the bag may give a clue and that they should not give up on the project. Pitt then turns and walks out of the hold. Out on deck Busby, Kemper and Nicholson are walking from the ship and down the gangway. The grim expression on their faces says it all. In *Titanic*'s ballroom, Pitt, Seagram and Sandecker are looking through the contents of Brewster's bag. Pitt is purposely lingering on a picture postcard. As Sandecker gathers up his own paperwork he comes clean with Seagram about the Byzanium and the *other* intensions that it could be used as a weapon of mass destruction. Seagram is in a state of shock. As Sandecker leaves the room, Seagram sits staring blankly… Speechless… Drained.

Scene 395-399a: EXT. INT. SEAMAN'S BAR NEAR DOCKS

Seagram is seated at a table of a bar near the docks. He is slowly getting drunk. Seagram is on a close-up talking, "If I felt the way Sandecker does I never would have started the damned project in the first place. I mean if it's all some kind of lousy game, who needs it?" Sitting opposite at the same table is Pitt. Seagram continues his drunken rant, almost happy that they were unsuccessful in finding the Byzanium. Pitt puts the old picture postcard on the table, sliding it towards Seagram. "It's not that easy. I won't let you wriggle off the hook like that" replies Pitt. Seagram acknowledges that he had already seen the postcard but Pitt pushes him again to look at the fine print on the rear of the card that reads, "A typical country church and graveyard in the county of Hampshire near the village of Southby." Pitt explains that they were wrong. It was never a man; it was a place.

Scene 399b: INT. DULLES TERMINAL

Pitt, Seagram and Sandecker walk towards the boarding area for British Airways. Seagram asks Sandecker if he has contacted the president yet. "Not yet" replies Sandecker. "No point in getting him all steamed up again till we know something for sure." Pitt agrees to call Sandecker from Southampton the following night.

Scene 399c-411: EXT. CHURCHYARD – ENGLAND – DAY

The vintage picture postcard of Southby church yard changes to the present day; the church in ruins and the landscape greatly changed. The graveyard has gone and is now an open grassy area with a granite monument standing in the center. Accompanying Pitt and Seagram is a vicar. "As you can see it wasn't just a bomb. A German plane crashed here carrying a full load of bombs. I'll never forget it. This whole area was like a crater, a hundred meters across and twenty-metres deep. Our parish graveyard was totally obliterated. But we've put up this monument with the names of all the people who were buried here." Pitt and Seagram scan through the names inscribed on the bronze plaque attached. They stop at one name.

Jake Hobart

April 3, 1913

Pitt and Seagram stare at one another. As they shake the vicar's hand they walk away and head towards their parked hire car. "Do you think it was there" asks Seagram. "We'll never know the answer to that question" Pitt replies. "I know we won't. But what do you *think*?" asks Seagram. "I think it was there" replies Pitt. "I think Brewster put it in a coffin and buried it. And it would be there yet if those bombs hadn't blown it to hell and gone." Pitt suddenly starts to chuckle. "What's so funny?" asks Seagram. "I knew a girl once" explains Pitt, and as he tells the tale of how this girl thought he was going to change the world but couldn't, he was out-numbered. "That's it." responds Seagram. "No more lectures. No more lessons. School's out?". "I wouldn't be surprised" says Pitt as they both reach the car, get in and drive off down the country lane. As the car disappears into the distance the view dissolves into a shot of the ocean as the *Titanic* bursts up from the depths to pause at the highest angle as the titles begin to role.

Chapter 23

Production Details

"That's right sir, we can't get divers down to the Titanic which leaves us with only one choice... We don't go to the mountain. The mountain comes to us!"

Dirk Pitt

With all the editing brought about by the concerns of the U.S. Government and the Navy, the films final editing by Terry Williams went on to remove much of the original intended screenplay. What was to end up on the cutting room floor had a profound effect on the movie as a whole. The cutting here and the cutting there resulted in a movie that was almost butchered out of extinction. But while the film was never to be a page to screen faithful adaptation of Cussler's best selling novel; while the extreme nature of how the production team were dealt with from higher management who, in turn, were dealt with heavily by governing officials; while the film ran so severely over schedule and budget and while the film encountered problem after problem; if that is all taken into account, what was delivered was a movie that was never meant to work. But because of all these wrong reasons it became a cult film in itself. And that final cut version which has been viewed for the past four decades has become a firm favourite for many.

THE MOVIE

Raise the Titanic opens with the elegant sweeping theme by John Barry that delivers *Titanic*'s charm in a musical format. Upon the screen a series of interweaving black and white period photographs tell the tale of *Titanic*'s construction, her maiden voyage and those who walked her decks. The images along with Barry's score symbolize the creativity and elegance of not just the ship but that of the Edwardian times without having to show the horror of the sinking that was yet to come. With the screen fading to black and the opening score coming to a close, the mood suddenly changes in an instant as the black screen turns to the murky blue of the depths of the North Atlantic Ocean as the sunken wreck of the *Titanic* emerges from the gloom like a spectral entity. As the view pans across the bow revealing the ships deck, the films logo of RAISE THE TITANIC glides gracefully upwards onto the screen. The music score is full of suspense bordering on a foreboding presence as *Titanic* suddenly disappears to be replaced by the broad sweeping aerial views of the bitterly cold snow-covered landscape of Svardlov. The scene reveals an American mining engineer who is frantically chopping and digging into the snow. His efforts reveal the entrance to a man-made mine shaft leading metres below the snowy landscape. Making his way down into the darkness of the shaft his torch light picks out the narrow-gauge wagon tracks that lead off down the tunnel. With his torch skimming the frozen walls and a Geiger counter ticking away sporadically, he stumbles upon a frozen corpse entombed in its icy grave. It is the body of the U.S. Army man, Jake Hobart, who was sent in to work the mine of its contents to then die in a storm in February of 1912.

The story shifts to Washington DC as scientist Gene Seagram and Admiral James Sandecker discuss the ongoing secret American defence system named 'The Sicillian Project'. For the defence system to work a vital component is needed - Byzanium, a very rare radioactive ore. The last known traces of the ore were thought to have been mined out decades previously on the island of Svardlov. With this in mind, the U.S. government sent in one of their undercover agents to track down the Byzanium. But he gets disturbed by a patrolling Russian soldier at the abandoned mine. As the mining engineer is chased, the soldier opens fire, wounding the agent. Suddenly there is a crack of gunfire, and the soldier falls to the ice. This marks the arrival of the American Naval Intelligence Officer, Dirk Pitt, who has been sent in to get the mining engineer off the island. Back at the Russian Embassy in Washington DC, the Soviets have been made aware of the United States intentions. With the wounded Koplin back on American soil, Pitt repeats the story told to him back to both Sandecker and Seagram. The ore was mined out in late 1911 by a team lead by an American agent, Arthur Brewster, and his colleague Jake Hobart. Now seventy years later what has become of the Byzanium? As Pitt investigates the story, he discovers that the team who extracted the ore were being watched and pursued by Russian agents, leading to a gun battle, and pushing Brewster and the Byzanium to Southampton Docks in England, and its journey across the Atlantic to America. Brewster had the ore with him and he had it put onboard a liner heading for New York. The last report that Brewster sent on to the U.S. Army contained a message reading, "Thank God for Southby", which Pitt assumes was a man, one of Brewster's team members. As for the ship that Brewster and the ore sailed on? R.M.S. *Titanic*.

With the realization that the ore is sitting over two-miles down at the bottom of the Atlantic Ocean, Pitt, Sandecker and Seagram have to face the prospect of attempting the impossible. "We don't go to the mountain. The mountain comes to us", explains Pitt to CIA Director Nicholson, Admiral Kemper and General Dale Busby. But the operation cannot continue forwards without the approval of the President of the United States. Following his meeting at the White House, Sandecker meets with Pitt and Seagram at his office to deliver the news. The president has given the go ahead to raise the *Titanic*. At the same meeting Pitt bumps into a former girlfriend, Dana Archibald, who not only works as a journalist but also is the partner of Seagram. Pitt approaches his former navy colleagues who will assist in the salvage operations. But he and Seagram come to blows when Seagram tries to undermine Pitt by requesting to view navy data. As the enormity of the operation becomes clear, Sandecker uncovers information that one of *Titanic*'s survivors is still alive in England. Pitt heads for St Ives in Cornwall where he meets with John Bigalow, a former crew member of the *Titanic*. Living his retired life in a pub he owns in the seaside town, Bigalow reminisces about the night the *Titanic* went down and tells Pitt about the 'crazy little fellow' with the gun who demanded Bigalow to take him down to the cargo holds. On display in the pub is his *Titanic* collection and the large White Star Line swallow tail flag that he pulled free from the mast as the liner sank. Taking it from the display case he hands it to Pitt asking that if he were to bring *Titanic* back up to sunlight would he put it back where it belongs.

The story now moves to the calm waters of the North Atlantic as a fleet of U.S. Navy vessels arrive in the location last reported by the stricken *Titanic* back in April 1912. In the water, submersible crews have descended into the depths to search the ocean floor, unaware of what they are actually looking for. This apparent secrecy is to prevent the news of the operation being leaked. But they begin to question the motifs of the expedition. As Pitt arrives on site, he spots that a Russian research vessel is in the area keeping watch on the American fleet of vessels. Pitt is certain that they do not know about the operation and will soon move on. Day after day, the sub crews continue searching the depths to no avail. Then disaster strikes when the submersible *Starfish* descends past its constructed diving depth resulting in a breach in the hull. As the sub slowly sinks deeper the crews try in vain to release the subs inner sphere. But it is too late. The sub implodes, killing all the crew. Back on land, a team of marine specialists experiment with a scale model of the *Titanic* in a tank to establish where she may have landed on the ocean floor. It is finally revealed by Seagram that they did not take into account the funnel that broke off as the *Titanic* went down. The missing structure, explained by Seagram, changes the overall streamline of the *Titanic* as she made her way to the sea bed. With the funnel removed, Pitt, Sandecker and Seagram, with the help of the marine scientist Dr Silverstein, watch the model on a video surveillance screen as it descends to the bottom of the tank to land within a new proposed search area. Seagram concludes they have been looking in the wrong place and suggests moving the operations team to a location ten miles further away. Pitt is sceptical of Seagram's findings at first, but the search teams move to Seagram's new position and take to the water, finding and recovering the encrusted remains of a cornet lodged between rocks on the sea bed.

Back in the preservation laboratory the cornet has been cleaned to reveal it belonged to a ship's musician named Graham Farley, who had worked for the shipping company the White Star Line, owners of the *Titanic*. Seagram was positive that *Titanic* was close by and in good condition. Pitt is more concerned to why his crews have failed in finding a ship that is 900ft long. Back at the Russian Embassy in Washington, news has been leaked to them by a spy among the American salvage crews out in the Atlantic. It is revealed that the United States were looking for the wreck of the *Titanic* which contains a rare ore inside her cargo holds that was mined from Russian soil. Now the U.S. Navy begins to suspect that their radio communications system between vessels is being intercepted. Do they have a spy on board? Meanwhile sub crews are back in the water and searching the ocean. Among the team is Pitt who is combing the sea bed some 12,400ft down in the *Deep Quest* and Master Chief Walker in the *Sea Cliff*. Suddenly their sonar equipment picks up something metal in their vicinity and as they head to the location, they come upon a huge steel cylindrical structure lying on its side and covered in layers of sea creatures. They have found the broken off remains of *Titanic*'s once towering funnel. After marking the position, the two sub crews continue onwards into the darkness. As the minutes pass the crews equipment falls silent. Where is the rest of the *Titanic*?

The two subs come to a rest so to recalculate their position. Suddenly the ocean floor directly ahead of them collapses into a mass of swirling sediment to reveal a canyon. Pitt and Walker slowly make the descent down into the trench. Is *Titanic* down here, hidden for all this time? As *Sea Cliff* and *Deep Quest* venture into the deep abyss, the subs sonar equipment and metal detector start to go crazy. Suddenly the needle of the metal detector jumps off the track as the ghostly shape of a huge ocean liner emerges from the darkness. Slowly the subs move upwards over the rusting hulk as their occupants view the video screens in disbelief. The decks are covered in silt. The steel hull is faded, rusted and covered in marine growth. But the liner looks intact. As the subs dance over the wreck, their lights reveal a huge gaping gash in the ships side. It is the fatal wound that brought the mighty vessel down. Finally coming to the stern where the huge rudder and propellers tower high above them, the subs make their slow rise up the hull plates as the ships name comes into view. The large raised letters that emerge triumphantly read; TITANIC.

During a dinner event at the Russian embassy in Washington, Prevlov is informed by his aid Marganin that the American research teams have located the wreck of *Titanic*. Prevlov issues Marganin to leak the story to the media on *Titanic*'s discovery and insists the leak to include 'The Sicillian Project'. Wanting to know about the source to the leak, Seagram confronts Dana who has published the story on *Titanic*'s discovery in her newspaper. As Dana refuses to give Seagram the source for the story, he speculates that it could be Pitt, but the argument leads to Seagram angrily walking off. With the news now public, Sandecker holds a press conference to discuss how the navy plans to raise the *Titanic*. But the press hound him over the leaked story of the Byzanium with concerns it could be used for warfare. Out in the Atlantic, lighting pods are being dropped down to the wreck site to illuminate the *Titanic* in her watery grave. Sandecker has now come on board the research vessel with news on the spy who has been intercepting communications between the navy ships. As the subs work on the wreck, Seagram has joined the crew of the *Deep Quest* to view *Titanic* and help with the floatation tanks dropped down from the surface. But disaster strikes as one of the tanks gets caught up in the twisted stump of the remains of the funnel. As *Deep Quest* pulls at the large structure, the tank comes free and lands on top of the *Deep Quest* pushing it down into the skylight of the *Titanic*, trapping the sub and its occupants.

On the surface, Pitt explains that the *Deep Quest* cannot be freed and that Seagram and the rest of the crew only have a few hours worth of air. The operation to salvage the ship has to be brought forward. Pitt's plan is to place extra explosive charges around the hull which he knows will rock the wreck free. The race is now on to raise the *Titanic*. On the ocean floor, the subs *Turtle* and *Sea Cliff* plant explosives around the wreck. With the minutes ticking away, the sub crews announce they have completed their tasks, and the alert is given to clear the area. As the navy vessels begin to move away from the spot they expect *Titanic* to appear, down at the wreck the floatation tanks are filled with air as the countdown begins. With the clock reaching zero and the detonation button pressed, a huge explosion rocks the hull of *Titanic* marking the first batch of explosives. One by one, the charges burst around the hull, slowly jarring the wreck free from the ocean floor. In the trapped *Deep Quest,* Seagram thinks that sub crews are trying to blast *them* free while not knowing of *Titanic's* speedy salvage operation underway. On the salvage fleet, a computer model recording the progress shows that *Titanic* is not moving. Then two late charges go off and *Titanic* begins to stir. As Pitt, Sandecker, and the rest of the team stare at the monitor, their anguish turns to excitement as *Titanic* begins to move.

Very slowly at first, and emitting painful sounds of buckling steel, *Titanic* begins her rise up from the ocean floor and the journey to the surface 12,000ft above. As she races upwards, she trails huge clouds of sediment behind her. Hull plates pop. Loose metal fittings clang. *Titanic* growls as if alive. Then, suddenly, a huge column of spray shoots clear of the sea and high into the air as the bow of the liner bursts clear from the ocean depths. Sounding like a mythical sea monster, *Titanic* hurtles up and out of the Atlantic Ocean as tons of sea water cascade from her decks and out from broken windows and portholes. As her bow comes down, her superstructure with the remaining towering funnels burst up into the sunlight. It appears there is no stopping her flight from the depths that have entombed her for nearly seventy years. And all around her there lay the navy vessels with their crews watching spellbound at the sight of the mighty rusting hulk of *Titanic*. However, one man is not that overly excited. Pitt is more concerned about the *Deep Quest* and her crew. As *Titanic* rights herself, Pitt calls out, "There she is", as the sub pops up amidst the churning waves and the hatch cover flips open to reveal Seagram and the rest of the crew who are now safely back home and unharmed after their ordeal. With the *Titanic* raised, she makes for a spectacular sight. Her decks are covered in silt and mud. Huge rivers of foaming sea water pour from her decks. Her railings are encrusted with marine growth. Her hull and funnels are stained. But she reveals a sense of beauty unparalleled to anything else.

As the navy vessels draw in closer to the raised liner, one of their helicopters drops Pitt down onto the muddy decks. He makes his way on to the promenade deck and into the surroundings of *Titanic's* once opulent ballroom with its elegant sweeping Grand Staircase. Pitt makes his way back to the stern and comes upon the flag pole protruding up from the rotten decking. From under his arm he produces the White Star Line flag that Bigalow gave to him back in Cornwall. Pitt ties the flag to the rusty wire and stands back as the flag unfurls in the breeze and flies from the stern of *Titanic* once again. Meanwhile, as Prevlov arrives on board the Russian research vessel that has remained in the area, the two deep sea tugboats arrive on scene to help with the salvage operations in towing the rusty derelict. But as crews on the *Titanic* battle with the sealed-up cargo holds, another problem appears on the horizon in the shape of a hurricane. Only one of the salvage fleet now remain on scene. But when a fake S.O.S. call is transmitted and picked up, the navy ship responds and leaves the *Titanic* and the tugboats to sit out the storm. From the Russian research vessel close by, Prevlov makes his way to the *Titanic* to offer Pitt and his team a solution disguised as a threat when he announces that Russia know about the stolen Byzanium sitting in the cargo hold. But Pitt and Sandecker had already anticipated Prevlov's move, and his plan to cease control of the *Titanic*. Pitt escorts Prevlov out to the promenade deck just as an armed U.S. submarine emerges from the sea to protect the *Titanic*. Now defeated, Prevlov leaves empty handed to return to the safety of his vessel and the journey back to the Russian embassy.

With the tugs ready, the towing lines strain under the pressure as the *Titanic* begins to move for the long trip to New York. A couple of days later, her arrival in New York is greeted by thousands of spectators and ships of all shapes and sizes as the rusting hulk is pulled past Liberty Island and up to the

Brooklyn shipyards. Now secured to the quay side, the right equipment can be brought on board to cut open the vault and extract the Byzanium. Down in the cargo hold, Pitt, Seagram, Sandecker, Admiral Kemper, CIA Director Nicholson and General Dale Busby look on as a member of the salvage team cut away the lock on the vault door. As the lock gives way, Pitt forces a crowbar into the door seam and begins to prise open the rusty door. The vault is dry. Sealed tight. Within the gloomy confides of the vault there sits seven wooden crates, and slumped in the corner is the mummified remains of Arthur Brewster. Pitt rips open the first crate. Inside is gravel. Seagram passes the Geiger counter over the contents. But nothing registers on the device. Again, Pitt rips open another crate to find nothing but gravel. Then another. And another. Nothing but seven boxes of gravel. What went wrong? Where is the Byzanium? In the surroundings of *Titanic*'s ballroom, Seagram puzzles angrily over the outcome of the salvage operation and of the lives and money lost. Then Sandecker reveals his thoughts on the Byzanium. If the ore had been found, and with all the innocent purposes that the American government had on building and operating a nuclear defence system in case of war, the superpowers that run the country may just use the Byzanium for other purposes. Not to prevent war but to start war with the aid of a Byzanium bomb.

Gutted by Sandecker's shocking revelation, Seagram exclaims that he is now glad the ore was never on-board *Titanic*, and that the Byzanium was not found. But Pitt, who has been sitting back, and who has been thumbing through the contents of Brewsters wallet to find, contained within, a postcard. As Sandecker leaves Pitt and Seagram to ponder over the operation, Pitt hands the postcard over to Seagram. It is an English postcard that depicts a graveyard. A graveyard in Hampshire. It was something Brewster had purchased but never mailed. On the reverse of the postcard is a publisher's printed caption that reads, "Typical country church and graveyard in the county of Hampshire near the village of Southby." Southby? They had thought that Southby was a man. But it wasn't. It was a place - Southby. Thank God for Southby. The location suddenly changes to that of a wind-swept coastal village and its graveyard nestled high above the white foaming sea. From amongst the headstones appears Pitt, Seagram and two grave diggers. One of the grave diggers stops at a weather worn headstone with the name Jake Hobart chiselled into the stonework. As the grave diggers head off to get shovels, Seagram removes a Geiger counter from his bag and passes it over the grave. The device emits a high-pitched crackle. Bingo! The Byzanium is sitting 6ft beneath him. Without opening the grave, both Seagram and Pitt now have the definitive proof of the location of the precious ore. Seagram now has to make a decision. A decision that could change the future for all. "Do you want us to dig it up?", asks the grave digger. "No!", responds Seagram. As Pitt and Seagram make their way out of the graveyard and Pitt jokes that Seagram has finally graduated as a Professor, the scene fades to the spectacular aerial view over the Atlantic Ocean as the *Titanic* emerges once again to John Barry's beautiful score.

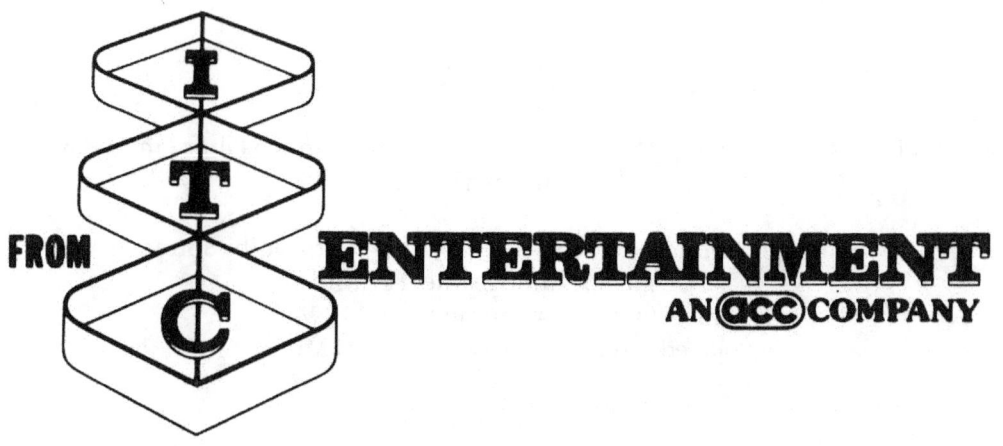

Lord Grade
Presents

A Martin Starger Production

Starring

Jason Robards
Richard Jordan
David Selby
Anne Archer

And

Alec Guinness

Executive Producer, Martin Starger
Produced by William Frye
Directed by Jerry Jameson
Screenplay by Adam Kennedy
Adaptation by Eric Hughes
Based upon the novel by Clive Cussler
Director of Photography, Matthew F. Leonetti
Production designed by John F. DeCuir
Music by John Barry
Film Editors, J. Terry Williams and Robert F. Shugrue

Filmed on Locations in San Diego, Los Angeles, Washington, D.C., Alaska, England, Greece and Malta.

Released by

Incorporated Television Company, Marble Arch Productions, Pimlico Films Limited with Associated Film Distribution

Filmed in Technovision and Deluxe Colour with Dolby Sound
Original Running time: 122 Min
Movie Premiere running time: 112 Min
Re-edited Theatrical Version: 109 Min

M.P.A.A. Rating: PG

Formats

Negative format – 35mm Eastman 100T 5247
Ultracam 35 cameras / Cooke Lenses
DeLuxe Laboratory, Hollywood (CA), USA
Theatrical release on 35mm – 8x 2000ft reels
Theatrical release on 70mm Anamorphic Blow-Up / Six-Track Dolby Stereo

Cast

Jason Robards . . . Admiral James Sandecker
Richard Jordan . . . Dirk Pitt
David Selby . . . Dr. Gene Seagram
Anne Archer . . . Dana Archibold
Alec Guinness . . . John Bigalow
Bo Brundin . . . Captain Andre Prevlov
M. Emmet Walsh . . . Master Chief Vinnie Walker
J. D. Cannon . . . Captain Joe Burke
Norman Bartold . . . Admiral Kemper
Elya Baskin . . . Marganin
Dirk Blocker . . . Meker
Robert Broyles . . . Willis
Paul Carr . . . CIA Director Nicholson
Michael C. Gwynne . . . Bohannon
Harvey Lewis . . . Kiel
Charles Macaulay . . . General Dale Busby
Stewart Moss . . . Koplin
Michael Pataki . . . Munk
Marvin Silbersher . . . Soviet Ambassador Antonov
Mark L. Taylor . . . Spence
Maurice Kowalewski . . . Dr. Silverstein
Nancy Nevinson . . . Sarah Martindale
Trent Dolan . . . Isbell
Paul Tuerpe . . . Klink
Sander Vanocur . . . News Commentator
Ken Place . . . Drummer
Michael Ensign . . . Lieutenant Northhacker
Craig Shreeve . . . Gunther
Brendan Burns . . . Carter
Jonathan Moore . . . Captain Parotkin
George Whitman . . . Beck
Hilly Hicks . . . Woodson
Mike Kulcsar . . . Russian Sentry
Alexander Firsow . . . Sloyuk
Mark Hammer . . . Polevoi
Ron David . . . Reporter #2
Franchelle Stewart Dorn . . . Reporter #3
Jon-Claire Lee . . . Reporter #4
Norvell McDonald . . . Reporter #5
Jim Scopelitis . . . Reporter #6

Gabrielle DeCuir ... Reporter #7
James W. Gavin ... Helicopter Pilot
Bert Drake ... Helicopter Passenger
Nicos Savalas ... Welch
Roy Evans ... Gravedigger #1
Tom Curnow ... Gravedigger #2
Clive Cussler ... Reporter (uncredited)
Steve Moriarty ... Reporter (uncredited)
Milton Selzer ... Dr. Vogel (uncredited)
Garth Inns ... Safe Cutter (uncredited)
Nik Mescherski ... Man at Soviet Embassy (uncredited)

Produced by

William Frye ... Producer
Martin Stager ... Executive Producer
Lew Grade ... Producer (uncredited)

Directed by

Jerry Jameson

Music by

John Barry ... Composer

Music Department

John Barry ... Conductor
Kenneth Hall ... Music Editor
Dan Wallin ... Score Mixer

Cinemaphotography by

Matthew F. Leonetti ... Director of Photography

Film Editing by

J. Terry Williams
Robert F. Shugrue

Casting by

Jane Feinberg
Mike Fenton

Production Design by

John F. DeCuir

Art Direction by

John DeCuir Jr

Set Decoration by

Mickey S. Michaels

Makeup Department
Cherie ... Hair stylist
Robert Dawn ... Makeup artist
Ramon Gow ... Makeup artist (Europe)
Robin Granthan ... Makeup artist (Europe)

Production Management
Malcolm J. Christopher ... Production Supervisor (Europe)
Robin S. Clark ... Production Manager
Dimitri Dimitriadis ... Production Manager (Greece)
Nikos Doukas ... Assistant Production Manager (Greece)
Ray Frift ... Production Manager (Malta)
Richard L. O'Connor ... Executive in Charge of Production
James Potter ... Post-Production Supervisor
Frederick Muller ... Production Manager (uncredited)

Second Unit Director or Assistant Director
Paul Chavez ... Second Assistant Director
D. Scott Easton ... Second Assistant Director
Bruce Hanson ... Third Assistant Director
Mike Higgins ... First Assistant Director (miniature unit)
Michael D. Moore ... Second Unit Director
Roy P. Stevens ... Second Assistant Director for UK and Greece
James A. Westman ... First Assistant Director

Art Department
Larry Clark Bird ... Property Master
Raphael Bretton ... Set Decorator (Washington, DC)
Susan Carsello ... Lead Person
Dick Frift ... Construction Coordinator (Europe)
Hank Kentop ... Supervisor of Construction
Daniel Maltese ... Set Designer
Peg McClellan ... Illustrator
Ian Whittaker ... Set Decorator (Europe)
Ken Zimmerman ... Property Master
Frank White ... Labour Foreman (uncredited)
William Ladd Skinner ... Set Designer (uncredited)
Tayie Rehem ... Scenic Painter (uncredited)
Ken Marschall ... *Titanic* Model Designer (uncredited)

Second Department
Dean Gilmore ... Production Sound Mixer
Robert W. Glass Jr ... Re-recording Mixer
Robert Thirwell ... Re-recording Mixer
John K. Wilkinson ... Re-recording Mixer
Glen Lambert ... Boom Operator
John W. Mitchell ... Sound Mixer (Europe)
Keith Pamplin ... Book Operator (Europe)

Ross Taylor ... Sound Effects Editor
Bill Thiederman ... Glen Glenn P.A.P. Systems
William H. Wistrom ... Supervising Sound Editor

Special Effects by
Ricou Browning ... Model Unit Director (Malta)
John Richardson ... Model and Mechanical Effects Supervisor (Europe)
Alex Weldon ... Special Effects Supervisor
Jimmy Thomas ... Special Effects
Norman Baillie ... Special Effects (uncredited)
Alan Barnard ... Special Effects (uncredited)
David Beavis ... Special Effects (uncredited)
Ron Cartright ... Special Effects (uncredited)
Mario Cassar ... Special Effects (uncredited)
David Harris ... Special Effects (uncredited)
Tony Dunsterville ... Special Effects (uncredited)
John Evans ... Special Effects (uncredited)
Scott Forbes ... Special Effects (uncredited)
Garth Inns ... Special Effects (uncredited)
Ted Koerner ... Special Effects (uncredited)
John Morris ... Special Effects (uncredited)
Joseph C. Sasgen ... Special Effects (uncredited)
Richard Stutsman ... Special Effects (uncredited)
John Richardson ... Special Effects (uncredited)

Visual Effects by
Michael McMillen ... Model Maker
Wally Veevers ... Matte Effects Supervisor (Europe)
Doug Ferris ... Matte Artist (uncredited)
Bob Spencer ... Matte Artist (uncredited)
Tad Krzanowski ... Model Effects (uncredited)

Stunts by
Loren Janes
Ivan Pulis ... (uncredited)

Camera and Electronics Department
Wayne Baker ... Assistant Camera
John Baron ... Key Gaffer
Jack Cooperman ... Director of Photography (full size underwater inserts)
Michael Ferris ... Model Unit Underwater First Assistant Camera (Malta)
Alan Gornick ... Underwater Cinemaphotographer
Bruce Hill ... High Speed Cinemaphotographer (Malta)
John C. Kirk ... Key Grip
Dennis Matsuda ... First Camera Assistant
Stan McClain ... Assistant Camera for Aerial Unit
Patrick E. McGinness ... Second Assistant Camera
Rexford L. Metz ... Director of Photography for Second Unit
Ralph Nelson ... Still Photographer
Louis Niemeyer ... First assistant Cameraman for Second Unit

Jeff Paynter ... Second Unit Focus Puller
Robert Steadman ... Director of Photographer for Model Unit (Malta)
John Tythe ... Gaffer (Europe)
Doug Willis ... Key Grip
Arthur Wooster ... Director of Photography (additional sequences, Europe)
Roland Lenoir ... Chargehand Rigger (uncredited)
David Wynn-Jones ... Focus Puller (uncredited)

Editorial Department
Martin Chielens ... Assistant Editor
Geoffrey Mackrill ... Assistant Editor for Malta (uncredited)

Costume and Wardrobe Department
John A. Anderson ... Wardrobe Supervisor
Dianne Cohoon ... Wardrobe
Babs Gray ... Wardrobe (uncredited)

Location Management
Mike Higgins ... Unit Location Manager
Philip Morris ... Assistant Location Manager
Stuart Neumann ... Location Manager (Washington, DC)

Script and Continuity Department
Ray Quiroz ... Script Supervisor

Transportation Department
Donald R. Casella ... Transportation Captain
Linda Cipperley ... Transportation
Tony Drosis ... Driver
Frank Khoury ... Transportation (uncredited)

Other Crew
Ellen Adolph ... Manager of Production Accounting
Riccou Browning Jr ... Marine Crew
Ron Cook ... Production Accountant (Europe)
Robin Demetriou ... Cast and Crew Chef
Richard Dixon ... Production Auditor
Jeffrey A. Humphreys ... Studio Utility
Miriam Holder Jacobs ... Production Secretary
Don Keach ... Technical Advisor
Don Walsh ... Technical Advisor
Gene Kraft ... Title Designer
Manuel Louis ... Boat Master
Nancy Mayer ... Production Coordinator
Marilyse Morgan ... Production Assistant (Malta and Greece)
Donald L. Nobles ... Technical Coordinator
Stefano Priori ... Location Accountant
Paul Taylor ... Key Production Runner for UK, Malta and Greece
Arthur Wilde ... Unit Publicist
Callum McDougall ... Production Runner (uncredited)

Trailers (known releases)

"The last great human adventure" #1 advance teaser #1 – 1:30 AFD – Released in the United States and selected European territories (spring 1980)
"The last great human adventure" TV spot trailer – 0:30 AFD – Released in the United States (July 1980)
UK full trailer – 3:03 – ITC – Released October 1980
"Impossible Task" 0:30 radio trailer AFD (1980)
"Undisturbed" 0:30 radio trailer AFD (1980)
"God Himself" 0:30 radio trailer AFD (1980)

Release Dates

USA... 1 August 1980
Argentina... 11 September 1980
France... 22 October 1980
UK... 24 October 1980
Finland... 31 October 1980
Denmark... 7 November 1980
Japan... 13 December 1980
Columbia... 6 January 1981
Sweden... 2 February 1981
Norway... 3 March 1981
Portugal... 10 April 1981
Australia... 7 May 1981

Also Known As (AKA)

Argentina... *Rescaten al Titanic*
Belgium (Flemish title)... *De berging van de Titanic!*
Belgium (French title)... *Renflouez le Titanic!*
Brazil... *O Resgate do Titanic*
Canada (French title)... *La guerre des abîmes*
Columbia... *El rescate del Titanic*
Denmark... *Hæv Titanic*
Finland... *Nostakaa Titanic!*
France... *La guerre des abîmes*
Germany... *Hebt die Titanic*
Greece... *Επιχείρηση Τιτανικός* (1981 release)
Greece... *Ανελκύστε τον Τιτανικό* (later releases)
Hungary... *A Titanic kincse*
Italy... *Blitz nell'oceano*
Japan... レイズ・ザ・タイタニック
Mexico... *Raise the Titanic*
Norway... *Hev Titanic*
Poland... *Podnieść Titanica*
Portugal... *A Guerre dos Abismos*
Romania... *Razboiul din adancuri*
Soviet Union (Russian title)... *Поднять Титаник*
Spain... *Rescaten el Titanic*
Sweden... *Lyft Titanic*
Turkey (Turkish title)... *Titanic Macerasi*
UK... *Raise the Titanic*
USA... *Raise the Titanic*
West Germany... *Hebt die Titanic*

Chapter 24

Premiere, Charity Events and those Damned Critics

"The film production schedule has never been stronger. Choice is invidious but if I were to single out one film for a personal mention, I would choose Raise the Titanic. *This was a very costly film which took three years to make and I am hopeful of a very great success."*

Lew Grade

By July 1980, a newly edited print of *Raise the Titanic* was now ready for screening, firstly to the press, followed later by the general release to the public. With all the cutting and editing it had to go through following the personal battles between the producers and the Pentagon, would this edit live up to all the media hype? But if they were to take any notice to all the media stories, be them good or bad, the film was being advertised and generating some interest. Afterall, the public enjoy *Titanic* movies… right? For the run up to the release ITC, AFD and Marble Arch Productions set about with the usual practice of advanced advertising starting in the latter quarter of 1979 as actors came on board with the project. This is a key process with any major film of this calibre, and with a £25m adventure movie getting ready to be screened; *Raise the Titanic* was *the* big film for 1980. Lew Grade had already injected a huge amount of money into the publicity for *Raise the Titanic,* with artworks created, one sheet, quad and day bill posters printed, double sided flyers, four page leaflets, booklets, foldout information sheets, brochures, black and white photographs, colour photographs, print packs with caption sheets, press packs containing information sheets on the movie, press colour slides and campaign press books, trailers, tv spots and radio commercials.

One of the earliest teaser trailers came out in spring of 1980 promoting the film to be the "greatest human adventure" that will treat audiences to the spectacle on August 1 when ITC raise the *Titanic*. Apart from the film's logo appearing at the end over stock footage of heaving seas, the remainder of the ninety-second trailer paid tribute to some of the greatest adventures of the twentieth century. By July, a thirty second TV spot for the U.S. market was released showing a number of scenes from the film. In the United Kingdom, a full three-minute trailer hit cinemas towards the end of September as the November release loomed. Around the same time in Britain, the film was to surface on television during the weekly children's cinema series *Clapperboard* that aired on the 10th November 1980 on ITV. The episode focused on *Titanic* on the big screen from the early 1929 British talkie *Atlantic* to the recent movie release of *Raise the Titanic*. Even ITC got in on the act of advertising their film in their own company-produced magazines aptly named *ITC Magazine*.

On July 23, 1980, the Los Angeles Times printed a quarter page teaser for their readers. It simply read, *"The Year of the Titanic"*. They certainly had high hopes for Grade's approaching $32m spectacular. The World Premiere for *Raise the Titanic* was set for the July 30, 1980. With the press reporting on the build-up to the release, they also focused on the public's reaction to the up and coming spectacle. In America, reporter Andrew Anthos for the *Los Angeles Globe* took to the streets on July 20 to speak with the public as the release date for the film's world premiere neared. And what was the word on the street? It was - *Titanic*.

Special Advance Screening

On the evening of July 22, a special preview showing of the film was screened to a selected star-studded audience at the Cinerama Dome on Wilshire Boulevard, Beverly Hills. For *Variety Daily*, journalist Army Archerd reported on the event for the following morning publication. The audience erupted with "cheers", he reported, "as the giant ship was raised from the Atlantic depths" which was reminiscent of the audience's enthusiasm that applauded during the special screening of the salvaging of the jet liner in *Airport '77*. However, this was no ordinary audience, as among them were some of Hollywood's elite including film legend James "Jimmy" Stewart with his wife Gloria; *The Time Machine* actress Yvette Mimieux; singing screen goddess Irene Dunne; Clint Eastwood and Sandra Locke; and Lady Sarah Churchill, the cousin of former British Prime Minister Winston Churchill. At this time, for America at least, $4 million had been spent to screen the movie come August 1, on 190 screens. This gamble was financed by distribution executive Leo Greenfield who saw much potential in *Raise the Titanic*. "But I've seen *Titanic*", he said, "and it's something else - an *epic*, that has to be made into an *event*."

The World Premiere

Raise the Titanic was never going to be a dull event with Lew Grade at the helm. For the World Premiere on 30 July, Grade opted to celebrate the event with three days of festivities starting two days before the main screening. The venue selected for the premiere was the Sack Cinema 57 in Boston, Massachusetts, that would have gala events before and after the screening. The events kicked off on Monday July 28 with a dinner in honour of Lord Lew Grade that was hosted by Mayor Kevin H. White and the executive vice-president of the First National Bank of Boston, William Thompson, at the banks Federal Street offices with 67 guests on the exclusive list that included Martin Starger, William Frye, Adam Kennedy, Jerry Jameson, Richard O'Connor and David Selby. In town was Clive Cussler and his wife Barbara, who had been specially invited to attend the World Premiere. Cussler was to have a busy couple of days promoting his novel which had been given the film tie-in treatment, and for Clive to spend time being interviewed by a host of reporters for news broadcasts and radio stations. That day, Cussler gave his first interview with Virginia Lucier of the *South Middlesex News* in the elegant surroundings of the dining room to the Ritz Carlton hotel, followed later for a luncheon interview with Jim Randall of *Newstape*. For the remainder of the afternoon, Cussler greeted book lovers at Waldenbooks, signing copies of his bestselling novel before ending the day attending the cocktail party hosted at the First National Bank.

The following morning, Cussler was busy again being interviewed for the local radio networks of WEEI-FM and WXKS, before being whisked away to attend a luncheon event hosted by the New England Broadcasters Association at Restaurant 57, then back out again to attend day two of book signings at Waldenbooks. That evening the Cussler's were picked up from the Ritz Carlton for an evening of entertainment. Starting with a party at the state home of Governor Edward King, it was swiftly followed by a celebrity dinner event in honour of Lord and Lady Grade, hosted by Abraham Friedberg, chairman of Loews Theatres. July 30 was the day of *Raise the Titanic*'s gala evening World Premiere event. Cussler started the day as a guest on the lavish one-hour special broadcast of the *Good Day* show by WCVB-TV.

The event was attended by a number of stars from *Raise the Titanic*; Edward Kamuda from the *Titanic Historical Society* and a live broadcast feed of *Titanic* survivor Marshall Drew from onboard the U.S.S. Constitution out in Boston harbour. At 11:30am Cussler spent the last day at Waldenbooks before heading back to the Ritz Carlton for a 90-minute Press Conference with thirty-one reporters present. At 6pm that evening the ceremonies started with a parade of floats, drill teams, drum and bugle corps, roller skating clowns and revellers who took to the streets starting the procession from City Hall Plaza to pass through downtown Boston to the doors of the Sack Cinema 57 on Stuart Street. As free champagne was handed to the guests, the excitement inside differed to what was going on outside in the street as protesters from the Disabled People's Liberation Front picketed outside the main cinema entrance, greeting each arrival to the Sack 57 theatre to the chants of "Sink Sack or raise ramps. Not the *Titanic*!", in protest over the cinema chain's lack of respect towards people with disabilities unable to access the cinemas.

An hour later and the champagne reception was in full swing as celebrities and dignitaries including Lord and Lady Lew Grade, Jason Robards, Richard Jordan, David Selby and his wife Claudeis Newman, William Frye, Jerry Jameson, Adam Kennedy, Clive Cussler and his wife Barbara, and the Hon. Kevin Hagan White, Mayor of Boston, attended the movies pre-show party as Boston's television network Channel 5's Frank "Bozo the Clown" Avruch entertained the crowds. At 8p.m sharp the Boston's Boys & Girls Club of West End House entered onto the stage for a brief moment to enlighten the audience with a history lesson marking a yearlong celebration of 350 years of Boston, before handing the night over to the World Premiere screening of *Raise the Titanic*. And as the chatter died down and the audience got comfortable in their seats, the first notes of John Barry's opening score filled the theatre as the curtains opened to reveal "LORD GRADE PRESENTS" on screen. At the close of the screening at 10p.m the party was then moved over to the Copley Plaza Hotel for a black-tie dinner event in the luxurious surroundings of the main ballroom as the special guests were treated a dinner similar to a menu course served on board the *Titanic*. After dinner, survivor Marshall Drew gave a brief account of the night the *Titanic* went down using his hand built 5ft model of the doomed luxury liner as a focal point to his accounts. The model, delivered during the day to the hotel, had made its journey, bizarrely, in a hearse of all things; delivered by a funeral director friend of Drew who promised its safe passage to the hotel. It is easy to imagine the disbelief from people who passed by as a model of the ill-fated *Titanic* was slowly disgorged from the back of a hearse. As the evening came to a close, Lew Grade was awarded as an Honorary Member to the *Titanic Historical Society* by one of the societies founding members, Edward Kamuda.

A Tale of Three Salvage Attempts

When *Raise the Titanic* hit theatre screens on the 1 August 1980, the public were oblivious that a longer version existed having only watched the publicly released 109-minute edit. And 40 years later the public are still unaware that other prints of the movie existed. While the editing process butchered much of the production's overall quality due largely to the interference of the United States Navy and government officials, the movie was still undergoing editing right up to the moment the clocks struck midnight on a new day and new month, August 1, 1980. Outside of the studio environment the first official print was shown on the evening of July 22 and the special preview screening at the Cinerama Dome in Beverley Hills with a running time of 122-minutes. With feedback obtained and with the Navy officials continuing to breath down the neck of ITC, the movie underwent another cut stripping it down to 112-minutes that was shown at the World Premiere screening in Boston. And yet, as the stars sat in their seats watching the movie unfold on screen, it was being cut again for the widely distributed public viewings. It is unclear to why the movie over a matter of days underwent such drastic change. But as the finalised cut, the version released publicly, was never shown to the Navy or Pentagon, it may be that the pressure to get it right plagued ITC and prompted a panic response to cut, print and release before any further delays came back to taunt ITC, its board of directors and shareholders.

But what became of these other two longer versions of Raise the *Titanic*? The 35mm print of the preview screening appears to have vanished without trace. That is not to say it is out there – somewhere. That leaves the 35mm print from the World Premiere. That has survived. The print is currently owned by one of the worlds most renowned film directors whose back catalogue of movies never hinted once of any interest such as the subject of *Titanic*. The print came unceremoniously to light in 2017 when it was screened as part of event of 35mm prints at the New Beverly Cinema in Los Angeles and shown on one night only in March that year as part of a trilogy of Jerry Jameson movies that also included *Airport '77* and *The Bat People* from 1974. The Beverly Cinema was first founded during the golden vaudeville era until major changes in 1978 turned the premises into the popular New Beverly where it continued to thrive for the next 30 years. One benefactor to the theatre is Oscar-winning filmmaker Quentin Tarantino who then became the new owner and head programmer to the Beverly and turning the cinema into a venue screening 35mm film prints that started in October 2014 including a bulk of prints from his own collections. Who would have thought that the man who brought us *Reservoir Dogs, Pulp Fiction, Django Unchained and Once Upon a Time in Hollywood* is the lucky proprietor of a unique and very rare version of *Raise the Titanic*?

The Cussler Calamity

During his time in Boston, author Clive Cussler had three days of opportunities in greeting fans at three of the Waldenbooks book stores; starting with the 384 Boylston Street store on the 28 July, next day at 383 Washington Street followed by 3 Center Plaza on the 30th; *Read the Book that made the Movie!!* A designated area had been hastily set up utilising AFD movie posters and a table breaming with heaped copies of the film tie-in of the Bantam printing of his paperback to handcrafted publicity board that read, "Meet Clive Cussler author of RAISE THE TITANIC!" While his time in Boston was eventful during those three days, things were to take an unexpected turn the evening of the film's premiere. As he took to his seat to watch this $32 million big screen adaptation of his best-selling novel, Cussler began to feel somewhat uncomfortable as the movie played out. What he was watching was no longer what he had originally wrote five-years previously. One can only imagine the sheer frustration at seeing such a butchered adaptation of his best-selling novel as the film rolled out before him in a packed theatre. This apparent Adam Kennedy adaptation of *his* novel was now far removed from its origins that the story had been turned into a dishevelled vulture picked carcass. But Cussler remained seated, hoping that, maybe, his onscreen presence as a press reporter asking a question to Jason Robards during the Mayfair Hotel sequence would at least heal some of the wounds. It was not to be. While Cussler appears in several extremely quick shots, his line, "and what will happen to *Titanic*?", was completely removed.

Why did they cut the line? Pacing maybe? That did not excuse what had been previously promised when that telephone call in August 1976 between Cussler, his agent Peter Lampack and Lew Grade, had verbally established an agreement that part of the deal would include a cameo appearance of Cussler along with the author delivering a line or two to camera. Already disgruntled by the first quarter of the film and its removal from his story, the now enraged Cussler got up from his seat and proceed to walk towards the theatre exit, leaving long before the *Titanic* erupted from the depths. The repercussions from his first professional dealings with the film industry were to stay with him for many years to follow.

> "People often wonder why I've never sold another book to Hollywood. My response is 'Not after the way they botched up *Raise the Titanic!*' The screenwriting was simply awful, the direction was amateurish and even the editing was pathetic. Only John Barry's musical score and the special effects were first rate. I'm not looking for a blockbuster motion picture, but I'm hoping for a production of quality, more of a classic then a run-of-the-mill car chase with special-effects explosions every five minutes."

If time is indeed a healer, Cussler was to challenge it when in 2004 he decided to give Hollywood one more chance at turning another of his novels into a big screen adaptation. Paramount Pictures picked up his 1992 novel *Sahara*, the eleventh in the Dirk Pitt series, for a 2005 release. While the film was more on the lines of a family friendly adventure, it lacked once again, much of Cussler's adventurous flare, making it the second film adaptation of his works and the last time he allowed any of his works to be turned into any screen adaptation.

Those Damned Critics

The day after the world premiere of *Raise the Titanic* the film critic's reviews were coming in; and what a mixed bag it was. *Variety Daily* who up until this point had been neutral on the production was quick to explore new depths in sinking *'Titanic'* calling it "the worst of Lew Grade's overloaded Ark melodramas. This one wastes a potentially intriguing premise with dull scripting, a lacklustre cast, laughable phony trick work, and clunky direction that makes *Voyage of the Damned* seem inspired by comparison." Their closing lines did pick up on one interesting aspect of the movie in that since the July 22 special preview screening in Beverly Hills some 10 minutes of footage was again cut from the production. While 10 minutes may not seem like a lot, those scenes that were cut clearly affected the overall appearance of the film to earn such unwelcomed criticism. But the verdict was still out as Friday 1st August would be the day *Raise the Titanic* hit those 190 screens across America. It was hoped that the public were not going to be as devious as the media critics and the film's success would be mainly down to them. It was only early days and so far, excluding the *Variety Daily* grounding upon the rocks, the film was receiving stark reviews courtesy of those early screenings. A few choppy waves were not going to spoil this voyage.

As *Raise the Titanic* surfaced on screen across the U.S, it touched down in Argentina on September 11 followed by France on October 22, and the United Kingdom becoming the sixth country to screen the movie starting on November 14. By the end of October, *The Hollywood Reporter* had reported that *Raise the Titanic* had already clocked up $7 million at the box office since its release date on August 1 and was now being made ready for its first televised screening sometime in 1981. The success of ITC's *The Muppet Movie* followed by its pay TV premiere in 1979 had shown that AFD were onto a winner, delivering quality film productions with *Raise the Titanic* now windowed for viewing sometime between August 1981 to February of 1982. Lew Grade was maintaining his confidence in ITC realising that if his big budget productions were not to be the money earners on the big screen, then there was another output that would generate a healthy income. In Great Britain, Grade had £25m riding on his *Titanic* adventure. His next step was to take the film and turn it into a charitable screening venture on British territories. *Raise the Titanic* had its UK premiere at the Dominion Theatre on the Tottenham Court Road, London, on the evening of Tuesday 28 October 1980. Like that of the screening back in July over in Beverley Hills, this too was a special preview event which included celebrities and the press, all of which was expected to attend at 8p.m for the 8:30 screening of Grade's Film of the 80s. Attending the event were a number of celebrities and dignitaries from film and television including Alec Guinness, Burt Kwouk who played the ever fighting Cato from the Peter Sellers series of *Pink Panther* films, and Robin Askwith, a regular face on British television and film including *Bless This House*, the *Confessions of* series of saucy films and *Carry on Girls* from the equally popular *Carry On* movies. One notable guest that evening who had been specially invited by Lew Grade was surviving 2nd class passenger Sibley George Richards who attended the event with his wife and who had taken the place of his older brother William who had previously turned down the offer to attend.

With stories coming in from America that *Raise the Titanic* was clawing its way across cinema screens, it was hoped that Britain's turn would be more lucrative, considering Grade's dominating presence with television. The reviews fared a little better but still the film was not living up to the expectations; "The characters may be as interesting as barnacles but what saves it from plunging to the bottom are the special effects" wrote *Daily Mirror* film columnist Arthur Thirkell. That weekend marked the start of winter, but as the days were to pass, *Raise the Titanic* started to suffer a cold reception as Grade's British fan base delivered a less enthusiastic reaction to the film. *Daily Star*'s showbiz reporter hailed the film with a simple headline grabbing "Abandon Script!" to then proceed with some positivity of "when Oscar time comes, the film's special effects wizards should be at the head of the queue", while concluding that the films ending may not have been seen if the audience had "sat through enough and taken to the lifeboats." Christopher Hudson writing for *The New Standard* remarked that the film "has a plot almost as splendidly idiotic" that even school children would find fault with it. Of course, the films special effects all came good if somewhat questionable as to why "not a single skeleton on board to satisfy our curiosity about the 1500 passengers and crew". He must have abandoned ship early to have missed the opening of the vault that contained the mummified remains of passenger Arthur Brewster. *The Guardian* was no better with slating Grade's "expensive non-answer to the problems of the British film industry." And if that wasn't enough, they closed with, "The rest, however, is exceedingly lumpen dross in which inept characterisation and a no-hope script are compounded by a complete lack of cinematic flair." Even the *Financial Times* questioned whether or not Michael Caine had been offered a part as it was right up his street; a cheeky dig at Caine's 1979 previous outing in Irwin Allen's less than ambitious *Beyond the Poseidon Adventure*.

There was something about the movie that attracted so much negativity to draw in reviews across the board that just didn't give the film any credit. It was almost becoming like an epidemic. Writing for the *Daily Express*, Ian Christie slammed *Raise the Titanic* with "If you find major disasters awe-inspiring you will no doubt be impressed by *Raise the Titanic*." Not so bad? He continues, "After all, it isn't every day you walk into a cinema and see $35 million go down the drain before your very eyes." The *Sunday Telegraph* went on to inquire if the $35 million cost was down to sheer expense of the water rates for filling up the tank in Malta? The American reviews were no better as the film coursed across the states. *The New York Times* questioned that if you take the adventure out of an adventure what are you left with? Kathleen Carroll for the New York *Daily News* remarked, "*Raise the Titanic* is the kind of movie that appeals mainly to gadget lovers and mechanical nuts who don't mind when the camera does nothing but pan across the impressive array of equipment, accompanied by the soothing music of John Barry." The *Evening Outlook* newspaper of Utah labelled the movie as a "*Titanic* film a disaster... It looks like bad acting, but it's not exactly. It's just non-acting." while the *Detroit Free Press* went with "*Raise the Titanic* is on its way back down." Interestingly enough the reviewer did point out in an almost apologetic way that "*Titanic* broke in two before it sank, and thus could not be raised whole." The *Providence Journal Bulletin* emphasized that the "movie about raising *Titanic* is unsalvageable as ship itself" while the *Houston Chronicle* cheekily referred to the film as a film that would increase popcorn sales as movie-goers would be driven into the theatre lobby to stock up on the snack *during* the screening.

But not all of it resembled a mid-Atlantic shipwreck. Dotted among the reviews came the odd tangible signs that some did take to the film. The *Birmingham News* of Alabama reported that despite the film's flaws, *Raise the Titanic* was a "grand family entertainment." and *The Indianapolis News* proudly claimed "*Raise the Titanic* an exciting film." One of the most prominent of those came from Margaret Hinxman for the *Daily Mail* with, "fifteen minutes I wouldn't have missed for anything". While she agreed that Adam Kennedy's script should have had more of the films multi-million-dollar budget thrown its way, she did positively note on the films raising sequence, "The whole operation takes about 15 minutes on the screen and it's worth seeing the film for that spectacle alone... I wouldn't have missed the sight of the barnacled empress of the sea nosing out of the water for anything." But of all the reviews published in Great Britain during November 1980, if there ever were an award for The Most Mundane Movie Review, then it would have gone to the *News of the World* with their "*Raise the Titanic*. What deadly secret did the giant liner take to the sea bed 68 years ago? Special agent Richard Jordan fights the terrors of the Atlantic in this action-packed drama." Did they watch another film?

Let's hear it for Old Ben

That November, regardless of how the film was doing in theatres, *Raise the Titanic* was going to end the year in style. It was decided that London would make for a good setting to raise money in aid of the Newsvendors Benevolent Institution; more commonly known as "Old Ben". Founded in Great Britain in 1835, with one of its presidents being Charles Dickens who chaired the charity between the years 1854 to 1870, the purpose of Old Ben was to assist in the time of need the elderly, widows, orphans and the sick as long as they had a link to the newspaper or magazine distribution around the city by helping in the form of grants, allowances and low-cost retirement housing. The location for the charity event was to be the prestigious 400-seater Leicester Square Theatre with *Raise the Titanic* as the fund-raising spectacle. The event would take place on the 12 November and screened in glorious 70mm Dolby stereo. Tickets for the event came in four price categories of £5, £10, £25 and £40 with all proceeds from the event going to Fleet Street for Old Ben. For the occasion the front of the theatre was dressed with the usual one sheet posters and front of house lobby cards while above the main doors a sat a large 40ft x 4ft illuminated signage board bearing the films title along with the leading actors names. But the most impressive display was mounted above the main entrance. It was a monstrous illuminated double layered artwork of the *Titanic* as she bursts up from the ocean in a composite style. From any angle the front of the theatre with that huge dominating glowing artwork looked spectacular and it could not have failed to impress.

What was equally impressive were the sponsors for this special occasion that included the cream of British businesses with such famous companies and brands as Stanley Tools, C&A, gin manufacturer Gordons, Radio Rentals, London Weekend Television, TV Times, Readers Digest, Debenhams, electrical giant Philips, Granada TV Rental, The Daily Telegraph and the Mirror Group of newspapers, Radio Times, Currys electrical retailers, The Guardian, Trusthouse Forte Hotels, furniture giants MFI, Financial Times, Dixons electrical retailers and the high street giant W.H. Smith. Their contributions to the cause made for more than a special night. While many proclaimed Lew Grade's *Raise the Titanic* had met an early watery grave, the wake from this *Titanic* adventure was to last a life time for many. Two days later, *Raise the Titanic* went on to have its UK nationwide release.

... meanwhile in Malta

One last charity event was to take place in Malta as *Raise the Titanic* was to be screened at the Plaza Cinema, Sliema, Malta. The special screening was organised by Moyra Mintoff, chairman of the Community Chest Fund, who appealed to the public to patronize the premiere of the movie to help raise funds for charitable causes. The evening of Friday November 21, 1980 was chosen with an 8: 30p.m viewing in the presence of the Prime Minister and Allen Keen, Managing Director of ITC. During the event a series of prizes were offered up for raffle with musical entertainment courtesy of local acts Joe Cutajar and The Falconers. All proceeds raised during the event were passed onto the selected charity organisations for equal distribution.

CANADIAN DISTRIBUTORS FOR:
TWENTIETH CENTURY-FOX CORPORATION LTD.
ASSOCIATED FILM DISTRIBUTION

BelleVue
Film Distributors Limited

HEAD OFFICE
277 VICTORIA STREET
TORONTO, ONTARIO M5B 1W6
TELEPHONE (416) 869-5949
TELEX: 06-22041

On April 14, 1912 the "unsinkable" White Star Liner Titanic struck an iceberg off the Grand Banks of Newfoundland and sank. Fifteen hundred people and a fortune estimated to be worth $250 million were lost with her. It has been the dream of many men to raise the glorious ship which lies at the bottom of the ocean - 12,500 feet below the surface. Now, Lord Grade present a Martin Starger production of "RAISE THE TITANIC", based on Clive Cussler's best selling novel.

"RAISE THE TITANIC", starring Jason Robards, Richard Jordan, David Selby, Ann Archer and Alec Guiness, will open at Canadian Odeon and other selected theatres on August 1, 1980, (August 29th in Montreal).

Please contact your local Canadian Odeon District Manager for theatres and times. If you should require additional information, please do not hesitate to contact Mary-Pat Gleeson, Director of Publicity/Promotion, AFD (Associated Film Distribution) in Toronto at 416-593-2021.

WINNIPEG, MAN.
20 STEVENSON ROAD
TEL. (204) 633-9411

MONTREAL, QUE.
250 ROSE DE LIMA STREET
TEL. (514) 935-6377

SAINT JOHN, N.B.
55 BENTLEY STREET
TEL. (506) 657-2610

CALGARY ALTA.
3904 - 1ST STREET N.E.
TEL. (403) 276-8601

VANCOUVER, B.C.
1644 WEST 75th AVENUE
TEL. (604) 263-2494

Early summer of 1980 and with July fast approaching, ITC and AFD ramped up the publicity for *Raise the Titanic*. This film production letter was distributed in Canada through Belle Vue on behalf of Twentieth Century Fox via AFD. *(Author's collection)*

Chapter 24: Premiere, Charity Events and those Damned Critics • 317

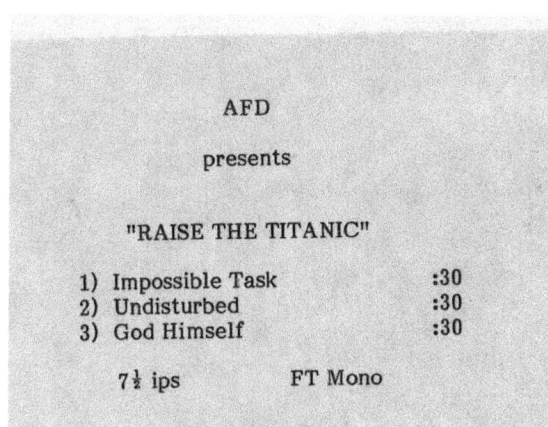

Original ¼ inch radio station audio tape featuring 3x 30 second audio trailers for *Raise the Titanic*. (Author's collection)

In the weeks leading up to the World Premiere, AFD began an advertising campaign aimed towards the public with the chance of one lucky winner of a competition bagging a brand new Alcort Sunfish sailboat. (Author's collection)

Sacks newspaper teaser leading up to their World Premiere screening. (Author's collection)

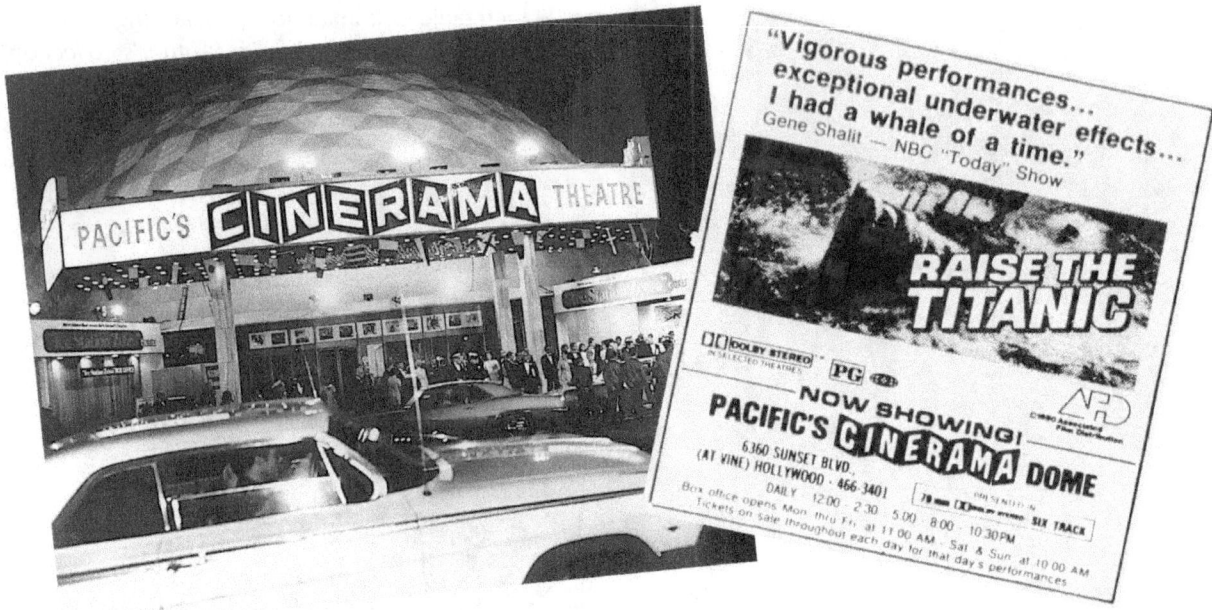

The prestigious Cinerama Dome, pictured here during the screening of *Ice Station Zebra* in 1969, would become the theatre to screen the star-studded special screening of *Raise the Titanic*. *(Author's collection)*

Hollywood legend James Stewart is accompanied by his wife Gloria to the star-studded special screening of *Raise the Titanic* at the Cinerama Dome. *(Los Angeles Times, August 8, 1980 – Author's collection)*

Leo Greenfield; Senior Vice-President, Marketing and Distribution in the United States for AFD. *(ITC – Author's collection)*

Chapter 24: Premiere, Charity Events and those Damned Critics • 319

~~Travelling~~ lling with John Markle   CAR # 5

SACK THEATRES

REVISION #1   7/17/80

Executive Offices
141 Tremont Street
Boston, Massachusetts 02111
(617) 542-3334

ASSOCIATED FILM DISTRIBUTION

"RAISE THE TITANIC"
****

Clive Cussler

Accommodations· Ground Transportation:	Ritz Carlton Hotel	(536-5700)
	Executive Service	(926-1600)

Monday, July 28, 1980

10·30-11.30 a.m.	South Middlesex News interview with Virgina Lucier (872-4321) Ritz Carlton Hotel, Main Dining Room
12-1:30 p.m.	Luncheon interview with Jim Randall of "Newstape" (893-7652) Ritz Carlton Main Dining Room
1:45-3:15	Bookstore Appearance: Waldenbooks 384 Boylston St., Boston
7·00 p.m.	Cocktails and Dinner hosted by Mayor Kevin H. White and William Thompson of the First National Bank, 100 Federal St.

Tuesday, July 29, 1980

10-10.30 a.m.	WEEI-FM interview with Nat Segaloff (262-5900) Hotel Suite
10:45-11·15 a.m.	WXKS interview with Joan Quinn Eastman (396-1430) Hotel Suite
12.00 - 2:00 p.m.	Luncheon hosted by New England Broadcasters Association 57 Restaurant, 200 Stuart Street, Boston
1:45-3:15 p.m.	Bookstore Appearance: Waldenbooks 383 Washington St., Boston
5·30-7.00 p.m.	Cocktail Reception hosted by Governor Edward King State House
7:30 p.m.	Dinner hosted by Mr. & Mrs. A. Alan Friedberg 42 Chestnut Street, Boston

(Continued on the next page)

Saxon Theatre Corp. of Boston—Saxon Distributing Corp.—Beacon Hill Theatre, Inc.—Boston Music Hall, Inc.
Sack Cheri Inc.—Sack Cheri II, Inc.—Sack Cheri III, Inc.   Subsidiaries of Cadence Industries Corporation

Part of Cussler's 2-page attending events list between the dates of 28 to 30 July. *(Author's collection)*

320 • *Raise The Titanic*

Clive Cussler's personal invitation pack sent to him for the attendance to the World Premiere of the movie, and to carry out a number of bookstore signings, radio and television interviews and special dinner party events. *(Author's collection)*

Bantam Books publishing campaign advertisement covering the film tie-in book and Cussler's other novels, *Iceberg*, *Vixen 03* and *The Mediterranean Caper*. *(Author's collection)*

Chapter 24: Premiere, Charity Events and those Damned Critics • **321**

Polaroid of Clive Cussler's *Raise the Titanic* book signing display at Waldenbooks, Boston, July 28 – 30. *(ITC – Author's collection)*

The two Bantam Books U.S film tie-in paperbacks printed and on sale during July 1980. *(Author's collection)*

322 • *Raise The Titanic*

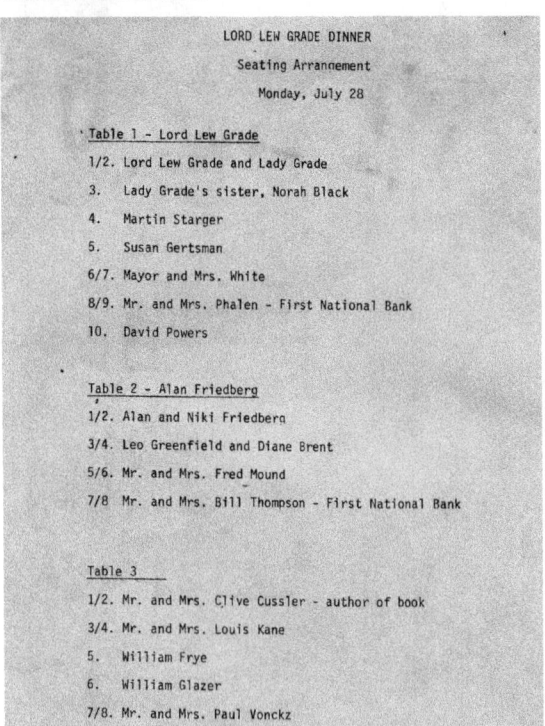

Cussler's invitation to the reception of Lord Lew Grade held on the evening of 29 July. *(Author's collection)*

LEFT: Rare Bantam bookmarker promoting the World Premiere and the Cussler novels. *(Author's collection)*

BELOW: Advertising poster for the World Premiere of *Raise the Titanic* on the 30 July in Boston. *(Author's collection)*

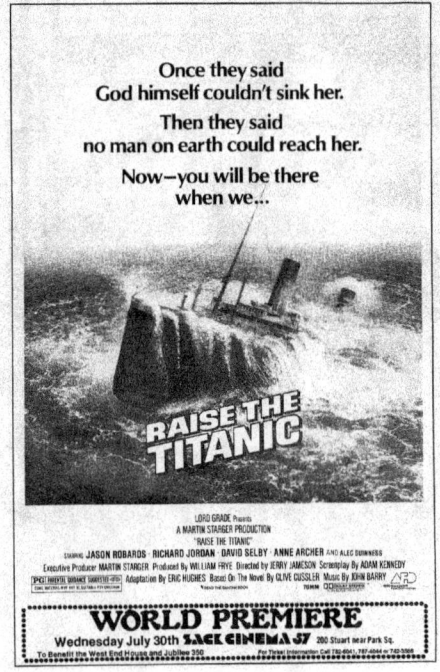

TOP: Cussler's table and guests seating arrangement list for the private function on the night of 29 July. Clive and his wife are seated at table 3 in the company of the film's producer William Frye. *(Author's collection)*

Chapter 24: Premiere, Charity Events and those Damned Critics • 323

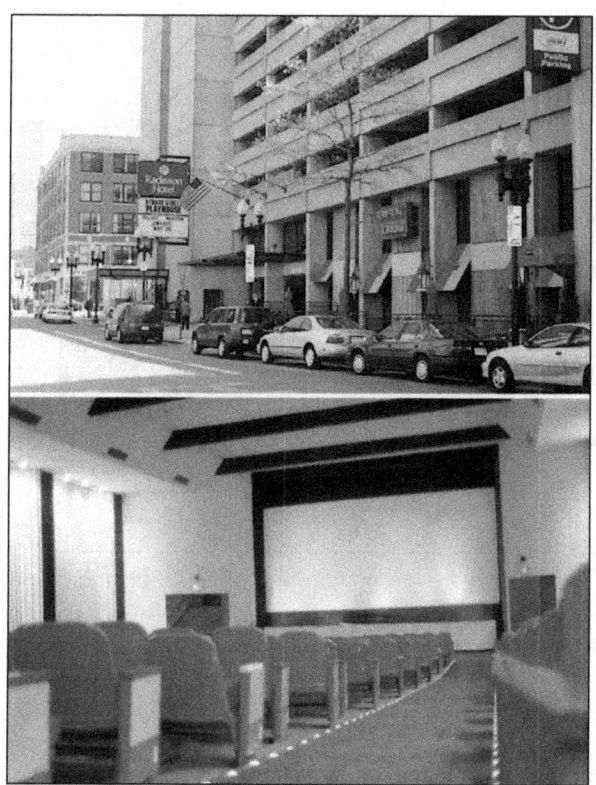

The former Sacks Cinema 57. It is pictured here in 2002 under the name of the Stuart Street Playhouse. *(Photographs: Top © Scott Norwood / Bottom © Dick Dziadzio)*

Jason Robards arrives at Sack Cinema 57 for the World Premiere. He is being escorted into the premises by Susan Fraine; Vice-President of Sack Theatres. *(The Boston Globe, July 31, 1980 – Author's collection)*

A rare survivor from the World Premiere. *(Author's collection)*

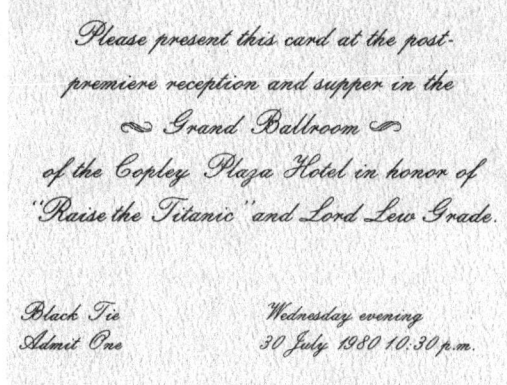

Clive Cussler's personnel invitation to the gala supper event following the screening of *Raise the Titanic*. *(Author's collection)*

324 • Raise The Titanic

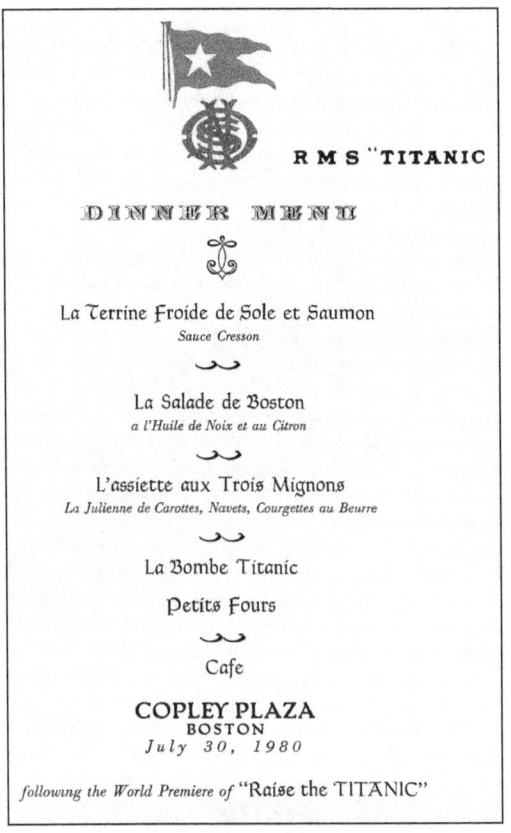

The menu card from Cussler's invitation pack. (Author's collection)

Titanic survivor Drew Marshall offloads his 8ft model of the doomed liner from, bizarrely, a hearse loaned to him during his brief stay over in Boston for the *Raise the Titanic* World Premiere events. *(The Boston Globe, August 1, 1980 – Author's collection)*

Survivor Drew Marshall stands alongside Jason Robards during the gala dinner event following the screening of the movie. *(The Boston Globe, August 1, 1980 – Author's collection)*

Official ITC promotional material from the summer of 1980 that includes the running time of 112 minutes for the World Premiere screening in Boston. When the movie went public on the 1 August, the running time had been cut down to 109 minutes to remain that way, even when the movie went to home entertainment releases on tape, laserdisc, DVD, download and Blu-ray. *(ITC – Author's collection)*

Chapter 24: Premiere, Charity Events and those Damned Critics • 325

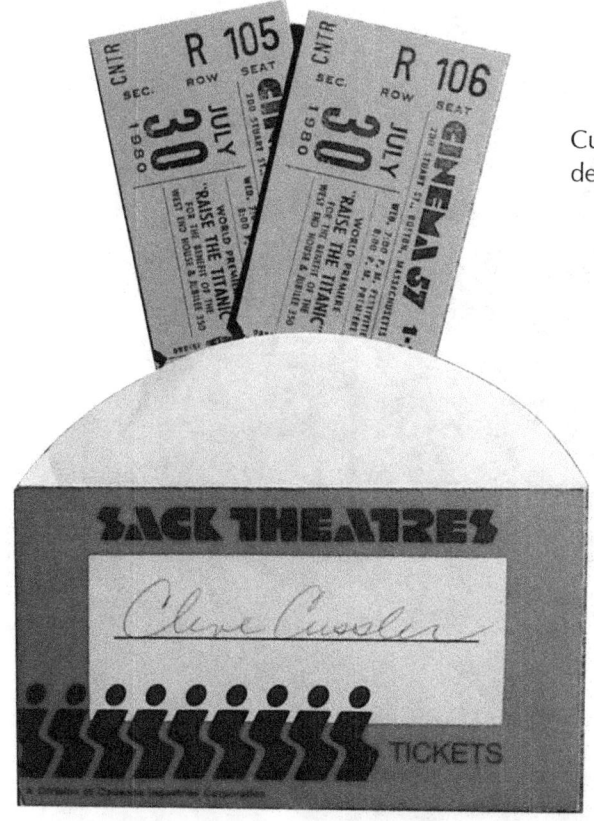

Cussler's tickets that lead to so much despair. *(Sue Connelly collection)*

Clive Cussler's far too brief appearance in the film as one of the press reporters. Seeing his line removed was enough for Cussler to exit the theatre before *Titanic* even broke the surface. *(ITC/ITV Studios)*

Central Park Fox cinema in San Antonio, Texas. *(Author's collection)*

As summer turned to autumn in London, Lew Grade was still pinning his hopes on *Raise the Titanic* being a late starter for ITC regardless of the questionable box office takings overseas. *(Author's collection)*

Newspaper cutting for the screenings at Freemont 3 Theatres in Springfield, Missouri. *(Author's collection – With thanks to Teresa Trower)*

Chapter 24: Premiere, Charity Events and those Damned Critics • 327

Press pass for the preview screening at the Dominion Theatre in London. (Author's collection)

Advertisement for the special charity premiere for the film at London's famous West End theatre. (Author's collection)

A rare and still complete charity ticket. (Author's collection)

You won't sell many newspapers there mate. A comical look at one of the doctored images for the "Old Ben" charity screening. (Author's collection)

The grand frontis to Leicester Square Theatre in London and the eye-catching custom *Raise the Titanic* display. *(Author's collection)*

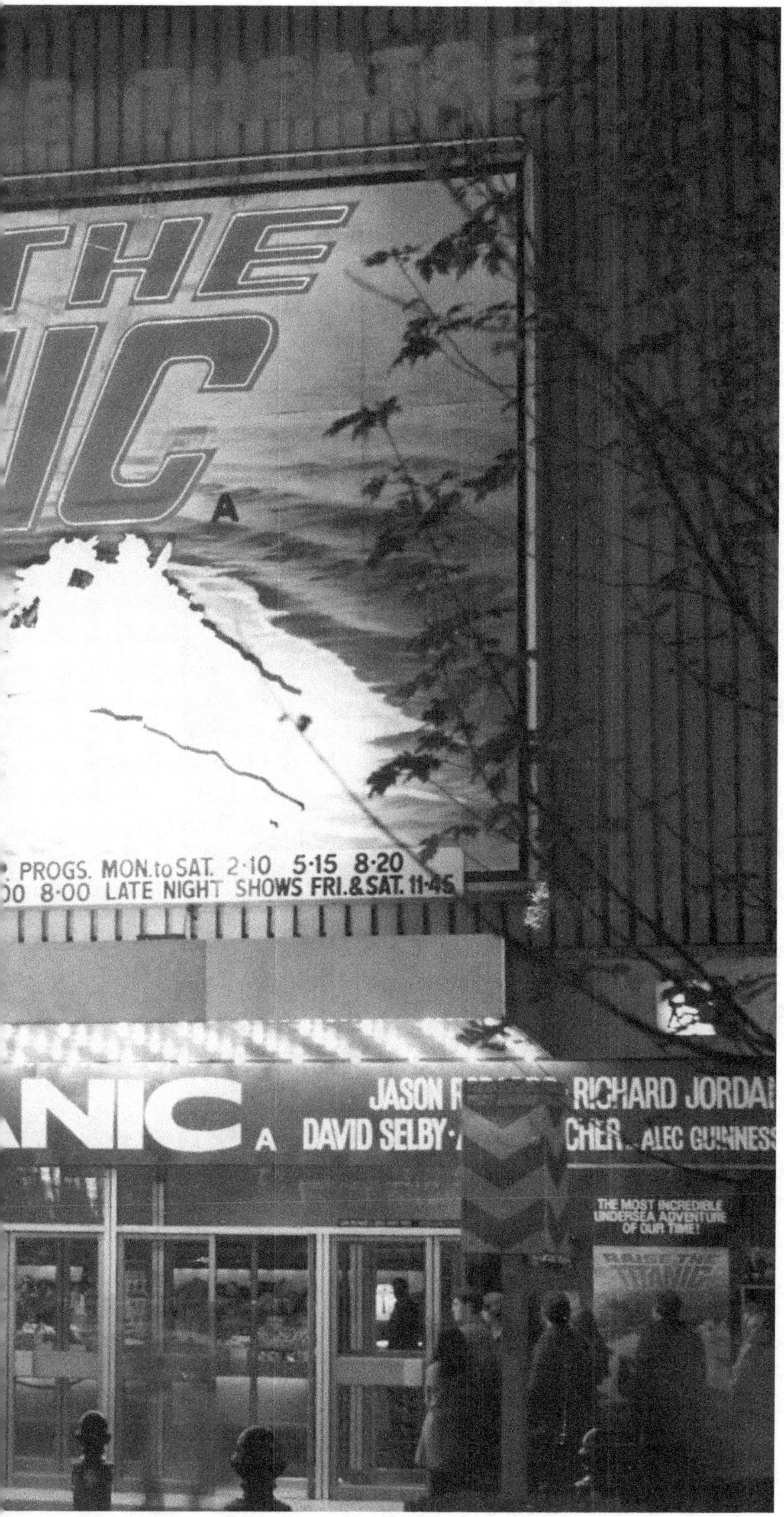
PROGS. MON. to SAT. 2·10 5·15 8·20
8·00 LATE NIGHT SHOWS FRI.&SAT. 11·45
DAVID SELBY
THE MOST INCREDIBLE UNDERSEA ADVENTURE OF OUR TIME!

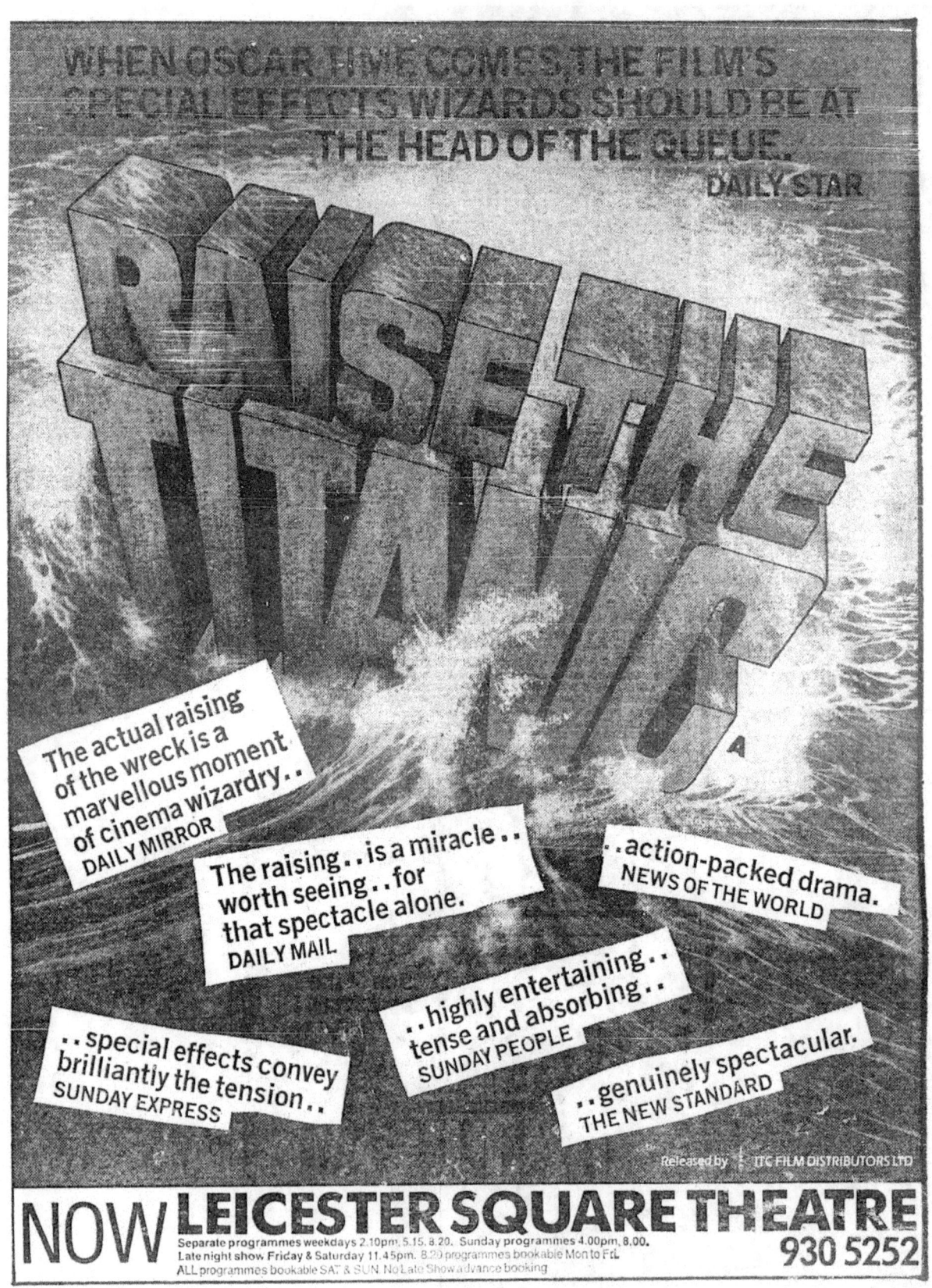

The Daily Star newspaper goes overboard with promoting the new film as it surfaces on UK shores. (*Author's collection*)

Chapter 24: Premiere, Charity Events and those Damned Critics • 331

Lew Grade arrives at the Leicester Square Theatre for an evening of entertainment, fund raising and the official launch of *Raise the Titanic* in the UK. *(Photograph © Paul Smith)*

Lew Grade (right) talks with *Titanic* survivor Sibley George Richards in the lobby of the Leicester Square Theatre prior to the screening of the movie. *(Jeanette Francis/Tony Richards collection)*

The "Old Ben" charity brochure. *(Author's collection)*

Examples of sponsors for "Old Ben". *(Author's collection)*

332 • *Raise The Titanic*

Montage of selected newspaper reviews for *Raise the Titanic* that sank the ship quicker than any iceberg could have. *(Author's collection)*

Chapter 24: Premiere, Charity Events and those Damned Critics

CHAPTER 25

The Art of *Raise the Titanic*

"I had nothing as a child. I drew on toilet paper with pencils"

Drew Struzan

To capture the public's imagination a number of respected artists were called upon to bring *Titanic* to life for use in promotional, advertising and poster work that would sell the movie to the masses. The early days of creating the concept artwork and promotional material for use during filming and leading up to the release worldwide, went on to show *Titanic* in various ways based around the information released by the studio and mingled with the imagination of the artists commissioned to carry out the artworks. A broad range of artists were called upon in creating works that were to symbolise the movie as a whole in just one piece of work. The artwork for the posters had to combine marine elements such as the ocean depths, or surface, with that of maritime matters in the form of ships. Given the two main factors to be used in capturing the look of a *Titanic* movie, it would have made some sense in hiring a maritime artist. Yet none were ever approached. It was probably a wise decision by the films art director in avoiding a stereotypical move in having the posters more generic and not taking any approach in having *Titanic* appear more photographic and overblown in detail that would render the poster more of a gallery piece than that of a standardised movie poster that cinema attendees were already accustomed too.

The Artists Behind *Raise the Titanic*

Drew Struzan

The choice of the artists behind the renderings was a diverse one with those approached to create works based around their scope in the industry. One artist who created some of the early promotional artworks for *Raise the Titanic* was the relatively new to the scene, Drew Struzan. Yes, *that* Drew Struzan. And for those who may not be familiar with his name it will be his artworks crafted for some of the most celebrated movies of modern times that you will be instantly familiar with; *Star Wars, E.T, the Extra-Terrestrial, The Goonies, Blade Runner,* the Indiana Jones series of movies, *Batteries Not Included, Back to the Future* trilogy, *The Muppet Movie, The Thing, Hellboy, Big Trouble in Little China, Harry Potter and the*

Sorcerer's Stone; the list goes on with Struzan amassing over 150 movie titles to his incredible career. Born in May 1947 in Oregon, Drew Struzan, at the age of 18, enrolled at the Art Center College of Design in Los Angeles to become an illustrator; a career choice he selected over being that of an artist of fine art, saying that "I need to eat" motivated his decision. "I had nothing as a child", recalls Struzan. "I drew on toilet paper with pencils – that was the only paper around." Following his graduation, he remained in Los Angeles where he got employment with a design studio creating album cover artworks for The Beach Boys, Roy Orbison, Bee Gees, Earth, Wind and Fire, Alice Cooper and Black Sabbath, with each album artwork earning him a steady $150 to $250. With a growing interest in his artworks Struzan set up his company, Pencil Pushers, and in 1975 his first movie poster appeared. Initially the posters were more for B-movie releases. But as soon as his talent and name circulated it did not take long until the big studios were calling on his craftsmanship. That came in 1977 when the Vice President at 20th Century Fox approached Struzan to create a portraiture poster for the studios latest release of *Star Wars*.

Struzan was contacted by Marble Arch Productions in 1979 to work on creating poster work for *Raise the Titanic* which was in its early stages of filming. What he created would set the bench mark for the other artist renderings that were to come when his first piece sent to Marble Arch Productions was a simple landscape format reference piece measuring 28 x 18 inches. Done in acrylics and coloured pencils the piece showed a low angle view as the stern of *Titanic* bursts up amongst a heaving sea and heavily laden sky. Later Struzan would copy the angle again for the first of three artworks meant for use in potential one-sheet releases. The first of these was a multi-view format that was a trademark of Struzan by using a number of publicity shots sent by the studio of the principle actors already contracted to the production. The artwork was mainly compromised of a view of the ocean as the stern of *Titanic* exits amidst the calamity of the rough sea. The sky was a combination of the Stars and Stripes representing the United States and the Hammer and Sickle emblem for the Soviet Union. U.S Navy ships and helicopters fill in left and right of the *Titanic* while Robards, Jordan, Selby, Guinness and Archer are included to the left allowing for text to be include to the right side of the artwork. The second piece produced by Struzan in full one-sheet format had a slightly different angle with a view of the *Titanic*, minus her number one funnel, resting on the sea bed with a heavy list to starboard as submersibles glide around the wreck. Placed center of the art was Jordan, Robards, Selby, Archer and Guinness with the view of the ocean surface with Navy ships and equipment and the repeat of the flags of the two waring countries. The final artwork submitted was in spring 1980 and was more a direct and faithful representation from the film showing an almost fully raised *Titanic*, her second funnel snapped away and the bow bulwark and additional tall vents in place on the bow. A large area was given over to another world beneath the waves with two of the film's submersibles positioned off to one side that would allow for text to be added by the studio.

Despite all his work, the studios decided not to go with his artwork, opting instead of the alternative works that came in from others artists. A decision that could have been down to Lew Grade and him keeping the film a much more British affair. Regrettably for fans of the film, and even Drew Struzan, his artworks for *Raise the Titanic* were never released in any type of print or poster medium, making them largely forgotten and hidden under the shadow of his more famous works.

Rodger Towers

Like any major movie studios ITC/Marble Arch Productions did venture into releasing a teaser poster for *Raise the Titanic* during mid 1979 as media outlets reported on the progress of the film. For the poster design they approached British artist Rodger Towers who was familiar with both portrait and landscape art. Towers has a background working in London's West End as a professional illustrator completing works for publishers, recording and film industry. He works with two basic styles which he describes as "loose" and "tight". The former being a washed-on tradition with paints while the latter is more a realistic and detailed style. For the *Raise the Titanic* teaser poster Towers took on the look in creating something more unique and what I personally think is one of the most appealing yet thought provoking designs for the production. Towers decision was to simply have the films *Raise the Titanic* logo as the focal point, replacing the *Titanic* as the object being salvaged and seen seconds after coming to the surface in a choppy sea and water cascading from each letter. The artwork was minimalistic in just representing a close up of the sea and the film name, yet it worked perfectly. The poster does share some traits with *Titanic* in that it was extremely short lived having been pulled from distribution with only several known copies existing, making the poster one of the more sought after film production promotional items ever made for *Raise the Titanic*.

W.E. Berry Ltd

For fans of the movie the name W.E. Berry may not be so familiar. Yet the name is associated with one of the most recognisable poster designs for the film. W.E. Berry is the first in this list of companies who designed the large British quad poster and accompanying tie-in for the book publishers Sphere. The artwork used is not entirely credited to Berry but it is credited to his publishing company W.E. Berry Ltd of Bradford, England, at the time was of the world's most popular publishing companies for movie posters for thousands of blockbusters to a huge array of film studios. Originally founded in 1922, W.E. Berry went on to print some of the most iconic posters ever to grace the lobbies of cinemas including the eye-catching designs for the early James Bond movies, *Oliver Twist*, *Flash Gordon* and *Star Wars* with their customer list containing those of the Rank Organisation, Paramount Pictures and 20th Century Fox. While the poster work for *Raise the Titanic* is recognisable, it is unknown to who the artist was behind the piece as nothing is to be seen on the painting. I can conclude that W.E. Berry Ltd, as the main publisher, used one of their own in-house artists to create the piece and with the artist employed by the company, it is the company who is behind the work; and what a stunning poster design it is. Created as a high elevation view it shows the bows of the *Titanic* as she appears from the swirling mass of sea, water pouring from her decks and portholes and under the rather optimistic header of "THE MOST INCREDIBLE UNDERSEA ADVENTURE OF OUR TIME".

The angle chosen should be familiar to fans as it is based around one of the publicity photographs of the actual model being raised. However, for the benefit of the poster, the artist has omitted the pair of tall ventilators that sit either side of the mast making the image familiar yet uniquely different and separate from the other releases. Along with varying formats of the poster, the artwork was used extensively for other promotional items including brochures, flyers, lobby displays, special press tickets and mini posters. It was even recreated as a monstrous illuminated display that was erected above the main doors of London's Leicester Square Theatre.

Dan Goozee

Dan Goozee (1943 – 1996) was a creative visual artist who was predominantly influenced by Pop Art leaning towards the use of conceptualism in his works delivering geometrical elements and polished lines to bring about significant changes to the art of the 1960s created by the Andy Warhol, Tom Wesselmann and Roy Lichtenstein culture. Goozee worked in both portrait and landscape medium with his most recognisable works during the 1970s and 80s with posters created for *Star Wars*, *Superman*, *The Poseidon Adventure* and some for the Roger Moore period of James Bond that included *Moonraker*, *Octopussey* and *A View to a Kill*. His previous commissions in science fiction art meant that Goozee was familiar with creating crafts surrounded by an almost alien environment. Taking inspiration from Drew Struzan's earlier rendition of *Titanic*'s wreck, Goozee would create his own version of the liner sitting within her watery tomb. Submersible lights tantalisingly reveal little details of the wreck; the iceberg damage down her hull side, the twisted remains of the broken forward funnel and the cargo hold on the foredeck; the darkness was oppressive while *Titanic* still possessed surreal beauty. Produced in a portrait format allowed the artwork to be used for one-sheet posters over in Japan that also included tickets, flyers, Chirashi mini posters and film tie-in editions of the Clive Cussler novel.

In the United Kingdom, the artwork was used for the sleeve to a press pack containing publicity photographs and synopsis sheet while over in America the artwork was carried over to a folder of press material released by AFD and containing a large number of publicity documentation and black and white photographs. As Britain opted to use the W.E. Berry Ltd painting for their Sphere tie-in novel, Bantam books in America went with using the Goozee art for their Cussler rerelease at the time of the movies launch in cinemas. What may come as a surprise to fans is that Goozee did not stay with creating just one piece of *Raise the Titanic* artwork. When he submitted his work in late 1979 Goozee included an alternate wreck version of the *Titanic* and created at a much lower angle, almost sea bed level, but in a less intimidating light that reveals much more detail when compared to his other work. The artwork did not make it to any posters or promotional material other than used as a background piece for a double page feature on the movie published in the ITC Entertainment publication; ITC Magazine 1980. The final artwork by Goozee was to be a striking scene of the moment *Titanic* is freed from the grip of the ocean floor for the journey to the surface. Created for use in Japan the artwork was used as the cover to the Towa published film brochure, one-sheet posters, flyers, Chirashi mini posters, tickets, promotional material, newspaper and magazine advertisements.

John Berkey

John Berkey (1932 – 2008) was born in Edgeley, North Dakota. He graduated high school in 1950 and went on to study at the Minneapolis School of Art which set him on course to freelance work throughout the 1960s and being commissioned by NASA to create artwork depicting the Apollo space program. His first introduction to the movie world came in 1968 when he turned down the opportunity to create the poster work for Stanley Kubrick's *2001: A Space Odyssey*. Success in the film industry came in 1974 when he produced the key art for Irwin Allen's disaster epic *The Towering Inferno*. This led the way to Berkey creating a series of now iconic movie poster artworks which includes *King Kong, Orca: The Killer Whale, Superman III, Meteor, Airport '79, Dune* and *Star Wars*; the latter being of great importance with Berkey producing several paintings based around his science fiction art which George Lucas used to pitch the film to studios. Berkey's artistic palette varied between space art, landscape works, maritime, aviation and historical themes, making him a versatile and diverse artist.

For *Raise the Titanic,* his submitted artwork featured what Berkey says "everything that happens in the movie, and more!", highlighting not just his passion for science fiction but that of sparking the imagination for countless admirers. The setting is fulsome but not overly exaggerated with a series of subs paused around the wreck as explosives and salvage tanks lift the sleeping steel giant from her resting place of 68 years. The artwork was used primarily for Australian daybill posters upon release of the movie but was carried over to being utilised on video, laser disc and more modern releases on DVD and Blu-ray.

Yves Thos

Born in Paris 1935, Yves Thos enrolled in the School of Graphic Art at the age of 16. Primarily a character painter and producing figurative contemporary art, Thos was first introduced to creating movie poster artwork when he was just 19 years of age painting for Pathé-Cinéma, a period that would later earn him a place in Cinema World Heritage. His most recognisable work was for the James Bond film *On Her Majesty's Secret Service* from 1969. The artwork Thos produced for the French poster of *Raise the Titanic* (*La Guerre des Abimes*) is a combination of his own interpretation and that of work originally from John Berkey, specially the reproduced submersibles. Thos decided to keep his rendering of the sunken *Titanic* extremely basic, shifting the liner to a more distant location while the submersibles were prominent in the foreground. Bizarrely, the English translation of *La Guerre des Abimes* comes out as *War of the Abyss*.

National Screen Services Corporation

Another much loved release was the National Screen Services Corporation one-sheet and accompanying daybill poster that was used in the United States. The poster design shared similarities to that of Britain's W.E. Berry Ltd in that it was the second publishing company to create their own designs and posters for *Raise the Titanic*. The design was an edited image from one of the publicity photographs taken in Malta of the model being raised in the deep tank. While much of the original was kept the National Screen services art department added a horizon point and painted in additional streams of water pouring from the foredeck. One of the refining features of the piece was the addition of the tagline that was taken from the Associated Film Distribution (AFD) promotional campaign:

First, they said God himself couldn't sink her.
Then they said no man on earth could reach her.
Now - you will be there as we...

... just a couple more

As *Raise the Titanic* screened across the globe, some European theatres had posters created outside of the official studio releases. Amongst them were the odd one's. While not officially approved by ITC, they did serve the purpose of promoting the film and equally promoting the talents of local artists. It is impossible to establish how many were made and how many exist to this day. But here are some examples of printed works with one being a well-known Japanese release from Towa and a colourful and somewhat action-packed Thailand one-sheet poster.

Publicity Campaign

Since the late Edwardian era, movie studios have supplied press-related materials to cinemas and distributors as a way to improve and promote a successful exhibition of the feature intended for public viewing. The period from the 1950s to the 1990s was the golden era of when studios pulled out all the stops in producing a huge array of publicity material that was destined for newspapers, magazines, supplements, and, of course, the exterior and interior areas of theatres. Along with posters and flyers the studios also produced a large amount of press packs that contained printed matter such as production details, actors and synopsis sheets. The larger sets of the press packs included a number of still photography from the production that ranged from actors to film crew, behind the scenes work to official movie scenes; most of which came with attached caption sheets. Some studios released campaign books that outlined the film in minor detail with suggested captions for their publicity photographs and options of images for newspaper and magazine advertisements, poster and lobby card sizes. The bigger studios could be bold in producing impressive cinema lobby display boards that came flat packed ready for assembly and mighty banners that could be tied up and displayed on lobby walls. The publicity material for theatres was listed out with a brief description of the item, sizes available and for what medium they were created for such as theatre or newspaper advertising. With each item there came a reference number in which the theatre, upon receiving the lists, could choose what material they wanted to display based on the floor space and display boards inside and exterior of the cinema. As the 1990s came to a close and a new century began it marked the decline of such material as studios began to decrease their budgets and cut back producing promotional items to focus towards the more conventional printed posters and online advertising. Today the campaign kits are extremely popular with collectors around the world with early sets from acclaimed blockbusters attracting premium prices; depending on the film franchise and its popularity.

As *Raise the Titanic* neared completion, ITC set out to release a number of press kits and campaign material that would promote to the maximum. For some it would seem that the studio put more attention in the campaign than the film itself with Lew Grade convinced that the name *Titanic* would be the films major selling point. ITC and their sister companies of Marble Arch Productions and Associated Film

Distribution started their campaign for *Raise the Titanic* as early as 1978 when the British book publisher Sphere introduced a banner that read, "THE MIGHTY ALL-ACTION SUPERSELLER! SOON TO BE A MAJOR FILM!", in which they added it to the cover of their paperback editions of Clive Cussler's *Raise the Titanic*. As filming commenced on the production the same banner appeared again on Sphere's 1979 rerelease of the novel and followed shortly afterwards with ITC's ill-fated teaser poster by Rodger Towers. By the beginning of 1980 ITC finally released the first teaser trailer that foretold mankind's greatest achievements; going to the moon, conquering Everest, battling the freezing climate of the Poles. By spring of 1980 the teaser poster campaign put to print what had already been teased in the first teaser trailer:

Challenging The Impossible...

1927
Man crosses the Atlantic on the first solo flight.

1953
Man climbs to the top of Mount Everest.

1969
Man conquers space and walks on the moon.

1980
Two-and-a-half miles beneath the Atlantic, Man, once again challenges the impossible.

Before spring came to an end, ITC had now begun to send out the posters for the movie that included a view of the *Titanic* accompanied with the final list of production details including actors, producer and director. With the campaign increasing the press, media outlets and theatres received their campaign packs for the movie to mark its arrival that summer. So, let us take a look at some of the campaign material produced for Lew Grade's summer blockbuster.

AFD Campaign Pressbook
United States
The AFD Campaign Pressbook was issued to theatres and media outlets such as newspaper and magazine publishers. Produced in large format (37 x 26 cm) the pressbook was printed in black and white on a total of 20 pages with the first three pages consisting of text covering the production. The remaining 17 pages covered the posters, newspaper, magazine and trade advertisements. And column shorts, B&W press kit/theatre display stills and inserts cards.

ITC Entertainment Production Card
United Kingdom
The ITC Production Card was produced and issued by ITC in London and issued in a 30 x 21 cm format colour card. The front of the card included the film's title, running time, photographic still and a brief synopsis. The reverse side included 4x small colour stills, cast list and credits list.

AFD Press Material (press pack)

United States

The AFD Press Material (press pack) was the largest of the press kits issued by the studio. The press kit came in three untitled versions with content varying depending on the size of the issued kit. As these kits were only marked with "PRESS MATERIAL – RAISE THE TITANIC", for the purpose of describing the contents better depending on the set issued, I will call them Deluxe, Standard and Basic. The standard kit included 31x B&W 10 x 8-inch gloss stills showing some scenes from the film, behind the scenes views, actors and some production crew. Each photographic still comes with a caption sheet glued to the reverse side of the still. A total of 83 pages of printed text are included on the actors, film credits, film production, director and screenplay author. Presented in a large format full colour card folder. A basic kit was issued in an identical folder but with only 16x B&W 10 x 8-inch gloss stills of selected content from the standard set but did include 83 pages of printed text and 16x caption sheets. The deluxe version is incredibly rare having only been distributed to executives of productions companies and studios. The deluxe kit came with the same standard kit photographs that included the 31x B&W 10 x 8-inch gloss stills with attached caption sheets in the card folder. The kit included the 83 pages of printed text on actors and film production but included additional material not present in the other kits on general captions. Completing the kit were 20x colour 12 x 10 cm slides of various behind the scenes views from the production.

The description here of these kits are based on those that are obtained as full sets. Over the years these kits have been broken up and the contents mixed up and sold off as separate pieces to fans and collectors of the film. As the years pass it is getting much harder to find full sets as distributed by the Associated Film Distribution company during 1980.

ITC Films International

United Kingdom

Published by ITC Entertainment, Films International is a 4-page large format full colour promotional brochure listing 21 feature films released and in development by ITC. The two main pages cover the movies *The Legend of the Lone Ranger*, *Green Ice*, *The Salamander* and *Raise the Titanic*.

Raise the Titanic UK Premiere Brochure

United Kingdom

Published by ITC and released under ITC Films International, the 27 x 30 cm full colour 8-page premiere brochure includes a number of publicity and behind the scenes photographs along with a film synopsis and production details.

ITC Magazine

United Kingdom

The ITC Magazine was published by ITC Entertainment only once a year starting with 1978 as a promotional publication. Their 1980 issue was a full colour magazine with card cover with 27 pages covering the company and their productions with 8 pages on *Raise the Titanic*.

ITC Entertainment Vol 3 Press Information Pack

United Kingdom

The ITC Entertainment Press Information Pack was a stapled set of production sheets that were normally found in the larger U.S press packs. Accompanying the pack was 7x B&W images and 2x 35mm slides that were housed in a card sleeve with the production notes.

Raise the Titanic Synopsis Brochure
United Kingdom
Published by ITC Entertainment, the 4-page A4 sized synopsis leaflet features an illustrated cover and two pages of text covering the story of the film, cast and production credits.

Raise the Titanic Charity Premiere Brochure
United Kingdom
Published by Premiere Metropolis Press Ltd the brochure contains 38 pages of advertisements in B&W and 8 pages devoted to *Raise the Titanic* with B&W and colour publicity photographs. Printed for the Charity Premiere of the movie screened at London's Leicester Square Theatre, Wednesday, November 12, 1980, the event was to raise money in aid of the Newsvendors Benevolent Institution which had been supporting newspaper vendors in times of need from when the charity was founded in 1839 and endorsed by the legendary author Charles Dickens.

ITC/AFD Promotional Foldout
United States
Published at the start of summer 1980, the ITC/AFD foldout was an oversized 4-panel production piece containing actors, production crew and production information that was distributed through the United States.

Raise the Titanic Japanese Promotional Foldout
Japan
Published by ITC Entertainment and Towa in Japan, the 36 x 34 cm colour and black/silver tone fold out consists of 3 panels totalling 6 sides of production information, film synopsis and publicity images.

Raise the Titanic Japanese Film Brochure
Japan
Published by ITC Entertainment and Towa in Japan, the film brochure contains 24 pages covering the film, production details and information about the *Titanic* using B&W/colour photographs from the film and publicity stills.

Advertising Slicks
United States
Similar to the press campaign pieces, the Press Advertising Slicks were issued by the studio as camera-ready advertising sheets for use in printed media such as newspapers and magazines promoting the film through a cinema chain or theatre.

Cinema/Theatre Press Advertising Sheets
World Wide Distribution
Released as part of the studio publicity campaign, the Cinema/Theatre Press Advertising Sheets were issued according to countries. Those distributed had a blank space where the cinema/theatre could add their own screening details. As the sheets were sent out for world-wide distribution, the same image wasn't necessarily used. Countries such as the United States, United Kingdom, Japan and Australia, had a certain image or artwork selected by the studio, printed out and sent out to the country. The sheets were used for magazines, but mainly newspapers.

Lobby Cards

In keeping with previous movie studios and the decades of released lobby cards produced for cinema lobby's and those used for front of house – a term for poster and lobby cards displayed in glass fronted wall mounted cases positioned on the exterior walls of the cinema, mainly around and above the main entrance – these cards usually came in four sizes; 10 x 7 inch, 10 x 8 inch, 14 x 10 inch and 14 x 11 inch and printed in both B&W and colour formats. ITC covered several countries in having lobby cards produced for display. The cards were issued in varying quantities that allowed theatre management to order accordingly depending on space set aside for promotional displays and advertising at the cinema complex. The lobby cards for *Raise the Titanic* were issued in sets of 8, 10 and 12 and printed in the language for the country they were destination for. However, not all countries were covered and those the film was sold too for exhibition were already on the list to receive the paperwork containing a list of promotional items available. The smaller venues who were late picking up the release could adapt pre-existing posters or lobby cards by removing the text and replacing it with their own printed material. The main countries issued covered were the United Kingdom, United States, Australia, France, Spain, Japan, Belgium and Italy.

Photographic Stills

A wide range of photographic stills were produced by ITC and Associated Film Distribution (AFD) that featured a number of scenes directly from the movie and a large number of behind the scenes images, many of which were scenes that were filmed and later cut during the final edits of the movie. Those of cut scenes make certain photographs released as publicity stills more collectible amongst the fan community. What makes collecting these still hard is that, like the lobby cards, the stills were released in sets of varying quantities and over the course of 40+ years these sets have been broken up and sold off as a single still or mixed sets making them a difficult and sometimes frustrating task for collectors. The stills were released in 10 x 7 inch, 10 x 8 inch and printed in both B&W and colour variants; the B&W versions were the more widely distributed version while the colour versions were only released in a set that came in a full colour card folder. The stills differed in style to the publicity photographs that were issued in the Press Material packs in that, unlike the Press Material photographs, they did not come with any borders or film logo, leaving just the front of the photograph as a gloss still. Stills produced by ITC for UK distribution were issued with captions sheets taped to the reverse of the photograph that included information on the movie while other versions were released without any of these caption sheets allowing for the stills to be distributed overseas as an image only option.

The more sort after colour set was published by ITC for the UK and came within a colour folder featuring artwork by Dan Goozee and featured a set of 16 full colour 10 x 8 inch borderless stills. The rarer of the coloured images were the 5 x 4-inch press publicity transparencies that numbered a total of 80 images. These transparency versions were not as widely available when compared to the other photographic sets due largely to the costs of manufacturing. But of the one's released they were included in some of the deluxe executive Press Material kits with the full set of 80 also available for the larger and more prominent press agencies based in cities. The most popular of the stills issued by ITC were the B&W versions which worked better for newspapers and magazines that were printed in the more economical monotone. The stills were released in sets of 8, 12 and 16 and printed in 10 x 7 inch and 10 x 8 inch versions. As interest in the film grew, ITC and AFD added to their existing list of stills by issuing the Press Material publicity photographs in sets separate from the press packs.

ITC Publicity Transparencies

The rarer of the imagery for *Raise the Titanic* are those of the original ITC company photographic transparencies that were captured specially for use in promoting the movie while also covering some of the behind the scenes to the production. These colour transparencies were issued to the larger and more established news agencies a month or two before the films public release. Some of the transparencies did end up in the deluxe Press Packs that were handed over to executives. But as separates, or even small sets, these transparencies are rarely seen publicly with the most residing in the archives of visual media companies.

Theatre Display

Film fanatics will remember visiting their local cinema complex and upon entering through the main lobby doors being greeted by one of two large cardboard standees promoting the next big studio blockbuster. I can still remember the life size standee of Arnold Schwarzenegger in his role as the T-800 for *Terminator 2*, adorned in his leather jacket, shades, holding on to the pump-action rifle and astride a Harley Davidson Fat Boy. There has always been something special about these kinds of displays that, no matter how old you are, still create a buzz of excitement. The golden age of these striking displays are now but a memory as more and more studios cut back on such lavish displays. But some of the major studios do still release the occasional monster display; the current *Jurassic World* franchise is one example. Not much is known about the extent of such displays that were commissioned by ITC when *Raise the Titanic* was ready for public release. Most of what was used were the traditional lobby cards, stills and posters. But there were some exceptions made. For American cinemas AFD released a flat card teaser standee promoting the films forthcoming summer release that could be used as a floor or counter top display. As critics reviews started to mount following the World Premiere in Boston, ITC and AFD did not progress forwards in financially supporting any further displays, relying on posters and stills to continue advertising the film.

In England, Lew Grade had invested heavily in promoting the film by having a titanic billboard display that dominated the exterior front of London's 400-seat Leicester Square Theatre. The display measured an impressive 40 x 20 feet version of the W.E. Berry Ltd artwork that was created in separate panels overlapped to give an illusion that *Titanic* was bursting out from the billboard. Above the artwork of *Titanic* was the film logo in large letters which was backlighted in red for a better visual during the evening. Grade and his London main offices of ITC chose the prestigious Leicester Square Theatre as the venue for the UK star studded premiere of *Raise the Titanic*. The theatre front was dressed with additional banners directly above the main entrance that spelled out the name of the movie and the main stars, while posters and lobby cards were used in the three front of house poster display boxes. For the premiere the interior of the lobby had been dressed with numerous W.E. Berry quad and one-sheet posters and film logo card placards.

... and the billboards?

The billboard poster campaign for *Raise the Titanic* is a grey area as very little is known on which artworks were used to advertise the movie. Given the dimensions of traditional street billboards it is most likely that a landscape format was chosen. The UK may have opted to use the W.E. Berry Ltd artwork being that it was created in landscape format for the quad posters while the U.S and other countries could have used Dan Goozee's painting as it offered the choice for being trimmed down. The only known image of one of the billboards comes directly from AFD and ITC. The artwork was based around Drew Struzans' conceptional art of *Titanic* being raised up by the stern and publicly released in the early summer of 1980 to advertise the movie coming to the Cinerama Dome on Hollywood's bustling Sunset Boulevard.

Chapter 25: The Art of *Raise the Titanic* • 345

(STRUZAN) Early conceptional art by Drew Struzan. *(Artwork © Drew Struzan – Original artwork in the Walter Winterburn collection)*

(STRUZAN) The second phase of Struzan's art for *Raise the Titanic* displaying his usual montage flare. *(Artwork © Drew Struzan)*

(STRUZAN) Artwork by Struzan for one-sheet posters featuring his montage signature of illustrating. He depicts *Titanic* with her first funnel removed. This early rendering by Struzan would serve as a guide for later artworks that were used by other artists. *(Artwork © Drew Struzan)*

Chapter 25: The Art of *Raise the Titanic* • **347**

(STRUZAN) Despite Struzan's art fitting perfectly with the look of this film, this was surprisingly rejected by ITC. *(Artwork © Drew Struzan)*

348 • *Raise The Titanic*

(TOWERS) Roger Tower's simple yet effective raising logo. *(Artwork © Roger Towers – Author's collection)*

(BERRY) W.E.Berry's instantly recognisable artwork. *(Author's collection)*

(BERRY) UK cinema lobby poster. *(Author's collection)*

(BERRY) Another rare printers' proof for the planned oversized bus stop advertising poster. *(Author's collection)*

Chapter 25: The Art of *Raise the Titanic* • 349

(BERRY) Rare printers' proof for the UK one-sheet which includes printers hand written notes on imperfections and alterations needed. *(Author's collection)*

350 • *Raise The Titanic*

(BERRY) UK quad theatrical poster. *(Author's collection)*

(BERRY) Spanish one-sheet theatrical poster. *(Author's collection)*

Chapter 25: The Art of *Raise the Titanic* • 351

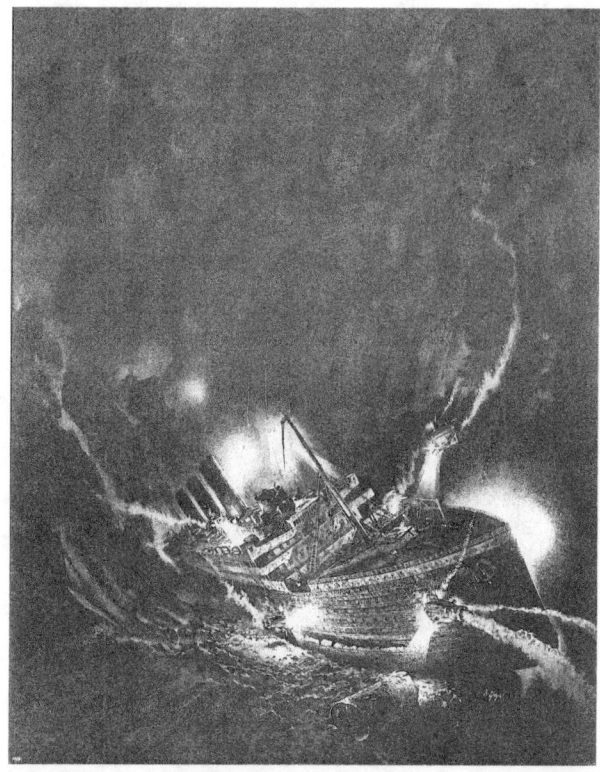

(GOOZEE) Dan Goozee's art for the U.S market distribution of the movie. And the rarer of his renderings that was used for the UK publication of the ITC Magazine. *(Artwork © Dan Goozee - Author's collection)*

(GOOZEE) The Goozee artwork in use on the joint UK and Japanese advertising market. *(Author's collection)*

(GOOZEE) Japanese theatrical poster. *(Author's collection)*

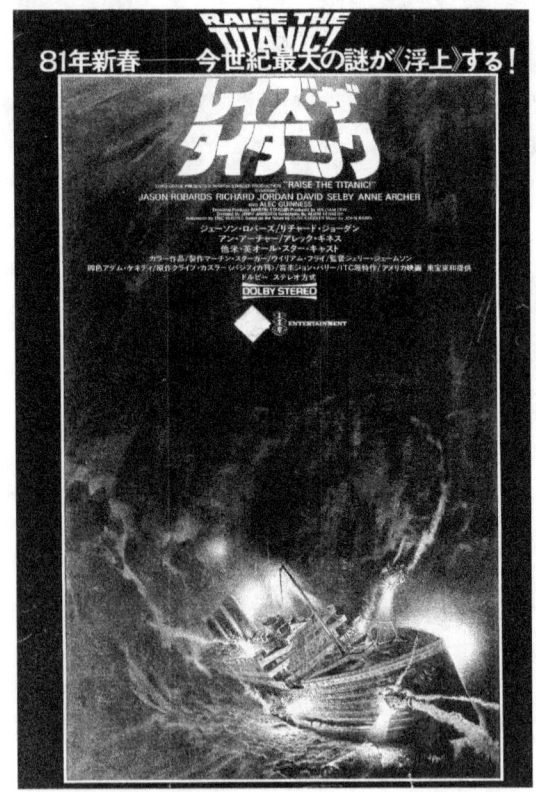

(GOOZEE) Japanese mini poster. *(Author's collection)*

(GOOZEE) French theatrical poster. *Renflouez le Titanic!* translates to *Bail Out the Titanic!* *(Author's collection)*

Chapter 25: The Art of *Raise the Titanic* • 353

(GOOZEE) Spanish theatrical poster. *Rescaten el Titanic!* translates to *Rescue the Titanic! (Author's collection)*

(BERKEY) The John Berkey artwork. *(Artwork © John Berkey – Author's collection)*

(THOS) French theatrical poster. *(Author's collection)*

(BERKEY) U.S theatrical insert poster. *(Author's collection)*

(NATIONAL SCREEN SERVICES) U.S one-sheet theatrical poster. *(Author's collection)*

(NATIONAL SCREEN SERVICES) U.S theatrical insert poster. *(Authors*

Japanese one-sheet featuring the TOWA company artwork that shares some similarities to the John Berkey work. *(Author's collection)*

Italian theatrical poster. You may think that this printing is featuring the Dan Goozee artwork. But it is not. The artwork is a copy of Goozee's work by another artist. *Blitz Nell'Oceano* translates to *Blitz in the Ocean*. *(Author's collection)*

Chapter 25: The Art of *Raise the Titanic* • 355

Another Italian theatrical poster by an unknown artist that shares some similarities with the W.E. Berry work. *(Author's collection)*

The action-packed Thailand poster. *(Author's collection)*

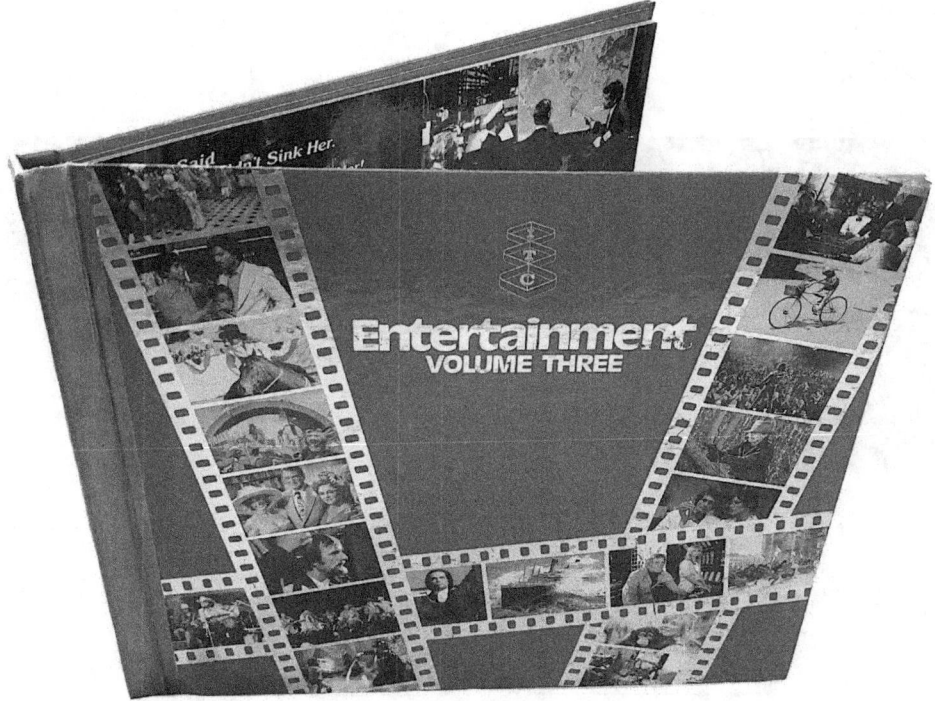

Rare ITC company movie display book that features a large number of their released and forthcoming film projects, including *Raise the Titanic*. *(Author's collection)*

356 • *Raise The Titanic*

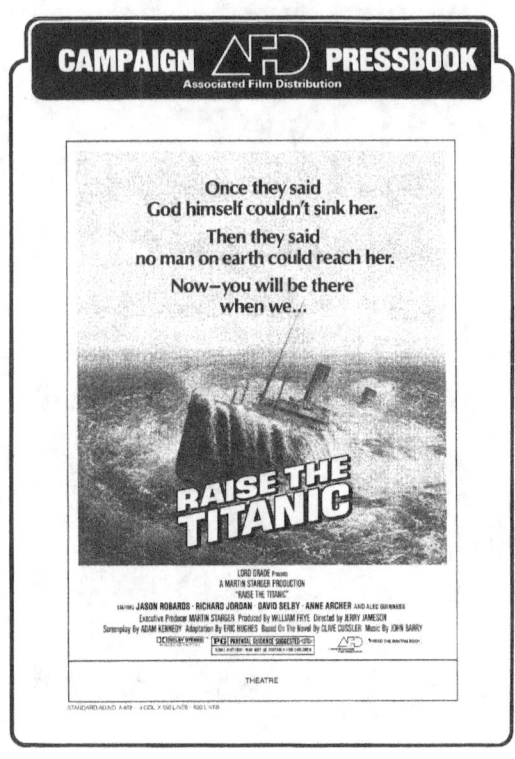

Cover of the AFD Campaign Pressbook. *(Author's collection)*

ITC Entertainment Production Card. *(Author's collection)*

Chapter 25: The Art of *Raise the Titanic* • 357

AFD full Press Pack. *(Author's collection)*

358 • *Raise The Titanic*

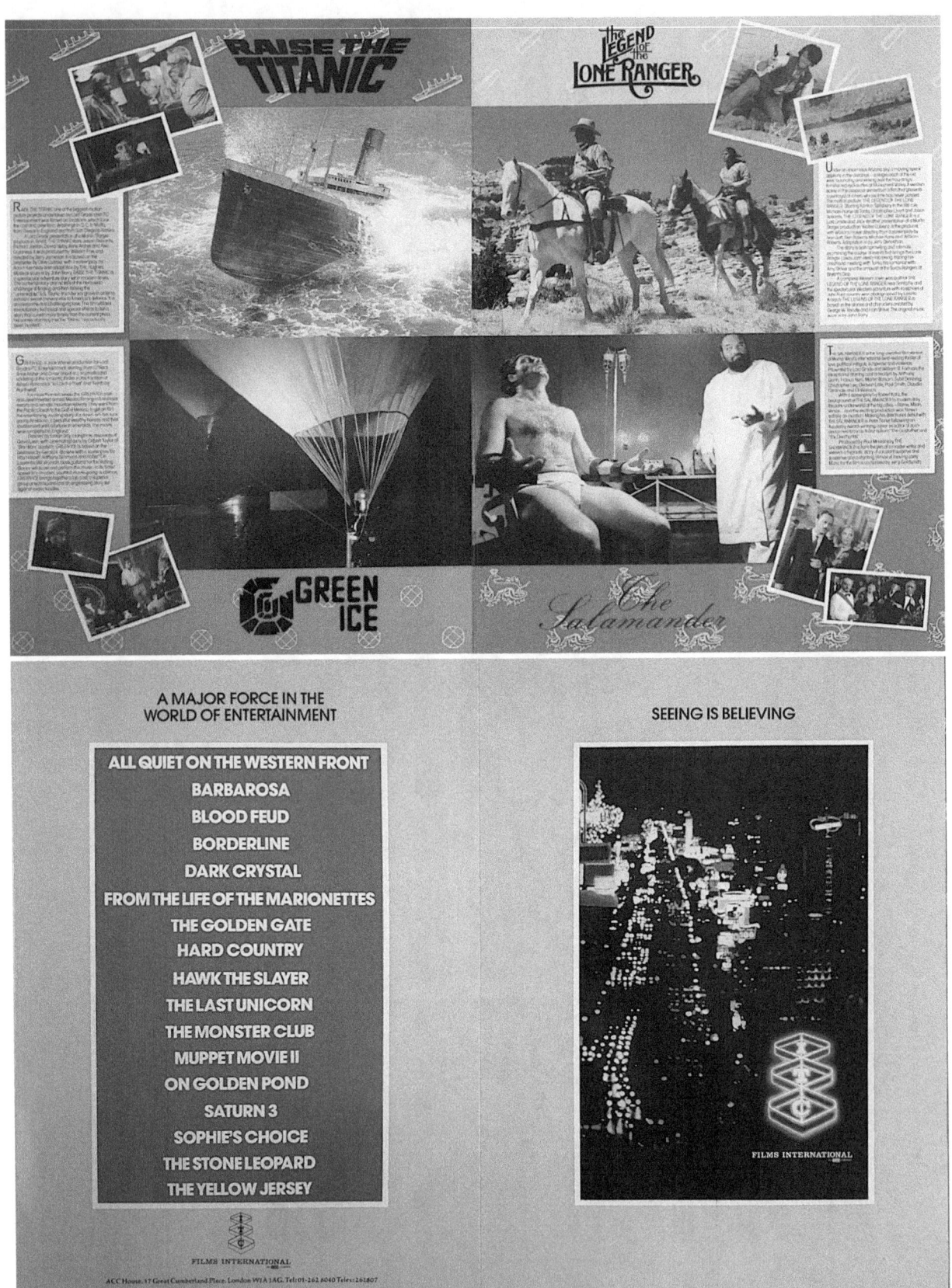

ITC Films International publicity brochure. *(Author's collection)*

Chapter 25: The Art of *Raise the Titanic* • 359

UK full colour Film Premiere Brochure. *(Author's collection)*

ITC Magazine 1980. *(Author's collection)*

360 • *Raise The Titanic*

ITC Entertainment Vol 3 Press Information Pack. *(Author's collection)*

  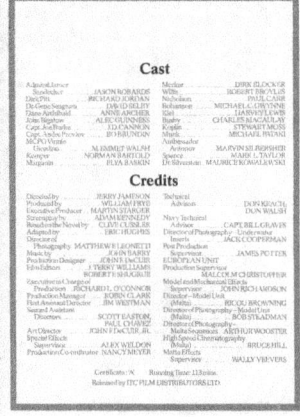 

UK synopsis brochure. *(Author's collection)*

UK Charity Premiere Brochure. *(Author's collection)*

Chapter 25: The Art of *Raise the Titanic* • 361

U.S Promotional Foldout. *(Author's collection)*

Japanese Promotional Foldout. *(Author's collection)*

Japanese Movie Brochure. *(Author's collection)*

362 • *Raise The Titanic*

U.S press Advertising Slicks. *(Author's collection)*

Example of the Australian press advertising sheet for the Hoyts cinema chain. *(Author's collection)*

Spanish Press sheet. *(Author's collection)*

Chapter 25: The Art of *Raise the Titanic* • 363

Example of varying cinema lobby cards. *(Author's collection)*

Example of photographic publicity stills. *(Author's collection)*

Raise the Titanic billboard close to Sunset Boulevard that was erected for the advance screening of the movie on the 22 July at the Cinerama Dome. *(ITC – Author's collection)*

366 • *Raise The Titanic*

Example of some of the rare publicity transparencies for ITC. *(Author's collection)*

AFD cinema lobby display issued for use in the United States and consisting of a large cardboard placard, double sided advance poster and AFD company logo card. *(Tommy Bernard collection)*

CHAPTER 26

It *would* have been easier if they had lowered the Atlantic

"But let me tell you, it wasn't a bad picture. There are two scenes which are worth the price of admission alone. And it took $8 million in America, the equivalent of about $40 million today. Some films don't even take $1 million. Also, it was the top-grossing film of the year in Japan. They went over the moon about it."

Lew Grade

Towards the end of October 1980, with the film's dismal box office takings weighing heavy on those in the offices at ITC, new feature films in the works as part of Grade's $100m motion picture investment, and those still in the production stages, were all relying on the success of *Raise the Titanic*. The spectacular publicity campaign for the build-up to the release had all but become deflated, resulting in the film raising more eyebrows than profits. And it had not gone unnoticed by company executives and shareholders. Grade's gamble on *Raise the Titanic* being the *big one* for the 1980s was rapidly sinking fast. Within the walls of ITC and Marble Arch Productions questions were being asked if Grade gambling the company assets away on so many feature films on the back of each other was a viable option from the offset. *Raise the Titanic* alone began with a £7m budget where the entire production was to be completed within that cost. As the months passed, Grade went on to increase the productions budget to £12m, then £15m, to finally complete the project at a staggering £25m, making *Raise the Titanic* not only the most expensive British film, but the world's most expensive film production. But Grade was refusing to be defeated. "*Titanic*'s a real gripper, so my advice to you is… hurry up and go and see it" said the *Movie Mirror* in December 1980.

As Christmas loomed, Grade still maintained faith in *Raise the Titanic* and that is was not the disastrous flop others were suggesting it was. Thankfully the $16m return from the U.S distribution for the film would hopefully reduce, if not silence, the critics within his own company. That December Grade flew out to Japan to finalise a deal to have the film screened at a number of venues across the country, confident the public would relate to the technological aspects of the film. Grade was right. By the 16 December it was reported that in the space of two weeks following it opening, *Raise the Titanic* had grossed $1.8 million through Toho-Towa putting the film in the No.1 box office spot to out-gross *The Shining*, *The Hunter* and *Airplane*. That success did not stop the press back in England claiming that Grade and his film empire were "cutting back". Speaking at his annual Christmas lunch for ITC he flatly denied that *Raise the Titanic* was a "disaster", quashing the press rumours and announcing his next "expensive" production to date would begin in April 1981 with Jim Henson's *Dark Crystal* and *The Great Muppet Caper*. With the festivities, over Grade was back to work in promoting *Raise the Titanic* as he worked towards having the film released in the UK on home video, predicting that the film would net over £7m in rentals alone. Despite Grade digging his heels in, there were others who were no longer convinced in his abilities and who wanted to see the back of Lord Lew Grade and his overblown expenditures that, as they perceived, reflected badly on not just ITC, ATV, ACC and AFD, but also those who had seats at the company board table. *Raise the Titanic*, so they thought, would be used as the straw that broke the camel's back.

As *Raise the Titanic* hit screens across the U.S in August 1980, Grade was already seeing another of his partially financed productions having its own run in theatres. *Can't Stop the Music* portrayed the story of The Village People and billed by its writer Allan Carr as the "Musical Comedy Smash of the 80s!". Grade had been led to believe this musical was to be the next big blockbuster. Carr indeed had a very good eye for musicals and Grade was sold the premise that *Can't Stop the Music* was to be the next *Grease*, Carr's previous cinematic hit from 1978. As the summer of 1980 drew to a close, *Can't Stop the Music* divebombed quicker than a German Stuka and Grade was not impressed having been sold such an expensive $20m turkey. It did not take long until Grade and Carr resulted in tearing strips from one another in the tabloids. The end result was that of a colossal financial failure for Grade whose company AFD had coughed up a substantial amount of the productions budget. By March 1981 the writing was most definitely on the wall for Grade as Associated Communications Corporation (ACC) reported its biggest ever loss in its history of some $24.6m attributed to AFD. Grade was quickly running out of plausible excuses for the shareholders who could no longer pretend that *Raise the Titanic* would ever claw back profits to exceed the productions overall budget in such a short space of time.

By now Grade's stance on the film was beginning to wane. "I believe in the law of averages" Grade said. "One of these has to be a blockbuster." In fact, ACC had committed to 39 feature films with only one ever doing well in America; *The Muppet Movie* from 1979. But it was not *Raise the Titanic* that was to bring about the decline of Lew Grade's British film empire. Investors were losing faith in being steered towards looking past the failures. It just wasn't good for business even if the UK already had a strong film heritage with blockbusters such as *Star Wars*, *The Empire Strikes Back*, *The Elephant Man* and *Chariots of Fire*. But these movies struck a chord with moviegoers and critics, something that the subject of *Titanic* on the big screen lacked during the late 1970s. The time just wasn't right. Even before *Raise the Titanic* had entered the postproduction stages, Grade had already had a taste of what audiences were thinking on the *Titanic* subject when EMI released *S.O.S. Titanic*. The production became a box-office failure. And what made matters worse was that the production had been financed by Grade's brother; Lord Delfont. Ironically, *S.O.S. Titanic* was to be more at home on the small screen when the television broadcasting rights were sold at the same time the film was submitted to home video distribution. The same would happen to *Raise the Titanic* when the rights for screening on television were sold to ITV in June 1982 for £500,000. As ACC began to wave its white flag, requesting negotiations to commence, investors to the company began selling off shares with all eyes turned towards Grade. But on the side lines there was one man who had been watching the slow demise of the company, waiting for the perfect opportunity to step forward and cease control.

The Australian Gordon Gekko

Part One

He was a man of substance, power, and with money and an eye for ruthlessly operating in business and getting what he wanted regardless of cost. Robert Holmes à Court was the Australian billionaire, an entrepreneur and one of the most feared corporate raiders of the 1980s. Holmes à Court had single handily built his empire up from nothing. And in the space of a decade had accumulated a net worth of $2b prior to the stock market crash of 1987. Like *Jaws*, Holmes à Court would wait in the shadows, watching how shares reacted to then rise up from the depths and snap them up. While his heavy-handed business approach paid off in some cases, he did fall flat with others such as his attempted takeover of Rolls Royce and the Times newspaper. Although some hid from Holmes à Court advances, others saw him as a means to an end to their financial woes, laying down a business proposition on the table before him. Grade became one of them. On April 30, 1980, Jack Gill, then the Deputy Chairman and Deputy Chief Executive of ACC, sat in a meeting with Grade. Gill had been keeping an eye on the losses over in America for the company's film distribution side as share prices plummeted to an all-time low. Gill brought to topic that Holmes à Court was in London, suggesting that a meeting could be achieved in doing a deal with him, maybe selling him something on the lines of a lucrative deal on cable and satellite television where all parties would benefit. Gill went ahead and arranged a meeting between the two giants for the following day. Grade was unaware that Gill, in an abuse of power, had already been keeping tabs on Grade's dealings as the company expenses continued to increase and raise suspicions.

Those on the company board were now being updated on the expenditures as Grade dwindled away the company profits on his adventurous journey in creating a solid platform for ITC and its sister company's in maintaining a prominent role in the movie industry. Grade's intentions were good. Always for and on behalf of the company. Grade, a veteran of old school ways in business, always had his past experiences to rely on when advertising his name as a brand in entertainment. There was no one else like him in the business that had such pedigree, and panache, especially when delivering a product. But those economical days of the 1960s and 70s were now long behind him. And while others were blissfully aware of this, Grade was not. He still maintained that you have to spend money, lots of money, to get a hit and reap the benefits. While this worked with lower budgeted television programming, the transition to movies was not working to his or the company's advantage. It was a gamble that unfortunately did not pay off and the company board and shareholders were demanding to know why.

Prior to Holmes à Court's arrival at Grade's office, Gill and two other men from ACC, Bill Michael, who operated the lucrative side of the company through Bentray Investments, and Ellis Birk, lawyer and business executive, met to talk about the situation boiling over at ACC. The tone of the meeting was not good as Ellis expressed "The situation is now very worrying, Jack. The debt equity ration in horrifying and the city are crazy at Lew for what he's done in the U.S." Gill responded that all three of them had to work together, "You know what an optimist Lew is and he just doesn't think it's as bad as we do." Gill continued "but we have the Starger problem", taking aim at Martin Starger, President of Marble Arch Productions over in the U.S. Bill Michael made his intentions very clear. "Clearly Lew's not going to listen; he never has. He's a stubborn old man, and in my view, we should get rid of him." Both Gill and Birk fundamentally disagreed with Michael's frank and hostile approach. "Bill, that's crazy" Birk responded, "it would kill him. It would be mad for the company, and how would you do it? Lew has the largest majority of the voting-stock." Gill and Birk parted company with Michael's and set off for lunch at the Montcalm London Marble Arch hotel, coincidentally where Holmes à Court was staying, to discuss Michael's offensive and disloyal outburst. Gill was now beginning to wonder about his own future with the company.

The following day, Gill arrived at the office several minutes before Holmes à Court, deciding it best not to mention anything of the previous days meeting with Ellis and Michael. The meeting lasted less than an hour with Holmes à Court appearing cold and distant. They talked business, television and newspapers. But it was at the close of the meeting that Holmes à Court dropped his bombshell. "What you're doing is all very exciting and I'm really pleased because I've just bought a million of your shares." Gill was left flabbergasted by the cheek and arrogance of the man. However, events were to change on the morning of December 18, 1980 as Grade was chauffeured past the Odeon Cinema at Marble Arch to see in huge lettering JACK GILL PRESENTS *HAWK THE SLAYER* on the buildings frontis. Grade knew nothing of this production which had been untimely financed by ITC. Upon realising that Gill was stealing his crown, Grade flew into a fit of rage, made worse that the cinema was just a stone's throw from Grade's main office. With Grade already under scrutiny from his own company with board officials baying for his blood over the financing of his movies, Jack Gill had over stepped the line in an act that Grade saw as hostile. As the company revealed to the press its biggest financial losses in its history, city investors and banks began to reel in the wake of the mounting loss. The newspapers soon began to turn on Grade expressing that he should just step down and retire once and for all. In his typical style, Grade responded to the media outbursts stating that he had no intentions of retiring any time soon, not until 2001 when he would be at the tender age of 94 years. And yet while all this drama played out, it diverted the attention away from Holmes à Court who stood back in the shadows, taking advantage of the situation and building up an ever-increasing stake in ACC shares.

Boardroom Blues

In July 1981, Jack Gill was reviewing ACC's operations over the past couple of years and focusing mainly on the film production side of the company. Martin Starger's contract stood out, particularly his salary. Grade had previously delighted in broadcasting that Starger was the highest paid executive in the UK. It came to no surprise that the deal, rendered by Grade, was netting Starger anywhere between $1m to $10m a year. Gill felt it was time to fly out to Los Angeles with Birk and Michael in tow and confront Starger with the necessary paperwork. The meeting backfired. Starger stood firm insisting that he was not planning on going anywhere anytime soon. Defeated, the three men made their way back to the UK; but not before Gill decided to take a much-needed holiday at the expense of the company and the businesses luxury yacht. In the meantime, Starger was on the telephone to Grade to report on them affronting him, of Gill wanting to replace Grade down the line by starting with clipping Grade's wings and relieving him of some of his current duties. Michaels, on the other hand, wanted rid of Grade – full stop. Angered and anguished by the betrayal, Grade carried on regardless, setting his sights on making a move on August 26 with a board meeting that was to include Gill, Birk, Michael, the Independent Television executive Norman Collins and Leo Pliatsky, board member of ACC. At first Pliatsky tried to stall the meeting pointing out that Birk was not present due to being away on holiday unaware that Grade had already made contact with Birk prior to the meeting. Grade's task was to remove Gill from his position as executive and terminate his contract, formulating a plan of compensation so not to alienate the present board and then restructure the board accordingly.

The air must have turned blue in that boardroom when Grade delivered his verdict. As the raised voices became a little calmer, Grade informed Gill that he would pay him his five-year salary in an act of good-will. As the rest of the board reacted it became apparent that Michael who had wanted Grade removed had voted in favour of Gill's leaving from the company. "A fine colleague you turned out to be, Bill" barked Gill as he made his way towards the boardroom doors. Collins turned to the other board members and joked "If Lew ever remakes *Jesus of Nazareth* and is looking to cast the role of Judas, he needs look no further than Bill." As the board members made their way out of the boardroom, Gill approached Grade in the corridor to shake hands. "Lew, you have six months", before walking the corridor to his office to clear his desk. That next day Grade called upon the press to run the story that Gill had resigned from ACC and while *The Sun* ran with the headline "LORD MUPPET SACKS RIGHT-HAND MAN", the *Financial Times* took the story more seriously with their headline "GILL RESIGNS: SHARE-PRICE TUMBLE AT ACC".

The Australian Gordon Gekko
Part Two

Following the meeting with Grade and Gill back in May, Holmes à Court had returned home to Australia to ponder his next move with ACC. He had no original intentions of taking over the company at this time. But he did care for the large percentage of shares he had with the company and could use this to his advantage. That day back in July when Gill was removed from ACC the news broke that one of the banks financing ACC had withdrew its credit due to the tumbling shares. As the weeks progressed and the news reached Australia that ACC was heading towards trouble, Holmes à Court purchased another block of shares. Grade saw no reason to be concerned as to him Holmes à Court was showing considerable interest in the company having purchased a million of the company shares. For Grade, that was a positive sign to have a wealthy businessman taking so much interest in ACC. After all, it was not like

Holmes à Court could seize control of the company... or could he? Grade also realised that Holmes à Court could not have purchased all those shares for the fun of it.

On the 11 September 1981, Holmes à Court flew back to London for a press meeting in the presence of Lew Grade and aided by four accountants and his lawyer. Grade congratulated Holmes à Court on "acquiring so many shares at what I think is a ludicrous price when you consider the asset value of the company." The press was speculating to what Jack Gill's pay-off was to be as months earlier Grade had agreed on a signed contract deal for Gill of £105,000 a year running for the next five years. The press had deemed the deal unethical given the circumstances surrounding the finances in question with ACC. Courtesy of the media the Gill drama was now being broadcast publicly across the UK through newspapers and news reports on television. The once proud British entertainment sector that had become a household name was being tarnished for all to see. The tipping point was the disclosure of Gill's lavish life style and the penthouse flat at ACC House in London and the apartments extensive refurbishment at the cost of company assets.

That December, Holmes à Court had now secured fifty-one percent of shares in a move that welcomed him onto the board at ACC. As Grade prepared to address the media over the new member to the company, he was besieged with questions on the aftermath of Jack Gill's departure and Gill's sumptuous pay-off deals. Gill was to receive £560,000 in cash; the option to purchase his house for £100,000 less than the current market value; gifted a Rolls Royce, Mercedes Benz and an Aston Martin, along with an additional yearly pension of £72,000. But if that wasn't enough to distract the press the announcement that ACC had made a half-year loss of £8m was certain to do the trick. The shareholders and pension fund holders erupted with outrage. Then on the 24 December *The Times* printed that ACC had lost over £7m in film-stocks. To Holmes à Court, ACC had become a mismanaged company that had been built up and suddenly run down by an old man. In January 1982 and some two weeks after his golden handshake deal, the Post Office Pension Fund who had shareholdings in ACC sought out an injunction through the High Court to stop Gill's pay-off from going ahead. Up until recently ACC had tried to operate under a private policy and with the medias broadcasting the exploits going on within, it did nothing to put the company in any form of a positive light. And still the revelations came. It was reported that Gill had purchased a Cessna jet for £2m and additionally acquired a private suite at the Park Hotel in Los Angeles; all with company money. It also emerged that both Grade and Gill had previously signed documents allowing them to purchase their homes at the price they were obtained by ACC and not the market value price.

That January Holmes à Court and Grade were to meet Martin Starger in person in a meeting that did not go down well at all. Holmes à Court, spurred on by Starger's absurd fees, did not favour the Grade-Starger business deal informing Starger that under no certain terms would he be renewing the contract. During the return flight to London, Holmes à Court laid it out to Grade that the board of directors were of low calibre and if Grade were to get rid of them, Holmes à Court would support his decision. And to sweeten the deal, Holmes à Court would give Grade a generous newly drafted contract and handsomely pay him for his troubles. But there was a catch. Because ACC was on the verge of bankruptcy, Holmes à Court wanted to be the main voice of reason that had full support from Grade in backing up any new decisions. This was not how Grade wanted things to go. And for the first time in his life he felt he had been forced into a corner from which ultimately would come with personal sacrifices. And so, for the remainder of the flight until Concorde touched down at Heathrow Airport, Grade hurriedly come to the decision to sell his voting-shares for ACC to Holmes à Court. In an undignified manner, Grade wrote out his exit plan on the back of a Concorde napkin as Holmes à Court looked on, hesitatingly passing it to Holmes à Court and bringing to a close 27 years of Lord Lew Grade's great British ITC entertainment empire.

The Battle for ACC

On the 13 January, Holmes à Court held a meeting to discuss his proposed take-over of ACC. Concerns were raised that ACC would no longer be in the hands of British directors. Holmes à Court had promised

Grade that he would keep him on with a title of Life President and retaining his current £203,000 yearly salary with a contract running until a review in 1984. As the press fell over themselves with the developing story little did they know that Jack Gill was ready to take the ACC company board of directors to court over the fresh decision to block his promised pay-off. With attention focused on the pantomime between Holmes à Court and Grade, ACC investors and pension holders had become tired of the whole debacle and turned their anger now towards Holmes à Court and his hostile takeover of a great British institute. A war of words soon mounted as the courts asserted pressure on him to pay-off Jack Gill once and for all. Leading newspapers laid it on thick in exposing the shocking truths unfolding within the walls of ACC and the board of officials who were living a life of luxury with little to no care towards the investors. In no time, both Gill and Holmes à Court became Public Enemy Number One. However, Holmes à Court was not content in just owning the larger percentage of the shares to ACC; he wanted the company in full. And so, he proceeded to secure the remaining voting shares.

A bidding war erupted in the law courts situated on Fleet Street. At first Holmes à Court tried to play down ACC's worth by undervaluing the company as a whole. But with ACC now seemingly on the market, Holmes à Court was not the only businessman interested in securing the company. As Holmes à Court kicked the bidding off with a friendly £36m on the table, up rose British property tycoon Gerald Ronson with a counter bid of £42m. The board of directors agreed that Ronson's bid had to be given fuller consideration. But as Holmes à Court was both chairman and chief executive of ACC, it was decided the position was untenable. Ronson requested to see the financial records for ACC. Holmes à Court, on the other hand, denied him of such pleasure. Yet again the whole sorrowful saga turned into another drawn out corporate media driven slanging match. Ronson wanted the company for personal reasons and felt that Holmes à Court, if he continued on with his role in the company, would no longer keep it operating as a whole but rather break it up for financial gain. On 13 February, Holmes à Court upped his bid to £46m prompting Ronson to retort that he was "not playing the game." Even Holmes à Court went on to admit that the business saga had become the "longest running comedy show in town."

Finally, both men came to an agreement in working together to iron out their concerns over the companies' financial woes. What was most important was that ACC's shareholders were to gain a better deal obtaining the best possible price for their shares. Part of Ronson's plan was to keep Lew Grade on as Life President, placing himself in a role as chairman and keeping ACC in business with Central Television, thus preventing any further redundancies. In return Holmes à Court left the day-to-day running to his deputy, Bert Reuter, and under the strict orders that he catalogued any further financial abuse within the company which could be used against any of the directors in the form of engineered fashion. All the company finances had to be signed off by Reuter. Even the company alcohol had to be locked away with it being allowed out during certain occasions under specific instructions. Even with all this utter farce being played out in front of staff at ACC, the company was still accumulating interest from other parties who wanted to buy and secure ACC for the future and remove it from the vice-like grip of Holmes à Court.

On the 22 March 1982, Holmes à Court made an unexpected return to London without any advanced notification of his journey. It came as quite a shock when he walked into the boardroom in the middle of a meeting between company directors who had, until then, presumed he was still in Perth. Realisation dawned on the directors that someone had tipped off Holmes à Court of their apparent attempt to offer the company to other parties with the hope they would purchase ACC as a whole. As Holmes à Court laid out on the table several pieces of documentation disclosing those who had agreed to go against him, the boardroom turned to uproar. Of those voicing their anger to the situation was Ellis Birk who pointed out the unethical and improper manner being displayed by Holmes à Court. "As you seem so worried about ethnics, Ellis", barked Holmes à Court, "you can hand back the keys to the Rolls Royce that the company paid for." Rumours began to circulate that the telephones at ACC House had been tapped and that during one meeting the board of directors had resorted to searching the boardroom for bugging devices. The following day, two of the company directors, Sir Leo Pliatsky and Lord Matthews, handed in their resignations. On the heels of them leaving, Holmes à Court jumped at the chance to put in another higher bid in an attempt to secure ACC by using one of his other companies, The Bell

Group, promptly forcing Ronson to declare on 23 March that he would no longer be pursuing ACC after already spending £250,000 in court costs in fighting Holmes à Court. With no other contenders coming forward to challenge him, Holmes à Court became the victor of the battle for Associated Communications Corporation. Only time will tell to the future of the company and the other associated companies consisting of ATV, AFD and Grade's much beloved ITC.

Exit Stage Left

During his time at the top, Lew Grade was considered to be Mr Entertainment in dominating television screens with his hit shows. His status as Britain's media mogul earned him a healthy pay rise when back in August 1978 his yearly salary went from £59,500 to £210,426, making him one of Britain's highest paid television executives. But by the middle of April 1982 Grade had become almost a shell of the man he once was as exhaustion by the stress brought about by the poor relationship with Holmes à Court took its toll. Of the original board of directors, only that of Lord Windlesham had remained. The others, Birk, Louis Benjamin and Norman Collins had abandoned ship to leave Grade behind. Grade had now become just a mere employee and open to scrutiny as Holmes à Court questioned Grade's expenses. Now the legal owner of the company, Holmes à Court asserted his authority, doing whatever he liked even if it meant humiliating Grade both privately and publicly. The end came on 17 June 1982 as Lew Grade cleared away his desk and walked out through the doors of the company that he had spent so much of his life building up. His departure sent ripples through the world of entertainment as the bitter take-over by Holmes à Court pushed those from the entertainment business to no longer remain silent. Comedian, television star and writer Spike Milligan vented his anger in writing a letter for publication to the *Financial Times*.

> Sir,
> Many people from the entertainment world will be depressed at the forced resignation of Lord Grade. It was Lew and Leslie Grade's agency that helped hundreds of us during the post-war variety years. But for them it would not have existed. They left it only when they realized TV was the coming thing.
>
> OK, so *Raise the Titanic* lost a lot of money. I ask you what company doesn't. What about British Leyland? At least Lord Lew never went cap in hand always begging for money. It was always on a business basis. What other chairman would you find at his desk at six and in the morning? Of course, he gave a large golden handshake; he was a big man, he is still a big man.
>
> Holmes à Court has got the company not because he is interested in show business, but because he is nothing more than a business magnate. I am appalled at the short memories of the world of finance. This man could have made it again and again if he was just given breathing-space.

Not all the bad air between Grade and Holmes à Court was that stale. When Grade was ready to leave ACC, he had promised to keep to his side of the agreement in promoting the companies financed movie, *Sophie's Choice*. Some months after departing from ACC and with Grade back at his own office in London's Audley Square, he was taking stock of his own business and trying to continue on as normal as a businessman never to sit back idle. Then he received the phone call from Holmes à Court asking if the two of them could have a chat. Arriving at Grade's office, Holmes à Court was acting like nothing had been untoward previously. Grade was not a man to hold grudges and with three months having passed since his last dealing with Holmes à Court, he was more concentrated on running his own company. The businessmen discussed productions with Grade raising some concerns about how *Sophie's Choice* was going to be presented. It was agreed between them that the film would open with the wording LORD GRADE PRESENTS as used previously with ITC's *On Golden Pond* (1981). *Sophie's Choice* had its world premiere in New York on the 8 December 1982 with the opening title credit reading, as promised, LORD GRADE PRESENTS. But come March 1983 when it was screened in Perth, Australia, home of Holmes à Court, Grade's credits were nowhere to be seen. Grade shrugged it off until April when he received another phone call from Holmes à Court requesting yet another face to face meeting.

Confronting Holmes à Court, Grade demanded to know as to why his name was omitted during the Perth screening. Holmes à Court played it down having said he had no knowledge of it considering their agreement a few months earlier. Whether Grade believed him was the least of Holmes à Court's worries. The heated departure of Martin Starger was not over as Starger pursued Holmes à Court through court, suing him over non-payments of money towards *Sophie's Choice* and *On Golden Pond*. Although Grade had been approached to give evidence in court, the opportunity never arose when the case was successfully settled out of court the day before proceedings were to start. As the months passed stories continued to surface on the unsavoury running of ACC as Holmes à Court continued his relentless power-driven assassination. It emerged that as a bribe to get singer Michael Jackson to perform at Holmes à Court's son's birthday party, he had sold the rights to the Beatles' songs to Jackson for an eyewatering £33m. Grade could do nothing but watch the circus show roll on by. He became dumbfounded when Holmes à Court let go of the companies £80 per-week tea girl, followed briefly by the sacking of the lift man who had worked with the company during Grade's reign of 25 years. For Grade, enough was enough. With over nine months left on his contract with the company, Grade up and left the dictatorship of Holmes à Court. Writing in his 1987 autobiography *Still Dancing*, Grade wrote "So much for Robert Holmes à Court - a major miscalculation in my life. To this day I cannot understand why he felt the way he did and why he behaved the way he did."

Titanic sinks *Titanic*

The years that were to follow offered Grade the time to ponder over the successes and the failures of the industry. For *Raise the Titanic* and its downward descent into the bleak waters of Davy Jones' Locker, Grade did have one person in mind who he blamed for the film's financial loss – his brother, Lord Delfont. Delfont was the Managing Director to the EMI division for entertainment. The brothers certainly had a flare for television entertainment. But where it faltered was the transition to the big screen. As Grade's *Raise the Titanic* was slowly withdrawn from theatres during 1981, Delfont's own cinematic financed creation *Honky Tonk Freeway* was released publicly becoming a box-office failure that it eventually lost more money than *Raise the Titanic* ever did. Delfont was no stranger to the subject of *Titanic* when he and EMI were responsible for the release of the $5m budget *S.O.S. Titanic* back in 1979. During the time Delfont financed the project he was blissfully aware of his brother's involvement in bringing Clive Cussler's novel to the big screen. Grade had concerns with his brother pushing forwards a low budget *Titanic* movie while he continued to pursue the release of his considerably higher budgeted *Titanic* spectacle. What made matters worse was that both were pencilled in for their release a matter of months apart. It was a risky business having two movies released in such a short space of time covering the same subject. Grade had to focus on *Raise the Titanic* being the better choice for the public. That did not stop the ill-feeling mounting between the brothers.

One major factor for both Grade and his brother was that they had joined forces in October 1978 to create AFD and cover the film distributions for both ITC and EMI on American shores. The company would have Grade as chairman and Delfont as vice-chairman with Leo Greenfield as the company marketing distributor. When Delfont announced his involvement with *S.O.S. Titanic*, Grade was quick to point out that his younger brother looked to be copying him. "He's getting on the bandwagon" said Grade. Delfont was equally quick to retaliate through the press, "I am not copying my brother. I've been working on SOS *Titanic* for over two years." During that time Delfont stumbled upon a dilemma that could have easily scuppered the movie. As *S.O.S. Titanic* focused on the sinking, the production was lacking one crucial element in which to tell the story; they had no *Titanic*, not even a working miniature. EMI had successfully secured the rights to film on board the former transatlantic Cunard liner R.M.S. *Queen Mary* which had been preserved and turned into a tourist attraction over in Long Beach, California. But what the liner could not offer were those scenes showing the flooding decks of the *Titanic* and the much-needed distance views of the doomed ship. The sound stage at Shepperton Studios offered the space for a section of the Boat Deck and bridge to be constructed that allowed for full scale lifeboats to be suspended from a gantry system above the set. But what was entirely missing was a scale model of the *Titanic*. Delfont had an idea and one he could only pitch to his brother.

Aware of the 55ft *Titanic* model under construction at the CBS Studio Center for *Raise the Titanic*, Delfont approached Grade to ask permission to use the model for *S.O.S. Titanic* when the model was still in its 1912 livery. While it would have benefited *S.O.S. Titanic* immensely, it was just not going to happen. Grade refused out-right. That, if it wasn't already clear, was going to cause more of a rift between the two brothers. Grade resorted to advising his brother to put the film on hold, as more was at stake with *Raise the Titanic*.

"I hear you're making a film about the *Titanic*?" Grade asked,

"That's right" his brother replied.

"You know I've been working on *Raise the Titanic*. Why are you doing this to me?"

"I'm sorry, Lew, I had no idea. What do you suggest?"

"Well, it's obvious, isn't it? You've got to stop yours", said Grade.

"I can't do it" replied his brother, "I'd lose a fortune."

Bernard tried to convince himself that there was enough room for two movies covering the *Titanic* saga. Delfont now had to look elsewhere for a *Titanic* miniature. Things would finally go his way when the British model making company Bassett-Lowke agreed to lend their 20ft *Titanic* that was in its final building stages at their factory for a client over in Canada. But there was a catch. EMI were only permitted to photograph the model and then matte the images into scenes. The model shots were eventually matted into several scenes in such a way that the finished shot was more amateurish than that carried out by a major studio. And yet, only one photograph of the model would be used to show the *Titanic* sinking. In the end Delfont turned to using a large quantity of unused test footage from the 1958 Rank Organisation movie *A Night to Remember* where each frame of the footage was hand-coloured by matte artist Wally Veevers who was also working with Grade over on *Raise the Titanic*.

Despite its flaws, *S.O.S. Titanic* had one advantage over previous films covering the disaster in that this was the first *Titanic* movie to portray the event in full colour while leaning more towards the lives on those on board. But all that colour and all that storytelling could not save the film. Delfont should have taken his brothers advice as reviews were nowhere near kind towards the production and the disappointing box office takings. "I told you so" must have been the voice rolling around in Delfont's head. Looking back on the film, Delfont wrote in his 1990 autobiography, *East End, West End,* that *S.O.S. Titanic* was a "disaster movie in every sense". Meanwhile the film was picked up for television screening, a better suited medium, followed by Japans Toho-Towa securing the rights to both *S.O.S. Titanic* and then later *Raise the Titanic*. In a stroke of luck, Toho-Towa went on to shelve the release of *S.O.S. Titanic* in favour of *Raise the Titanic,* allowing Grade's post-disaster film to become Japans biggest box office success for that year. In his autobiography *Still Dancing,* Grade would have the final word on the Grade vs. Delfont battle of the *Titanic*'s,

> "I really believe that the failure of the film was inadvertently, and ironically, due to my brother Bernie. He was the Managing Director of EMI's Entertainment Division and had a production company based in America that was making movies and mini-series for television. One of these projects was a four-hour version of *SOS Titanic* – a story about the sinking of the *Titanic*. It was shown on television and was a real flop."

An Unexpected Return

As Lew Grade walked down the steps from ACC in June 1983, one would assume that at the age of 77, he would have thrown in the towel and put his feet up to enjoy the rest of his life. But that was *not* Grade. He caught the attention of American television writer and producer Norman Lear who brought in Lew Grade to head the London division of the Embassy Communications International in the distribution of films and television programmes until the Coca-Cola Company purchased the business in June 1985. Now back on his feet, Grade followed with launching the Grade Company in which during that time he was given the position of vice-president to the Loews Theatre Group franchise who owned and operated a cinema chain right across America. Through the 1990s, Grade would tell the story to the media of how he was at his office desk come 7am, to enjoy smoking that day six Monte Cristo 2's costing £12.50 each. And for a special treat, one Monte Cristo A with a £36 price tag. "I don't drink, I don't gamble, I don't go on holiday", Grade said. While things were looking up for Grade, the past was to come back to taunt him when he received news that Robert Holmes à Court had passed away suddenly from a heart attack at his home on the morning of September 2, 1990. By 1995 Grade had once again built up a strong reputation where those who still honoured his time as the head of ACC pre-1980 continued to support his adventures. Despite Holmes à Court selling off the rights to ITC, EMI and AFD, the latter being snapped up by Universal Studios, miraculously ITC had survived to continue operating under a new license revealing a ray of light on the horizon.

ITC had been purchased by PolyGram in 1995 for $156m to form another variant of ITC Entertainment. Upon purchase, PolyGram began to look for someone with experience to head the company. One man's name kept coming up; Lord Lew Grade. In an unforeseen set of circumstances Grade was back in the London offices of ITC and the familiar territory of an empire he created many years ago. He remained in that position until his passing on the 13 December, 1998; just 12 days before his 92nd birthday. That December, PolyGram sold on the rights of ITC to the Seagram Company Ltd, a parent company to Universal Studios. Then in January 1999 ITC was sold again to the British organisation Carlton Communications for a cool £91m with the deal including the rights of the programme library of all ITC, ATV and AFD licensed films and television programmes, and to render ITC as a defunct company. With the passing of Lew Grade and the dissolving of ITC as a brand, it marked the sad end of an era for classic British television.

But as one flower dies, another one blooms. The passing of Lew Grade and the dissolving of ITC may have ended a remarkable era, but it opened the doors to a new period of remembrance towards the back catalogue of classic British television that was originally created by Grade and ITC. The London based Network on Air was created in 1997 to preserve the legacy of classic television programmes released through Grade's entertainment companies. In conjunction with ITV, one of Grade's former creations, Network would see the release of over 3,000 titles from the vaults of ITC, AFD and ATV including their restored theatrical version of *Raise the Titanic* in a special edition release.

Twenty-five years after Grade's passing, his entertainment legacy continues to thrive. Holding cherished moments for the many and creating many more for the new generations yet to come. Grade was confident that *Raise the Titanic* would eventually come out on top despite all his comical banter that it would have been cheaper to have lowered the Atlantic. And yet, over 40 years later, his £25m gamble in raising the legendary lost liner has defied all odds to become a firm favourite among fans of classic ITC; of classic Lew Grade, and of classic British television. And over the past 40 years, Grade's quip of, "Raise the Titanic? It would have been cheaper to have lowered the Atlantic", is still cited time and time again when the subject of the movie comes to light. Would it really have been cheaper? It may well have been. But one thing is certain, it would never have been as entertaining if they had gone to all that trouble.

ATV House, the former offices of ITC and Marble Arch Productions, that is located at Cumberland Place in London and just a stone's throw from Hyde Park and the Marble Arch. Today the building is a residential property of high-end apartments and penthouse suites. *(www.buildington.co.uk)*

378 • *Raise The Titanic*

Company letter header. *(Author's collection)*

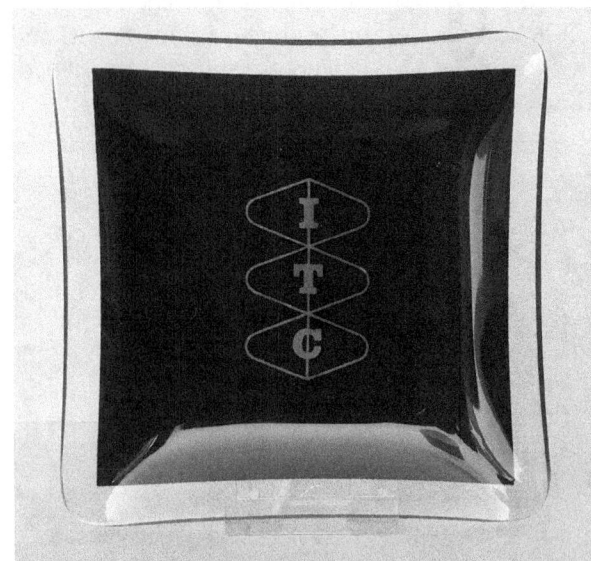

Late 1970s ITC company glass desk clip tray. *(Author's collection)*

Lew Grade at his London ATV House office desk in 1980. *(Author's collection)*

Chapter 26: It *would* have been easier if they had lowered the Atlantic • 379

Grade's deal with Toho-Towa finally paid off as *Raise the Titanic* was lapped up by Japanese moviegoers, pushing the film into its only box office success through tremendous ticket sales. *(Author's collection)*

Carr on location during the filming of *Can't Stop the Music*. *(IMDb)*

Allan Carr's *Can't Stop the Music* which would become another AFD disaster movie to cast a shadow over Grade back in London. *(IMDb)*

Robert Holmes à Court *(Author's collection)*

Jack Gill *(ITC – Author's collection)*

RIGHT: Martin Starger *(ITC – Author's collection)*

Jack Gill's ITC funded motion picture *Hawk the Slayer*. *(IMDb)*

Lew Grade and Robert Holmes à Court discussing business in early 1981. *(Mirrorpic)*

Martin Starger in his AFD office in California, June 1980. *(Los Angeles Times, June 12, 1980 – Author's collection)*

Happier times for Grade and ITC during a visit to Pinewood studios in 1974. From left to right; Bruce Gyngell (deputy managing director of ATV), Lew Grade, Bernard J. Kingham (ITC executive in charge of productions) and *Thunderbirds* creator Gerry Anderson. *(Author's collection)*

382 • *Raise The Titanic*

Grade addresses shareholders and the press, September 1981. Robert Holmes à Court can be seen at the conference table - fourth person seated from the right. *(Author's collection)*

Grade had no choice but to argue his corner on the gamble in committing so much money into the companies lavish film expenditures. To the board members, shareholders and press, the poor box office takings of several of his films had placed the company into an uncertain future. *(Mirrorpic)*

Chapter 26: It *would* have been easier if they had lowered the Atlantic • 383

A clearly exhausted and stressed Lew Grade leaves the board meeting. *(Author's collection)*

As the woes of Grade and ITC played out in newspaper columns, satirical British cartoonist Stanley Franklin gave his spin on events. If Grade was struggling to hold onto the publicly loved entertainment sector, maybe Prime Minister Margaret Thatcher could be the one to come to the rescue. *(Original artwork © Stanley Franklin – Author's collection)*

Lord Bernard Delfont *(Author's collection)*

The ill-fated EMI tv-movie *S.O.S. Titanic*. *(Author's collection)*

Actress and model Antoinette O'Reilly, who plays an unnamed 3rd class passenger, stands alongside the 20ft Bassett-Lowke model of the *Titanic* that would be photographed and used in *S.O.S. Titanic*. *(Author's collection)*

With Grade refusing Delfont's request to use the *Raise the Titanic* model for *S.O.S. Titanic*, EMI were left to find other means. Matte artist Wally Veevers, who would also work on *Raise the Titanic*, used a number of still photographs of the Bassett-Lowke model (images 1, 2 & 3) where he matted the shots together for several scenes. Veevers would also hand tint unused footage from the 1958 Rank Organisation movie *A Night to Remember* (image 4) for the brief sequences of the doomed liner. *(EMI / Rank Organisation)*

He's no muppet. Grade with one of his much-loved British family entertainment exports. Grade's return to the ITC brand in 1995 would see the king of entertainment back where he belongs. *(ITC Publicity photograph - Author's collection)*

Lord Grade takes centre stage at a company press conference in the summer of 1980 as he promotes *Raise the Titanic* in the UK. Speaking to the press he remarked 'Everybody doesn't believe that we'll raise the *Titanic*. But here's us bringing up the *Titanic*. You see it? You see it coming up more. And now here it is. It's up... the *Titanic*. I think its $35m well spent – I hope." *(Author's collection)*

CHAPTER 27

Lost and Found

"This is Pitt. Bring on the surprise package."

Seasoned fans of *Raise the Titanic* could possibly recite much of the movie scene by scene, even dialogue by dialogue. I know I can. But what was released to the public was far removed from what was planned and filmed. The editing of the film by Terry William's and Robert F. Shugrue resulted in much content being purposely removed as the studio pushed for the tightening up of the production for the public release. These removed segments came from the feedback of the U.S. Navy, the Pentagon and those who had viewed the film during special screenings prior to the world premiere screening in Boston. As the release dates neared, the pressure to get out a version of the film that supported the feedback already received may have benefited those who were sceptical of some scenes. But in the long run, it created so many plot holes that the *Titanic* herself could have been lost down one of them. Those removed scenes, regardless of what the studios thought best at the time, did tie-up many parts of the movie and answer some of the questions that went on to appear after the public release. Some scenes cut were the result of it being explained in another part of the film such as Sandecker replying to the press conference reporter that the iceberg gash would be covered over with "special metal plates." What many may not be aware of is that the scenes of the iceberg damage being plated over was filmed and made it right to the very end, to then be pulled because it conflicted with both the feedback and Robards spoken line.

The choice in removing some content focused more towards scenes that did not include much character screen time, especially those scenes with less dialogue. Many of the cut scenes were special FX segments that occupied running times lasting a matter of seconds to those going into a minute or more. The studios jump decision to edit out much content came from the feedback of the screenings by those largely there to watch a movie, as a movie, and less in the role of a *Titanic* enthusiast. As the studio focused more in getting a return on their product, if that meant cutting scenes to tighten up the overall look and running time of the film, then that is what they had to do. Blinded by the decision to please others; those others not being fans of the subject, could be looked upon as one reason the film became the press titled "clunky" production that it is still referred to forty-years later. The critics of the time pointed out that the scene of the submersibles picking up the steel plates, holding them over the iceberg damage and welding them onto the hull took up too much screen time and added nothing new for the viewer who had been told minutes before that the hull damage would be plated over. Why see it when we were already told about the procedure? But that is what the fans wanted to see. It was storyboarded. It was approved. It was filmed. It was edited into the movie as a sequence and it was then cut, and fans were none the wiser that such content ever existed. Unfortunately, that sequence was not the only one removed from the production. The removal of scenes reduced the movie from one with a running time of over two-hours to that of one hour and fifty minutes.

If all the removed scenes amounted to somewhere between 10 to 15 minutes of footage, what was covered in those scenes and sequences would make some difference if edited back into the movie for a future release on disc or offered as separate deleted scenes for a special features section. And that is where the problems begin. After forty-years, none of these deleted scenes are known to have survived other than the all too brief piece here and there released back in 1980 and used in a television feature along with the occasional still used for publicity reasons. The studio owners of the film have nothing in their archives other than publicity images and a trailer. It is now left to others to turn Dirk Pitt and go adventure hunting for the lost treasures from *Raise the Titanic*.

Maiden *Voyagers*

It still remains unclear to what actually became of all these deleted scenes during the days and weeks following the movie's release. What is known is that some have been unearthed courtesy of other sources. And while these scenes originate from the publicity days of the movie, they are the only known clips still in existence. The weeks leading up to the cinematic release of *Raise the Titanic* in the summer of 1980 did use fleeting shots that were published in newspapers, magazine articles, press release photographs and trailers, hinting at scenes that would eventually fall foul to the editing. During my own forty-years obsession with this movie I have searched high and low for any trace of these scenes to present them here for fans of this cult classic. While this is not a list of all the removed content it is the largest gathering of known material brought together for the first time to create a clearer picture of what was, what should have been and what could have been released.

Before we look at the scenes that did survive the test of time it is imperative that I clear up one confusion that has circulated for some years concerning footage that was used in the science fiction show *Voyagers*. The American television series followed the time travelling adventures of Phineas Bogg and his young sidekick Jeffrey, as they travel through history using a small handheld device called an Omni. Episode 15 titled *Voyagers of the Titanic* was broadcast on February 27, 1983 and featured the time travelling duo going back to 1912 to rescue the stolen Mona Lisa painting from a thief who had boarded the *Titanic*. Footage of onboard life was filmed in Long Beach using the deck and interior areas of Cunard's former liner *Queen Mary*. The views of the sinking *Titanic* would come from two big budget films; the 1953 Fox movie *Titanic* and other segments from a previously unseen production. It is the latter that is of much interest as the footage used for *Voyagers* did come from the film production of *Raise the Titanic*, but not in the context first thought. Each scene was only a matter of seconds in length but it was enough to show that the model used was the 55ft *Titanic* from that production. The segments consisted of scenes of the funnels belching out smoke, distant views of the liner with a heavy starboard list, lit up in lights as the dark silhouettes of people move along the promenade deck. As an explosion fills the air the second funnel lifts off the deck in a cloud of sparks and comes crashing down into the sea.

The segments used from both productions were given a blue tint, understandable when the black and white footage from the 1953 film was required to match up with the more newer colour footage from the *Raise the Titanic* production. To keep with consistency the colour footage was treated with the same blue tint. But what is the origins behind the used sinking footage from *Raise the Titanic* and why did it appear in this particular television series? It is no secret that *Raise the Titanic* was to include a prologue set during the cold night of April 1912. The footage filmed in the surface tank in Malta during the summer of 1979 had already been previewed by the studio and edited into a sequence ready to be used with live-actions scenes with actors. When the prologue was dropped the footage was still the property of the studios even during the time of filming and editing of the series *Voyagers*. One thing that the footage used in *Voyagers* does show was that the clips used were taken from a series of outtakes that were initially rejected during the editing process. It is common practice for any studio to carry out such takes for the sake of safety and viewing them to select the best scenes for use during the productions final editing phase. An identical process was carried out in 1979 when the film studio behind the tv-movie *S.O.S. Titanic* executed unused outtakes from the 1958 Rank production of *A Night to Remember* where the black and white footage was hand coloured frame by frame by matte artist Wally Veveers. Using such methods meant that studios working to a set budget could pay for the use of footage which would be considerably cheaper to do than go through the process of having miniatures built completely from scratch. The outtakes used in *Voyagers* are always referred to as being segments from the actual deleted prologue. This has never been the case. But what these segments do offer is a fascinating glimpse into what the film makers tried to achieve but sadly never fully accomplished due largely to the critiques of the studio executives.

Raise the Titanic: The Known Scenes

Between spring and mid-summer of 1980, the movie went through the usual stages of publicity with a number of official press packs, photographs, column shorts and trailers, released to seduce the public's imagination during the time of *Titanic*-fever in 1980. The media outlets such as newspapers and magazines circulated the usual images supplied by ITC included those of the main characters, the odd image of the *Titanic* model or the views of the fictional ballroom created on board the *Athinai* over in Athens. But certain stills did make it into print that were part of the film to then later disappear as the movie hit theatre screens. During the course of the production a lot of photographs were taken specifically under the guise of behind the scenes and for the purpose to sell the movie as well as documenting the production and using them over the years to sell the film on the varying media outlets such as VHS, laser disc, DVD, Blu Ray and download. By searching through the wealth of vintage publications, the odd scene can still be found, hinting to what was eventually cut during the final editing process.

Sourcing potential surviving clips is more complicated as the owners of the movie no longer hold such footage. It is left to the lengthy search of archival programmes with the hope that *something* may have been used. What a lot of these movie review shows frequently do is to play certain approved clips that were already used in trailers screened across cinema chains and those edited for television use. For example, the British weekly televised film show *Clapperboard* did cover the topic of *Titanic* appearing in movies with a section covering the new release of *Raise the Titanic* during the airing of the episode on the 10 November, 1980. But it is unclear if the episode ever featured any footage that did not make it into the publicly released version as a lot of these older recorded productions made by television corporations either degraded over time to the point of the print being unwatchable or in the case of some classic archival BBC material the tapes were wiped and recorded over as the demand for new programming increased. At the time of publication, the only known deleted footage comes from two official sources; the 1980 mockumentery *The Last Great Human Adventure* and a 30-second advanced teaser trailer released in America.

The clips used in the 30-second tv-spot are more thought-provoking even though they are a mere split second on screen. This time the scene of salvage crews working on the piping for the foam was carried over from the mockumentary for public viewing. Among the familiar shots that made it into the lengthier main trailers at the time of the film's release were a small selection that never survived the editing of the released production. A close-up of the *Deep Quest* with the lifting and welding device in its claws is shown as the sub crews weld the steel plates to *Titanic*'s hull. As the *Deep Quest* continues to lift up the plates and press them against the hull to then weld them in place, the *Sea Cliff* moves into position to drop one of the plates onto the sea bed at the base of the wrecks hull.

Since the release of the movie the only footage available commercially from the *Raise the Titanic* production period are some of the outtakes used within the episode of *Voyagers of the Titanic* released as part of the 5-disc DVD boxset on the Universal-Playback label in 2007. The tv-spot trailer has never made it to video with the only known recording taken from the television aired broadcast. It is unclear to what became of the deleted scenes once they hit the floor of the editing facility. In 1999 three frames cut from the deleted sinking prologue were discovered when they appeared in an auction sale of film memorabilia. The edited model footage for the prologue is rumoured to be in the private collection of a shipping historian in America who had supplied information for the film during its production. The footage, as the story goes, was handed to the historian as part payment for their services. Despite tracking down the alleged owner, I was unsuccessful in obtaining any validation of its existence without having to pay, heavily, for the privilege. With alarm bells ringing, I opted to walk away, leaving the question open to whether the footage still exists to this day.

One thing that is certain is that the clips used in the tv-spot and mocumentary are unusable in any context due to the poor quality and the 4:3 frame ratio. The split-second running time of each one does not warrant any distributor investing in cleaning them up for use as extras in special features contents on disc. The 30-second tv-spot if presented in its original form of a trailer would be plausible if the original tape was found and cleaned up. But since the movie's release in 1980 and the hype created by the *Titanic*'s discovery in 1985 and the global phenomenon created by the James Cameron blockbuster, if these clips had ever survived they would have been made public by now; unless they were destroyed as the film foundered at the box office during a time before movie goers began to demand for extended editions of their favourite movies.

The Last Great Human Adventure

As part of the films ongoing publicity, the studios opted for the unusual approach in promoting the production to high end clients. They approached the Hollywood based company Kaleidoscope Films, one of the largest producers of movie trailers in the industry. The twenty-three-minute mockumentary was done in a documentary style feature that combined some behind the scenes filming on the production of *Raise the Titanic* in which acclaimed television host Doug Llewelyn interviews Jason Robards as he acts out the role of Admiral Sandecker while mixing in interviews with the films production crew. Another element of the mockumentary was the inclusion on the development of the real-life expedition to the wreck site by Texan businessman Jack Grimm that was scheduled for the summer of 1980. The mockumentary is interesting in that it includes footage taken during the filming process on *Raise the Titanic* with locations on board the *Athinai* in Greece and highlighting some of the film process of converting the former cruise liner into the barnacled rust stained *Titanic*. The feature also includes some intriguing views during filming on board the U.S Navy fleet out in San Diego bay, from interior views to those out on deck. It is the series of scenes – deleted scenes from the film – and a small selection of John Barry tracks that did not make it into the final edit of the movie that makes the production much sought after for the fans of *Raise the Titanic*.

The deleted clips that appeared in *The Last Great Human Adventure* featured scenes of the U.S. Navy salvage crews as they assemble the flexible piping that will be connected to the pumping tanks on board the naval vessels. At the surface, the piping is lowered over the ships side and dropped down to the wreck 12,500ft below where submersible crews then attach the pipes to a set of portable pumping stations that feed the foam through hoses connected to *Titanic*'s lower compartments. The next segment of footage showed the numerous steel plates which were used to cover over the iceberg damage being dropped down to the ocean floor. The plates, stacked side by side, make their way down to the wreck while attached to a set of parachutes similar to those used on the lighting pods, salvage lifting tanks and depth charge cases. Once on the sea bed, the submersibles then remove them from their landing spot and carry them over to the hull ready for fitting.

"I was hired to host that show", reminisces Llewelyn. "I got to go to Athens in order to film aboard a ship the producers had been given permission to use by the Greek government. The ship was being doctored to make it look like it had been on the ocean floor for more than 60 years when it was brought to the surface in the film. We spent several days in the harbour in Piraeus shooting on board the ship. We were then supposed to go to Malta, where there is the largest deep-water filming tank in the world. However, the tank was out of operation when we arrived in Athens, and after spending 2 days waiting for it to be fixed, we got orders from Hollywood to come back to LA. It was a great gig!"

Surprise Package

Terry William's and Robert F. Shugrue's editing of the movie had resulted in much of the originally filmed sequences becoming litter on the cutting room floor. Since the film's release in the summer of 1980 only a couple of frames of those cuts have ever been discovered. Early drafts of the screenplay tell one tale of how they planned to have Clive Cussler's novel adapted for the screen while another, a recently rediscovered treasure-trove, finally reveals a totally different adaptation to that released in August 1980. When I set out to bring together the many stories of how *Raise the Titanic* came into being, I never envisioned that one day I would learn of the discovery of the movie's storyboards, having come to terms that they had been destroyed or lost without trace over the forty-years passed. Then by a stroke of luck, I was contacted by someone in the entertainment industry with the message, "you will want to speak with this guy." That contact proved instrumental in getting a far greater understanding of this much universally resented production. The purchasing of a storage locker in America had unearthed a wealth of movie production material in which the new owner of the contents was categorising for private and auction sales. And of the hundreds of boxes inside this locker, one contained a substantial amount of original *Raise the Titanic* storyboards. This once in a lifetime opportunity was a no brainer for me. And within 24 hours, I had secured the entire crate.

The storyboards, concept artworks and sketches amounting to over 700 pieces, although not complete, when put together detail a version of *Raise the Titanic* thought never to have existed and one that makes for interesting comparisons between what was considered and what *was* delivered. To take the story from the pages of the book to be fulfilled onscreen required much imagination and storyboarding from the hands of accomplished visual artists. The execution of visualising *Raise the Titanic* went to art director and production designer John DeCuir and his son John DeCuir Jr. Both father and son were assigned to work together on *Raise the Titanic* with DeCuir senior in the position of production designer while DeCuir junior worked as the art director. Their vision of the story is unique, capturing numerous elements of the novel in cinematic form in the all too familiar traits of the DeCuir's. And now, it leaves me to present to the reader in descriptive form some of the previously lost storyboarded sequences for this adaptation of Clive Cussler's bestselling novel, *Raise the Titanic*.

***

THE PROLOGUE: APRIL 1912 – *PART ONE*

Scene. 1 - 18

From the darkness of the night, a bewildering object emerges. It is cold, monstrous and threatening. As metal and ice make contact it is quickly replaced with voices of desperation and panic mingled with the sounds of distress rockets booming overhead in unison with the venting steam of the doomed *Titanic*'s steam whistles. From her boat deck the lifeboats packed with passengers swing haphazardly from their davits as they strain under pressure. As hysteria mounts among the passengers and crew a large explosion rips through the night as one of the boilers succumbs to the inrush of the icy cold water. Hard on the heels of the detonation from below decks, the number 2 funnel erupts in a cloud of sparks to come crashing down onto the boat deck and the fully laden lifeboat, sending the wooden craft and its poor occupants tumbling headlong into the sea below. Out on the boat deck the figure of a man emerges from the confusing mass of people; it is Arthur Brewster, shabbily dressed and clearly in a hurry. Entering through a door, he appears on the landing beneath the huge glass dome of the 1st class grand staircase. Quickly he pushes his way through the hordes of passengers and crew ascending the stairs as he, on a mission, is desperate to reach his destination somewhere on the lower decks. Brewster comes out onto the enclosed promenade deck in time to witness crewmembers trying to smash the glass of the window to create access to the lifeboat that is making the journey down from the boat deck. Running aft he enters the interior once again and makes his way to the aft staircase passing passengers who are trying desperately to retrieve their items from the Pursers Office.

Descending further he enters into the crew area of the vessel and the labyrinth of corridors, stairs and barriers while trying to avoid being seen. He stumbles upon a crew manhole cover that leads down to the engine room uptake; a large open space built up of stairs and catwalks. What is his purpose? Raised voices alert him to engineering staff fighting with the ships ever fluctuating electricity as lights flicker and generators struggle. Rushing past them unnoticed he enters into an open area of the hulls interior that is stacked with crates and slowly filling with seawater. It is one of the cargo holds. Standing just yards away is crew member John Bigalow, *Titanic*'s officer in charge of cargo. Brewster rushes upon Bigalow and produces a small handgun that he brandishes at the crewmember forcing him to lead him to a location of the cargo hold and a large vault. Handing over the keys to the dishevelled passenger. Brewster unlocks the vault door and pulls it open. Turning to face Bigalow before telling him to save himself. Bigalow quickly retreats and runs from the flooding hold. As the man enters the vault, pulling the door behind him, Bigalow hears the muttering words of, "Thank God for Southby", which abruptly cuts off as the steel door slams shut entombing the mysterious passenger inside for all of eternity. *Titanic* raises her stern skywards and slips beneath the waves and heads down towards the ocean floor. As she lands on the sea bed kicking up sediment she fades into the blackness as the title **RAISE THE TITANIC** appears on the screen.

EXPLORING THE DEPTHS: *SEA CLIFF*

Alternative for Scene. 99

The artificial light from an alien craft descending from the world above suddenly disturbs the blackness of the ocean depths as the D.S.V. *Sea Cliff* glides into view nearing the sea bed at 12,000ft. Inside the confides of the pressurized sphere, the ocean exploring occupants, now tired and exhausted, strain their eyes for any tell-tale sign of the lost *Titanic*. As the submersible skims over the sediment it disrupts a sleeping creature that churns up the silt creating a blanket of murk that envelopes the *Sea Cliff*. As the view clears it reveals a congregate of slender eel-like creatures that dart up and down in the lights of the sub. The forward-facing cameras pick up the outline of large jellyfish massing together as the sub glides through their path. Deep-water shrimp, illuminated now, dance in swarms almost blotting out the view from the *Sea Cliff*'s viewport that is being used by NUMA crewmember Mullins. As he photographs the spectacle outside the sub he is briefly distracted looking to his colleagues and missing the moment a large deep-water shark glides past the viewport. Finally, he returns to the porthole to be greeted by a group of rattail fish suspended in animation and staring blankly back at him.

FLYING FISH

Scene. 114 – 117

Far out in the North Atlantic the salvage fleet make their way to another new location within the triangle where *Titanic* sank. As the vessels slice through the waters, they are proceeded by a swarm of flying fish that leap up from the ocean, take flight for a few feet to the splash back down into the water to reappear again seconds later. On the bridge wing of one of the navy vessels, the officers point out the spectacle unfolding ahead of them as the small fish guide the vessels to their destination.

THE BOULDER FIELD

Scene. 116 - 125

The crew of the D.S.V. *Turtle* are testing their equipment as the sub reaches 15,000 feet. As they switch on the starboard high intensity lights, they instantly explode from the pressure. Suddenly from out of the darkness a huge mountainous formation appears. The *Turtle* has stumbled upon a vast boulder field. As the crews slowly and carefully navigate around the hazards the lights of the sub bounce off the almost polished surface of the rocks. The crew continue on over the boulder field with the rocks now starting to become smaller. The magnetometer, a metal detector attached to the bow of *Turtle*, starts to pick up something metallic sitting within the rock piles ahead of them. As the *Turtle* slows down the crew see nesting between layers of rocks a peculiar object. It is a musical cornet.

RETRIEVING THE *SEA CLIFF*

Scene. 125 - 130

From the depths a small craft emerges. As it nears the surface a series of splashes form in the sea as frogmen roll backwards from zodiacs released from the stern ramp of the salvage vessel. They swim down to the ascending *Sea Cliff* at it reaches the surface. The divers then systematically connect lifting cables to the eyelets on the hull of the sub as the craft bobs around in the swell. Suddenly the cables snap tight as *Sea Cliff* is pulled from the sea like a fish on a fishing line and swung inboard of the salvage vessel and lowered down onto the deck.

DROP TEST MODEL

Alternate Version
Scene. 131 – 132

At the marine laboratory, Dr. Silverstein explains to Pitt and Seagram what is going on in the testing pool. The men are standing in a high ceiling room with computers at one end, a large steel walkway with stairs above them and a steel concaved wall with three large thick glass windows that look right into the huge tank filled with water. From above, a white model of the *Titanic* emerges as it streams past the window and towards the floor of the tank. As it lands, two divers appear and attach a pair of cables to the large model for the scientists above on the platform to lift the replica back to the surface.

ICEBERG ALLEY

Scene. 133 – 137

Far out in the North Atlantic Ocean the stillness of the night is suddenly broken by the sounds of an approaching helicopter. On board are four occupants; the pilot, a U.S. Navy crewmember, Gene Seagram and Dirk Pitt. The cold air circulates the interior of the helicopter as the Navy crewmember, secured by a safety line, leans out of the open door to view the spectacle far below them. In the brightness of the helicopters searchlights a vast ice field is revealed emerging from the ocean mist. Towering icebergs like mountains, cold, stark and threatening, drift with the tides having travelled through the Labrador Current from Greenland. Seagram is transfixed to the window as Pitt explains the ice graveyard far below and how these towering ice beasts come to die as they branch out into warmer waters.

GLACIAL DEBRIS

Scene. 155 – 156

In their search for the *Titanic*, the submersibles *Sea Cliff* and *Turtle* stumble upon an area of the sea floor littered with monstrous glacial rocks that are highly polished and reflective. These towering giants were deposited from passing icebergs that slowly melt as they travel through the warmer waters.

THE CORNET

Scene. 159 – 165

After the metal detector has picked up something metallic below them, the crew of the *Turtle* spot the object sticking up from the rock piles. As they move in closer, they notice it is a horn of some kind. Hovering over the sea bed, two robotic arms unfold from beneath the sub and pause over the object before one of the arms opens its claws and slowly creeps upon the mystery item to take a hold and prise it from the rock pile. Suddenly the object slips, drops to the rocks below and bounces and rolls down the pile coming to a stop metre's away. The *Turtle* draws in again as the metal fingers of the arm grip the object once again. As the arms lifts the item closer to the camera the crew identify it as a musical cornet. Pleased with the discovery the operator places the cornet into a basket attached to the second extended arm.

THE FUNNEL INCIDENT

Scene. 195

Deep in the depths of the ocean the submersibles *Deep Quest*, *Sea Cliff* and *Turtle* continue on with their search for the *Titanic*. As they glide across the seafloor their motors kick up a large silt storm blocking their visibility. The disturbance interferes with the subs monitors and radar equipment. The crew are unaware of what is awaiting ahead of them in the darkness. From the churned up sediment the *Turtle* enters a chasm of steel some sixty-feet in length. It is the remains of *Titanic*'s funnel that has landed on a rocky outcrop of the sea bed. As *Turtle* passes through the interior of the funnel, it snags up a piece of the funnel rigging and drags the funnel to the edge of the ledge to the outcrop. As *Turtle* breaks free from the cable the funnel continues to slide forwards and over the edge of the ledge, missing the *Turtle*, but not the approaching *Sea Cliff* that is located at the bottom of the underwater cliff face. From above, the funnel falls vertically down to close in around the *Sea Cliff* like a spider caught in a drinking glass. As quickly as it appeared, the funnel topples to land on its side once again as the unscathed *Sea Cliff* reappears from the kicked-up sediment.

TITANIC FOUND!

Alternate Version

With a rumble, a section of the ocean floor collapses beneath the hull of the submersibles. As the sediment cloud clears, the subs begin their slow descent down into the canyon. With the metal detector jumping from its track and the lights of the subs piercing the blackness, a curved shape begins to appear. It is the stern of a sleeping steel giant. As the subs move closer the stern nameplate fades into view exposing the shipwrecks name as TITANIC. Slowly the subs move up the hull and pass along the wrecks side giving little sneak-peak views of the rusting hulk. As the subs reach the bow the lights pick out the ships name once more before they leave the wreck to the cold abyss. With the subs lifting up from the wreck they drop a series of small light flares as if to illuminate a route to the wreck.

SALVAGE LIFTING TANKS

Inserts

Scene. 224 – 243

From the interior loading bay of the *Modoc*, the Hydrozene salvage tanks are lifted onto barges that are then towed out from the navy vessel by tugboats. As the tugs near the location above the wreck site, a helicopter lifts the tank from the barge, positions it over the surface and the lifting cables let go to send the tank plunging down into the sea and its journey down to the ocean floor. At the bottom, the tanks, attached to their parachutes, land around the wreck. One by one, the submersibles move into position and lift up each tank, carrying it over to the *Titanic*. Other subs are busy welding the steel plates over the iceberg damage and attaching the mounting frames to the hull that will hold each tank. Also arriving from the surface are a number of pumping stations that are placed around the perimeter of the wreck to have sub crews connect a series of pipes from the pumps and over to the salvage tanks attached to the *Titanic*. One by one more tanks arrive, more pumping stations, more piping and more steel plates. The three remaining funnels have now been capped off with canvas covers as the *Turtle* pumps the salvage foam into the stacks. The *Titanic* is now ready to be raised.

PLATING THE HULL

Scene. 225 – 228

Steel plates rain down from above. One by one they touch down onto the sea floor, to collapse flat in an eruption of sediment. From the murk appear the submersibles as they come to collect a plate and move them over to the hull of the *Titanic*. As each plate is pushed against the hull, a blinding flash of light erupts from the welding machine attached to the front of the sub.

SALVAGE FOAM

Scene. 226 - 234

With crews finishing up on plating over the iceberg damage, the time has now come to fill the ships lower compartments with the salvage foam that will add 20,000 tons of additional lift in raising the wreck. At the surface, naval crews are busy connecting miles of piping together, manoeuvring over the side of the naval vessel and slowly lowering into the sea. Along with the piping, a number of specially constructed pumping units are also lowered down into the ocean, and allowed to float at a certain depth level as more piping is attached and passed down to the sea bed and connected up to yet more pumping stations positioned around *Titanic*'s hull. From the pumping stations a series of pipes with special connectors have been attached to hull portholes as the foam is pumped from the storage tanks at the surface, down the pipes, through the pumping units on the sea bed and into the hull of the *Titanic*. As the foam works its way around the lower interior spaces of the wreck, it activates with the sea water expanding into a solid substance dispelling much of the water from within the hull.

CAPPING THE FUNNELS & FITTING THE TANKS

Scene. 235 - 243

At the wreck site the submersibles *Deep Quest* and *Sea Cliff* are busy working on *Titanic*'s three remaining funnels as they cap the tops of the stacks with large covers that will help with the salvage operation for when the salvage foam is pumped into the towering structures. Once they have completed the task, they then join the *Turtle* in moving the Hydrozene tank anchorage frames over to the wreck, lifting them up into place and securing them to the hull. Then the subs lift up the Hydrozene tanks and attach each one to the *Titanic*.

LIGHTING RIGS DEPLOYED

Scene. 239

At the stern of the U.S Navy ship *Modoc*, crews are hooking up the series of salvage lighting rigs and sliding then along the hoist tracking to the open stern and ramp of the vessel. From there, each light is lowered into the sea, then released to sink to the ocean floor.

SALVAGE TEST

Alternate Version

Following the discovery of the broken funnel and then the main hull, NUMA carry out a salvage test to establish that their equipment is operational. The crew turn their attention to the detached funnel. With a tow cable attached to the funnel and the broken stack pumped full of salvage foam, the *Sea Cliff/Turtle* drags the funnel up off the sea bed and up towards the surface.

DEEP QUEST GETS STUCK

Scene. 246 – 266

Down at the wreck site crews are busy making *Titanic* ready for salvaging. The *Deep Quest* is working its way around the third and fourth funnels and heading towards the stern of the ship. Unbeknown to the crew inside, they are heading directly towards danger. As the *Deep Quest* passes over the open section of the A-Deck promenade it moves between the port and starboard electric cranes with their cargo derricks frozen at peculiar angles. The crew, oblivious to the unnatural surroundings, accidentally clip part of the cargo crane derrick with the *Deep Quest*, to become snagged in the wreckage. The crew increase the power of the sub's motors to free the vehicle, but it does not go to plan. The steel frames of the cargo crane derricks suddenly break their rusty cables sending the derricks crashing down on top of the *Deep Quest* and pinning it down to the deck. As the lights flicker and crews try to make sense of what has just happened, sparks suddenly erupt from the controls and a haze of smoke fills the interior of the *Deep Quest* forcing the entrapped crew to don safety gear. Nearby the *Sea Cliff* comes to the aid of the stranded *Deep Quest*. Extending its retractable arms, the *Sea Cliff* attempts to lift the cargo derricks up. But the crane arms refuse to move. It then takes hold of the broken steel cable of the crane and starts to pull. Again, the derricks still refuse to move. With nothing else they can do to help; the *Sea Cliff* begins its journey to the surface.

SEA CLIFF GETS STUCK

Alternate Version

Sea Cliff is working around the broken remains of *Titanic's* funnel when the subs manipulator arm gets tangled up in a broken piece of funnel rigging cable. The crew try to free themselves by putting the subs motors into reverse. As the sub struggles and weaves about, it appears it cannot free itself. But then the cable suddenly gives way sending the *Sea Cliff* hurtling backwards. As the sub crashes backwards into the skylight over the grand staircase, the situation is made worse when the entangled funnel rigging pulls and snaps off a large chunk of remaining funnel steam pipe that is protruding up from the deck and sent hurtling towards the *Sea Cliff*, striking the sub and pinning it down even more into the skylight.

DEEP QUEST GETS STUCK

Alternate Version

Scene. 246 – 269

Deep Quest is making its way around the rigging of the fourth funnel and out towards the stern of the *Titanic*. As the craft passes under the raised cargo derricks, the hull of the sub strikes a piece of debris attached to the underside of the cargo crane. Caught up on the wreck, the crew put the motors to full power in the hope of freeing the sub. Suddenly, the sub breaks lose. As it moves forwards, the hull hits the cargo derrick, sending the structure crashing down onto the hull and pinning the *Deep Quest* down onto the wreck. *Sea Cliff* appears from the darkness, grabs a hold of the derrick arm of the crane and begins to try and lift it clear of the downed sub. But the crane arm refuses to move. The *Sea Cliff* tries again. This time they have wrapped a section of towing cable around the cargo crane arm. As *Sea Cliff* pulls, the cable suddenly snaps. As there is nothing else they can do, the crew of the *Sea Cliff* begin their journey back to the surface.

THE ANCHORS

Scene. 246

On the bow of the *Titanic* the *Turtle* is busy at work preparing the wreck for salvage. Hovering over the anchor chains, the cutting equipment slices through the links as the port and starboard anchors are freed from the hull and drop down to the sea bed. *Turtle* then turns towards the bigger anchor sitting in a well at the tip of the bow. Reaching out with its manipulator claws it takes a hold of the anchor shackle and starts to pull the anchor up from the deck. But the anchor is too heavy to be completely lifted and so the *Turtle* releases its grip allowing the anchor to slam back down onto the deck.

GHOSTLY APPARITION

Scene. 255 – 257

Down on the sea bed the crew of the *Sea Cliff* are working around the wreck of the *Titanic*. As they take in the haunting beauty of the vessel, they are unaware of the ghostly apparition of a lady with long hair and flowing dress who manifests and glides through the sub's interior. As soon as she appears, she is gone.

MERKER IN HANDCUFFS

Scene. 265 – 268

Merker, who has been uncovered as the spy leaking information to the CIA, is escorted to the awaiting helicopter on the stern of the navy vessel. In handcuffs he is guided aboard the helicopter as personnel close the door behind him. As the helicopter lifts up from the deck it is eagerly watched by Pitt, Seagram and Sandecker. Seagram then heads towards the bridge where he meets Captain Burke as both men then watch the helicopter through binoculars as it flies away from the area.

ANGERED PITT

Scene. 282 – 291

Sea Cliff is hoisted out from the sea, swung in board of the navy vessel and lowered down onto the deck. From the open hatch appears Pitt who is greeted by Sandecker and Burke. Pitt is angered from seeing the *Deep Quest* trapped in the wreckage of *Titanic*. In the chartroom the men look over shipbuilders plans of the *Titanic*. Pitt explains the situation, marking off on the blueprints his hasty plan of action. Pitt wants to lay explosives around the hull of the wreck and blow it clear of the ocean floor. Still angered, Pitt exits the chartroom, walks out onto the bridge of the vessel, and, peering over the side, he says aloud "Seagram, you chowderhead."

FAULTY HYDROZENE TANK

Scene. 301 - 309

As the storm intensifies and the sea swells up, the raised hulk of *Titanic* is buffeted around in the heavy seas that could compromise her overall stability. The situation becomes worse when one of the Hydrozene tanks at the stern of the *Titanic* malfunctions resulting in the wreck to list. From the waterlogged deck above, a rope ladder has been attached to a section of structure and slung over the side of the hull directly above the faulty Hydrozene tank. Peering over the rusty railing is Seagram and Pitt who are shouting out orders to a lonesome figure riding the tank like a rodeo cowboy. As the sea swells up and swamps the tank the crewmember struggles to reattach an all-important hose that connects the tank to pumps supplying the gas. As the salvage crewmember battles the waves the hose connection finally clicks back into place. A surge of seawater throws the crewmember off balance sending him reeling against the hull. As the ladder sways uncontrollably, Seagram desperately tries to steady it as the crewmember makes the perilous jump towards the rungs. As he makes contact and pulls himself up another heavy swell rolls up on *Titanic* submerging the tank and swallowing up the crewmember in its path. As the swell rolls away, the ladder is exposed, the rope snapped and tattered, its occupant is nowhere to be seen. Pitt pushes the button on the remote box to activate the pump to the tank; but nothing happens. Seagram urges Pitt to try again. Pitt angrily punches down on the box as the pumps systematically spring back to life; but at a cost.

DEEP QUEST SAVED

Scene. 310B – 314B

From the helicopter that hovers just feet above the aft well deck of the raised *Titanic*, Dirk Pitt emerges and jumps down onto the silt covered timbers and directly heads straight towards the *Deep Quest* that has somehow become freed from the cargo cranes to then get entangled under the docking bridge on the stern. Pitt scrambles up the hull and unlocks the hatch of the *Deep Quest*. He is greeted by Seagram who crawls up out of the blackened interior, clambers up onto the hull, and throwing his arms up in the air, he is acknowledged by cheers and whistles from the surrounding salvage vessels.

RAISE THE *TITANIC*

Scene. 318g – 318t

From the decks of the salvage fleet the crew watch in amazement as the surface of the sea churns and bubbles wildly. Suddenly the bow of *Titanic* erupts from the ocean as the unsinkable legend claws her way higher and higher. With water pouring from her decks, windows and portholes, the hull slams down into the ocean as the waves swallow the hull entirely leaving just the three funnels visible. As the floatation tanks take over again, the hull, on an even keel, slowly starts to rise revealing the sodden and rust stained shipwreck. A roar of excitement fills the air from ships horns and cheering crowds of crew who are lining the railings of the salvage fleet. Pitt and Sandecker are watching from a higher deck. "There she is", responds Sandecker. Pitt has more concern in his voice, "Yeah… but where the hell is the *Deep Quest*?" As *Titanic* levels off and crew get ready to head out to the ship to secure it, Pitt and Sandecker are unaware of the activity happening behind them. Some distance from the salvage fleet a Soviet submarine has surfaced. Prevlov, who is onboard the *Mikhail Kurkov*, boards the ships helicopter where he is flown out to the waiting submarine.

PITT BOARDS *TITANIC*

Alternate Version

Scene. 319 - 322

With water still pouring from her decks, the salvage fleet have closed in around the raised *Titanic*. Crews come aboard with the pumping equipment. Pitt is among the crew who board the derelict. As the helicopter drops him down on the stern well deck, Pitt makes his way to the superstructure and up to the boat deck. As he passes the empty lifeboat davits he enters through a door and onto the boat deck level of the 1st class grand staircase with its ornate but badly stained dome. With water still sloshing around the room, Pitt walks back out onto the boat deck and heads towards the bridge where he pauses, thinking what it must have been like on the night of the disaster when the iceberg was spotted. He turns and heads aft again to emerge on the poop deck at the stern with the *Deep Quest* still partially lodged under the docking bridge. Pitt approaches the rotten stump of the flag pole protruding from the deck. From his coat he pulls free the White Star Line pennant that Bigalow had given him. Using a piece of twine from the packaging that contained the flag, Pitt ties the red pennant to the stump as the flag unfolds in the wind. With the feeling of being watched, Pitt turns to see Seagram standing alongside the *Deep Quest*.

TITANIC INVADED

Alternate Version

Scene. 331 - 372

The hurricane is now receding. The sea is becoming calmer. The tug crews are now reconnecting their lines back to the bow of the storm battered *Titanic* in preparation for the long journey to New York. But they are still not alone as among the silhouettes of the U.S Navy vessels is the Russian vessel *Mikhail Kurkov*. With the area still under a blanket of fog, a metal giant has emerged from below. It is a Soviet submarine and it is armed with torpedoes and a gun crew. The hatch cover of the conning tower opens as a number of crew appear, some armed, others with cutting apparatus. They enter a small dinghy and make their way towards the raised *Titanic*. Now onboard, the Russian crew split up into two teams with one heading forwards to the bow and the other entering into the interior. Down in *Titanic*'s cargo hold Pitt and his team are cutting through the hardened salvage foam to clear a path to the hold containing the vault. They are unaware of Prevlov and his team are also making their way down to the holds. Like a game of cat and mouse, a U.S submarine has also appeared under the cloak of the fog to position itself between *Titanic* and the Soviet submarine. From the submarine a team of U.S Navy S.E.A.Ls emerge in zodiacs and make their way towards the *Titanic*. Arriving alongside the derelict, they climb aboard a stern Hydrozene tank and climb the ladder that is hanging over the hull side. At the bow the one party of Russians have cut the towing cables that connect the *Titanic* to the pair of tugboats. Meanwhile, the captain of the Soviet submarine has sent out the fake distress call and watches as the U.S Navy vessels respond by leaving the *Titanic*.

Down in the lower compartments of the *Titanic*, Prevlov and his party are closing in on the cargo hold from one side of the vessel as Pitt and his crew approach from the other side. Finally, the Russian crew break through into the hold and Prevlov approaches the vault. Moments later Pitt and his crew arrive, coming face to face with Prevlov. But they are not entirely alone. From the gloomy interior the Navy S.E.A.Ls appear. Prevlov and his crew are outnumbered. Defeated, the Russian crew are rounded up. But Prevlov needs to know. He wants to see the contents of the vault. The lock is cut and the vault door is forced open to reveal the mummified remains of Arthur Brewster and the wooden crates containing the vital cargo. But Prevlov is denied his prize as he and his crew are guided out of the hold, up to the deck and put aboard a Navy helicopter that lifts off from the *Titanic* and disappears into the fog.

THE HURRICANE STRIKES

Alternate Version

Scene. 333 – 347

The two tugboats arrive alongside the *Titanic* as the storm quickly approaches the area. On the bow of the *Titanic* crew are battling the winds and choppy seas as they pull the towing cables up from the tugs and onto the wreck, wrapping the cables around deck mounted mooring bollards. Below them the tug boats, one either side of the bow, are being pitched about like toys. Every now and then they get slammed against the hull of the *Titanic*. With the storm intensifying and the salvage fleet battling the elements, they are being watched from afar as Prevlov, on the bridge of the *Mikhail Kurkov*, gives the order to send the fake distress message.

TUGS IN TROUBLE

Alternate Version

With the Russians breathing down their necks, and the stability of the raised *Titanic* causing concerns, the NUMA team and the U.S Navy now face the next peril as the hurricane slams down upon them. The Hydrozene tanks are struggling with the heaving seas along with the crews of the two tugboats that are connected to *Titanic*'s bow. On board the waterlogged wreck, Pitt and his team are being thrown about in all directions as the storm intensifies. But the situation is a lot worse for the tug crews. With each heavy swell the tugs are drawn downwards to abruptly come to a shuddering stop as the steel lines connecting them to *Titanic* become taught. Each wave that rolls over the open deck of the tugs swamp the crew, knocking them from their feet. With each heavy swell the tugs are pulled closer and closer towards the huge towering hull of the *Titanic*. With the fear of being sucked under the bows of the wreck, the crew cease upon the chance to remove the towing cables, freeing them from the escalating danger. As the cables are detached, Pitt, Seagram and the rest of the salvage team are now left to sit out the storm on board the unstable *Titanic* as the tugs and navy vessels move to a safer distance.

HEADING TO THE CARGO HOLD

Alternate Version
Scene. 350 - 354

With *Titanic* on the surface, Pitt and his team begin the task of digging their way through tons of hardened salvage foam as they make their way down to the cargo hold in search of Brewster's vault. The job is long, tiresome and backbreaking, but the crew finally break through and enter the hold with its rotten contents of sacks, boxes and the rusting Renault car that belonged to First Class passenger William Carter. Just beyond is the vault and its secrets within waiting to be unlocked.

PIER 12: NEW YORK

Scene. 384 - 385

At Pier 12 in New York sits the *Titanic*. On the quay are press reporters and sightseers. From the crowd appears Dana. She is there to reconcile her love for Gene. From the interior of the ship appears Pitt who greets Dana on the gangway. As he tells her about Seagram being on board, Seagram then emerges and makes his way towards Dana, guiding her to one side so they can talk in privacy. The couple then embrace for a passionate reuniting of their relationship.

***

History Repeating Itself

THE PROLOGUE: APRIL 1912 – *PART TWO*

Grade's decision to pull the opening sequence was not something he did on a whim. Grade was against the idea of any sinking sequences from the very start of the production in 1977. During the early stages of preproduction with Stanley Kramer in charge, Kramer's bold vision for the movie was to have the sinking of the *Titanic* as fundamental to the film as the raising sequences were to be. Kramer wanted to make the sinking scenes lavish by taking advantage of the model work in progress at the CBS Studios and create something more realistic than previously envisioned with previous movies such as the 1953 Fox production of *Titanic* and the Rank Organisation's *A Night to Remember* from 1958. As tensions mounted between Kramer and Grade, Kramer still pushed for bigger sets to get onto celluloid a grandiose view of the sinking of the *Titanic*. "It's been done", snapped Grade. "This is a film about bringing it up, not sending it down!" All this back and forth bickering between the two giants of the film industry was not positive and Kramer was the first to see the cracks appearing in the production. His decision to walk was ill-timed for the film considering how much Grade and his companies had already invested. But for Kramer it was for the best as the production issues on *Raise the Titanic* slowly strangled his already highly respected movie-making background. And yet as Jerry Jameson boarded the project it was still on the cards to film the model sinking.

    The rewrites of the screenplay still featured the 1912 opening right up to the revised script in August 1979. As Grade was against the idea for showing the sinking of the liner from the early period of the production, whatever he was saying it was being ignored as someone other than Grade was giving the go-ahead to continue with getting the sequence to film during the summer of 1979. Possibly Martin Starger? Maybe Grade who was aware of how the films budget was being spent wanted to make an example of what he had been saying from the very start, proving a point on the unnecessary increase on things that the film did not require as those in executive positions at ITC, Marble Arch and ACC watched from the side line taking notes on another of Grade's overblown movie adventures that was draining the company profits. It may also be that Martin Starger was pushing to include the sinking sequence keeping it close to the opening of Cussler's novel. But one thing is for certain, Grade was going to have that final say and regardless of the costs that sequence was never going to make it into the final edit of the film. It is evident that Grade stuck to his words about the film telling the tale on the raising of the *Titanic*. Grade stuck to his decision about not wanting it present, even though some of the reasons behind these decisions were aimed more towards how the scenes did not look good on film. The response from those who viewed the sinking sequence was enough for Grade to make his point and act upon it. As Grade had said from the start that it was not required, the mixed reviews of the footage, be them good or bad, was enough for Grade to cease upon the opportunity, "I told you it was a bad idea."

We know what was planned. We even know what was storyboarded and how the sequence was going to play out on screen. But these are based on the early versions of that sequence with information gathered from the screenplays, storyboards and footage from the outtakes that appeared in *Voyagers*. But what is not fully known is the running time of those sequences as nothing has survived that give a hint to the prologue's duration. That is not to say that the clues never existed; as they did. An interview with Richard O'Connor during February 1980 brought up the subject of the 1912 sinking sequence where the footage was to be used in the capacity of a *behind the credits* flashback scenario showing *Titanic* in her death throws. These three words were meaningless back in early 1980 and it does seem that no one picked up on what they represented at the time. Now forty-years later these same three words become apparent in meaning when a number of other factors are added to them.

The 3m:36s opening sequence of the released film is made up of three segments, the photomontage, rolling title and aerial view down to the island of Svlardov as credits appear on screen before ending on Koplin digging in the snow. The *behind the credits* running time for the footage suggests that it would not exceed more than the normally expected five-minutes screen time and with the sequence they did use coming in at 3m:36s, a total of 1m:13s was given to credits appearing over the Svlardov footage. When taking into account the 73 seconds of credits over footage, that same 73 seconds matches the running time for one of the deleted John Barry tracks from *Raise the Titanic* that appeared in *The Last Great Human Adventure* mockumentary of June 1980. Shipping historian Charles Ira Sachs who had worked on the production in the role of *Titanic* consultant expressed that he had seen the prologue footage in its original state. Ken Marschall also confirmed that he too had seen the prologue footage prior to the movies public release in August 1980. While Marschall could not recall to what was shown and to the running time, Sachs, on the other hand, claimed it ranged between 5 to 12 minutes. While 12-minutes is excessive given that it does not fit in with the storyboarded scenes and the screenplay from August 1979, it could possibly be a rough-cut and not the prologue in its completed state. But Sachs also stated that he had seen a shorter version prior to the films public release which ties in with the 5-minute running time making it more credible and more in line with the possible 3m:36s designated to open the film and introduce Koplin and the mine.

The reported *behind the credits* sinking prologue back in February 1980 is the strongest indication to what could have been used, which following on from the movies 31 July 1980 world premiere that resulted in around 10 to 15 minutes of footage edited out from the entire film during tightening up of scenes for general release based on the feedback from the critics. The sinking prologue was not present during the Special or the World Premiere screenings in July 1980. But if it had of appeared in the film, what could it have looked like? One can only speculate based on the evidence to hand and the tantalising trail of breadcrumbs left behind over the past forty-years.

On the screen appears LORD GRADE PRESENTS A MARTIN STARGER PRODUCTION which then fades to black. The movie opens with John Barry's *Raise the Titanic* main theme title as the series of black and white period images takes the viewer through a photographic record of the building and maiden voyage of the *Titanic*. As the main title music ends and the screen turns to black, it is replaced by the night sky as distress rockets burst onto screen, panning down to a view of the *Titanic* listing to starboard as icebergs surround the stricken vessel. As the disaster unfolds in a series of colour flashbacks the credits began to appear, STARRING JASON ROBARDS, RICHARD JORDAN, DAVID SELBY, ANNE ARCHER, AND ALEC GUINNESS. The rest of the credits continue on as the *Titanic* sheds her funnel and slips beneath the waves for the journey into the abyss. As the ship lands on the ocean floor the title RAISE THE TITANIC rolls up onto the screen to fade off into the scene showing Seagram and Sandecker exiting the gate of the White House. The entire sequence from start to finish was to run no longer than the estimated 3m:36s.

The sequence of Koplin digging in the snow, entering the mine, finding the corpse of Hobart, to then be chased by the Russian sentry was originally to appear *after* Seagram and Sandecker explain to CIA Nicholson, General Busby and Admiral Kemper about the mineral being on the island of Svlardov. As Koplin runs from the mine to be then brought down by the gun shot, Pitt emerges from the ice and kills the sentry, picks up Koplin and carries him off towards the ice floes. In the end the sequence was edited into three main parts and used in the movie; Koplin finding the mine, Seagram and Sandecker explaining about the mineral and Koplin being chased, shot and rescued by Pitt. None the less, the changes that *Raise the Titanic* underwent, the large number of scenes cut and sequences changed conclude that the film greatly differed to that of what was finally released to the general public.

Producer William Frye at the AFD productions office in California. Around him are a number of wooden scale models of the salvage vessels for *Raise the Titanic*, a large pre-production artwork of *Titanic*'s wreck (left) by John DeCuir and a wide array of production art and storyboards. *(Author's collection)*

Chapter 27: Lost and Found • 403

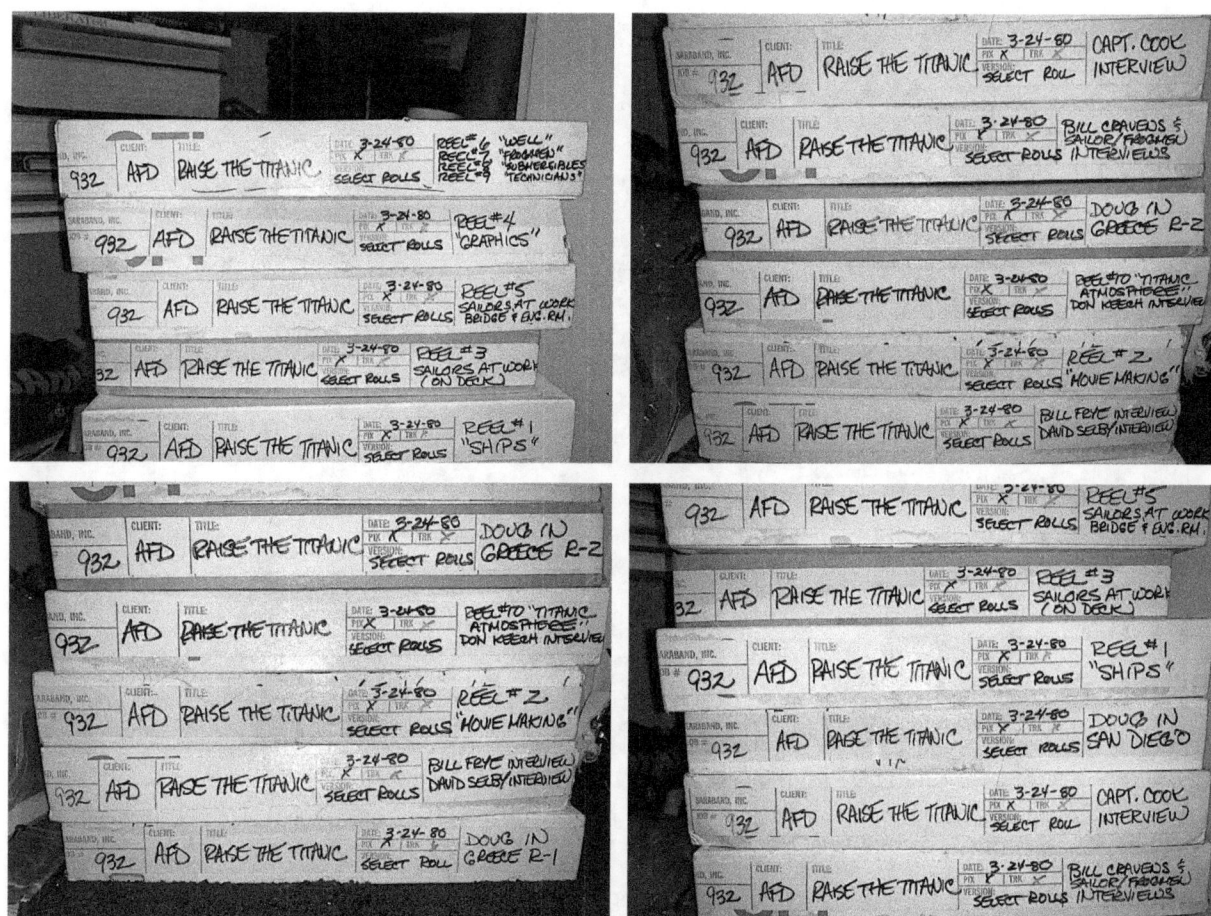

What treasures are there to be found on these reels? Now over 40 years old, the cardboard boxes holding the reels give a tantalizing hint to what was put onto celluloid. *(Jim Olson collection)*

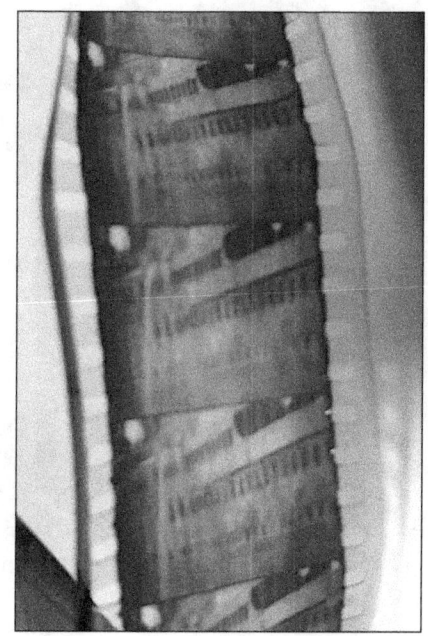

A recent find in Malta of reels taken during the filming at the studio tanks reveal a low-level portside view of the large *Titanic* replica moments after raising. *(Jean Pierre Borg collection)*

The time travelling duo from *Voyagers*; Phineas Bogg (Jon-Erik Hexum) and Jeffrey Jones (Meeno Peluce). *(NBS Publicity – Author's collection)*

The first in a series of stills taken from the *Raise the Titanic* sinking footage that would end up being used as stock footage in *Voyagers of the Titanic*. *(ITC – Author's collection)*

With a slight list to starboard, smoke venting from her funnels and lifeboats hanging from their davits, *Titanic* slowly succumbs to the cold waters. *(ITC – Author's collection)*

Chapter 27: Lost and Found • 405

Lifeboat #15 begins the perilous journey down the side of the doomed *Titanic*. *(ITC – Author's collection)*

The bow takes a plunge as the sea consumes the bridge and swallows up the first funnel. *(ITC – Author's collection)*

The second funnel is suddenly lit up as an explosion rips through the night. *(ITC – Author's collection)*

In a shower of sparks and thick smoke, the funnel collapses. *(ITC – Author's collection)*

Chapter 27: Lost and Found • **407**

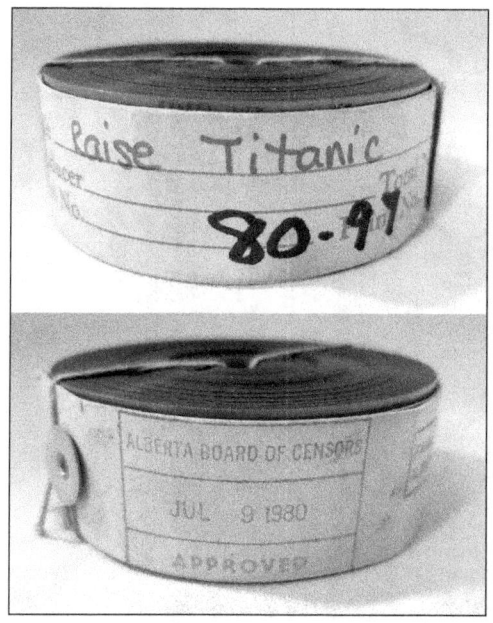

Seagram demonstrates his laser defence system. *(ITC - Author's collection)*

Original advanced 1980 teaser trailer for *Raise the Titanic* that, at the time, contained a small handful of clips that would later be removed from the film for its public release. *(Author's collection)*

Sandecker and Seagram leave the White House after a meeting with the President. This scene was to be the opening to the film following the 1912 prologue as both men try to convince the President that things are getting heated between the U.S and the Soviet Union. *(ITC – Author's collection)*

Marganin and Prevlov discuss the results from the aerial photography sent to them showing a U.S ship in the waters off Svlardov, raising concerns that something untoward is happening. *(Author's collection)*

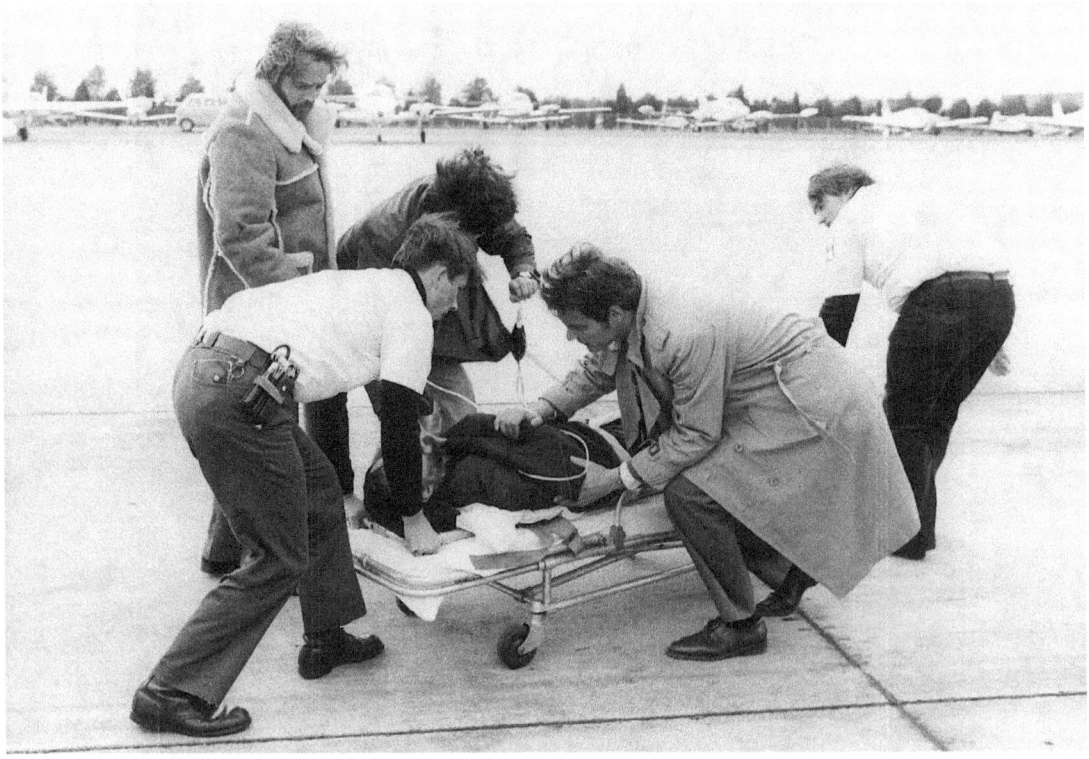
Seagram tries again to get information from the wounded Koplin. *(ITC – Author's collection)*

With *Titanic* now raised, the crew of *Deep Quest* safe, Pitt and Seagram finally see eye to eye and celebrate the resurrection of the ocean legend. *(ITC – Author's collection)*

Television guide advertising the series *Clapperboard* that for the 10 November 1980 episode covered *Titanic* on the big screen including *Raise the Titanic*. *(Author's collection)*

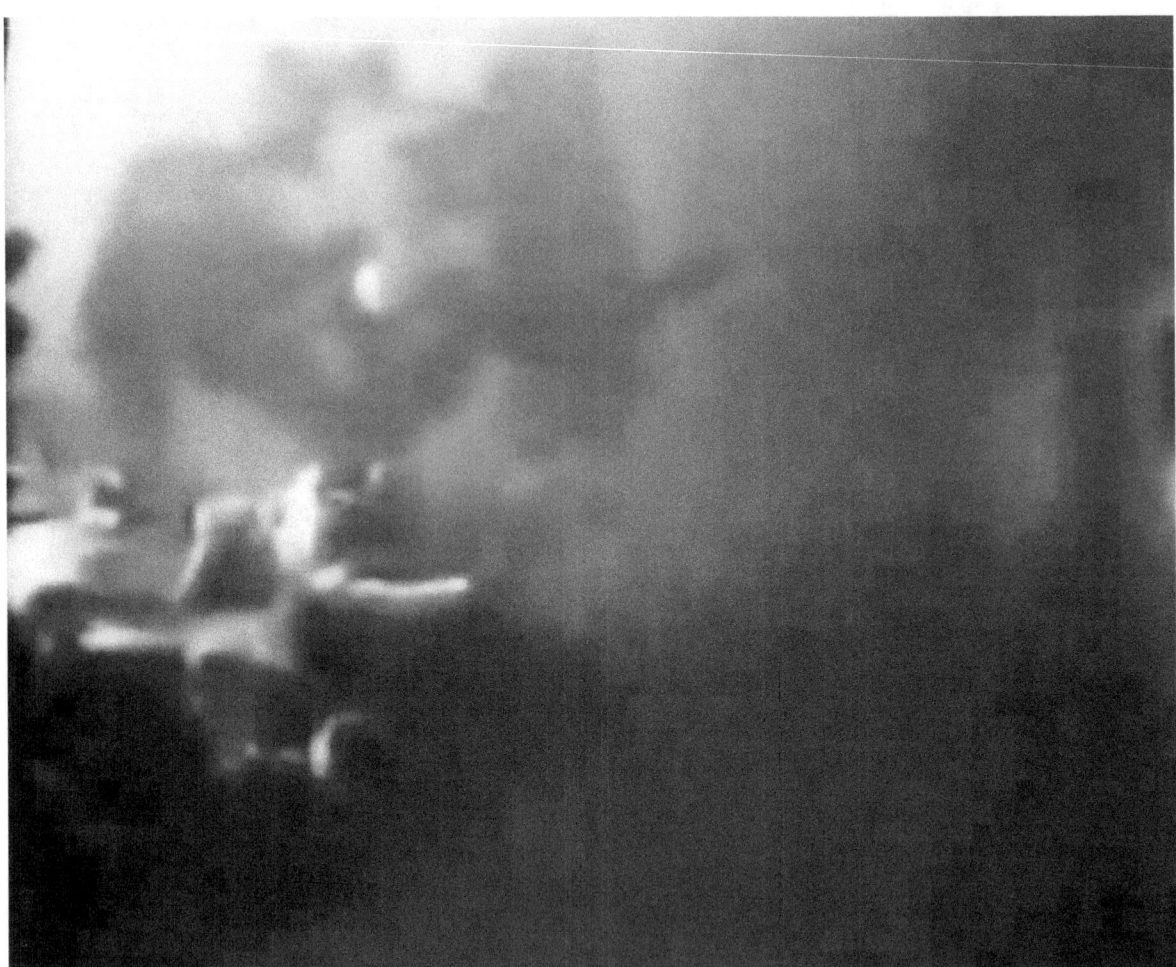

Carrying one of the large steel salvage plates in its manipulator claws, the *Sea Cliff* comes alongside the *Titanic*'s starboard hull to place the plate over an area of the iceberg damage. *(ITC – Author's collection)*

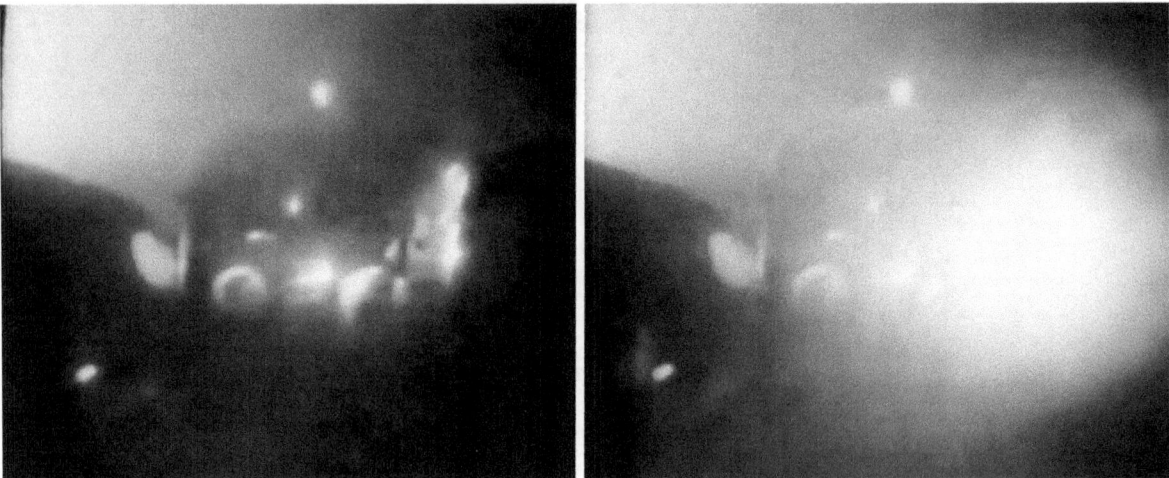

With the salvage plate held against the hull, the *Deep Quest* with its welding rig attachment begins the long job of welding the plate to the previously fixed plates. *(ITC – Author's collection)*

Chapter 27: Lost and Found • 411

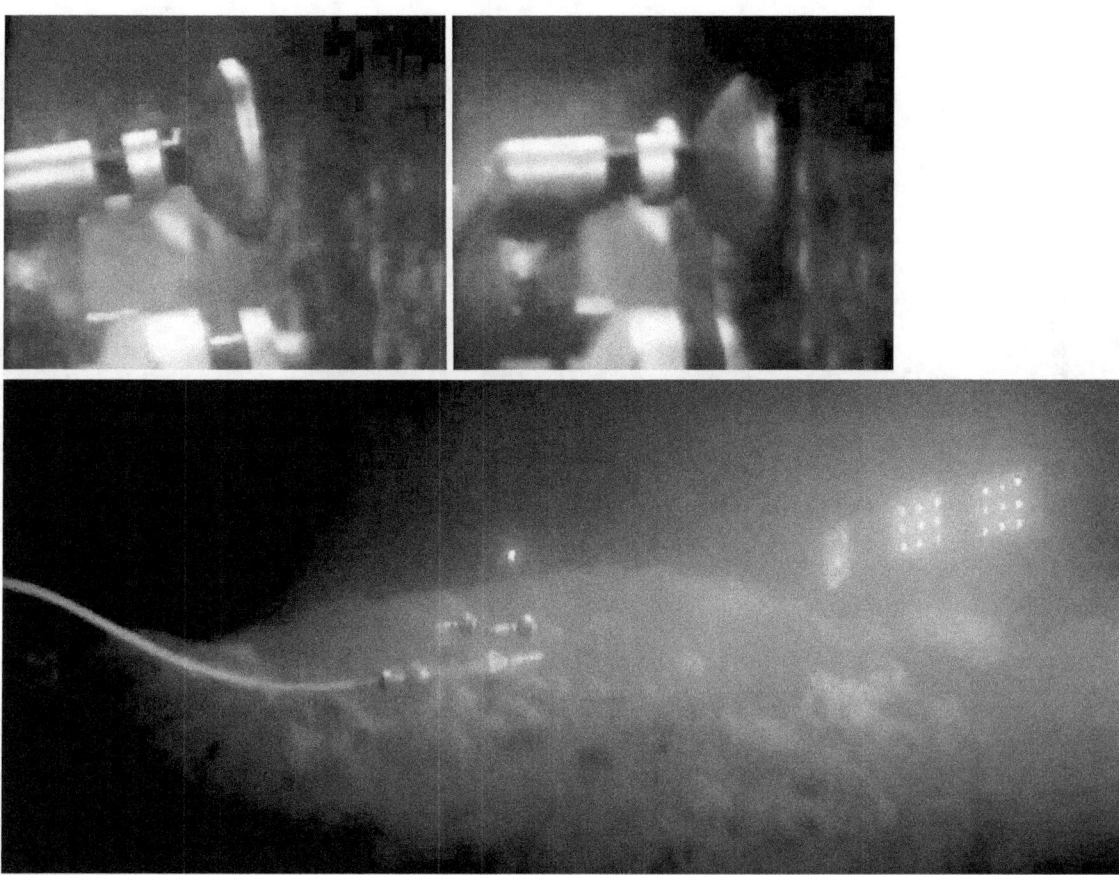

One of the salvage foam hose connectors is seen being fixed in place to the hull of *Titanic*. After a series of holes are drilled into the lower sections of the hull, a foam pipe is connected to the ship where pumping units positioned around the wreck then pump the foam into the *Titanic*. One of the pumps did briefly make it onto the screen during the sequence when the explosives go off. *(ITC – Author's collection)*

Title header from the extremely rare 1980 ITC company promotional film. *(ITC – Author's collection)*

Attached to a framework and stacked in pairs, the salvage plates that will be used to cover over the iceberg damage arrive on the ocean floor. *(ITC / The Last Great Human Adventure – Author's collection)*

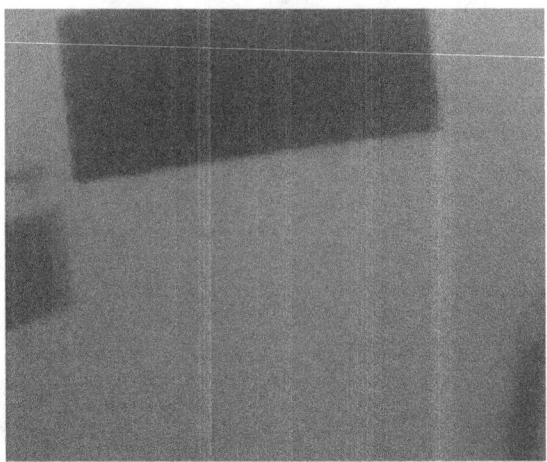
From the surface over 12,000ft above, more salvage plates descend into the murky waters of the Atlantic. *(ITC / The Last Great Human Adventure – Author's collection)*

On board the *U.S.S. Denver*, salvage crews are busy connecting up the salvage foam pipes to the vessel's storage tanks. From there, crews trail the pipes over the side of the vessel and down into the sea. *(ITC / The Last Great Human Adventure – Author's collection)*

Salvage crews pass the foam pipes down from the decks of the *Denver* and into the water where each length will be connected together and passed down to the wreck. *(ITC / The Last Great Human Adventure – Author's collection)*

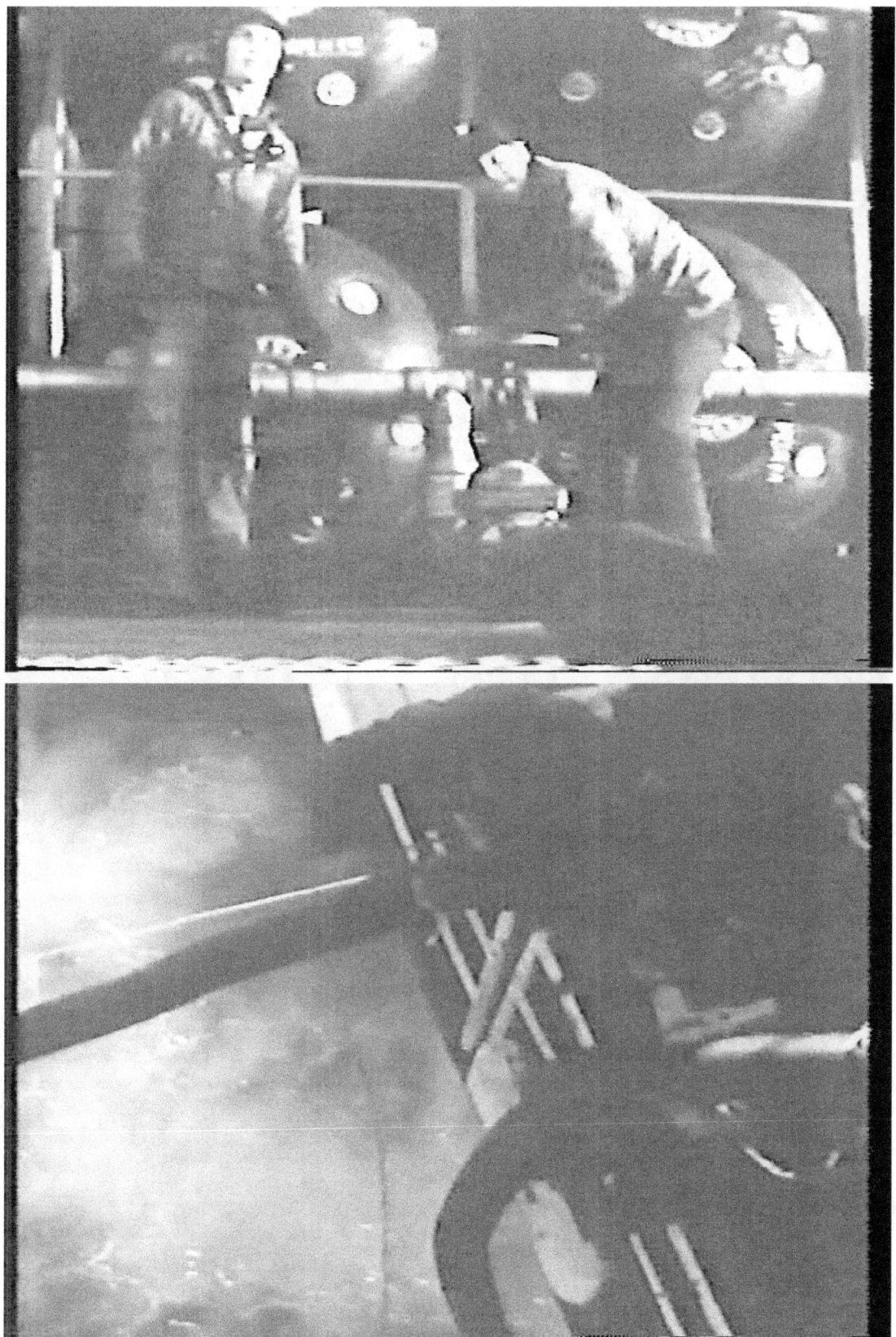

With the "All Clear" given, the crews open up the taps as the foam passes from the storage tanks, through the pipes and down to the pumping stations around the wreck. *(ITC / The Last Great Human Adventure – Author's collection)*

414 • *Raise The Titanic*

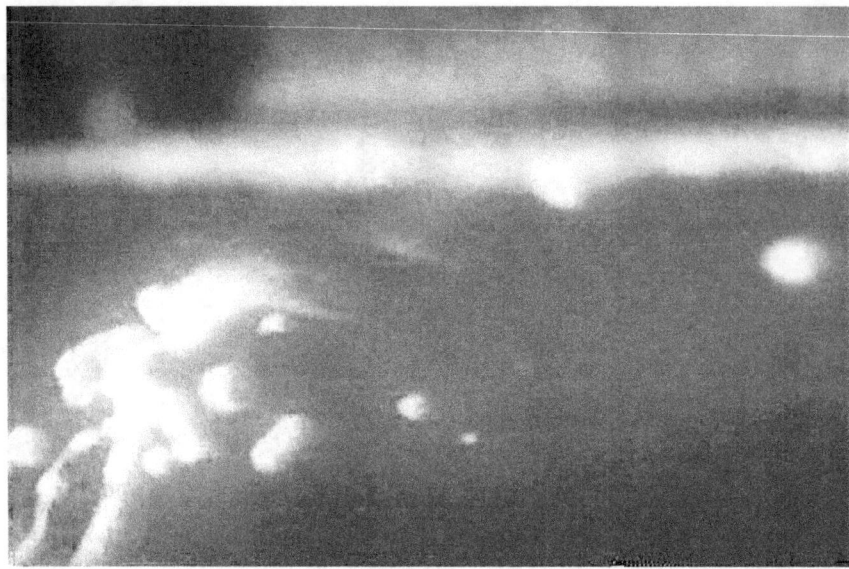

Down at the wreck, one of the foam pipes accidentally disconnects from the hull of the *Titanic*, spraying the foam as the hose weaves back and forth like a snake. *(ITC / The Last Great Human Adventure – Author's collection)*

Pitt, Seagram and Sandecker discuss the damage caused by Merker following his arrest for being a spy. *(ITC – Author's collection)*

Captain Joe Burke in the comms room as he talks with Pitt who is down at the wreck and reporting back to the surface that the *Deep Quest* has got itself jammed into *Titanic*'s skylight. *(ITC – Author's collection)*

Pitt and Sandecker discussing the salvage operation in Captain Burke's cabin. *(ITC – Author's collection)*

Chapter 27: Lost and Found • 415

Koplin stares down at the body of Jake Hobart who is entombed in ice. *(ITC – Author's collection)*

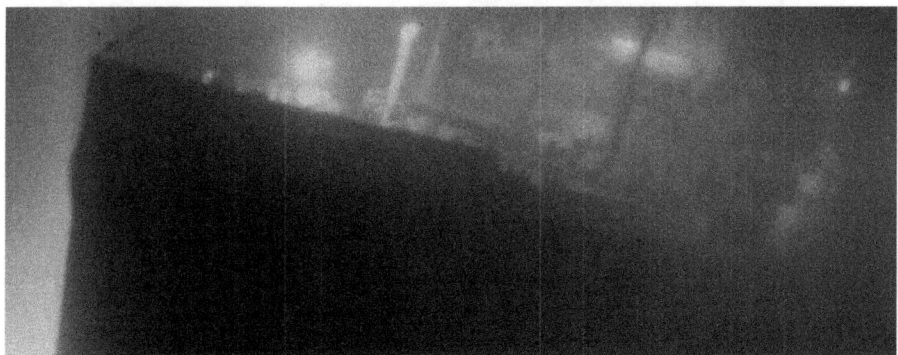

Listing heavily to port, the sunken *Titanic* is made ready for salvaging. *(ITC – Author's collection)*

After being lost for 39 years, the discovery of many original storyboards for *Raise the Titanic* not only answered many questions about the film but also showed another version that had previously never thought existed. *(Author's collection)*

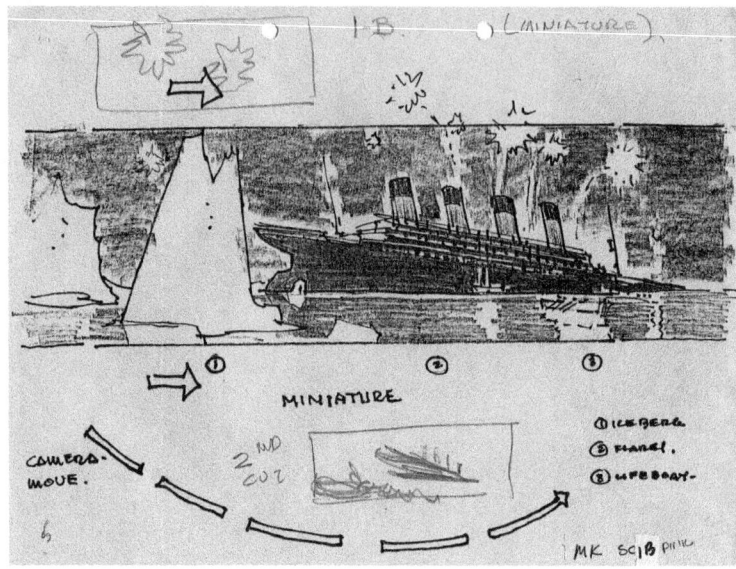
The Prologue 1912 *(Author's collection)*

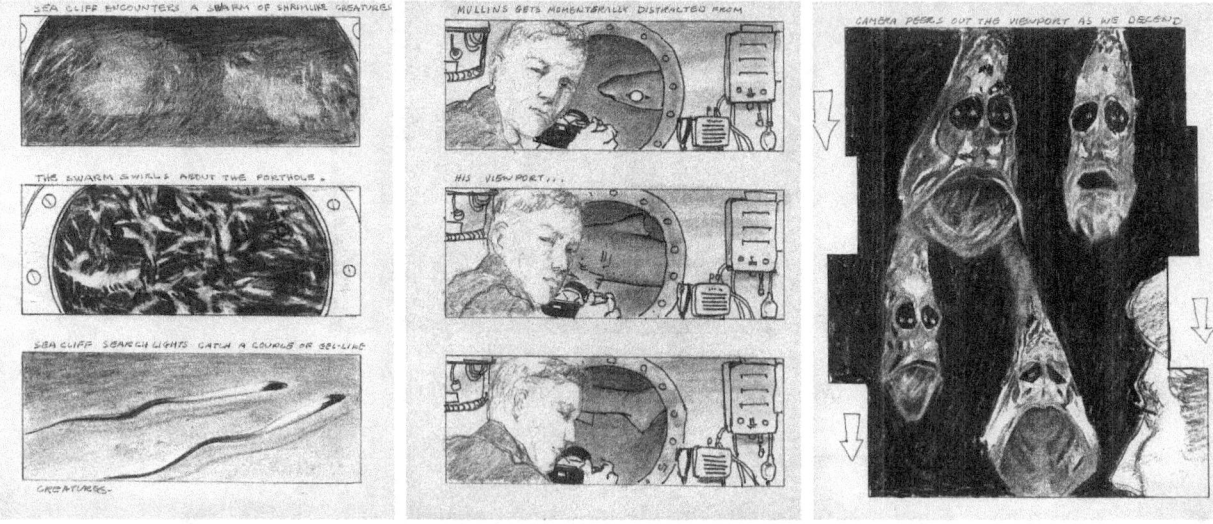
Exploring the Depths: Sea Cliff *(Author's collection)*

Flying Fish *(Author's collection)*

Chapter 27: Lost and Found • 417

The boulder Field *(Author's collection)*

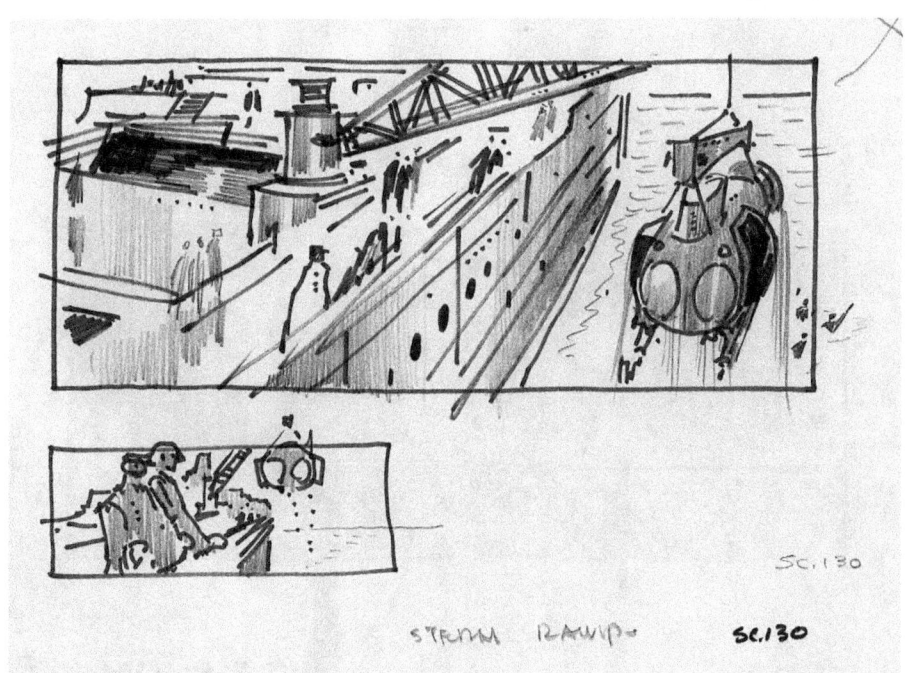

Retrieving the Sea Cliff *(Author's collection)*

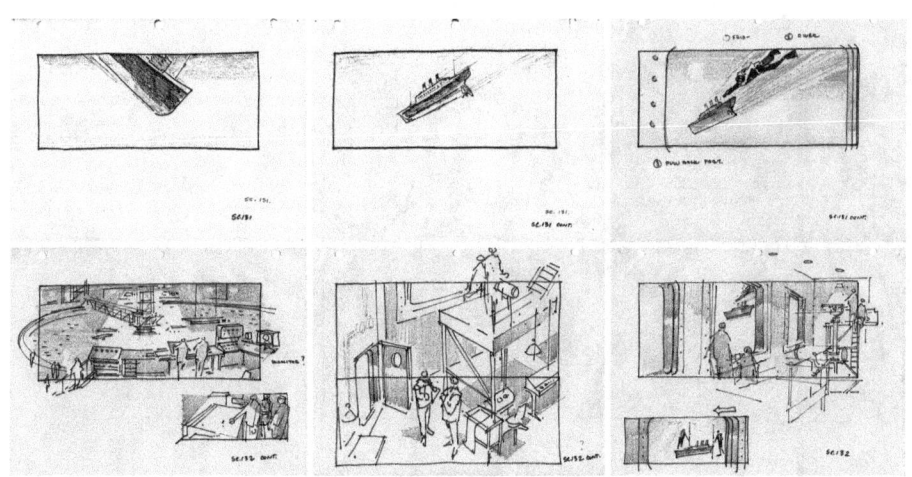

Drop Test Model *(Author's collection)*

418 • *Raise The Titanic*

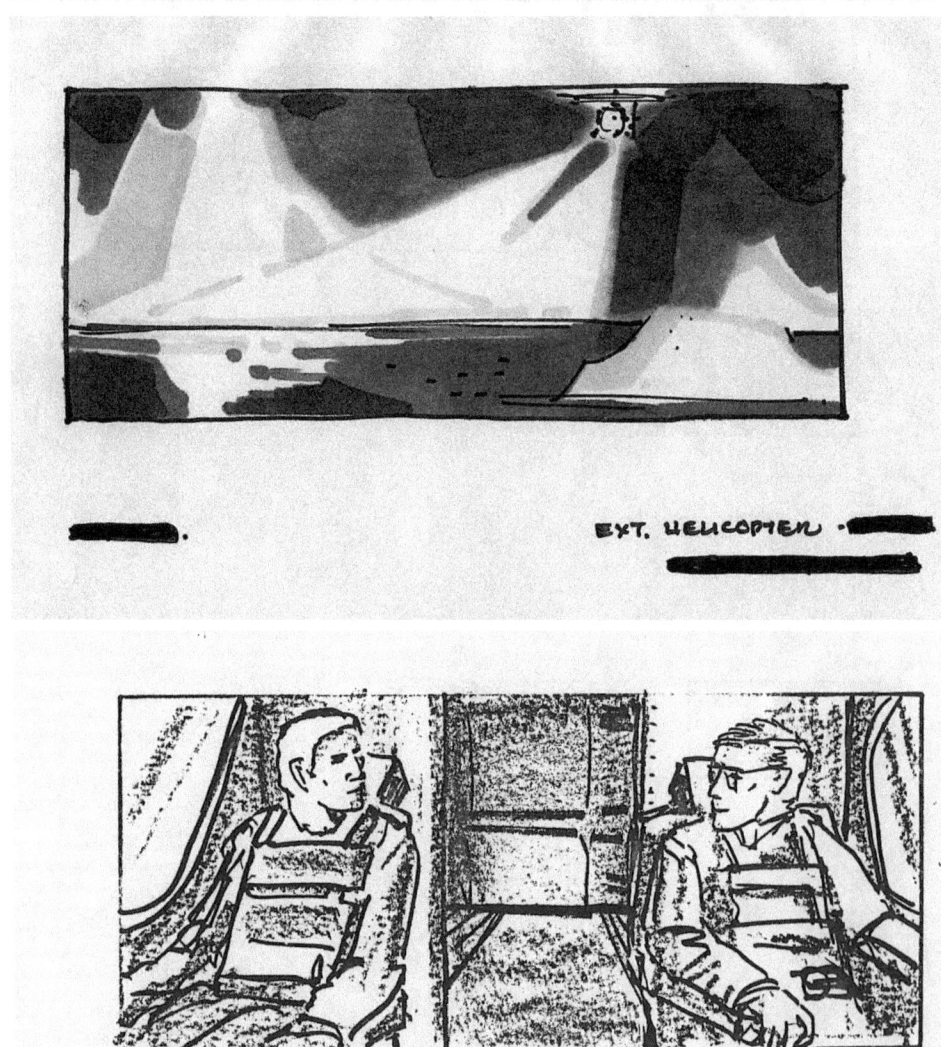

Iceberg Alley *(Author's collection)*

Chapter 27: Lost and Found • 419

Glacial Debris (*Author's collection*)

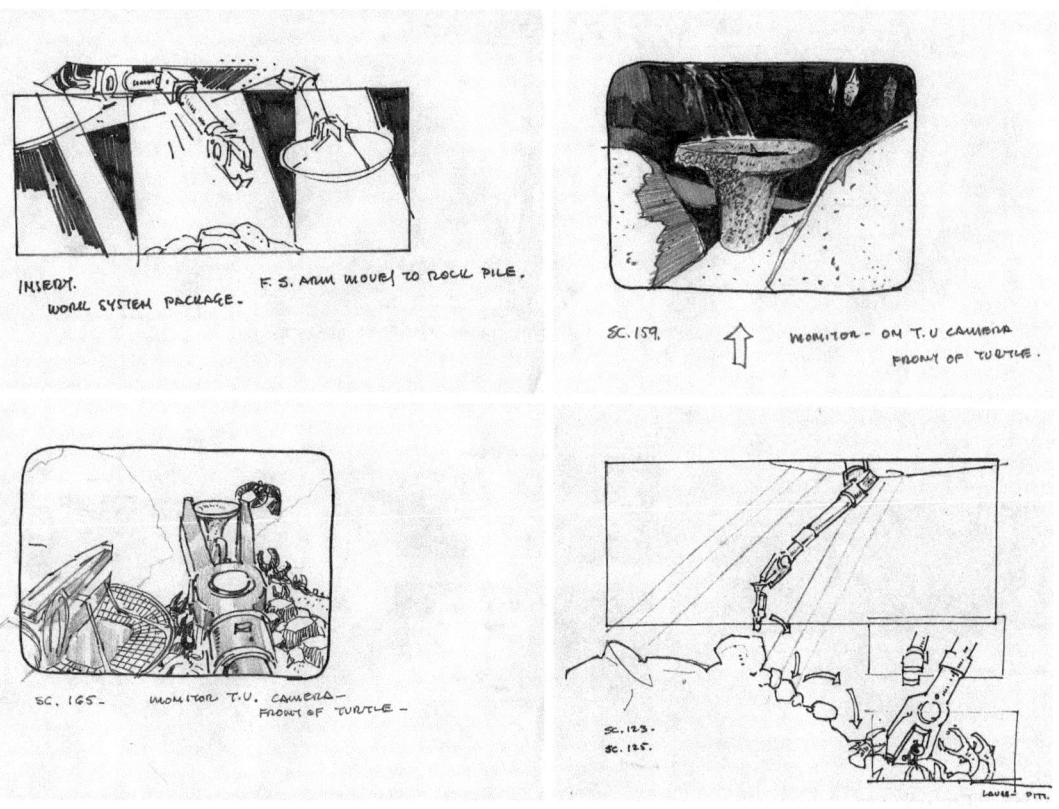

The Cornet (*Author's collection*)

420 • *Raise The Titanic*

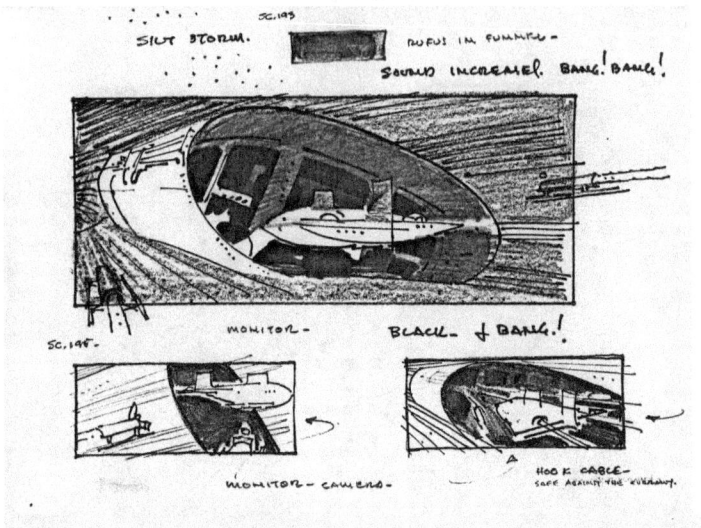

The Funnel Incident
(Author's collection)

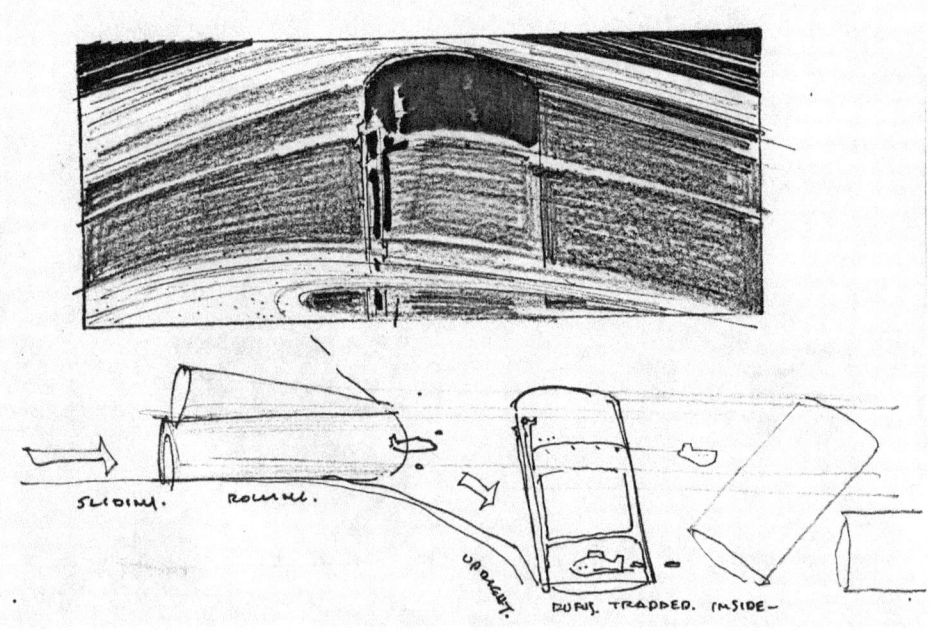

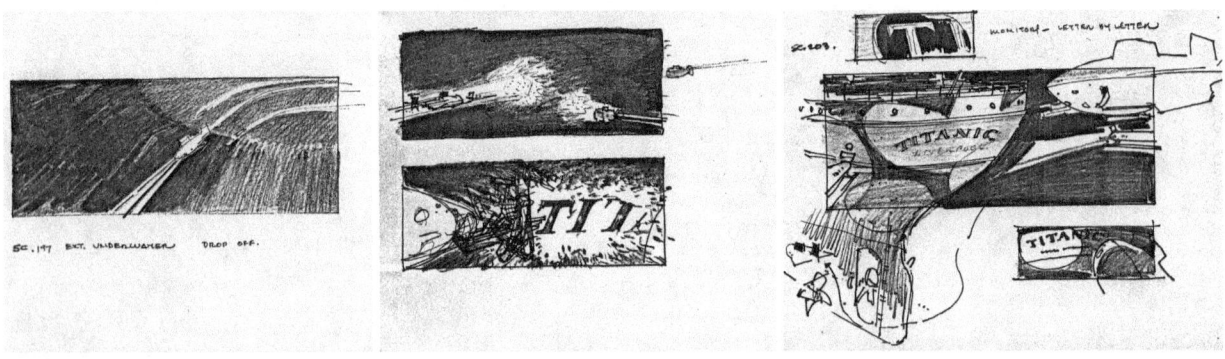

Titanic Found! *(Author's collection)*

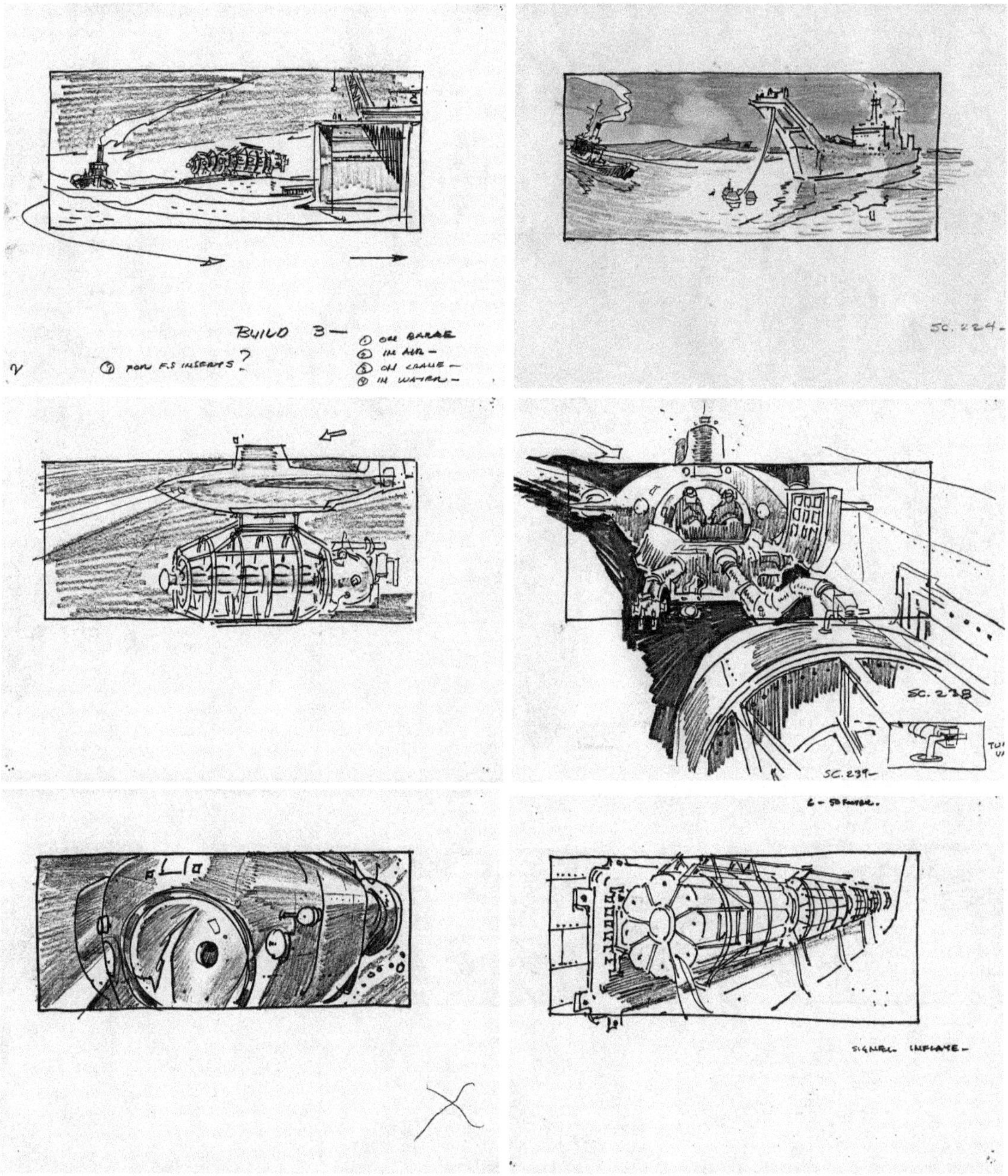

Chapter 27: Lost and Found • **421**

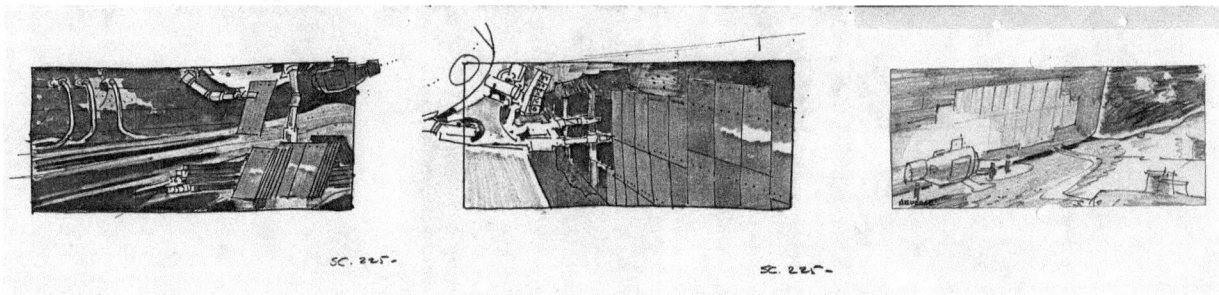

Salvage Lifting Tanks *(Author's collection)*

Plating the Hull *(Author's collection)*

422 • *Raise The Titanic*

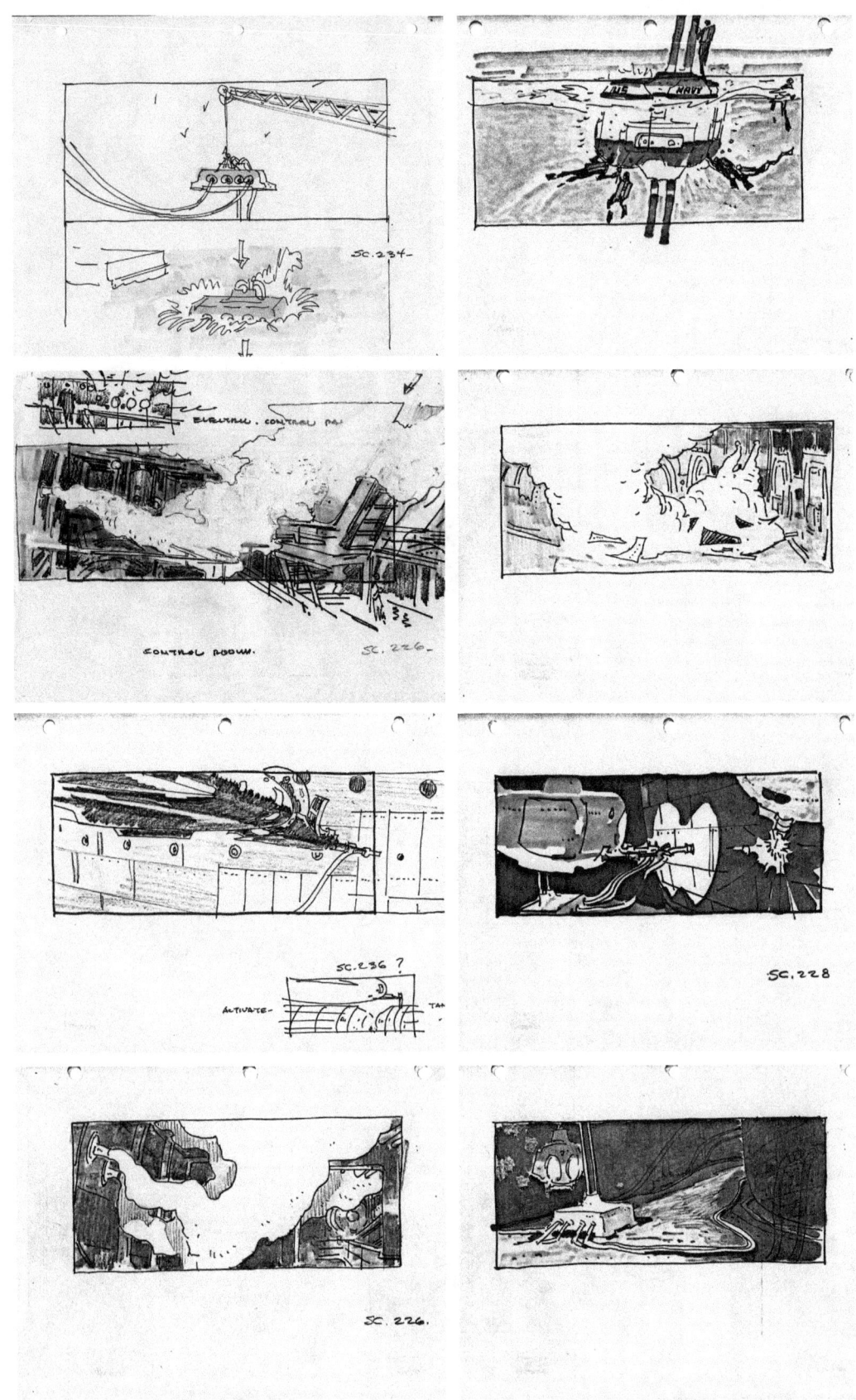

Salvage Foam *(Author's collection)*

Chapter 27: Lost and Found • 423

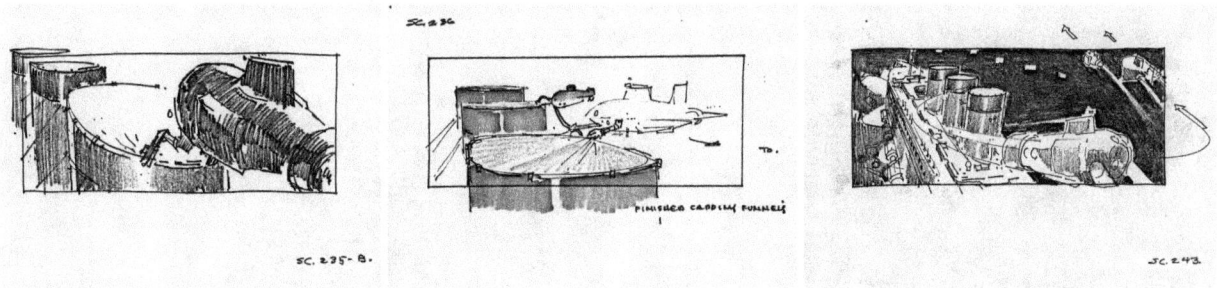

Capping the Funnels *(Author's collection)*

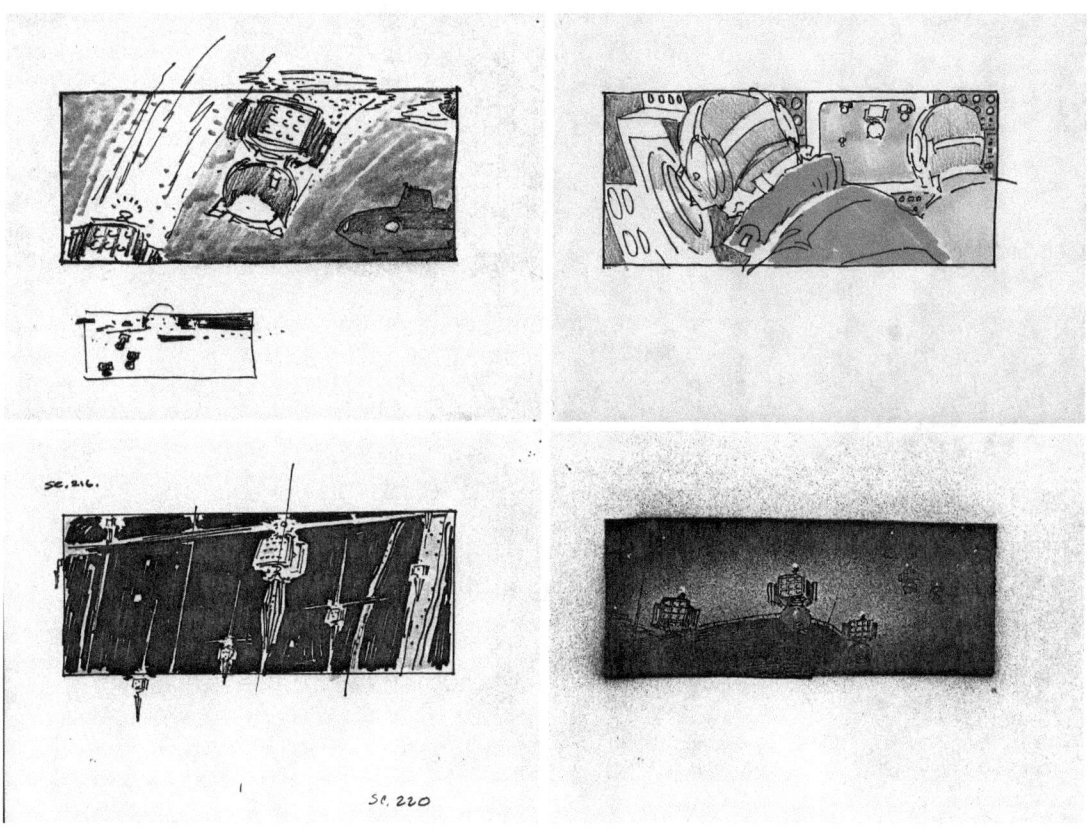

Lighting Rigs *(Author's collection)*

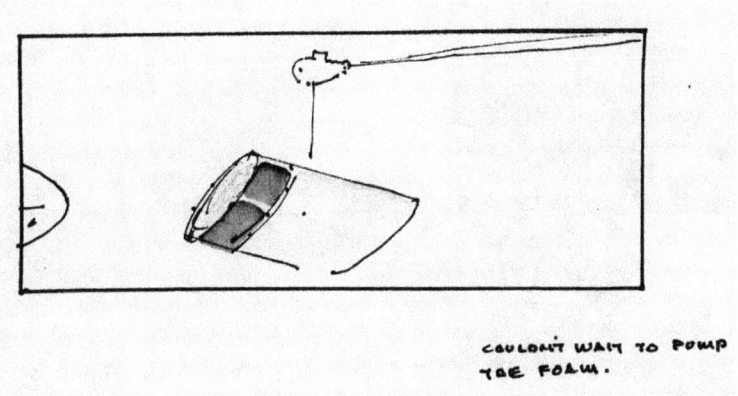

Salvage Test *(Author's collection)*

424 • *Raise The Titanic*

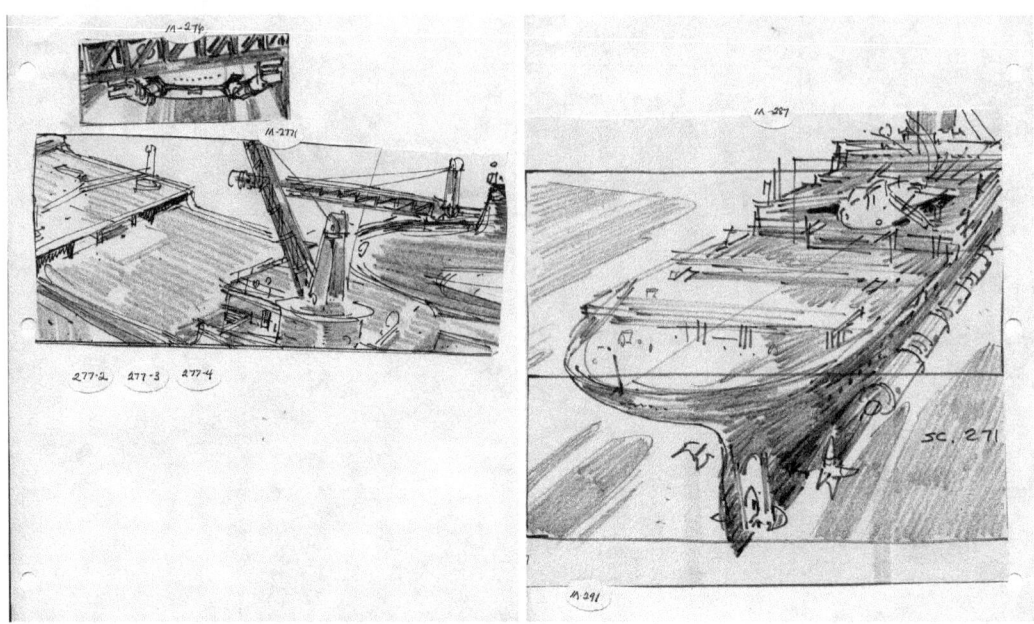

Deep Quest Gets Stuck *(Author's collection)*

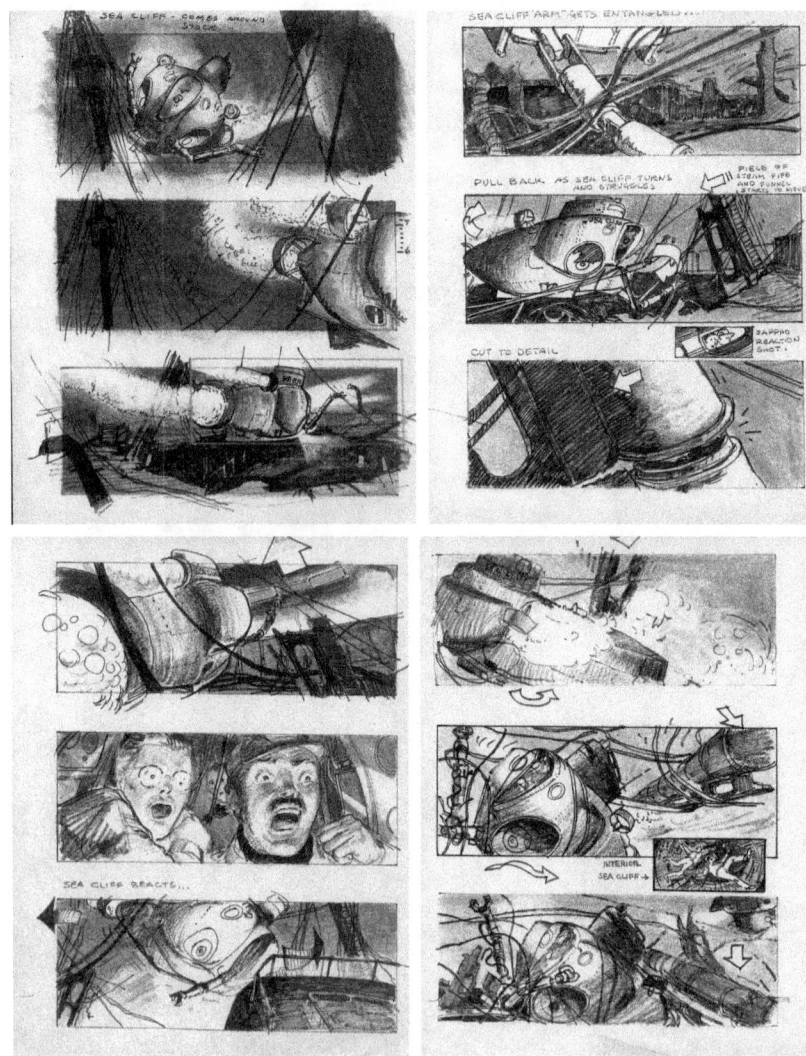

Sea Cliff Gets Stuck *(Author's collection)*

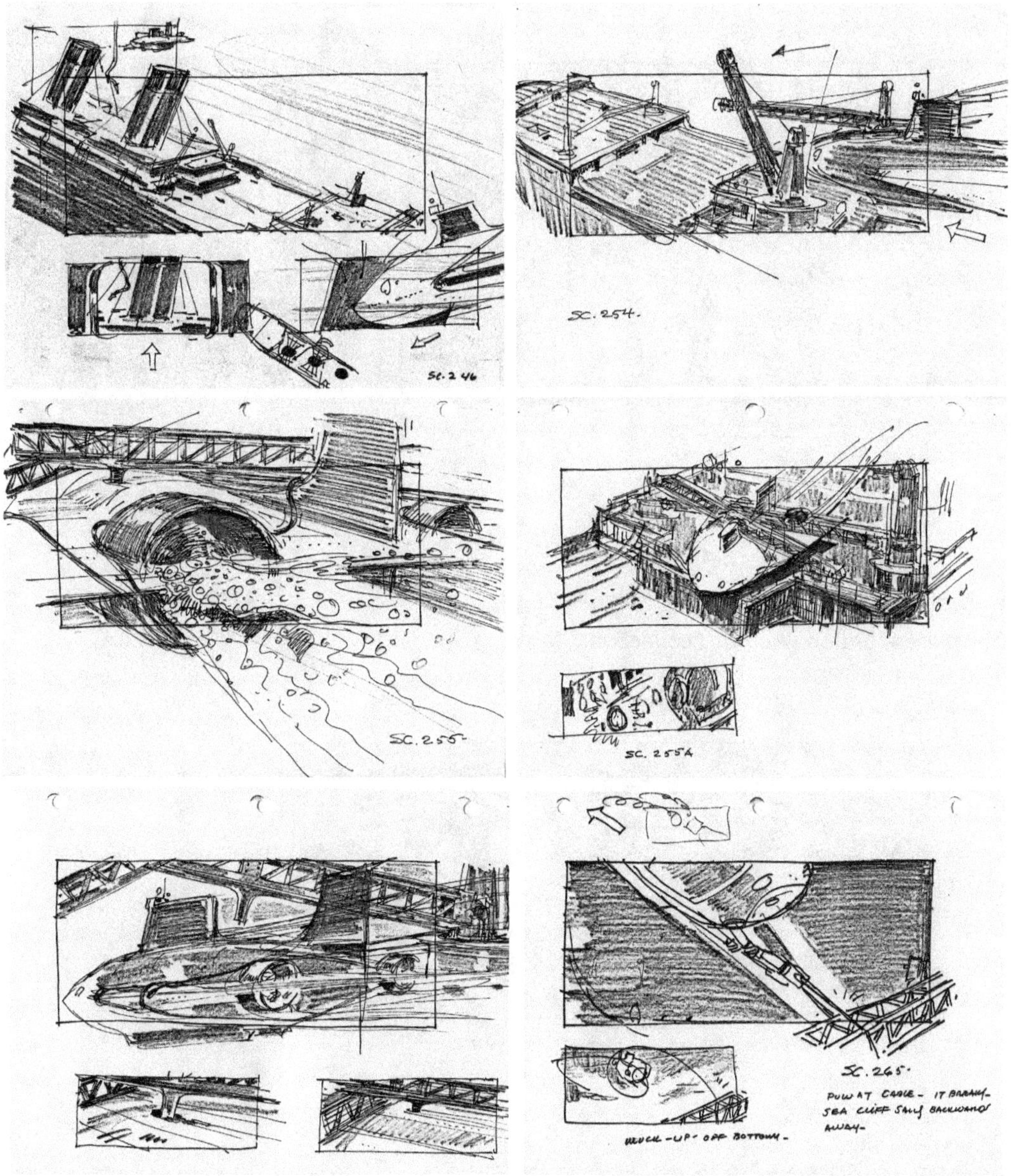

Deep Quest Gets Stuck – Alternate Version *(Author's collection)*

The Anchors *(Author's collection)*

426 • Raise The Titanic

Ghostly Apparition *(Author's collection)*

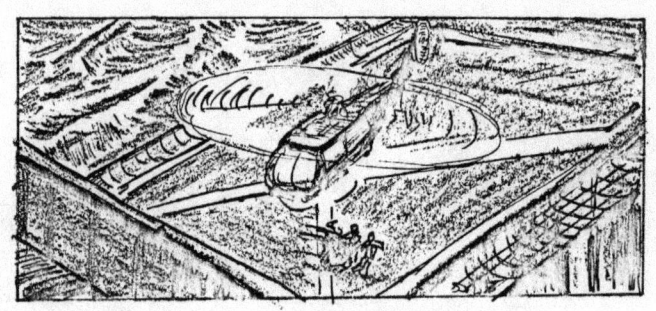

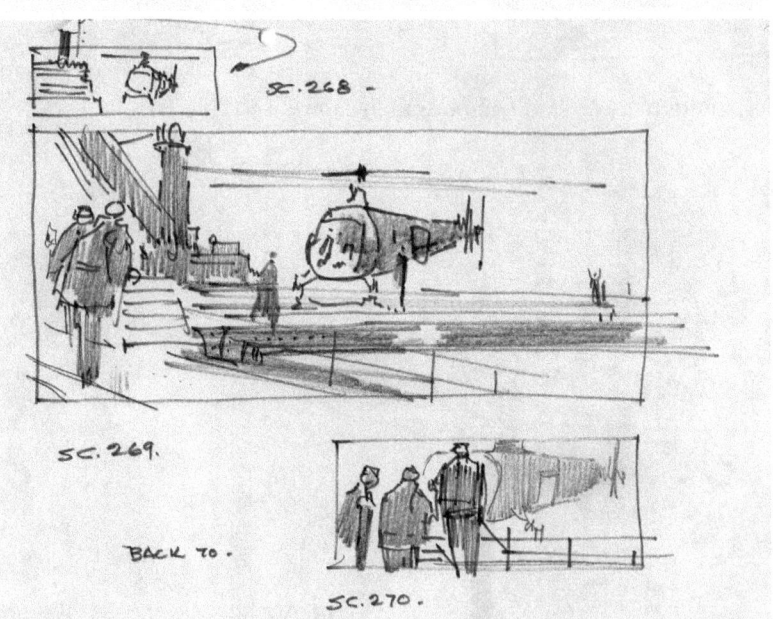

Merker in Handcuffs *(Author's collection)*

Angered Pitt *(Author's collection)*

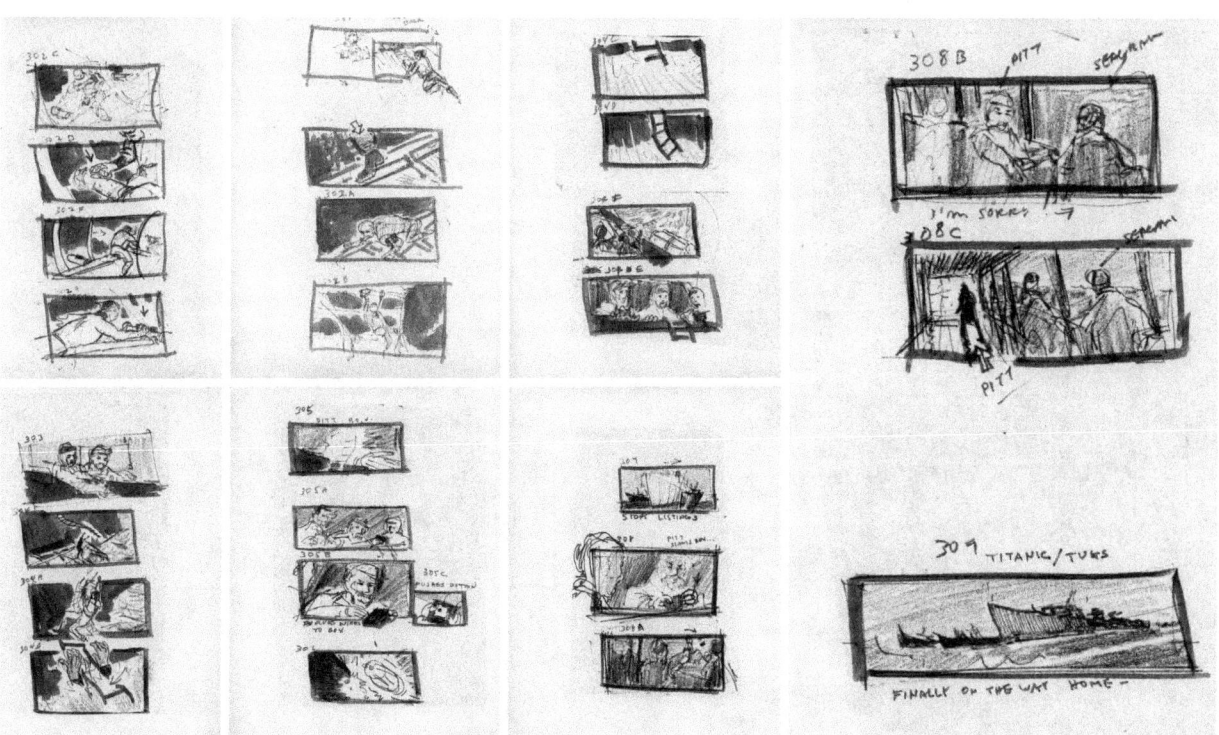

Faulty Hydrozene Tank *(Author's collection)*

Deep Quest Saved *(Author's collection)*

Raise the Titanic *(Author's collection)*

Pitt Boards *Titanic* *(Author's collection)*

Chapter 27: Lost and Found • 429

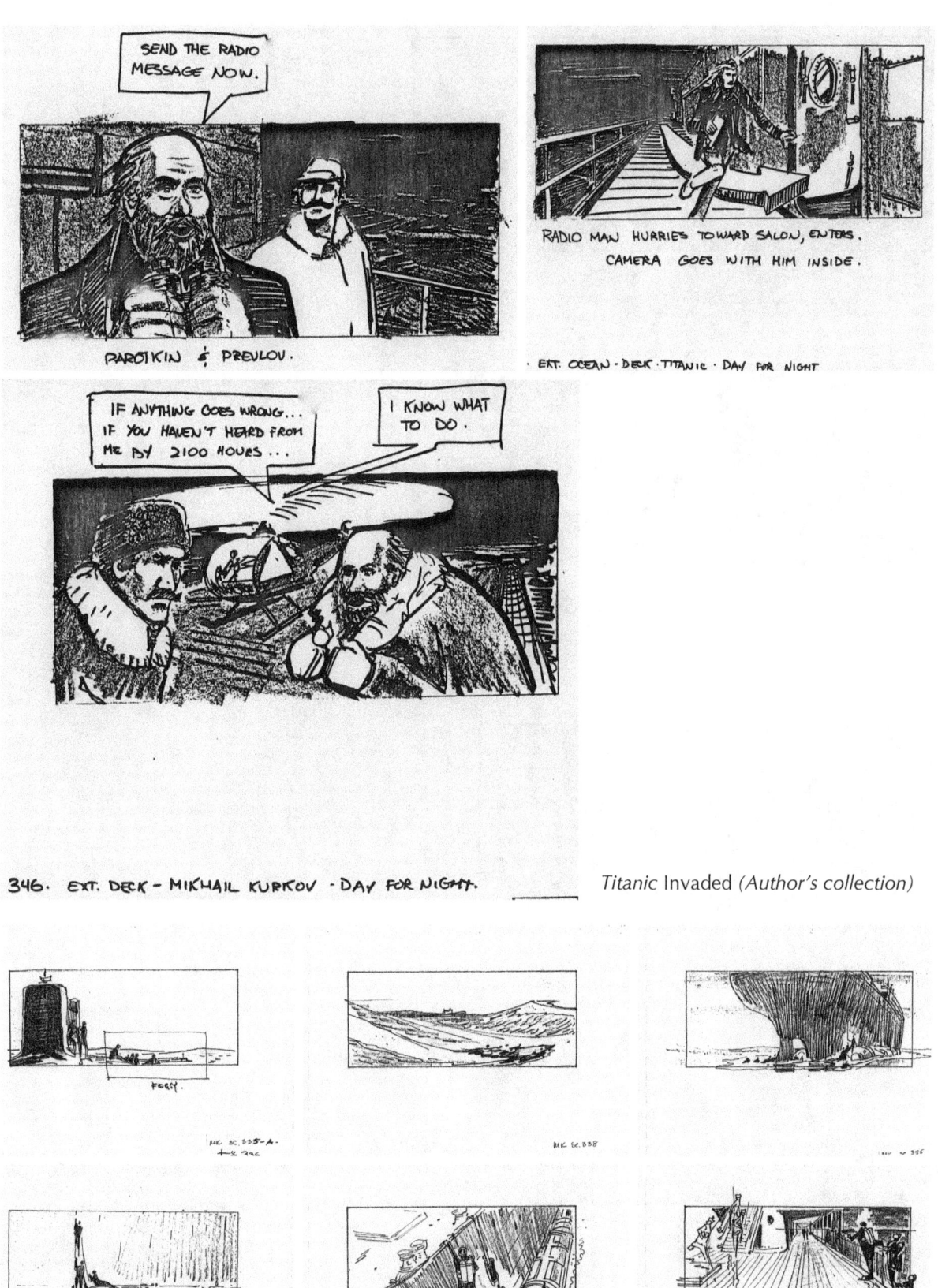

Titanic Invaded *(Author's collection)*

430 • *Raise The Titanic*

Hurricane Strikes
(Author's collection)

Tugs in Trouble *(Author's collection)*

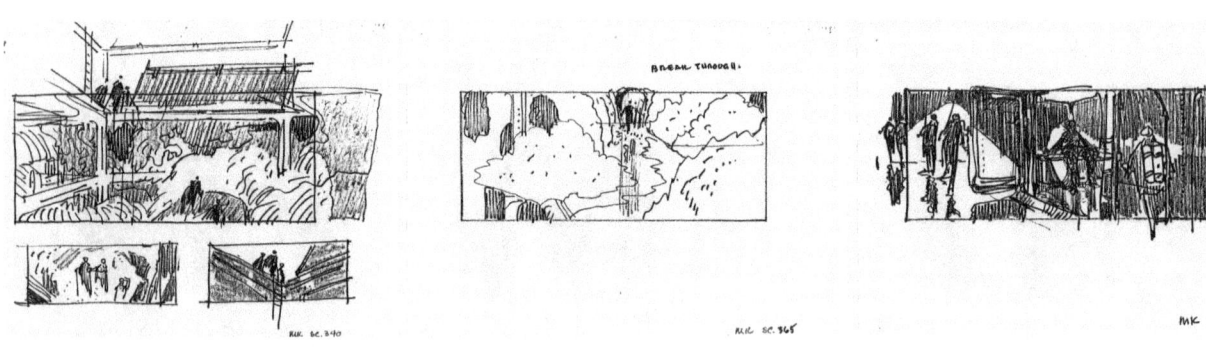

Heading To The Cargo Hold *(Author's collection)*

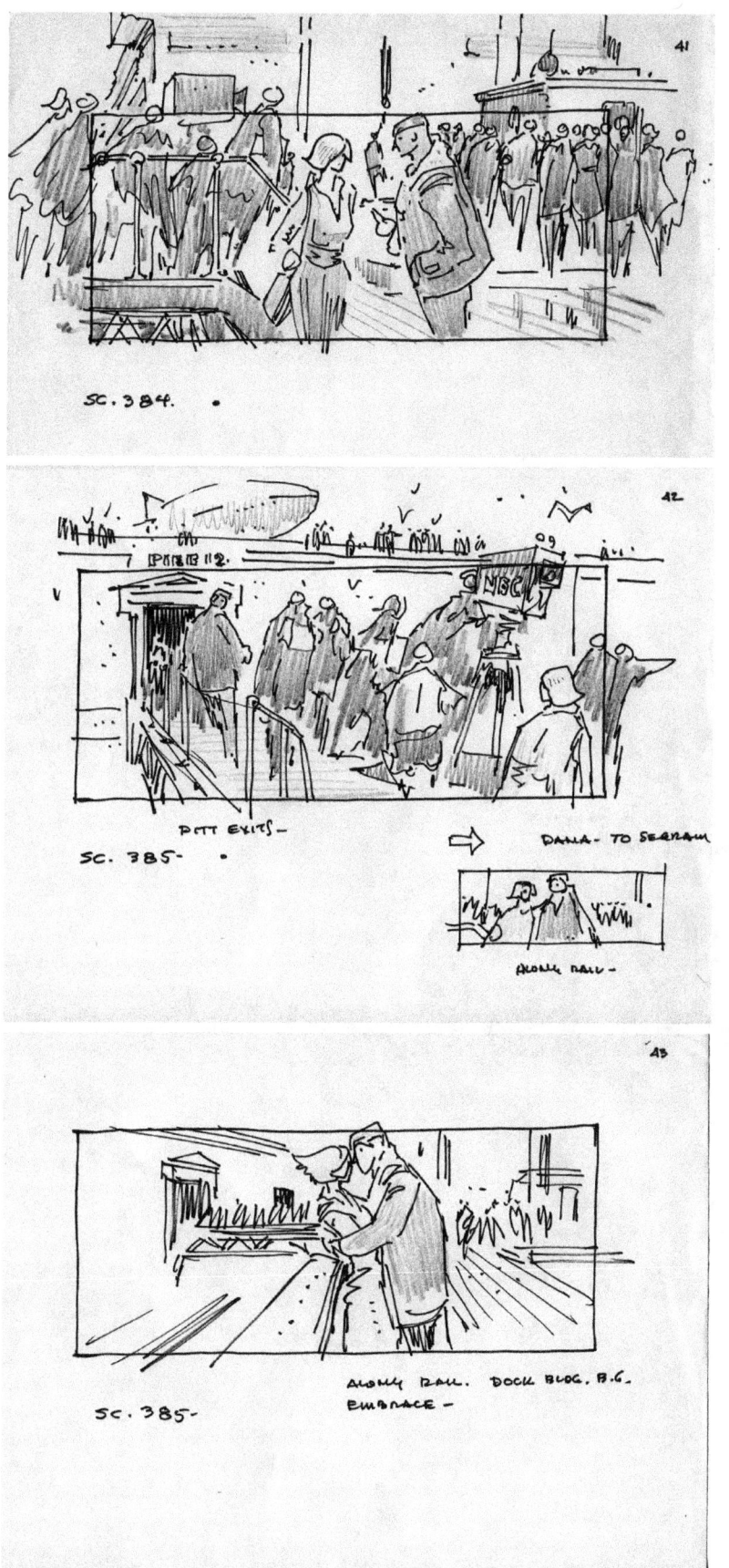

Pier 12 *(Author's collection)*

CHAPTER 28

The Last Voyage of the "unsinkable" *Titanic*

"The history of Raise the Titanic *is one of strange coincidences and unforeseen circumstances – something which all too often occurs in the making of films"*

Lew Grade

After the discovery of *Titanic* on September 1 1985, the interest began to build up once again as previously released films and books were republished along with new works. Of course, the interest in *Raise the Titanic* resurfaced too as newspapers and magazines used imagery from the film to emphasize that the wreck could be raised in similar ways to that of the movie. By 1987 that fantasy soon began to quickly dwindle as photographs and data from the wreck site emerged showing that in reality the once grand liners hull lay broken beyond any chance of salvaging. But the subject of *Titanic* was never forgotten as year after year the wreck provided the endless fascination through the salvaging of her artefacts from the vast debris field that stretched out between the broken bow and stern. If you were to assume that a film on the raising of the world's most famous ocean liner made four decades ago would have fallen out of favour with fans considering what we know now, you would be wrong. *Raise the Titanic* has sailed on to become a cult classic with many in the film industry still pointing out on how well much of the model work still holds up to this day, despite the complexity of filming with such large miniatures under difficult circumstances.

How Much?

When filming had finished on *Raise the Titanic* during mid-May of 1980, Lew Grade and his film company requested that the models of importance were to be put into dry storage until further notice. Grade's Malta offices of Pimlico Films which was part of his London's main ITC headquarters, had occupied one of the buildings at the Mediterranean Film Facilities for the duration of the *Raise the Titanic* production. On the 22 July an agent had been appointed in dealing with the disposal of the equipment with their role in overseeing not only the cataloguing of items but also the sales of the materials. Office equipment was gathered up for forwarding back to London while film equipment was catalogued and valued in both bulk lots and as separates so they could be sold on for use in other productions. The lists compiled were comprehensive with each inventory categorizing items from certain studio buildings; model shop, painters' shop, welders and fabrication shops, electrical shop, rigging and special effects stores. Even storage boxes and crates made the list including their contents from ¼ inch drill bits right through to 103 lengths of ¾ water hose. Almost hidden among the thousands of items listed in the 90-page inventory are some prominent film pieces of great importance including the 55ft *Titanic* hull and superstructure, the U.S. Navy vessels, the 9ft *Titanic* model, two tug boats and a New York fire boat, remote controlled helicopters including the crashed "Prevlov" version, several submersibles including duplicates of *Deep Quest*, *Sea Cliff*, *Turtle* and *Starfish*, and one of the *Titanic* stern models and boat deck section with deckhouse, funnels and damaged skylight.

Sections of the inventory were copied and put together to form a list of items and equipment that were up for sale. These lists were more for studio personnel and persons working in the business and were not openly available for the general public, although some smaller props that were previously in storage walked out of the studio gate when they became the memento of an employee who was working at the studio at the time. The catalogue contents varied with entries consisting of a box of mixed FX paints for $5, a palette of 18x steel cable reels for $600 or a crate containing 78x pipes with fittings for £7,410. Even all the diving wetsuits and diving regulators with gear, some 135 items, could have been yours for a bargain basement price of $300. And the bargains did not stop there. The entries in the list of miniatures built and used in the movie are the ones that amaze and raise more than just an eyebrow. The big models of the *Titanic*, tugs, fireboat and navy ships were not part of any auction or any terms of sale. But what was offered were smaller models with equally smaller prices. Crate MP40 contained 4x remote controlled helicopters including the crashed "Prevlov" craft, the chopper that flies over the stern of *Titanic* when Pitt is dropped to the deck and two spare craft, all of which could have been yours for a bargain $100 for the crate. Crates MP22 contained 8x miniature Hydrozene tanks, the same tank that Jason Robards uses in the press conference scene, with the buyer being able to walk away with a pair for $12. If one of the miniature salvage foam pumping stations for $5 did not whet your appetite, what about a choice from four of the *Deep Quest* submersibles ranging between $6 to $9 depending on condition, or a choice from two of the *Sea Cliff* models at $8 each or one of either of the *Turtle* models for $9 each. It is hard to believe that such intricate and beautifully detailed models could be offered up for so little considering the shear costs involved in building them. But their relatively low value was not in comparison to the more desirable larger *Titanic* replicas. Omitted from the catalogue's sale list was the 55ft fully hulled *Titanic* replica, the two tugs and fire boat, the four navy vessels and set pieces. The 9ft *Titanic* did make the list but was subject to being valued for its worth. In the end, that model became the property of Robert Holmes à Court where it was shipped over to Australia for use in one of his themed establishments. In the meantime, the larger models were separated from the other stock and placed in dry storage within the grounds of the studio facility.

Storage Wars

The story of *Raise the Titanic* was not to end the moment Grade lost control of ITC. The next chapter was to turn out to be frustrating and a very sad ending for one of the largest *Titanic* models ever constructed. As the movie entered the postproduction stages, the main assets, the large array of models, required storing and safe keeping until the project was wrapped up. With any large film studio, the sets and props built and filmed quickly become an issue once filming has come to an end. The storage of such pieces takes up considerable space, can be costly if they are requested to be stored under dry circumstances or require moving over the duration of storage. In 1997 when filming had come to a close on the production of James Cameron's *Titanic*, the Baja film studio in Mexico had to clear the sound stages and exterior stage lots for the next Hollywood film to hire the use of the studio. The eighteenth instalment of the James Bond movie franchise had booked the use of the studios Stage One set which was the huge water tank facility. The tank was to be used for a numbered of scenes set at sea as Bond dives down to a recently sunk Royal Navy warship and what would be the films ending as Bond takes out a stealth ship built by a ruthless media mogul. But before any of these scenes could be filmed, the tank had to be cleared of the 770ft *Titanic* set piece from the Cameron production. It was disposed of in the only way they studio could work and that was to completely demolish the set with tons of materials dumped onto surrounding areas of land around the studio parameter while combustible items were piled up and set alight. This is a process carried out at hundreds of other studios on thousands of other productions ever since the early years of cinemaphotography. A fully operational film facility had to be ready for the next customer and continue to operate as a studio and not as a theme park.

The location chosen to store the larger models from *Raise the Titanic* was the St. Dominic Counterguard building of the 280-year-old Fort Ricasoli that was built on the east side of Malta's Grand Harbour. The fort was constructed over a twenty-eight-year period with work starting in 1670 by the Order of Knights of the Hospital of Saint John of Jerusalem and was used during the French invasion of Malta in 1798, the French siege of Valletta 1798 – 1800 and during the defence of Malta against the Italian attack on the harbour during World War II. After the war, the fort was handed over to the Maltese government where it was used as a storage facility of raw materials that arrived in Malta. Over the past several decades areas of the fort became abandoned and derelict with some of the fort being pulled down to make way for new building developments that included the film studio and more recently the 2007 SmartCity Malta complex. The remaining buildings to the Fort are still largely intact if in somewhat a dilapidated state and out of bounds to the public. By mid-1980 as filming concluded on *Raise the Titanic*, the larger models were transported the short distance from the main studio grounds to the large limestone structure of the St. Dominic Counterguard building. Originally the stone vault was constructed to store vast amounts of grain for the Knights of St. John and its 15ft thick walls made the Counterguard building impregnable to attack. Arriving at the Counterguard building the superstructure of the large *Titanic* model was removed, placed to one side for the hull to be manoeuvred into the building. Once the hull was inside the stone vault, the superstructure was laid on the ground alongside it, leaving enough space to allow the navy vessel models to be pushed into place along the opposite wall. With all the major models now in dry storage, all that was left now was to close the huge steel doors and weld them shut, entombing the replica *Titanic* within.

As *Raise the Titanic* foundered on the big screen during summer into winter of 1980, over in Malta the models sat safe and secure inside the limestone vault. By September 1981 after spending more than fifteen months locked up in the Counterguard building, it was time for the doors to be unsealed and the tomb exploited. "You'll have to give us an hour to cut through the welding", said Narcy Calamatta, managing director of the Mediterranean Film Facilities. Each of the steel doors required two people to pull them ajar enough to get enough traction to push them fully open. Greeting the explorers were the sad remains of one of the world's most famous ships. Her name still present on the bow proclaiming her as the *Titanic*. But this was no discovery with a promising ending. Lew Grade's gamble on his underwater adventure from the year previously had already sealed the fate of these spectacular models as they remained part of the fixture and fittings of considerable value for ITC. And with Grade being dragged over hot coals in London, and as shareholders to his film companies demanded to see a return on their investments with Grade and ITC being spotlighted in the media as being near to the brink of collapse, it was the slow box office returns from *Raise the Titanic* that quickly became the straw that broke the camel's back. *Raise the Titanic* was being portrayed within the film industry as one of several highly questionable Grade financed projects that had drained company profits in full view of the company executives. By September 1981 as Grade and his company's future hung in the balance and more money coming from the company accounts in the form of a £500,000 farewell cheque to Jack Gill, the storage costs for the models in the Counterguard building were not being settled, and the building's owner wanted a resolve on the issue. As the models were not the responsibility of the Mediterranean Film Facilities, let alone them being responsible for the upkeep and storage of the models, the owner of the Counterguard turned to the film facilities to have them removed from his property. With the storage costs not being met by ITC, and the Counterguard required for use, the decision was painfully easy. The film studio did not have any spare dry storage space for such large film models. And any space they did have was hired by visiting film productions. There were no other options available. The models had to be stored outdoors until they were claimed by ITC or any of the parent companies. That day they were hauled out of the building and moved back to the film studio and seated down in the open storage area grounds alongside the marine studio building where they would remain, exposed to the ever changing climate of Malta, until 1991.

The *Titanic* Years: 1982 – 2019

Following on from the models of *Titanic* and the four navy ships being ejected out into the elements of the Maltese weather in the autumn of 1981, the two tugs remained in storage as the Mediterranean Film Facilities found them of use for other productions. It is unclear as to what became of the tug boats and fire boat over the next three decades. No remains were present at the studio when the current owners took over the facility. It may be that they were sold on for parts, or changed beyond any recognition and remain in storage somewhere else. It may also be that they were stripped of parts to the extent that they ended up being scrap materials and disposed of as the studio depended on the storage space. The four navy vessels suffered the same fate as the 55ft *Titanic* as they shared the same storage space out in the open. From September 1981 the navy models were stripped of parts for use in other projects before they deteriorated, and in most cases, becoming the victims to souvenir hunters. By 1989 the navy models were devoid of smaller fittings. As the wooden decks rotted out the heavier upper structures began to collapse down into the hulls. The hull remains of the four navy ships were relocated to another part of the studio grounds sometime in 1993 where they were brought together and stacked on top of one another.

What became of them at the start of a new century no one knows. But one rumour is that the hulls of the navy models were secured by a marine agency and deliberately sunk to act as artificial reefs. When and where is a mystery, if there is any truth to the rumour. The whereabouts of the fully hulled 9ft *Titanic* model is another entry for the mystery book. While the timeline of this model is very short what is known is that the model was put into dry storage at the Mediterranean Film Facilities and was not sold off during the films inventory of items from July 1980. Then sometime around 1984 the new man in charge of Lew Grade's companies, Robert Holmes à Court, shelled out just under $5,000 Australian dollars in purchasing the model to display in one of his themed amusement facilities in Perth. The model remained in Australia following his death in 1990 and is rumoured to be in dry storage somewhere in Sydney. Yet despite years of researching including the assistance of colleagues overseas, no leads have led to the discovery of this particular *Titanic* model. And if it has survived, it is making sure not to reveal its location anytime soon.

The 55ft *Titanic* was certainly destined to go through a more eventful life style over the course of forty years. Being dumped outside was not even going to spoil any opportunity to be in front of the camera once again. In February 1986, the very much stripped model became the focal point for the press when the *Sunday Times* paid $850 in crane hire and crew to put the model back in the waters of the warm Mediterranean Sea to obscurely document the legendary liner as the world still embraced the real liners discovery five months previously. After its brief sea encounter in February 1986, the model was seated back into its storage cradle and delivered back to the studio where it was dumped among the navy ships next to the marine studio building. By 1989 the model had lost almost all of its resin cast deck details and deck railings. The masts were completely gone along with the rigging. The cargo cranes, anchors, propeller blades, ventilators, skylights, stern docking bridge, the cast resin window frames, the compass tower, funnel whistles and the remains of the second funnel had all been removed. The eight-years that had gone by had not been kind to the materials of the model as the steel deckhouses began to rust out, the decks had buckled and separated allowing for the many resin deck details to be pulled freely away and taken as souvenirs. With the decks now in a severe state of decay, the heavy steel superstructure with the three remaining funnels began to push down on the structure, resulting in the decks breaking away and buckling downwards under the shifting weight. What exaggerated the collapse even further was the removal of steel sections of the superstructure containing windows for use in other model builds in progress at the studio. With these sections purposely removed, the weight above them meant it was only a matter of time before the structure completely failed. But despite her wounds there was still life left in the old girl.

In 1991 the German television production company Laser produced their four-part TV-movie *Burning Shore,* a war drama based on the 1985 Wilbur Smith novel of the same name that was set in 1917 during World War One. The story follows Centaine de Thiry, a beautiful French socialite who loses her home during one of the German bombardments. Learning of the loss of her fighter pilot fiancé, Centaine enrols as a nurse and embarks on a hospital ship bound for South Africa. During the voyage the hospital ship is attacked and sunk by a German U-Boat. Centaine survives the sinking and continues on to South Africa where she begins a new life. For the brief sequences of the hospital ship at sea, the production company turned to the Mediterranean Film Facilities for help and the use of their water tanks. The fact they had a large-scale ocean liner model sitting in the studio backlot doing nothing may have swung the final decision. The studios surface tank was selected to film the scenes. With the tank having a depth of four-feet, the *Titanic* model could be controlled better.

The production budget did allow for some much needed repairs to be carried out on the *Titanic* model. The missing masts were replaced with, of all things, galvanised scaffolding poles. The models missing second funnel was replaced as the film production crews unbolted the pre-existing fourth funnel and moved it down to the location of the second funnel. A new fourth funnel was then constructed from sheet plywood wrapped around a wooden inner frame and bolted down in place. As the model was only to be filmed from one perspective, a broadside view, they painted just the starboard side of the hull, superstructure and funnels in white. The funnels were finished with thick black bands positioned across the center while the hull included a long red stripe and markings signifying her role as a hospital ship. While the new paint scheme was not entirely accurate, she did share an unmistakable resemblance to *Titanic*'s other sister, H.M.H.S. *Britannic,* that was tragically lost after she struck a mine in the Aegean Sea during November 1916. The model was rigged to be dragged across the furthest side of the surface tank allowing the foreground to be occupied with a U-Boat exterior set and later with full size lifeboats with actors and extras while the liner takes on a list without the need to fully submerge the model.

On the closure of filming for *Burning Shore,* the *Titanic* model was moved back to its steel cradle and a new location in the studio grounds on the side of the road that weaves between the two main filming tanks. Once again, the model was left to the elements as the white paint applied in 1991 peeled and faded over the years. It was the storms that battered Malta during September 2003 that were to prove extremely destructive. The freak storms that dropped onto Malta during the second and third week of September had heavy winds and thunder storms and downpours so torrential that the wave of destruction across the island was so severe that cars were swept from the roads, properties were badly damaged from flash floods and mud slides. Lightning struck a manufacturing factory of fireworks turning the building to rubble when it exploded. The average rainfall recorded in Malta during an entire month of September prior to 2003 was 40mm. That September both Malta Weather and the Meteorological Office recorded a staggering 260mm in rainfall. As residents and businesses of Malta cleaned up and repaired the damage, what could not be saved was the *Titanic* model which had took the full brunt of the storm. The heavy upper structure with funnels gave way as the remains toppled down into the already weakened structure of the hull, crushing down the metal floatation tanks inside and ripping away the rotten steel supports within the hull. The model now looked like a cross between an abstract art exhibit and a 55ft long blotched fibreglass dumpster.

In 2011 came the story that the model had been moved with rumours that it had been hauled out to sea and dumped into the waters off Valletta turning it into an underwater haven for marine life. However, there was no truth to the story. The hull with its twisted and broken contents had indeed been moved and to a new location just metres away and tucked almost out of sight at the base of the deep tank where over the next few years the undergrowth would almost consume the relic. The hull would remain there until mid-2019 when the studio, under its new owners, began major studio refurbishments including the clearing out old disused outbuildings within the grounds and clearing away areas of land around the studio and tanks. The *Titanic* hull was sitting in one primary location for redevelopment and needed removing. With the help of contractors, the hull was carefully lifted from its spot, lowered onto a flatbed haulage trailer and trucked to its current home within the grounds of Fort Ricasoli.

Not for the Taking

As a movie prop, the *Raise the Titanic* miniature was never built to be a museum piece. It was constructed, it was used and it was disposed of like any other large-scale movie prop. What made the matter worse for this model was that no one person owned it. The prop was paid for by a film company and built as a film prop to be used on screen. Once filming had finished, it was destined to be used for other projects that would see the prop changed, stripped and even sacrificed. It was due to the outcome of the movie's release, the rapid decline of ITC and the props problematic scale, that lead to the model to remain in existence to this very day. Another factor was that the film prop did not belong to the Mediterranean Film Facilities in those early years. It all became a complicated matter in establishing who the actual owner was; the collapsed ITC? The Holmes empire who took over the back catalogue of previously filmed ITC programmes and movies? The model's drawback was its size. And with such a huge film piece there came the spiralling costs. With it being connected to a publicly seen cinematic flop, it kept many of the business suits quiet while distancing themselves from the financial headache that was *Raise the Titanic*. Afterall, if you fail to acknowledge that it exists, there are no accumulating bills, so they thought. With the broadcasting company over in London now turning a blind eye, the model continued to sit in Malta, becoming someone else's problem. The years that would follow had many come forward inquiring on the status of the model and to if it could be purchased and saved. The Mediterranean Film Facilities may have the model in their grounds and them being its unpaid caretaker, the studio was, theoretically, stuck between a rock and a hard place. Each time the model required moving it was done so at the cost to the studios.

The prospect of saving the model, even in the mid-1980s, was not feasible and afforded no financial gain for anyone who was to secure it. Stripped of its details, the cost of recreating the parts outweighed any costs of securing the model in its current state. Even during filming, the model was already deteriorating as it spent weeks submerged in salt water that slowly warped timbers, softened adhesives and rusted up exposed metal not treated. With the corrosive salt water soaked up into every part of the model it would slowly begin to breakdown over the coming months in dry storage. When those storage costs were not paid, the owner of the facility rightfully had the model moved outside where it would remain. The complications over who owned the model was the least of peoples concerns. If during the early 1980s the studio had handed the model over to someone to restore, the costs of transporting, storing and restoring the model would outweigh the cost of the model's original construction. At 55ft in length the model would require a building of 80ft in length to store it for the restoration process. Once the model was restored then it has to be housed somewhere, and most museums, public funded museums, simply do not have the foot space or the budget for such a huge display piece. It would appear that in the 40 years that have passed no offers were ever taken seriously as they lacked the fundamental facilities and finances to save the prop. But any potential would-be-buyers still had the biggest hurdle ahead of them; the fact that the model never belonged to the Mediterranean Film Facilities, so it was not their property to sell. Only the passing of 40 years would see circumstances change.

But not all is lost. While there is very little remaining of the original build of 1980, there is the potential to preserve what is left of the hull by seating it securely upon a transportable chassis while the interior of the hull is fitted out with a steel skeleton frame. The fibreglass matting of the hull when cleaned would be coated inside and out with a clear sealant resin to act as a barrier on the fibreglass shell and reduce deterioration. With the hull secured and suspended upon a chassis the internal steel framework would allow for additional weight to be applied in a separate superstructure with decks, funnels and vents, all made from light-weight durable materials. The project would be costly but feasible if done correctly and professionally. But that final say in the matter rests with the studio as they have now ceased control of the remains to one of the world's largest models ever constructed of the R.M.S. *Titanic*.

Reappraisal of a Flop

Raise the Titanic marked the end of old school moviemaking of the 1970s and ignited the fuse for a new decade which by the end of it would have a new modelling tool in its arsenal that threatened the future of miniatures; the introduction of CGI technology. Models, actors and music aside, what *Raise the Titanic* still continues to define today is that of a movie that was so badly done and ill received it becomes an entity of its own and an example of how *not* to create a movie. You only have to go online to see the endless click-bait articles of *The Biggest Movie Flops of all Time* that list the usual suspects; *The Adventures of Pluto Nash* (2002), *Battlefield Earth* (2000), *K-19: The Widowmaker* (2002), *Land of the Lost* (2009), *Town & Country* (2001), *Stealth* (2005), *Sorcerer* (1977), *Red Planet* (2000) *A Sound of Thunder* (2005) and of course *Raise the Titanic* and Cussler's other movie adaptation, *Sahara*. They appear like winning entries into this brutal hall of fame. But what exactly is a movie flop? A box office flop is usually defined in two ways with one being a highly anticipated film production that, upon cinematic release, is significantly unprofitable during the course of its theatre run. The other is that of a production that fails to exceed both production and marketing expenses. It does not necessarily mean that the production is terrible from start to finish and every minute in between. I tend to learn towards the latter of the two where *Raise the Titanic* is concerned. But does the film deserve such harsh recognition?

Ever since its release in the summer of 1980, *Raise the Titanic* has been on a rollercoaster of a journey as it became symbolic for all the wrong reasons; it's dismal box office takings being used as an excuse to tar the film as a flop and use it as a genuine example of how *not* to make a movie. The film may not have been the blockbuster it was intended to be. But the movie never became the flop that many have labelled it over the decades. Calling *flop* on a film because the box office takings were less than the films overall budget has become part and parcel of many who set out to discredit a production because that is what they are paid to do as a critic. With the use of the internet and the many social media platforms available, anything is open to being critiqued specially when there is a demand and an audience for it. It was really no different back in the 1970s and 1980s with the exception that the media platforms open to the critics were the colossal amounts of newspapers and magazines distributed world-wide in the years long before the birth of the world wide web. Lew Grade observed in 1981 that most movies don't even gross $1m on their opening weekend. How times have changed. These days, studios can now spend twice as much on the company bar tab during a premiere screening of their latest flick. The $150m budget spent on the Denis Villeneuve directed science fiction sequel *Blade Runner 2049* resulted in the movie bringing in more than $259m worldwide and generating a healthy $109m in profit. But that did not stop critics hating on the film's disagreeable $32m box office opening weekend during October 2017 as they had anticipated considerably more. Regardless of the film's grand visuals the critics slapped the *flop* sticker on it whereas weeks earlier they had praised the production to the masses. Ridley Scott, director of the original *Blade Runner* from 1982, even went as far as saying that the film bombed blaming the movie for being far too long and slow paced. The press was no different back in 1980 as the troubles following *Raise the Titanic* was announced in the tabloids in a mixture of praise through to despair. As the film struggled from the offset, the press revelled in the misfortunes as for them it was a sure-fire way to fill up page columns.

What went against *Raise the Titanic* was the time it was released. The studio would feed the press with stories which the press in return would publish. On the back of the film was the real-life adventures of Texan business tycoon Jack Grimm who was pushing his summer 1980 expedition to find the real *Titanic*. If the stories were not about the movie or Grimm, it was the numerous fanciful salvage ideas of using bags, balloons and ping pong balls. And if that was still not enough, the public were being sold another movie on the disaster with *S.O.S. Titanic*. By the summer of 1980 it was becoming apparent that the *Titanic*-overload was beginning to weigh heavy on the public. *Titanic* has always drawn in the crowds with the subject of her one and only voyage generating such a frenzied fascination that thousands of books were put to print, hundreds of magazines published covering the ships, her passengers and crew and the opportunity of becoming a member of a society devoted to preserving her memory. But what all these shared was the common interest in bringing together thousands of *Titanic* enthusiasts from all around the world. Turning it into a specialised subject that was considerably less in statistics when compared to the general public who were being expected to support another version of the *Titanic* story that did not involve her tragic demise.

Titanic may have had a fan base in 1980 but it was not enough to sustain ticket sales and put customers in theatre seats, especially when those ticket sales were reliant on a larger percentage being the general public. And if the subject was falling out of favour with the general public then the takings at the box office would be greatly affected. Lew Grade had envisioned his *Titanic* as being a film of such spectacular magnitude he even went as far as claiming that the production would become *the* movie of the entire decade. He was so sure that the name *Titanic* alone would be the only publicity selling tool that the movie required to generate queues that encircled the block outside the cinema chains. There were queues that summer with crowds flocking into the cinemas. They just weren't there to watch *Raise the Titanic*. Instead the attention was on the second thrilling instalment of the *Star Wars* franchise. It was of no importance that *Raise the Titanic* starred Alec Guinness in a memorable cameo appearance in the role of a salty sea dog who survived the *Titanic* disaster. To the movie world Alec Guinness was Obi-Wan Kenobi and that was where he would be more fondly remembered. With *Empire* taking box office by storm on its release in May 1980 the release of *Raise the Titanic* a couple of months later had the production succumb to the advance of Darth Vader. *Star Wars* was far more appealing to the popcorn munching audience than that of an overblown and over budget story about a sunken shipwreck that had gone down more times than a sunset.

The more the tabloids exploited the movies financial woes, Grimm's laughable expedition, Lew Grade's woeful endeavours to sail his doomed *Titanic* into movie history and the unrest overseas with the Soviet-Afghan War, *Raise the Titanic* and its Cold War aspect lost the attention of the audience. In hindsight the *if only* rule would be the better way of summarising the entire production. *If only* the film had stuck to its budget. *If only* the film had not experienced directors' troubles. *If only* the film had been released prior to 1979. *If only* the screenplay had stayed more faithful to the novel. *If only* the movie was not competing with other *Titanic* projects at the time. If only, if only, if only. So, does *Raise the Titanic* still deserve such harsh recognition in being brandished a flop? The only critic whose opinion is trust worthy and valid is your own. The movie is not without fault. No movie is regardless who did them or how much money the studios invested in the production. In the case of *Raise the Titanic*, this movie captured my attention and not once did it ever fail in letting go. And after forty-years I still enjoy the film for what it is; a work of fiction that is not meant to be taken seriously or as reality. It is fun, it is adventurous but more importantly it is a time capsule of a year that I lived through and fondly remember. Those positive memories are priceless even if it cost a film studio over £25m to create them.

Earning Cult Status

Raise the Titanic was a product of its time. Despite its flaws, it is a remarkable adventure in storytelling using old fashioned techniques while trying and succeeding in raising a legend on screen. In the end *Raise the Titanic* did claw back its £25m. It may never have been the success on the big screen that many had hoped for. It was the small screen where it fitted right at home to become a popular classic among viewers. When the film premiered on ITV in Britain on Thursday 27th October 1983, following its purchase for £500,000, it was watched by more than ten million viewers to eventually become one of ITV's largest viewing figures for that year. The films television debut, its release to VHS and other home entertainment formats slowly pulled the waterlogged *Raise the Titanic* out of the red and into the black. But it was all too late for Lord Lew Grade and his much-loved ITC and parent companies.

And yet, despite all its faults, *Raise the Titanic* has gone on to become a cult film in its own right, now largely looked upon as another fabled tale on *Titanic*'s enduring legacy. The film was not the first or last to be hyped up to then be let down by the critics. Master of horror John Carpenter was scalded over his 1982 science fiction horror adaptation of *The Thing*. The film bears some production resemblances to that of *Raise the Titanic* such as overly long filming schedules, budget issues and then the public flogging by film critics. Carpenter recalled in an October 2012 interview with *Time Out* how he was gutted at how the film was being hated by fans of science fiction during the 1980s. And now, four decades later, it has an unprecedented cult following and regarded as the defining sci-fi horror of its genre. While *Raise the Titanic* lacks any form of shape-shifting aliens, the film has taken those well-known elements of *Titanic* and crafted into a story a compelling piece of science fiction that will be impossible to achieve in reality. As the film ended its run at theatres during the first quarter of 1981, and the unrest over the complications between ITC and Lew Grade died down, *Raise the Titanic* was snapped up for release on home media entertainment for the purpose of clawing back some of the abysmal box office losses. The sales on VHS, laser disc, Super8, video CD and in more recent times DVD, digital download and high definition blu ray, have proved that the movie has never lost its appeal to the small screen audience. Just like Cussler's novel, *Raise the Titanic* has never been out of print having been distributed across many countries including the United Kingdom, United States, Australia, Germany, Spain, France, Denmark and Japan; the country which really embraced the film and was the only country the movie broke box office records. The movie even went on to have regular screenings at 35,000ft for passengers on board Malaysian Airlines as part of their onboard entertainment packages.

A Tale of Two *Titanic*'s

Titanoracs, a term given to die-hard fans of the subject, always bring up the question as to why the *Raise the Titanic* model was never saved when the film models from the 1953 and 1997 movies remain to this day as displays for the public. Unlike the model from *Raise the Titanic,* those two movie representations of *Titanic* were box office successes in which the 20th Century Fox studios benefited greatly. In helping with their preservation was the fact these two film models were considerably smaller than Grade's monster boat. However, it is to be remembered that the 40ft *Titanic* built by the Shawcraft company for the 1958 Rank Organisation production of *A Night to Remember* was built, sunk and then later broken up after production had completed.

The 1953 Fox production used a 28ft constructed model of the *Titanic* which, at that scale, was more workable and easier to store in the undercover back lot of the Fox studios. The model was to be reused for another 20th Century Fox production, *Gentlemen Prefer Blondes* from 1953 and which starred Jane Russell and Marilyn Monroe. As a Fox film, the model was already there at the studios, and for this production, the model unit could alter the model for the needs of the film. The *Titanic* was converted from that of a four funnelled ocean liner to a three-funnel ship. With the additions of new lifeboats and davits with new deck ventilators manufactured, the model was transformed to represent the Cunard-White Star liner R.M.S. *Queen Mary.* The model was restored back to *Titanic* where in the 1970s it was on public display in an Atlantic Ocean waterline setting at the Northtown Center Mall in Blaine, Minnesota. When the shopping mall was put up for sale in 1985, the model was secured by the *Titanic Historical Society* and donated to the Marine Museum at Falls River, Massachusetts, where it remains to this day on public display.

For the James Cameron movie, several miniatures were built for use on screen which included the full scale 45ft *Titanic* replica, a scale bow wreck, and large models of the stern which was used for the final sinking scenes including the moment the ship breaks in half. The wreck model still exists along with some of the stern sinking prop, the wreck belonging to James Cameron along with the 45ft hero model which forms part of the studio attraction at the Manhattan Beach Studio Media Campus in California. But during the period from 1997 to more recent times the 45ft model was used for displays, with one such public display in Australia that resulted in the model being cut in half so it could fit into the museums attraction hall. Its return back to America had the model gathering dust at the Manhattan Beach Studio alongside the wreck miniature before undergoing restoration for better display.

It was the success of these films that paved the way for their survival. The size of the models helped with their future preservation too. But unlike that of what befell the huge *Raise the Titanic* prop, these miniatures could have fallen foul to being destroyed. Luckily, that never happened. The future is always unpredictable. And while these miniatures have lasted into the 21st century, there is no guarantee on their future. But what does help their survival is the slow decline in the manufacturing and use of practical FX as more and more productions turn to the use of CGI. There may be a time when such practical FX are no longer needed. Turning these film relics into fascinating time capsules of a period in film making where artistry in the physical media brought about some of the most cherished and best loved movie miniatures to ever grace the big screen.

Pimlico Films Limited

a subsidiary of Associated Communications Corporation Limited

ACC House
17 Great Cumberland Place
London W1A 1AG

telephone 01-262 8040

Directors
Lord Grade
B.J. Kingham
Peter Lucas
A.D. Brook

Agents for Marble Arch
Productions Inc.

30th September, 1980

Technovision Limited,
c/o Twickenham Studios,
St. Margarets,
TWICKENHAM, Middx.

Dear Graham,

"RAISE THE TITANIC" - Underwater Camera Housings

You are probably still aware that the underwater housings specially developed and built in the US for the above production are still out in Malta awaiting disposal. Whilst I am aware that we have discussed this previously it occurs to me that the following may be a mutually agreeable arrangement:

(1) That Technovision pay for the temporary importation for a twelve month period and the incumbant freight charges from Malta to Englandwhich could be arranged through our Freight Agents in Malta

and

(2) That this amount be setagainst future hire of this equipment.

It will further be necessary to work out a further hire and/or purchase agreement with Marble Arch Productions Inc. once this amount has been covered by subsequent outside hire.

Should an agreement be reached on this subject, or if you have some other proposal you would like to make, perhaps you would let Gerard Fitzsimon know at the above address, when some deal may be arranged.

Kind regards,

Yours sincerely,

Malcolm Christopher

Registered Office: ACC House 17 Great Cumberland Place London W1A 1AG
Registered in England No. 482139

It is September 1980 and the woes continue to plague Lew Grade's companies. *(Author's collection)*

Pimlico Films Limited
a subsidiary of
Associated Communications Corporation Limited

ACC House
17 Great Cumberland Place
London W1A 1AG

telephone 01-262 8040

Directors
Lord Grade
B.J. Kingham
Peter Lucas
A.D. Brook

TO WHOM IT MAY CONCERN: 22nd July 1980.

Dear Sirs,

This is to authorise Mr Roy Maisey to act as an agent on our behalf in the sale or disposal of equipment held in Malta.

All cheques should be made out to Pimlico Films Ltd. "Raise The Titanic" Production Account and paid into the Bank of Valletta, Republic Street.

Yours faithfully,
For and on behalf of
PIMLICO FILMS LIMITED

MALCOLM CHRISTOPHER
Production Supervisor.

c.c. B. Kingham
      D. O'Connor
      R. Cook

Registered Office: ACC House 17 Great Cumberland Place London W1A 1AG
Registered in England No. 482139

The letter dated 22 July 1980 that was sent to a number of officials working at the Mediterranean Film Facility in Malta notifying that ITC had given the go-ahead for Roy Maisey to be the agent in the sales and disposal of film equipment and props in Malta from the production of *Raise the Titanic*. *(Author's collection)*

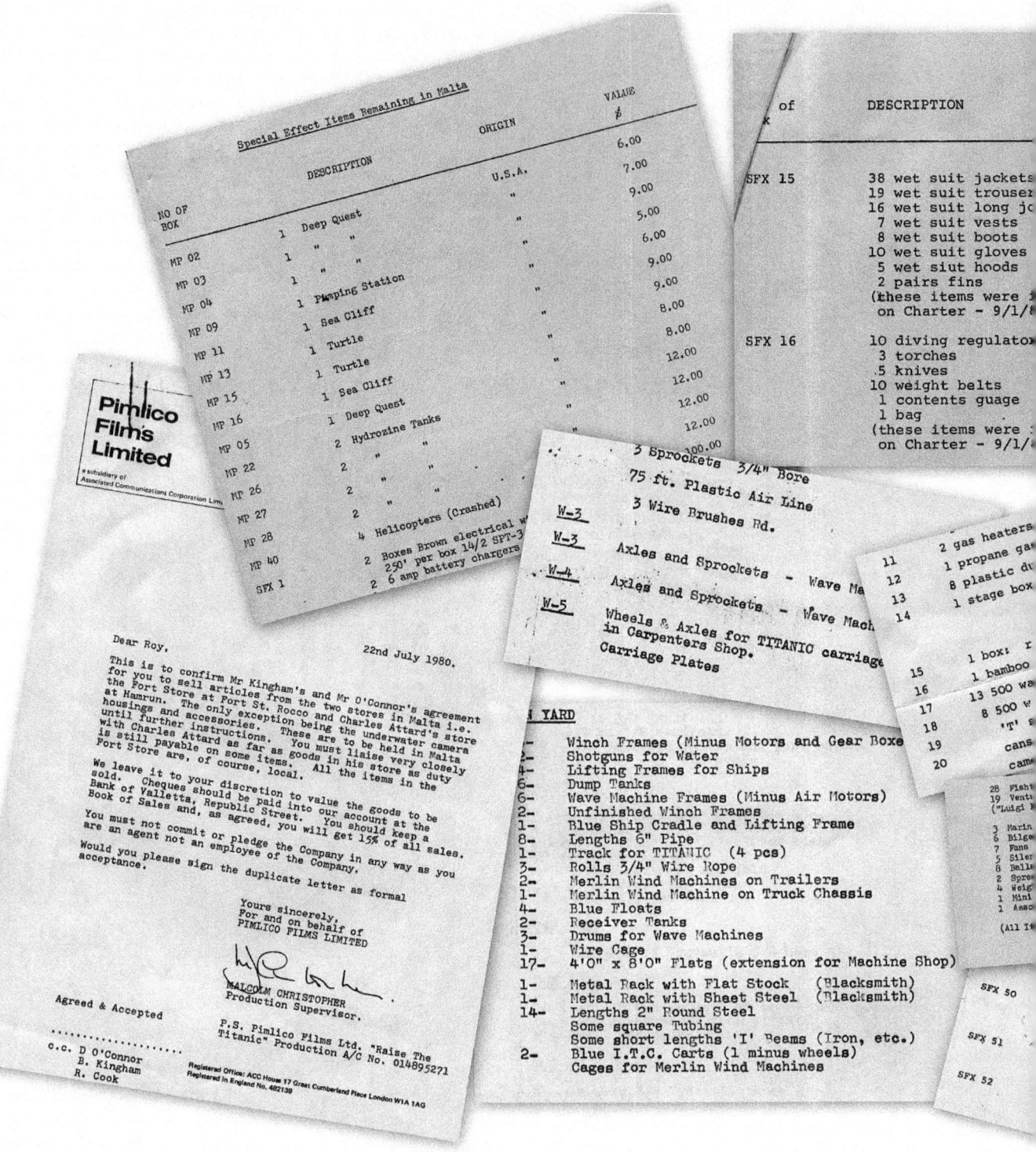

Sample of pages from the ITC *Raise the Titanic* film production stores inventory at the Mediterranean Film Facility that was first compiled between May to October 1980. Among the 103 pages are items ranging from the huge 55ft *Titanic* right the way down to 3x wire brushes. *(Author's collection)*

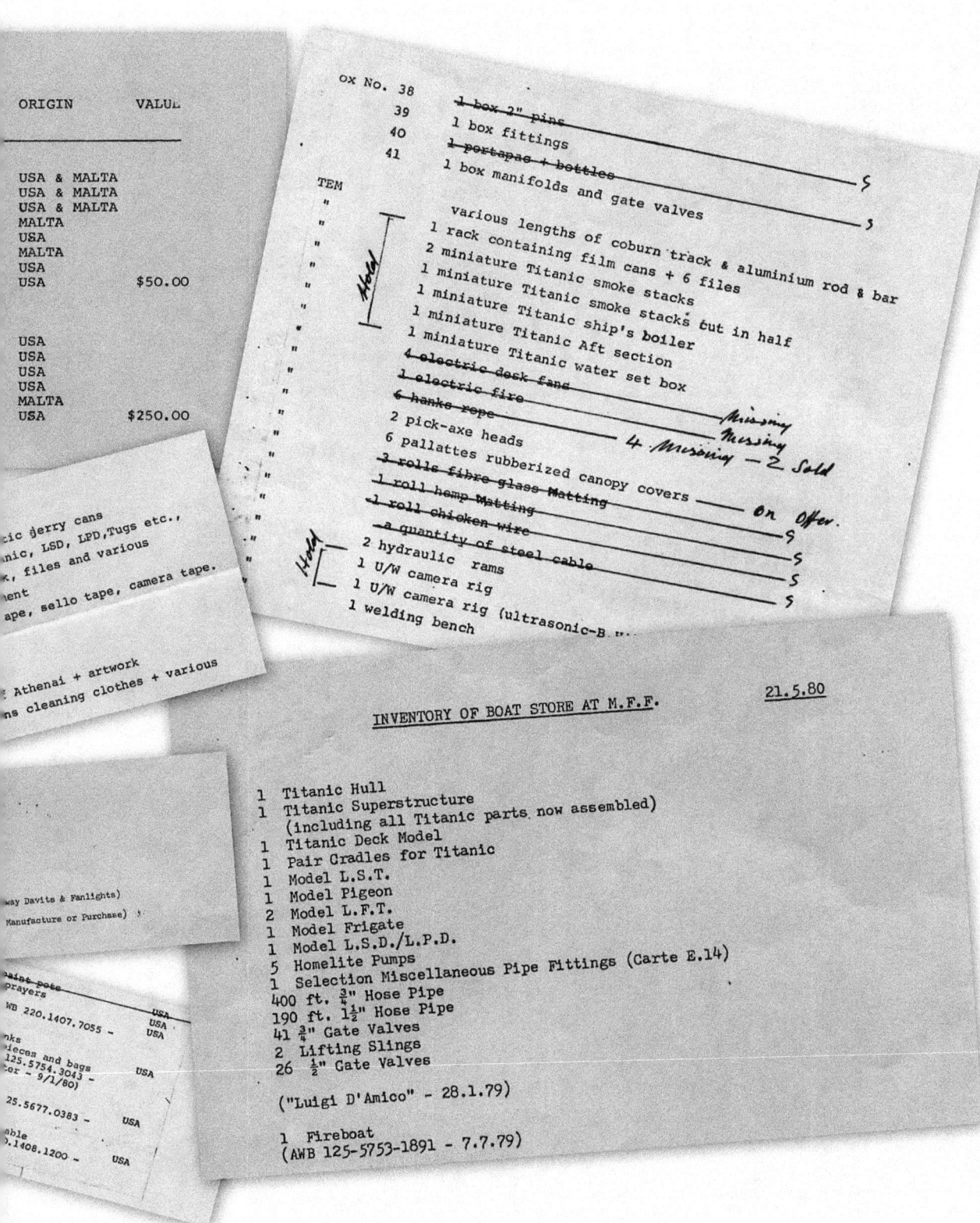

BOTTOM: The St. Dominic Counterguard building that became the storage home of the *Titanic* model between the summers of 1980 to 1981. *(Photograph © Jean Pierre Borg)*

The interior of the Counterguard building. This view is taken from the main door to the structure. The location of the *Titanic* was to the right with the hull placed alongside the wall, the removed superstructure sat down on the floor down the middle of the building while the navy vessels were placed along the wall to the left. *(Photograph © Jean Pierre Borg)*

Chapter 28: The Last Voyage of the "unsinkable" *Titanic* • 447

This view is looking from the rear of the building and towards the main doors. *(Photograph © Jean Pierre Borg)*

The Counterguard building in September 1981 following the cutting open of the heavy steel doors to gain access to the movie contents inside. *(Author's collection)*

The owner of the Counterguard stands along- side the superstructure of the *Titanic* model. With ITC neglecting to pay the storage costs and with a year having now passed, the building was required for other uses. *(Author's collection)*

February 1986 and the *Titanic* model floats in the waters of Marsaskala bay, Malta. *(Author's collection)*

Chapter 28: The Last Voyage of the "unsinkable" *Titanic* • 451

The model is lifted out of the waters of Marsaskala bay following a brief photo opportunity. *(Author's collection - With thanks to Teresa Trower)*

It is 1988 and the *Titanic* model sits in the backlot of the Mediterranean Film Facility. To the left is the deckhouse set built and used for the scenes of the trapped *Deep Quest*. To the right and pushed to the rear of the studio lot are the remains of the Navy vessels, all but stripped of parts. *(Photograph © Mike Seares)*

After seven years outside the model is showing a lot of deterioration, speeded up by the removal of parts and the brutal salt air of Malta. *(Photograph © Mike Seares)*

The stern of the model in 1988 showing that each letter of the ships name and port of registry had been chiselled off by souvenir hunters. *(Photograph © Mike Seares)*

The *Titanic* model became a must-see attraction for holiday makers visiting Malta during the 80s and 90s. *(Photograph © Colin Cook)*

It is 1989 and the masts have now gone. *(Photograph © Commodore Ronald Warwick)*

Chapter 28: The Last Voyage of the "unsinkable" *Titanic* • 455

The *Titanic* model painted up to mimic her sister H.M.H.S. *Britannic* and sitting in the surface tank with a foreground model U-Boat at the Mediterranean Film Facility for the filming of the WWI drama *Burning Shore* in 1990. *(Joe Sciberras collection)*

Two shots from *Burning Shore* of the sinking *Britannic*. The effect of the fire was created by a controlled contained fire behind the model on the edge of the surface tank. *(Laser Productions)*

The model in late 1991 showing the quickly deteriorating *Britannic* paint scheme. *(Joe Sciberras collection)*

1996 starboard broadside view of the model as its sits on the side of the road that passes between the two tanks at the film studios. *(Photograph © Simon Mills)*

This photograph taken in 1996 shows the deterioration of the superstructure and upper decks. With sections removed from B-Deck, the superstructure has dropped down under its own weight and decay. *(Photograph © Simon Mills)*

By 1996 the bridge area had all but gone. *(Photograph © Simon Mills)*

The *Raise the Titanic* miniature looking rather sorry for itself in the summer of 1996. *(Photograph © Simon Mills)*

Photograph taken in 2004 of the severely storm damaged *Titanic*. *(Photograph © David Lawrence)*

Less than two-years later and the change is startling. The funnels have collapsed down into the superstructure along with the heavy structure giving way and falling down onto the floatation tanks inside the hull. *(Photograph © Steve Rigby – Author's collection)*

Chapter 28: The Last Voyage of the "unsinkable" *Titanic* • 459

The tremendous change to the model is evident here following the severe storms that battered Malta in 2003. This view is looking from the rear of A-Deck promenade and looking forwards towards the bow. The structure to the left with the railings still attached is the tank room deckhouse that sat between funnels three and four. *(Photograph © Steve Rigby – Author's collection)*

Another view looking along the starboard A-Deck promenade. The windows to the right are those to what would be the 1st Class Smoking Room. The wooden structure laying across the top of the deckhouse is all that remains of the #4 funnel internal frame. Note the aft staircase weather covering just visible through the window in the foreground. *(Photograph © Steve Rigby – Author's collection)*

460 • *Raise The Titanic*

Ten-years have passed and the model, now moved to the foot of the deep tank embankment, is slowly becoming lost in the undergrowth. *(Photograph © Jean Pierre Borg)*

Resembling more of a garbage container, this view taken from the bow and looking aft towards the stern shows the mass of debris from the rotten remains of this once great replica. *(Photograph © Jean Pierre Borg)*

Chapter 28: The Last Voyage of the "unsinkable" *Titanic* • 461

Would an adaptation of *Raise the Titanic* have worked if the film idea did not come into being until after the real discovery of the wreck in September 1985? This mock-up poster was created by the author in mixing the actors from the original 1980 movie to the condition of *Titanic* as she was found. *(Artwork © Jonathan Smith / ITC)*

Two years after the release of the movie on the big screen, *Raise the Titanic* was to prove its popularity come October 1983 when over 10 million people in the UK alone tuned in to watch the film on the small screen during its television movie premiere. *(Author's collection)*

Promotional artwork by Duncan Mil from October 1983 as *Raise the Titanic* made its UK television premiere attracting over 10 million viewers. *(Artwork © Duncan Mil - Author's collection)*

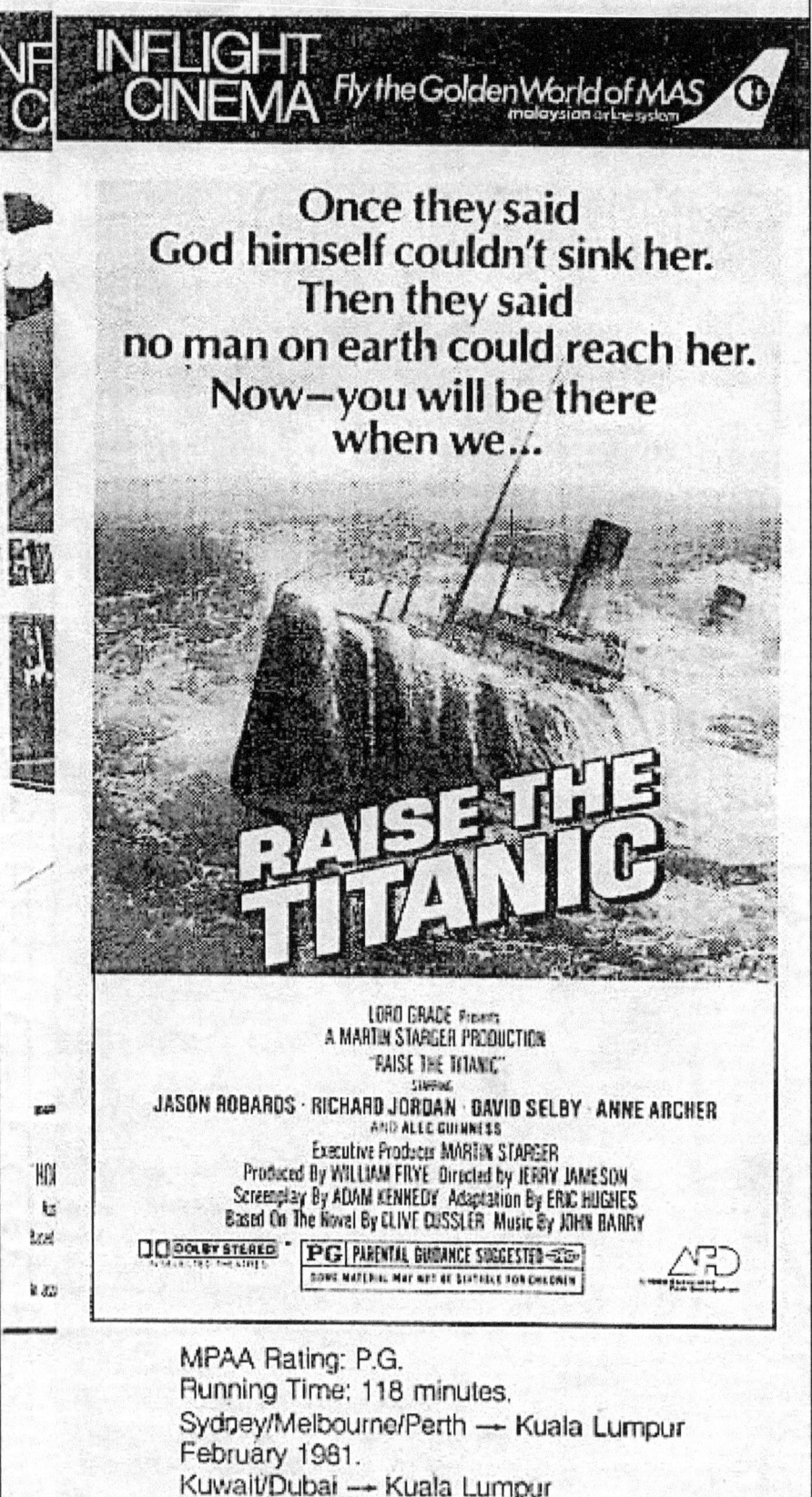

On a flight at 30,000ft and stuck for something to watch? *(Author's collection)*

CHAPTER 29

Brewster's Vault: Collecting *Raise the Titanic*

"Alright! Let's get those boxes out of there and get them opened up."

General Dale Busby

Even before the release of the movie in August 1980, fans of the Clive Cussler novel, and later the film, had already began collecting whatever material they could find. It did not matter if it was a book store advertising poster, a newspaper cutting or one of the many released publicity stills. There was always something that fans back then and today could add to their collections. Collecting *Raise the Titanic* is a relatively easy thing to do if you know what to look for, where to search for the items and have a general idea of what is available. Previous chapters in this book have hinted to what was released and what is still out there, and in most cases, what was produced in quantity to those more collectible and rarer. As the film's box office failure put an end to any possible merchandising, the only option for memorabilia is searching for any of the advertising material released by the studio pre and post movie release making the search sometimes challenging.

Unlike other blockbusters of the time, *Raise the Titanic* was not a money earning product in which collectibles could be manufactured and sold. It certainly was no *Star Wars*. The collectible side of the movie is dependent on publicity and press material released between late 1979 to the movies release in August 1980 that includes cinema lobby cards, movies posters in one-sheets, quad and inserts. The larger press packs by AFD that contains over 30 black & white publicity photographs distributed to news agencies do occasionally appear on auction sites along with the Press Campaign book and the popular Japanese press book. The more widely available pieces of ephemera are the several film-tie in editions of the Clive Cussler's novel published between 1978 to 1981 and featuring cover artwork from the film and earlier 1978/1979 printings featuring generic artwork with a printed banner on one side of the cover announcing the novel is soon to be a major motion picture. With Lew Grade focusing more on spending millions on advertising, it never occurred that the subject of *Titanic* could be key in generating additional sales for the studio. There was a window of opportunity for the studio to create merchandise and make it available far in advance of the movie's release which could have been beneficial for both fans and the studio. But in hindsight it was one less expense Grade and ITC could have done without come 1981.

From a personal perspective I have collected on the subject of *Titanic* since the late 1970s and during that time I have traded in collectibles covering the liner and her two sisters; *Olympic* and *Britannic*. And while items come and go, it is *Raise the Titanic* that has proven to me to be the most fun, the most challenging, but more importantly the most fulfilling. It doesn't matter what your hobby is, when something captures your imagination and your heart, it is the fun of the chase in searching for that one or more items to expand and complete your collection. Whether you are thinking of starting a collection or a seasoned pro, hopefully this chapter will give you an idea to what is out there waiting to be discovered.

Cussler's *Titanic*

There is a wide variety of collectibles out there on Clive Cussler's *Raise the Titanic* that cater for your personal taste and budget. If you are new to collecting a good starting point is obtaining a 1976 first edition of the novel published by Viking Press in the United States or Michael Joseph in the United Kingdom. A number of *Raise the Titanic* book collectors like to add the various editions from the many countries to their library with those focusing on first editions/printings to those collecting for the book cover art. Autographed editions of Clive Cussler's *Raise the Titanic* are common. The more sought after is those signed in the early days of the novels release in 1976 and again in 1980 during the movie adaptations release. These editions vary depending on the books overall condition and Cussler's signature as the author just signed his name during the book launch and bookstore publicity campaign due to time restraints. The most desirable of the signed editions is Cussler's now infamous "Get it up!"; his signature with accompanying *Titanic* doodle. Unique items on the book are those from the promotional period which included bookstore display posters, publishing company badges, counter top display cards and the advanced reading copy (ARC) of the novel.

One interesting piece of memorabilia connected to the novel was the comic strip adaptations that were printed in newspapers and magazines following the release of the Cussler novel. An early version published in the United States was for the children's *The Trib Comic Book* between 8 October 1977 with a weekly issue over eight weeks until 26 November. Presented in colour and black and white, the illustrations were created by the legendary comic book artist Frank Bolle (1924 – 2020) whose works through the 1950s, 60s and 70s are admired by comic collectors around the world. In 1977 a Spanish edition of Cussler's *Rescaten El Titanic* was released as a condensed version by D'Artagnan and featured multiple comic book-style illustrations based on chapter actions giving a unique look into the story. When the novel went into print with the UK publisher Sphere in 1978 the promotional material included a colourful store poster of artwork created solely for the poster. The 1978 Sphere paperback resulted in a simple yet effective advertising badge that had printed a simplified version of the Chris Foss *Titanic* artwork surrounded by the authors name, book title and Cussler's to be iconic "Get it up!" line. Due to popularity among fans of the 1978 paperback, science fiction artist Chris Foss released his best loved artwork for *Raise the Titanic* as a limited-edition print through his website at www.chrisfossart.com.

Movie Memories

Items on the movie are more excessive compared to that of the book as the bulk of collectibles come from those products released as publicity material before, during and after the film's release. The official printed theatre lobby posters are most popular with movie fans as they are ideal for framing and wall mounting. Lobby cards and publicity stills are more budget friendly and given their size can be easily displayed in frames or A4 display books. Again, on the lower end of the price range are mini posters printed and published overseas including Japan, France, Belgium and Italy. A firm favourite with many new to collecting *Raise the Titanic* is the 1980/81 Japanese film brochure that contains a lot of images from the film and a small handful of publicity shots. But while there is a lot out there that was mass produced by the studio for publicising the film, there are items that are far rarer and extremely hard to find.

Of these are props from the actual movie that have miraculously survived to this day. Collecting movie props is big business that attracts a cult following in itself as fans of a particular film or franchise want something that was made for and used in the production with screen used props fetching premium prices depending on the production and the size and physical appearance of the prop made for the production. Production made items from *Raise the Titanic* rarely come up with many having perished or become lost over the five decades that have passed. After filming had finished on James Cameron's 1997 blockbuster 'Titanic', the exterior and interior sets built for the production were completely destroyed. The huge 770 feet exterior *Titanic* set was cut up weeks after filming had finished to allow for the complex to lease out the studio for the next motion picture. Only a small number of items that were storable and displayable were kept. But some props from the movie did make it into auctions when the American vintage clothing and accessories company J. Peterman purchased a large quantity of items that was sold through their auctions and catalogues. In 1980 such films like *Raise the Titanic* did not have that option, and with the studio reusing or destroying the props, finding any that have survived to this day is like looking for proof of Big Foot.

Over the course of forty-years collecting on *Raise the Titanic*, I have only seen a handful of actual props that have survived to this day. Putting aside the rotten remains of the 55ft *Titanic* hull over in Malta, of the known props that have survived are one of the cast resin lifeboats that was used for the movies sinking prologue. Two known examples of the $1:16^{th}$ scale three-panel NAVY lighting pods have survived; one of which is in my own private collection. It is rumoured that one of each of the *Deep Quest* and *Sea Cliff* $1:16^{th}$ models have survived and in the collection of a shipping historian in America, while some questionable lifejackets reputedly made for live action scenes with extras in lifeboats for the film's prologue sequence have come up for sale over the years. Of all the items that occasionally surface are originally printed scripts that differentiate in value depending on condition and if they were used and annotated by an actor or crew member on the production.

One item that frequently appears online via a well-known auction site is the game *Raise the Titanic*. Often wrongly accredited as being associated with the movie, the game is actually a cash-in on the recovery of artefacts from the real wreck of the *Titanic* which had begun in the summer of 1987 by the French exploration team IFREMER. Released by games manufacturer Hoyle in 1987, *Raise the Titanic* is a family board game where up to 4 players can play against each other in exploring the wreck and attempting to raise the ship with the help of question cards, trinkets and a Monopoly-style board.

Collecting Cussler

Outside of the world of *Raise the Titanic* there is a rapidly growing fanbase of those who collect the other masterful works of Clive Cussler. The extensive library of Dirk Pitt, NUMA, Oregon, Isaac Bell and Fargo adventures meant that each product was promoted in some form or other by the publisher. Older publications from the 70s through to the 90s are ideal for beginner's due to the broad spectrum of Cussler novels available from companies who deal with new and used books. First editions of earlier Cussler books are desirable among collectors but not always essential if you are new to collecting. Picking up a used paperback release is a good budget starter which if liked can be updated with a hardback edition. There are some book editions that cater for the more serious collectors who demand that certain special piece. The 1973 edition of *The Mediterranean Caper* is regarded as the corner stone in Cussler memorabilia as only 32,000 copies from the 50,000 printed were sold. Another sought after book release is the 1977 Bantam International Edition of *The Mediterranean Caper* that was issued shortly after the release of *Raise the Titanic*. The edition is more collectible among fans of Cussler's work due to the cover artwork featuring a naked Pitt in the sea with nothing but snorkel and diving goggles. Later reprints were corrected in repositioning the books title and authors name covering Pitt's modesty.

As your book collection expands there is always the choice of taking your favourite book release from the shelf to the walls with publishers' posters, counter displays, floor standees or hanging banners. Occasionally original pages from manuscripts come up for offer with those pages signed by Cussler, making them a perfect piece of memorabilia for framing. For those wanting more than just books and paper ephemera, some of the older promotional items created by the publishing houses for bookstore display ranged from baseball caps for the 1999 release of *Atlantis Found* or more uniquely an inflatable airship for *Cyclops* from 1986. And for those who really want to add something really luxurious, how about the limited edition DOXA SUB 300T wristwatch from 2002, reissued to celebrate the 35th anniversary of their original SUB 300T and promoting the release of Cussler's best-selling non-fiction book *The Sea Hunters*. Afterall, if James Bond can wear an OMEGA, then our hero Dirk Pitt can wear a DOXA.

The Home Cinema Experience

Raise the Titanic has been released on almost all types of media from 8mm film to today's high definition Blu-ray disc. The first release of the film came in 1981 when it was rushed out on VHS and Betamax video tapes and the new media of the time, Laserdisc. It was an attempt to maximise a return for ITC during a troubled year for its board of directors and shareholders. And yet after the questionable box office takings during 1980 into 1981, the release of the movie on home video would see *Raise the Titanic* become an instant favourite and a top selling product. The United Kingdom saw the first release of the film on tape when it was handed over to Precision Video with sales of the movie on VHS, Betamax and laser disc. It comes as no surprise as to why Precision Video was so quick to receive the film for public release as the distributer was owned by Lew Grade under his Associated Communications Corporation (ACC) company. A few months later the United States followed with their release on VHS and Laserdisc on the Magnetic Video label. The releases kept on coming through the 80s and 90s with the film put to tape and Laserdisc and distributed by Spectrum Video, Channel 5 Video, CBS-FOX Video, Phillips Video, Polygram Video and King Video. The old Laserdisc releases do make for wonderful pieces of decorative art if collected and displayed in 12 x 12 inch album vinyl frames.

As a new century dawned the film was put over to the latest media of DVD with releases in many of the main countries. Some of the earliest DVD releases came in 2003 when Carlton, part of the ITV franchise, put the film to disc with other countries including Australia, United States, Germany, Denmark, Finland and Japan. The content of the releases was kept to a minimum with the film, and depending on release, the odd trailer. It was not until 2007 when the UK distributer Network on Air released the movie on DVD that finally contained a 'Special Features' section of images, stills, press material and notes. In 2015 Network on Air released the movie on Blu-ray in a new high definition transfer from the original UK theatrical release and accompanied with a booklet of linear notes and a 'Special Features' section of material, old and new, transferred over from their previous 2007 release, but this time to include the isolated film score by John Barry. The following year the U.S. distributor Shout! Factory released their own high definition version of the film that also included the full theatrical UK trailer and a new twenty-minute *Making Of* featurette. With the increase in popularity of productions being transferred to 4K and 8K ultra high definition, it is questionable if *Raise the Titanic* will ever be enjoyed in that format.

In terms of collecting the feature film it is the celluloid media that is the most desirable for collectors. The most popular of the releases came from Durann Film Services Ltd who were based in Dudley, England. Durann was the go-to entertainment company that catered for film fans to enjoy their favourite movies of present and past by taking home the feature film on reel-to-reel. *Raise the Titanic* was among the popular sellers for the company with the film being transferred over to 8mm in Super8 CinemaScope on 4x 600' reels and a special digest version with a running time of 54 minutes was released on 2x 600' reels. The releases were presented in carboard cases with colour printed artwork from the movie with the exception of the digest version that included a Silver Screen Collection banner over blue-tinted or sepia-tinted picture sleeves. Durann also went on to release a more condensed version of the film running in at 25 minutes and featuring the best sequences from the movie in something that resembled a deluxe extended trailer.

The circumstances which led to the film being released through Durann was one of an accidental encounter. By the early 1980s there had been a decline in the sales of 8mm productions as VHS and Betamax became the most reliable source of home entertainment media. It was during a trade fair in London when Durann's company founder Derek Simmonds, while washing his hands following using the gents, recognised the suited gentleman using the next wash basin. It was none other than Lord Lew Grade. Simmonds engaged in conversation with Grade over film releases. During the couple of minutes of discussion, Grade had promised to allow *Raise the Titanic, Capricorn One, Q: The Winged Serpent* and *Hawk the Slayer* to be a part of the Durann company catalogue. Keeping to his word Grade had a contract drawn up ready for Simmonds to sign at Grade's London ITC office. Paperwork signed; Grade concluded the meeting. "Perhaps you'll have better luck with *Raise the Titanic* than I did!" The decision was a positive move as the quality of the four movie releases through Durann revitalised the 8mm film market.

It's a Small World

As the movie gains more and more popularity among cult movie buffs, *Titanic* enthusiasts and fans of Clive Cussler's works, the question on what merchandise directly connected to the film still crops up frequently. Only two movies were ever adapted from Cussler novels; *Raise the Titanic* and the 2005 Paramount Pictures adaptation of *Sahara*. This chapter has covered to this point the promotional material and book tie-ins for *Raise the Titanic*, the only official ephemera released for the film, albeit somewhat publicity material. Cussler fans did finally have the chance in obtaining official merchandise when *Sahara* was released. Putting aside both press and promotional material the film production did produce a couple of collectibles that were available off the shelf. Created by 21st Century Toys and released under The Ultimate Soldier action figure series, they replicated the film's two main characters; Dirk Pitt (Matthew McConaughey) and Al Giordino (Steve Zahn) in 1:18th scale figurines. Additionally, the movie's Willy's Jeep with scaled Pitt and Giordino was released in a much larger 1:6th scale by 21st Century Toys and a smaller 1:24th scale tank and helicopter with figurines. With *Sahara* also hitting rock bottom at the box office it makes the short-lived run of the action figures imperative to Cussler fan collections. With no *Raise the Titanic* franchise it has been left to fans to create their own unique collectibles depending on their preferred taste.

Over the years there has been a steady increase in *Raise the Titanic* fans picking up *Titanic* model kits and changing the plastic kit to resemble the ship from either the film or basing the wreck on Cussler's book description. A number of custom built models and dioramas have appeared online lovingly recreating a scene or two from the film; the moment the liner emerges from the ocean in a cascade of water is one that captures many model builders imagination. As no kit has ever been produce of the movie version, it is left to the model maker in obtaining a pre-existing *Titanic* model kit and purposely degrading the look of the kit parts during assembly. There is no specific kit option as many of the manufactured *Titanic* model kits out there can be used as the main foundation for the movie or book replica; and there is a good range of plastic model kits out there to choose from; Revell, Minicraft, Academy and more recently the new Trumpeter *Titanic* kit. The plastic injection moulded kits range from the most workable of scales such as Revell's 1:700 scale (15 inches), to Minicraft's larger 1:350 (30 inches) and Trumpter's monster 1:200 scale (53 inches) giving the builder a varied option of sizes depending on how they want to display them. Of the builds I have completed over the years I have turned to all the popular scales as the releases are supported with third party detailing sets of photo etched parts that are more commonly known as PE sets that are produced from brass sheets to replicate the pre-existing plastic parts in better scale and extra added realism. While these sets can improve the overall look of the build, they do not include any of the required details in turning your standard *Titanic* model kit into something that resembles the film model. This all comes down to you, the model builder, in your skills of taking something factory produced and turning it into something it was not originally intended to be.

Raise the Titanic movie Replicas

I first turned to replicating the *Titanic* from the movie in the late 1980s following the increase of interest on the back of the discovery of *Titanic*'s final resting place in September 1985. The model finish was basic and based around a number of VHS screen shots from the movie to alter the construction kit.

A commission build in 1996 had me turning a 1:350th scale Minicraft kit into a raised *Titanic* in a setting moments after she has stabilised in a swirling sea made from modelling putty and layered gloss paint lacquer to resemble streams of water pouring off her decks. After joining a *Raise the Titanic* fan website in 2001, I decided to build my own display model in 1:350th scale, but in a online step-by-step guide for those interested in turning their hands to recreating the film version. The adventure turned out to be a success with numerous fans following the build and using it to create their own unique versions of *Raise the Titanic*. While many of those commissioned builds have come and gone, the build of 2002 still remains a firm favourite among the many who have used it as their primary source of information for their own builds. In 2011, the model was featured as part of the *Modelmakers Showcase* of *Titanic* builds in professional modelmaker Peter Davies-Garner's informative book, *Titanic and Her Sisters: Olympic and Britannic,* by Seaforth Publishing, which covered the many kits and builds currently in circulation at the time of publication.

The replicas did not stop there with the 2002 build. I followed on years later producing a diorama in 1:700 scale depicting the raising of *Titanic* as she makes her journey to the surface. Using a kit bashed Revell *Titanic* the diorama features a seabed with pumping equipment dotted about it as the *Titanic*, paused several feet above the sea bed, is angled upwards for the journey to the surface. Complete with photo etched detail sets and custom-made parts, the model includes the steel plates over the iceberg damage, sixteen Hydrozene salvage tanks attached to her hull side and the *Deep Quest* lodged into the skylight. Another favourite diorama build was done in 2020 replicating the broken remains of *Titanic*'s second funnel from *Raise the Titanic*. Built in 1:200 scale the funnel is seated upon a small display base dressed as the ocean floor and laid on its side as depicted in the movie; its torn steel plates, three-bar grating at the top of the funnel, steam pipes, whistles and crew ladders and finished with layers of FX paint. One could almost hear Bohannon remarking on the funnel's discovery; "Whatever it is it has about ten-layers of sea critters on it." The biggest build project to date is another complete *Raise the Titanic* movie replica in 1:200 scale making it the largest to date. The build depicts *Titanic* at the time of her discovery in the movie and bearing the jagged and buckled plates from her encounter with the iceberg sixty-eight years previously. While the build is a private project, I am hopeful that one day it will be on public display as the movie builds up its fanbase.

... one or more for consideration?

Not necessarily associated with the movie, fans may be surprised to learn that you too can own your very own *Sea Cliff* – in miniature. The Japanese plastic model manufacturer Takara produced a series of ready built and painted miniature display models of ships including a wide variety of submarines and submersibles. Titled the *Ships of the World*, one of the submersibles released in their series was the D.S.V. *Sea Cliff* in 1:144th scale. Copied from the original submersible, of which the *Sea Cliff* in *Raise the Titanic* was also replicated from, the Takara release makes for an unlikely and rare collectible to add to anyone's collection. And for the *Titanic* enthusiasts, Takara also included in their series a perfect 1:144th scale miniatures of the submersibles *Alvin, Nautile* and *MIR 1* and *MIR 2* that have dived the wreck between the years 1986 to 2005.

Fans Remember *Raise the Titanic*

The following is a selection of mini-stories from fans of *Raise the Titanic* from around the world. Here, fans reveal their personal relationship with the story, the film and what it means to them.

***

It's hard to imagine how a box office disaster could have helped to shape my life, but it did on many levels. I was introduced to *Raise the Titanic* during the summer of 1980 when my grandfather and I spent a day at the theatre. We missed our original choice. And as I turned to walk out, I was confronted with the bow of a ship breaking the surface. Having a developing interest in diving, I chose to see the film. By the first fade of the introduction I was hooked. I soon not only became enraptured with the story of *Titanic* herself but also the determined outlook and attitude of Dirk Pitt as well! I adopted his line "We don't go to the mountain. The mountain comes to us" and have used it as my own personal mantra. Since first seeing the film I've worn out 7 VHS, 14 DVDs and 3 Blu-ray copies as I use it as a play list whenever I'm writing a *Titanic* related project. Thirty-eight years later I've become an established historian among the community who was friends with a few of the remaining survivors as well as members of the various dive team and expedition leaders but, even these days whenever I put the movie on, I'm the five year old boy once again watching the ship rising from the waters.

William Brower, Florida (author)

* * *

For me, the movie, *Raise the Titanic*, did just that. It served to raise the *Titanic* from the depths of the pages of history and breathe life into a legend.

David Ashley Bubb, Pennsylvania

* * *

Raise the Titanic: Maybe it's the greatest Alternative History film of all time, yet really it is the secret dream of all *Titanic* lovers realised; to see the R.M.S. *Titanic* afloat once more and complete her maiden voyage to New York.

Adam Lively, United Kingdom

* * *

As an enthusiast of all things *Titanic*, I could not wait to see the movie, and to finally see *Titanic* reaching New York. She was a beautiful ship and the movie did a fine job of recreating the fictional story of her salvation. John Barry's theme is with me every time I read anything about her.

Terry Moore, Seattle

* * *

On the night of September 10, 2001, I surfaced from the *Titanic* after a magical day of biology and forensic archaeology, 2.5 miles down on the bed of the Atlantic. Unfortunately, the problem with magical days, down there, is that sooner or later you have to come back to Earth. I ended up, during the next weeks, studying the collapse of the stern and the damage to the steel, in preparation for an almost identical study in the wreckage of the World Trade Center - not very far from where the White Star Offices had been located in 1912, where families had been gathering, all those years ago, trying to find out what happened to loved ones where we were... while we, at sea, were trying to find out what happened to family near the old White Star location, in New York (not all of my family had survived 9/11). This past fall, while channel surfing, I caught the end of the film, *Raise the Titanic* - that scene with the ship being towed near the Brooklyn Bridge, and the Twin Towers standing behind the old girl. Tears do not come easily to me, but suddenly I was weeping.

I ordered the paperback of Clive Cussler's novel and read it for the first time since 1980. I had not previously, during these decades, appreciated the amount of research and pure heart Cussler had put into the novel on which the film was based, and how prophetically true, parts of his story turned out to be: A musical instrument intact (just like Howard Irwin's clarinet), the boiler being discovered before the ship itself (just as during the French/American discovery mission), and what one actually feels, looking through those empty portholes while sitting in a submersible on the deck. One of my kids, home from college, caught me in the act of getting all misty-eyed, while reading the novel. For Christmas, family members bought me three copies of Cussler's first edition - and the film, of course.

Charles Pellegrino (author)

* * *

I fell in love at first with *Raise the Titanic* when I was 13 after discovering it in an Italian language, divided in seven or eight parts on YouTube, and was very impressed with the plot, soundtrack, sequences and the idea of the *Titanic*'s wreck intact and salvageable. I cried the first time I saw the raising scene. Later I found Jonathan Smith's marvellous collection, especially his fantastic replica model of the *Titanic* from the film. Increasing my interest in *Raise the Titanic* I then bought a 1987 Italian edition of the original Clive Cussler novel. Even though the movie was not well accepted, I think it's a great movie which deserves to be remembered at least for the raising sequence and a shocking, thrilling, wonderful novel.

Walter Nones, Italy

* * *

Raise the Titanic was the first Clive Cussler book I read. As a fan of the *Titanic* itself, seeing any book with its name in the title captures me. Little did I know it would not only lead me to becoming a lifelong fan of Clive Cussler, it also enticed me to be a lifelong reader. The book itself is my favourite of all that I've read in my lifetime. The opening chapter is gripping and a real hook to carry you forward and read more. The story is amazing and looking back at the time it was written the *Titanic* wasn't discovered yet so nobody knew what to expect once it was found. The movie was, and still is, most enjoyable. The point in time when the *Titanic* breaks through the surface brought chills as it did in the book! All-in-all both are great adventures!

Mike Branigan, USA

* * *

A couple of years after joining the Royal Navy the word that was going around the mess desk was this Clive Cussler book *Raise the Titanic!* I acquired a copy and read it. In the early eighties the movie was making its rounds through the fleet, as a cine operator I had the privilege of showing it, the anticipation was immense, every one made it to the mess hall early for a change. Well the 16mm projector started rolling. As the movie dragged on, we eventually got to the ship rising and breaking surface, at which time there was the almightiest cheer, I never thought too much about it at the time. My dad had bought it on VHS and watched it again. Then in 1995 I moved from Doncaster, England, to the States to set up a new home in Phoenix, Arizona. I met Clive at the Poisoned Pen for a book signing and it re-ignited my Cussler interest. Then in 2012 I met the late Wayne Valero of the Clive Cussler Collectors Society where we compared notes. I now have posters, books, and practically all the different media it was recorded on and still enjoy the movie.

Walter W. Winterburn, Phoenix, Arizona

***

When I first watched this movie in the early 80's I was still pretty young. But I knew the history of this grand ship. And it was before they found her in pieces. It means to me that the love for this ship was so great that someone really wanted to find her. I really was hoping that they would find her in one piece.

Sandy Saling, Kentucky

***

From the mountains of Colorado to the shores of England and Ireland, *Raise the Titanic* will take you on an adventure. *Raise the Titanic* was the second book I read by Clive Cussler and sealed my obsession with The Grand Master of Adventure. I read every book over and over, but *Raise the Titanic* is my favourite. I even read it to my children when they were young, and it started my youngest son into a love of history, and a major in college. Together our love of *Raise the Titanic* has turned into a fascination of both the book and the film. I thank Clive Cussler and *Raise the Titanic* for giving us a lifetime of adventure.

Delinda Peterson, United States

***

My wife bought *Raise the Titanic!* for me in 1976. It was my first Cussler book, and she knew I had always loved ships and maritime history. Just pages in, I was hooked and currently have every book that Clive Cussler has written. Robert Ballard's 1985 discovery of the wreck was still years off, and in the end that made no difference – the story stands on its own merits. I learned to appreciate Clive's plots, sub-plots, and attention to detail that continues to this day. When Lord Lew Grade's film was announced in 1980, I was thrilled – although the picture turned out to be somewhat disappointing, with Jason Robards and Sir Alec Guinness being about the only good casting choices. However, the musical score was excellent, and the shots of the ship surfacing made the entire picture worth it. So, mediocre movie or not, it's still a great Clive Cussler novel.

David B. Reeves Cicero, NY

***

Raise the Titanic has been with me since first watching it in 2002 on an old VHS video that was on sale in an old town. Despite all the flaws it had (because I knew later on) I still look at it as one of my favourite films about the *Titanic* to this day. It's so ironic that the film was made in 1980, the same year *Star Wars Episode V* came out but only five years before the real *Titanic* herself was found in 1985. It all started somewhere in 1999 or 2000 when I saw many posters and a VHS video of the film at a cinema one time. It interested me but wasn't sure what the film was about due to lacking of understanding because of my autism. It was then in 2002 when I got an old VHS video on sale about the film and bought it. The footage was in original 1980 style. When I first watched it, it forever changed my look on *Titanic* with the scenes of the subs finding the ship, the famous raising scene and when the *Titanic* is towed into New York. It all looked so realistic because of the spectacular special effects. The music by John Barry also gripped me too. It was unlike any other of the *Titanic* films I had watched before since this one was to be a modern-day film whereas the other films had been based on the sinking of the great ship.

Later, after researching, I discovered it was based on a novel by Clive Cussler; now my favourite author. I have come to know that *Raise the Titanic* is much more than just a thriller action film based on a best-selling novel, but also something really special that has attached me to it ever since. Even though the movie was a flop back in 1980 I still enjoy watching it on DVD and, like many fans, I'm one of them who had wished the *Titanic* appeared as she did in the film, to be intact and brought back to the world of the living.

Glen Barker, Birmingham, United Kingdom

* * *

I first caught *Raise the Titanic* channel flipping as a 5-year-old, landing on the channel just as the waves started to form at the surface. Although *Titanic*-obsessed, I could not fathom the idea of the *Titanic* being raised in modern times, much less see it in such an awe-inspiring spectacle. I relished in the glorious but all-too quickly fleeting moment, as the *Titanic* triumphantly returned. Unfortunately, that was the last time I would see it for over 5 years — no video stores in the U.S, much less my native Macedonia, ever carried the movie. As I grew up, the memories of seeing the mighty *Titanic* raised from the depths in my youth eventually became almost unrealistically blissful. At that point, I did not even remember the scene itself, but rather the emotions from seeing it, much like a dream. It was not until Christmas of 2004 that "Santa" gifted me a copy of the movie that I was able to experience the rush of emotion all over again. After 5 years of painstaking patience, no words can ever describe the moment of once again seeing *Titanic* erupt from the waves.

Mario Hristovski, Cincinnati, U.S.A

* * *

Raise the Titanic was the movie that introduced me to Clive Cussler, marine archaeology and dodgy model shots! It got me reading other Cussler novels like *Vixen 03* and *Dragon*. It made me interested in other wrecks, the stories behind their fates and discoveries, like S.S. *Persia* and *Empress of Ireland*. It also gave a daft 7-year-old the chance to re-enact model shots from the film in his bath tub, with any toy ship that was remotely similar to the *Titanic*. When I was 12 years old I even went as far to do a fan comic strip of the raising scene at the end of the movie. Despite the film's faults and troubled production history, I will always remember the wonderful crane shot across the *Titanic*'s decks, before the wide shot of the ship to John Barry's underrated music score.

Alex McDonald, United Kingdom

Chapter 29: Brewster's Vault: Collecting *Raise the Titanic* • 475

Two of the author's custom-made large badges. *(Author's collection)*

Limited Edition and numbered *Raise the Titanic* film collector's packs that contain 30 unique reproductions and newly created collectibles consisting of behind the scenes photographs, mini prints, postcards, storyboard, letter, collector's cards, bookmarks, vinyl sticker, production crew tag, NUMA card and World Premiere ticket. Available from *www.raisethetitanic.co.uk (Author's collection)*

476 • Raise The Titanic

Some collector's like to broaden their collecting prowess by focusing on one object that inadvertently has a unique collectability. Cussler's novel has never been out of print since its release in 1976. During that time the book has come with hundreds of varying cover designs and artworks that make for great collecting. *(Clive Cussler's Collector's Society – Montage by Jonathan Smith)*

Cussler's classic and much loved "Get it up!" *(Author's collection)*

Chapter 29: Brewster's Vault: Collecting *Raise the Titanic* • 477

UK Sphere 1980 paperback film tie-in. *(Author's collection)*

Sphere Australian 1980 paperback film tie-in. *(Author's collection)*

U.S Bantam 1980 film tie-in paperback. *(Author's collection)*

U.S Bantam Book Club edition 1980 film tie-in paperback. *(Author's collection)*

Italian edition published in 1988 that was still using film promotional images. *(Author's collection)*

This scarce 1977 Argentinian edition of the novel is a condensed version of the story but is uniquely packed with comic-book style illustrations that make it the only book version of the novel to be fully illustrated. *(Author's collection)*

Selection of the *Best Sellers* series featuring an adaptation of Cussler's *Raise the Titanic!* with artwork by the legendary artist Frank Bolle. *(Author's collection)*

Chapter 29: Brewster's Vault: Collecting *Raise the Titanic* • 479

The Chris Foss artwork created for the Sphere paperback release of the novel that would be used from 1977 into the mid 1980s. *(Author's collection – Prints available from www.chrisfossart.com)*

The 1980 Japanese TOWA film publicity brochure is a firm favourite for collectors old and new being that it is one of the more common brochures still available. What makes this particular example extremely rare is that it is signed by Anne Archer, Jason Robards, Richard Jordan, David Selby, M. Emmet Walsh and Elya Baskin. *(Author's collection)*

Film magazines from 1980 are another collectible. A number of those published between July to December 1980 feature articles of varying sizes on the movie. Not many of these magazines included the movie on the cover making them harder to find. It would take the collector to flick through publications from that time to see if the contents included *Raise the Titanic*. With Japans embrace of the film, *Titanic* appeared on the cover of the November issue of *Kinejun* (Motion Picture Times) with a healthy article on the film inside. *(Author's collection)*

480 • *Raise The Titanic*

Scarce Japanese movie tie-in edition of Clive Cussler's novel published in 1980. *(Author's collection)*

Even today the novel is still very much in print in Europe. The latest Japanese release of the Cussler novel even arcs back to 1980 with an artist rendering of the *Titanic* depicted in the film. *(Author's collection)*

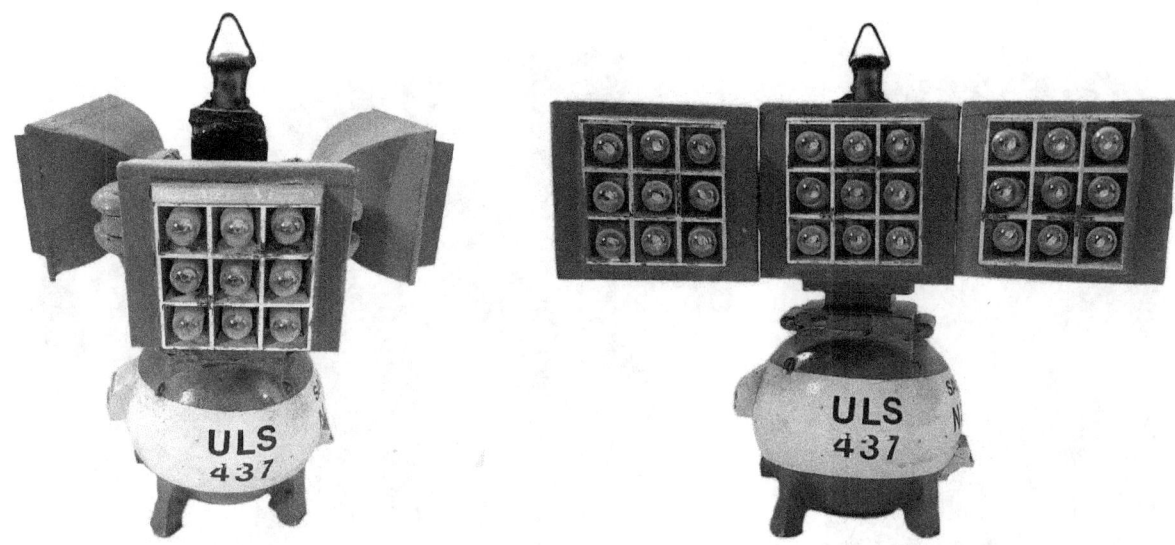

One of the surviving and still fully working 1:16th scale NAVY Salvage Lights. *(Author's collection)*

A single fairlead roller mooring unit from the starboard stern of the *Raise the Titanic* model that was removed in the late 1980s. At this point in the model's history the miniature still had much of its wreck FX paint still attached. *(Author's collection)*

The crow's nest bell from the model that became a souvenir for one of the films FX team upon the completion of the movie. *(Mario Hristovski collection)* RIGHT: Also removed from the model in the early 1990s is this mooring bitt (bollard) that came from the forecastle on the bow and can be seen in a number of shots of the model being raised. *(Author's collection)*

Resin cast door from the tank room deckhouse and a Sirocco electric vent motor from one of the boat deck ventilators. *(Author's collection)*

Rescued from the model following the severe storms of 2004, this is all that remained of the steelwork from the portside forecastle of the model. *(Author's collection)*

Chapter 29: Brewster's Vault: Collecting *Raise the Titanic* • 483

Movie Memories. The authors scrapbook that began life in 1978. At the time the eight-year-old Jonathan had no idea of the journey he would take and the importance of such a simple scrapbook would have on his life. *(Author's collection)*

Eight-page souvenir magazine from the Boston World Premiere. *(Author's collection)*

Magazine advertising pages make for ideal prints to mount and frame. *(Author's collection)*

484 • *Raise The Titanic*

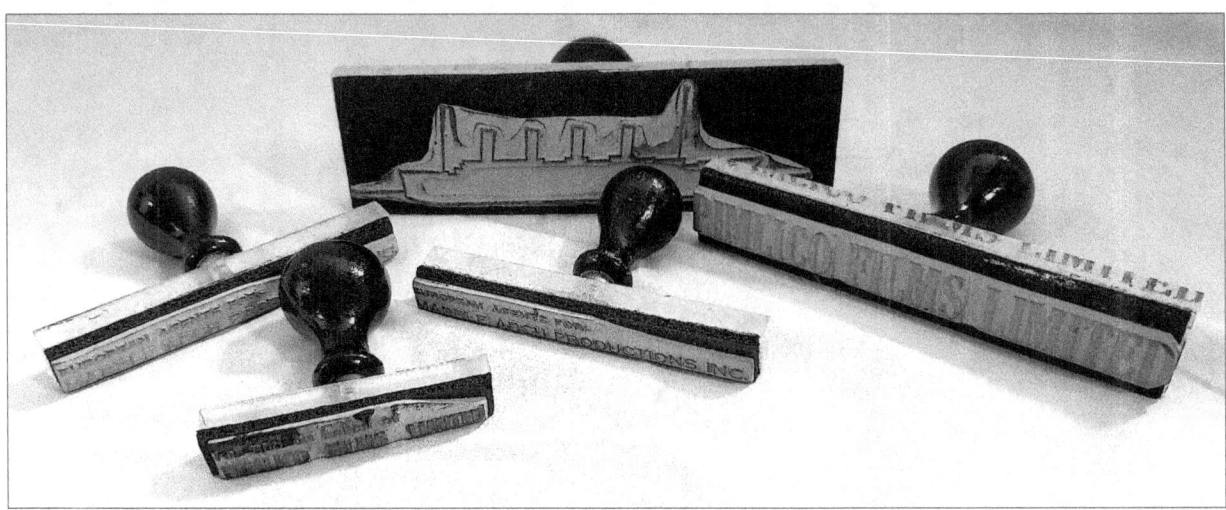

A more unusual lot of collectibles are these original ITC company rubber ink stamps that came from the films production office at the Mediterranean Film Facility during the filming of *Raise the Titanic* between the years 1978 to 1980. *(Author's collection)*

Raising *Titanic*, dashing hopes. The 1987 Hoyle board game that is often wrongly accredited as being connected to the movie. *(Author's collection)*

Early 1980 ITC film company belt buckle promoting the film. *(Kurt Kaufmann collection)*

Chapter 29: Brewster's Vault: Collecting *Raise the Titanic* • 485

Collecting Cussler can be fun, fulfilling, rewarding and at times budget friendly and expensive. There is a wide range of items out there just waiting to be found that can become the foundation to build a collection upon. *(Dave Hodgson collection)*

The DOXA Cussler range of wrist watches where owners can instantly become their hero, Dirk Pitt. *(Colten Vanosdale collection)*

Of the two movies adapted from Cussler's novels, *Sahara* was the only film where the studio invested in official merchandise. *(Walter Winterburn collection)*

Chapter 29: Brewster's Vault: Collecting *Raise the Titanic* • 487

Official studio t-shirts, baseball caps and bandanas. *(Walter Winterburn collection)*

21st Century Toys 1:6th scale Willy's Jeep with Dirk Pitt (Matthew McConaughey) and Al Giordino (Steve Zahn) action figures. *(Greg Nicholls collection)*

Just some of the varying medias that *Raise the Titanic* has been released for home entertainment viewing that includes video tapes, laser disc's, DVD and Blu-ray. *(Author's collection)*

488 • *Raise The Titanic*

British video rental store poster for the 1981 release of the movie through Lew Grade's company Precision Home Video. *(Author's collection)*

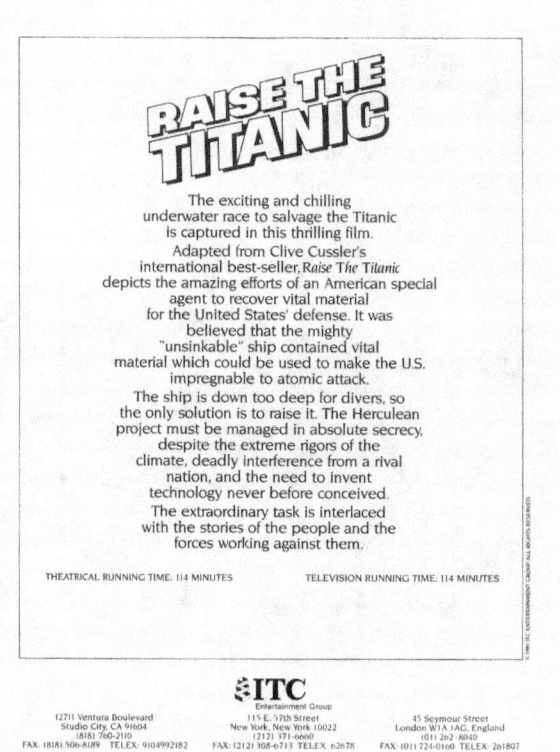

Double sided ITC Entertainment Group company large format card from 1989 promoting the companies release of the film on video during the period of Grade being back in the company. Note the incorrect spelling of Anne Archer's forename. *(Author's collection)*

Chapter 29: Brewster's Vault: Collecting *Raise the Titanic* • 489

Unused and still sealed up promotional t-shirt from 2005 that was issued in Australia when the movie first had its DVD release. *(Author's collection)*

The 2007 and 2015 DVD and Blu-ray release of the movie through Network on Air. Of the current releases of the film, these two versions are the only official releases containing an extensive special features section. *(Used with permission from Network on Air)*

490 • *Raise The Titanic*

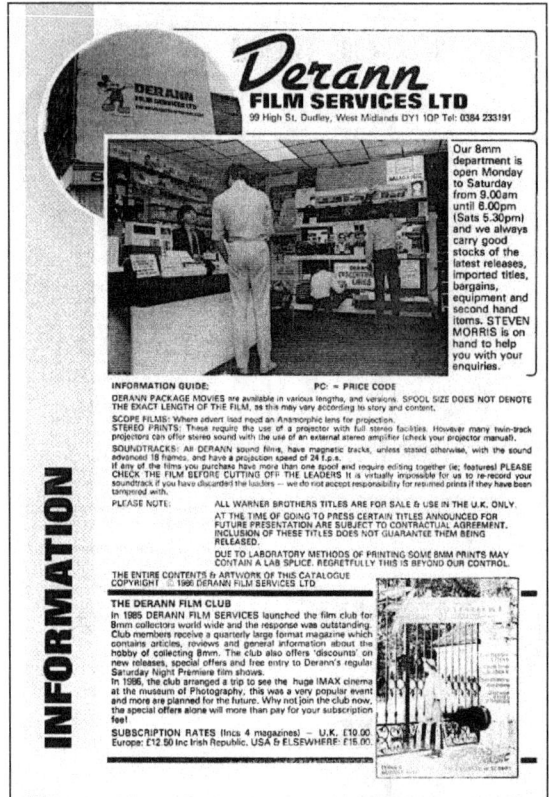

Derann Film Services Ltd; one of the UKs largest manufacturers and distributors of films on 8mm and 16mm reels. *(Ged Jones collection)*

Derann company advertisement for *Raise the Titanic* on their Super8 (8mm) film reels. *(Ged Jones collection)*

Keeping it British with *Raise the Titanic* on glorious Super8. *(Ged Jones collection)*

With the movie no longer on theatre screens, many screenings continued through private sectors with schools, leisure facilities and public halls with enough room for a screen and the seating of 30+ persons. *(Author's collection)*

Chapter 29: Brewster's Vault: Collecting *Raise the Titanic* • 491

21st Century Toys 1:18th scale Dirk Pitt (Matthew McConaughey) and Al Giordino (Steve Zahn) action figures. *(Dave Hodgson collection)*

The authors custom built NUMA research vessel. Using a technique known as kit-bashing, a pre-existing model kit of the research vessel *Le Suroit* released by Heller, was altered and added too to represent the NUMA company vessel from the Dirk Pitt adventure series. *(Author's collection)*

Another of the authors custom builds. Built in 2002, this faithful movie replica started life as the best-selling Minicraft *Titanic* model kit. After several months and a huge amount of modifying and aging, the final outcome was a 30-inch replica of the *Titanic* as seen in the movie. *(Author's collection)*

The Sleeping Giant. Submersibles float around the sunken remains of the *Titanic* as their lights pick out the once lost liner. Using a photograph of the authors 30 inch *Raise the Titanic* replica, artist William Barney has cleverly transformed the image into a new piece of art. *(Original photograph © Jonathan Smith / Digital alteration by William Barney)*

Chapter 29: Brewster's Vault: Collecting *Raise the Titanic* • 493

Still a work in progress. The authors 1:700th scale *Raise the Titanic* takes shape for a diorama depicting the moment the wreck starts to lift off the ocean floor with the salvage tanks attached to her side. *(Author's collection)*

Another of the authors works in progress on a build. This time a large 1:200th scale (53 inches) replica. This version is to be an exact duplicate of the model as seen and used in the movie. *(Author's collection)*

The authors 2020 custom build of the "Smokestack" diorama. Built to 1:200th scale, the funnel is a faithful miniature display of the funnel depicted in the movies sequence leading up to the discovery of the main hull. At 1:200 scale, the funnel is just under 12cm in length. *(Author's collection)*

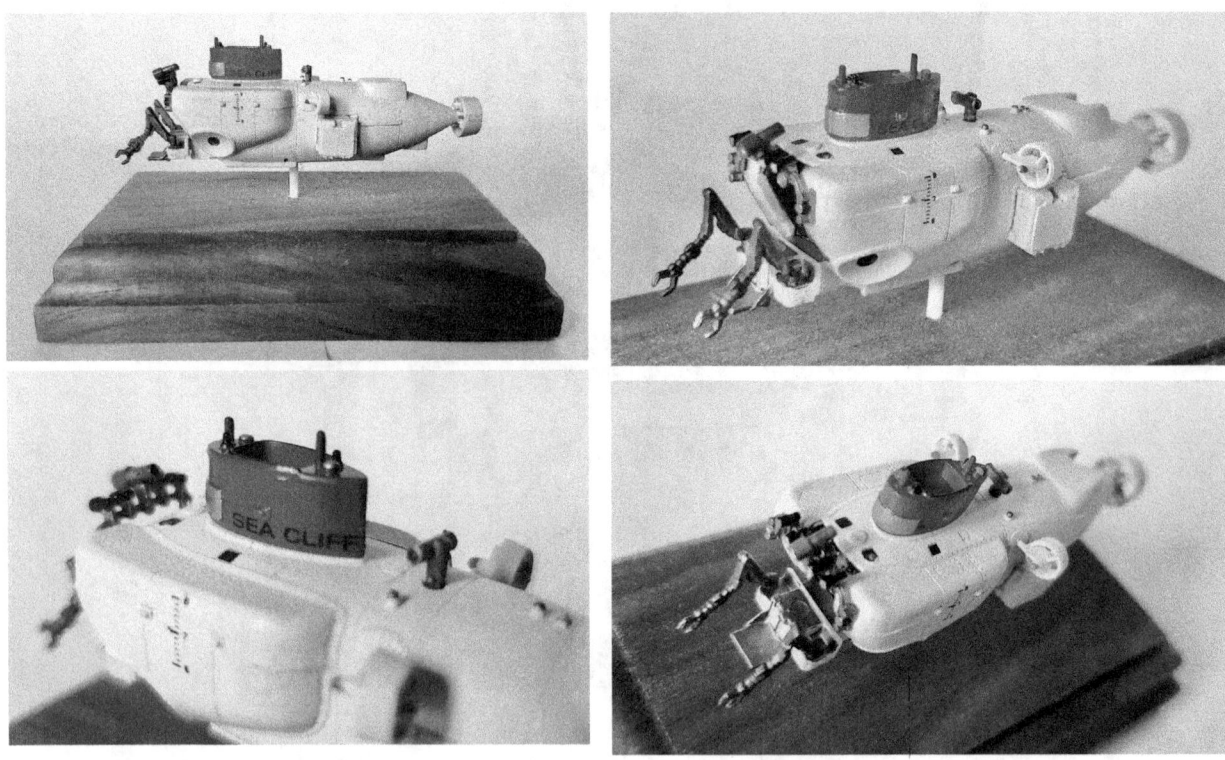

D.S.V. *Sea Cliff* by Takara models. *(Author's collection)*

CHAPTER 30

The Last Great Human Adventure

Project Titanic 2021

One reoccurring question amongst the *Titanic* community where this film is concerned is to why the model was never preserved after filming had completed. It is easy to assume that because some film models have survived long after the production has been released, *Raise the Titanic* should go the same way. If *Raise the Titanic* had become the blockbuster that Lew Grade had hoped for, there still was no guarantee that the *Titanic* model would have survived into the mid-1980s. The early days of negotiating between Lew Grade and Clive Cussler on *Raise the Titanic* had Grade showing much interest in adapting other Cussler works that were published prior to *Raise the Titanic* that included *Iceberg* (1974) and *Mayday!* (1973). The press had already been made aware of Grade's interest in Cussler's other earlier works as Grade announced his plan to have a series of films to rival the James Bond franchise. But what would become of the *Titanic* model? The other vessels built for *Raise the Titanic* would have been subject to change to fit within the story of the film in production. The *Titanic* model did not fit in with the other film projects and as a purposely aged derelict the model would have already been stripped of parts for use in other sea faring adventures filmed at the studio; this being dependent on ITC having survived with Grade at the helm.

At a time when studios relied heavily on miniatures and their parts, the model was already in the process of being stripped of details come late 1981 following its removal from dry storage to the exposed backlot of the studio. While collectors go to extreme lengths to find and secure props from movies, these monster props, such as a 55 feet 10-ton *Titanic*, was never going to be someone's prized possession. When taking into consideration how many films have been made using miniatures to how many of those film miniatures have been completely destroyed, it is remarkable that the *Raise the Titanic* model, despite its unlucky fate of being used as a Mediterranean garden ornament, the miniature could have gone the same way as many other miniatures in being disposed of in a crude manner. The model was, simply put, just too big, too heavy and too cumbersome for anyone to do anything constructive with. The Mediterranean Film Facility were never the owners of the model. They were put in a position of being unfortunate caretakers who had to foot the bill when the model got in the way of a production and required moving elsewhere within the studio grounds.

As the years passed away, so did the models look. The steelwork rusted, then rotted, then collapsed. After 40 years out in the ever-changing Mediterranean weather the model succumb to the environment to essentially become a 55ft fibre glass hull that was used as a way to store any old studio materials. An undignified way for such a graceful replica of the world's most famous ocean liner.

"PROJECT TITANIC"

In the summer of 2019, something stirred among the wild undergrowth at the foot of the deep tank facility. Lifting straps, that had been slung around the fibreglass remains of the *Titanic* model, took the strain as the hull was lifted up and lowered down onto a low-loader trailer. The journey was to be short, just a quarter of a mile. But it was the beginning of a new chapter in the legacy of the model. The studio, now under new ownership and management, had received a healthy investment to update the facilities and grounds. The *Titanic* hull was removed from the deep tank embankment to allow the area to be cleared for new building work to commence. The model was placed down within the grounds of Fort Rikazoli, away from the public and heavy machinery that was operating in the film studio grounds a short distance away.

There is a familiar saying that goes, "better late than never". No truer words could be said. Behind the scenes, discussions were taking place on the future of the hull, and, if anything could be done to preserve what is left. I was approached to give my input on the potential preservation on the hull. In February 2020, I submitted my own preservation and partial restoration proposal to the studio. After months of consideration, the studio agreed to the proposal, and in June 2021, after many meetings, backed by the Malta Film Studio Commission, *Project Titanic* began. The proposed plan is to clean the hull. Carry out the essential repairs and stabilize the structure where it can be professionally preserved. A new internal frame would be constructed and fitted within the contour of the hull to allow the hull to be suspended on the frame; the frame acting like an internal skeleton that would also take all the additional weight to follow during the next stage of the restoration.

In late May, 2021, the clean-up work began on the hull where over a ton of debris and junk was removed. Luckily, a number of original features have survived over the course of four decades. Although they are not in any condition to be reused, they will form part of *Project Titanic* where casts will be taken and copies made for use on the build. With the hull cleared of debris, it will be stabilised for its return journey back to the Malta Film Studio where the process of stripping, cleaning and repairing can begin, while the framework and superstructure and upper deck details are reproduced with all work being carefully carried out by a team of professionals at the film studio. Once completed, the newly restored *Raise the Titanic* film model will go on display within the grounds of the Malta Film Studio where visitors can view what will still be, the world's largest model of the mighty *Titanic*.

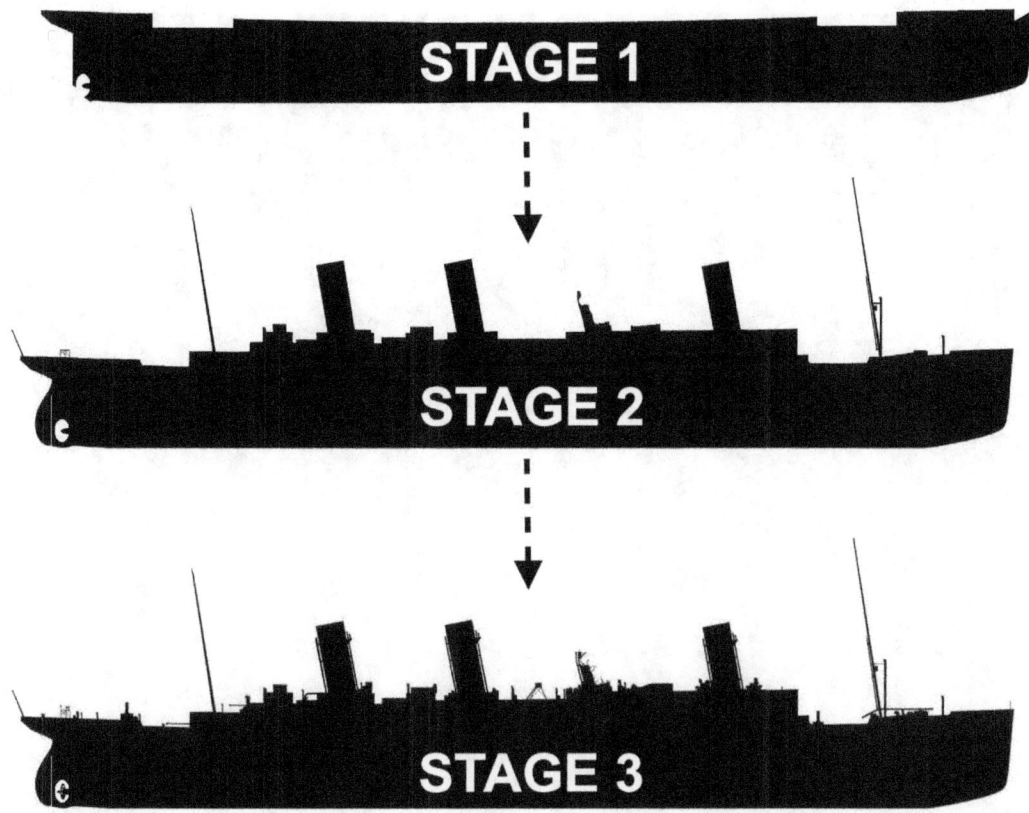

ABOVE: There could be a positive future for the model remains after plans were unveiled in 2021 to preserve the hull and add to it over the coming years. BELOW: But before that can begin, the model had to be removed from its current location and moved to safer grounds. *(Illustration © Jonathan Smith – Photograph © Jean Pierre Borg)*

498 • *Raise The Titanic*

Summer 2019 and the hull of the *Titanic* model is lifted from the base of the deep tank embankment and swung over to a low-loader for the short journey to Fort Rikazoli. *(Photograph © Jean Pierre Borg)*

Over a ton of debris was removed from the interior of the hull. Each load was checked for any surviving relics that could be used as reference before it was tipped into the skip. *(Photograph © Jean Pierre Borg)*

The weather covering from the rear staircase that sat between funnels 3 and 4 that can be seen in the movies fly-past sequence. *(Photograph © Jean Pierre Borg)*

Chapter 30: The Last Great Human Adventure • 501

This view is looking from the bow and towards the stern. The rectangular holes were cut into the hull bottom when the model was converted into the wreck for mounting on the lifting rig. On the bottom left of the image, the hull shows the extra strengthening braces put in place for when the hull side was cut out for the installation of the iceberg damaged hull plates. *(Photograph © Jean Pierre Borg)*

This view is looking from the stern and towards the bow. Again, a section of the hull bottom has been cut away for the main mounting point of the lifting rig. *(Photograph © Jean Pierre Borg)*

502 • *Raise The Titanic*

The interior side of the starboard hull showing the porthole cut outs and two of the internal supports added in Malta during the model's conversion to the wreck. *(Photograph © Jean Pierre Borg)*

This view looking from the starboard side of the bow highlights the sixteen vertical braces that were installed when the model underwent its conversion into the wreck in Malta. *(Photograph © Jean Pierre Borg)*

Chapter 30: The Last Great Human Adventure • 503

Early 2020 and the model sits outside the ruins of Fort Rikazoli. *(Photograph © Jean Pierre Borg)*

Only time will tell to what extant the preservation will be to return this movie ghost of the past back to something worthy of public display for years to come. *(Original photograph © Jean Pierre Borg / Photo-editing by Jonathan Smith)*

Chapter 30: The Last Great Human Adventure • 505

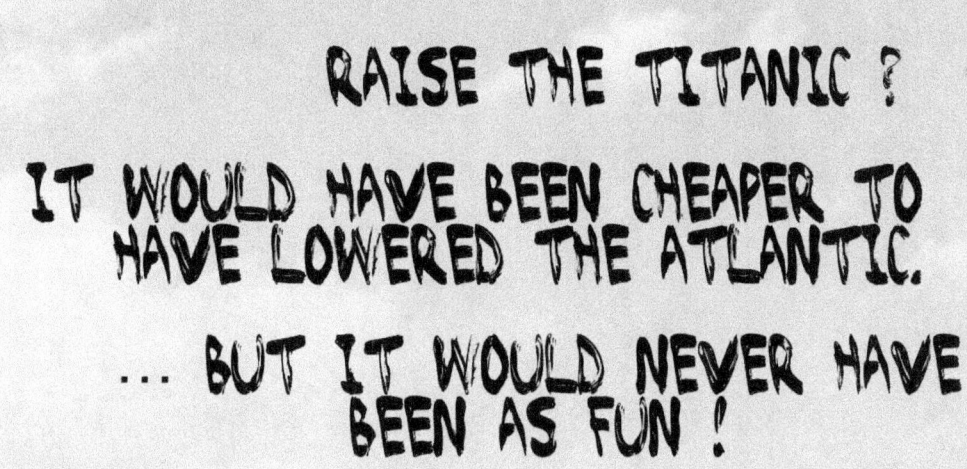

RAISE THE TITANIC?
IT WOULD HAVE BEEN CHEAPER TO HAVE LOWERED THE ATLANTIC.
... BUT IT WOULD NEVER HAVE BEEN AS FUN!

Afterword

It is no secret that *Raise the Titanic* still divides opinions between those who have a love of the film and those who prefer the novel over the movie. As a lifelong fan of the film, and while writing this book, I have tried to balance the scales on the production and present for the first time the many hurdles encountered in bringing the story to the big screen. And yet after forty years, the film still gets bad reputation from those who delight in pointing out that the film flopped without giving the production a second thought or stating as to why they feel it did. But is it fair to condemn the film into a Top 10 category of the World's Biggest Movie Flops like many of these polls do? Movie productions have come a long way since 1980. And yet, for the older generations, it is the great practical effects movies from the 1930s right through to the 1990s that still have a special place in the hearts of countless moviegoers. Today's modern audiences expect such delights because this is the era of movie making where they expect technology to deliver extraordinary visuals at the cost of computer software and those who worked feverously upon the keyboards and digital drawing pads. We also live in a time where $100m budgets budget movies are the normality. But it is the older films like *King Kong, The Poseidon Adventure, Blade Runner* or *Star Wars,* that remain much loved for those of us who grew up in those decades watching magic unfold on the screen regardless if that voice in the back of our head reminds us "Hey! That giant ape is a man in a suit."

For the many, these old films, the methods used to bring them to the screen, have a feeling of nostalgia in the same way a vinyl record does when compared to a digital download. Now, after 40 years, this misunderstood movie is best remembered for the *Titanic* model and the breathtakingly beautiful raising sequence that still captures the public's imagination. And while todays special effects are largely the product of computer imagery, *Raise the Titanic* and its array of miniature work is still looked upon by those in the film industry as a remarkable snapshot in practical effects and a prime example of how impressive the period of miniatures can captivate its viewers decades later. Was the £25m used to bring Clive Cussler's novel to the big screen worth it? I hope the reader can close this book with a better understanding to how the film came about, why it was delivered in the way it was, and the monumental task the production crews faced in bringing the story to the big screen. And maybe that £25m was worth every penny when the grandeur of *Titanic*'s everlasting legacy was captured in such a unique way. As the real *Titanic* continues to crumble in the bitterly cold and crushing depths of the North Atlantic, her sad demise is recorded for future generations as man-made crafts hover over the decaying remains like vultures over a carcass. Her collapsing decks and hull sections tantalisingly reveal a time long forgotten in memory but now subscribed to the pages of a history book.

She was hailed as the greatest of the works of man. Later to become a symbol of man's arrogance over nature. Her sinking was a turning point in society as the winds of war churned up across Europe marking the departure of the Edwardian era. And yet her name, *Titanic*, still conjures up a mixture of excitement, intrigue, sadness and an overwhelming desire in wanting to travel back in time and walk the decks of this once luxurious ocean liner that was hailed unsinkable, a marvel of opulence, of confidence and marine engineering. It seems fitting to me that I should conclude my 40 year obsession with *Raise the Titanic* by quoting Alec Guinness' fictionalised *Titanic* crewmember who, through the artistry of movie magic, once walked those pine decks, scaled those graceful gilded staircases and survived one of the most famous shipping disasters in maritime history.

"What a lovely thing she was. Standing as high in the water as one of your skyscrapers. Longer than two rugby fields. And furnishings to match the finest mansions in England. She was one of a kind. No question about it. And God himself they said couldn't sink her. Then in two-hours she was gone… and fifteen-hundred souls with her."

Bibliography

Ballard, Robert D., *The Discovery of the Titanic*, Madison Press Books, Canada, 1987
Bottomore, Stephen, *The Titanic and Silent Cinema*, The Projection Box, UK, 2000
Chester, Lewis, *All My Shows Are Great: The Life of Lew Grade*, Aurum Press Ltd, London, 2010
Cussler, Clive, *Raise the Titanic*, The Viking Press, New York, 1976
Davis, Clifford, *How I Made Lew Grade a Millionaire and Other Fables*, Mirror Books, London, 1981
Delfont, Bernard, *Bernard Delfont Presents East End, West End*, Macmillian Publishers, London, 1990
Falk, Quentin & Prince, Dominic, *Last of a Kind: The Sinking of Lew Grade*, Quartet Books Ltd, London, 1987
Grade, Lew, *Still Dancing*, William Collins Sons & Co, London, 1987
Grimm, Jack & Hoffman, William, *Beyond Reach: The Search for The Titanic*, Paul Harris Publishing, Edinburgh, 1981
Kramer, Stanley, *A Mad, Mad, Mad, Mad World: A Life in Hollywood*, Aurum Press Ltd, London, 1998
Leonard, Geoff, *John Barry: The Man with the Midas Touch*, Redcliffe Press Ltd, Bristol, UK, 2008
Mills, Simon, *The Titanic in Pictures*, Wordsmith Publications, Buckinghamshire, UK, 1995
Parks, James, *A Day at the Bottom of the Sea*, Crane, Russel & Company, New York, 1977
Read, Piers Paul, *Alec Guinness: The Authorised Biography*, Simon & Schuster UK Ltd, London, 2003
Richardson, John, *Making Movie Magic: A Lifetime Creating Special Effects for James Bond, Harry Potter, Superman & More*, The History Press, Gloucestershire, UK, 2019
Suid, Lawrence H, *Guts & Glory: The Making of the American Military Image in Film*, The University Press of Kentucky, 2002
Suid, Lawrence H, *Sailing on the Silver Screen: Hollywood and the U.S. Navy*, Naval Institute Press, Maryland, 1996
Nesmeyanov, Eugene, *The Titanic Expeditions: Diving to the Queen of the Deep 1985 – 2010*, The History Press, Gloucestershire, UK, 2018

Websites & Organisations

www.raisethetitanic.co.uk
www.maltafilmcommission.com
www.cusslersociety.com
www.cusslermuseum.com
www.hunley.org
www.kenmarschall.com
www.drewstruzan.com
www.titanichistoricalsociety.org

www.britishtitanicsociety.com
www.titanicverein.ch
www.titanicinternationalsociety.org
www.seacitymuseum.co.uk
www.titanicbelfast.com
www.nmni.com
www.pcpmalta.com
www.aylonfilmarchives.com

LIMITED EDITION  COLLECTOR'S PACK

THE MAKING OF THE MOVIE — RAISE THE TITANIC

Once they said God himself couldn't sink her. Then they said no man on earth could reach her. Now --- you are finally here to see the raising of the legendary ocean liner. To accompany the release of RAISE THE TITANIC: The Making of the Movie, Titanic historian and author Jonathan Smith has selected a number of rare items from his personal archive and reproduced them for film fans, collector's and Titanic enthusiasts. This deluxe collector's set features a number of reproductions taken from the original ephemera in the authors collection and highlights a part of the movies production from 1976 to 1980 that was not widely available to the public.

RAISE THE TITANIC: The Making of the Movie Collector's Edition is strictly limited to only 500 sets world-wide, making it a cherished collectible with an interest in the old days of movie making, special effects and Titanic on film that fans can enjoy for years to come.

CONTENTS

- Specialty bookplate signed by the author, numbered, embossed and ink stamped
- Collector's Edition sticker that can be attached to the cover of the book
- Set of 10 behind the scenes images from the production of Raise the Titanic
- National Underwater Marine Agency (NUMA) salvage operations identification card
- Letter sent from the book publisher Viking Press to Raise the Titanic author Clive Cussler announcing that his novel is going to be published
- Colour publicity card from 1980 of the raising of the Titanic
- 1979/80 ITC film crew equipment tie-on tag
- Film logo vinyl sticker
- Arthur Brewster's 1912 "Thank God for Southby" postcard
- UK cinema front-of-house promotional poster art card
- Viking Press Raise the Titanic book publishers trade information card from 1976
- U.S insert poster design collector's card # 1 (raising Titanic)
- U.S insert poster design collector's card # 2 (seabed Titanic)
- 1977 Raise the Titanic bookmarker design collector's card # 3
- 1980 Bantam Books Clive Cussler novels bookmarker design collector's card # 4
- 2021 Raise the Titanic raising wreck collector's card # 5
- 1978 "A PROJECT TO STAGGER THE IMAGINATION" advanced ITC promotional print
- 1980 storyboard depicting the discovery of the Titanic in the movie
- Deleted sinking scene from the film's intended 1912 prologue
- Hydrozene salvage tank schematic
- Admiral Sandecker's press conference Titanic profile plan
- July 30, 1980 World Premiere ticket for Raise the Titanic

ORDER YOURS TODAY AT

www.raisethetitanic.co.uk

www.ingramcontent.com/pod-product-compliance
Lightning Source LLC
Chambersburg PA
CBHW082019300426

44117CB00015B/2275